IMAGE COMICS PRESENTS

THE LEGEND OF
SLEEPY HOLLOW

WRITTEN & ILLUSTRATED BY
BO HAMPTON

ADAPTED FROM A STORY BY
WASHINGTON IRVING

LETTERING BY
TRACEY HAMPTON

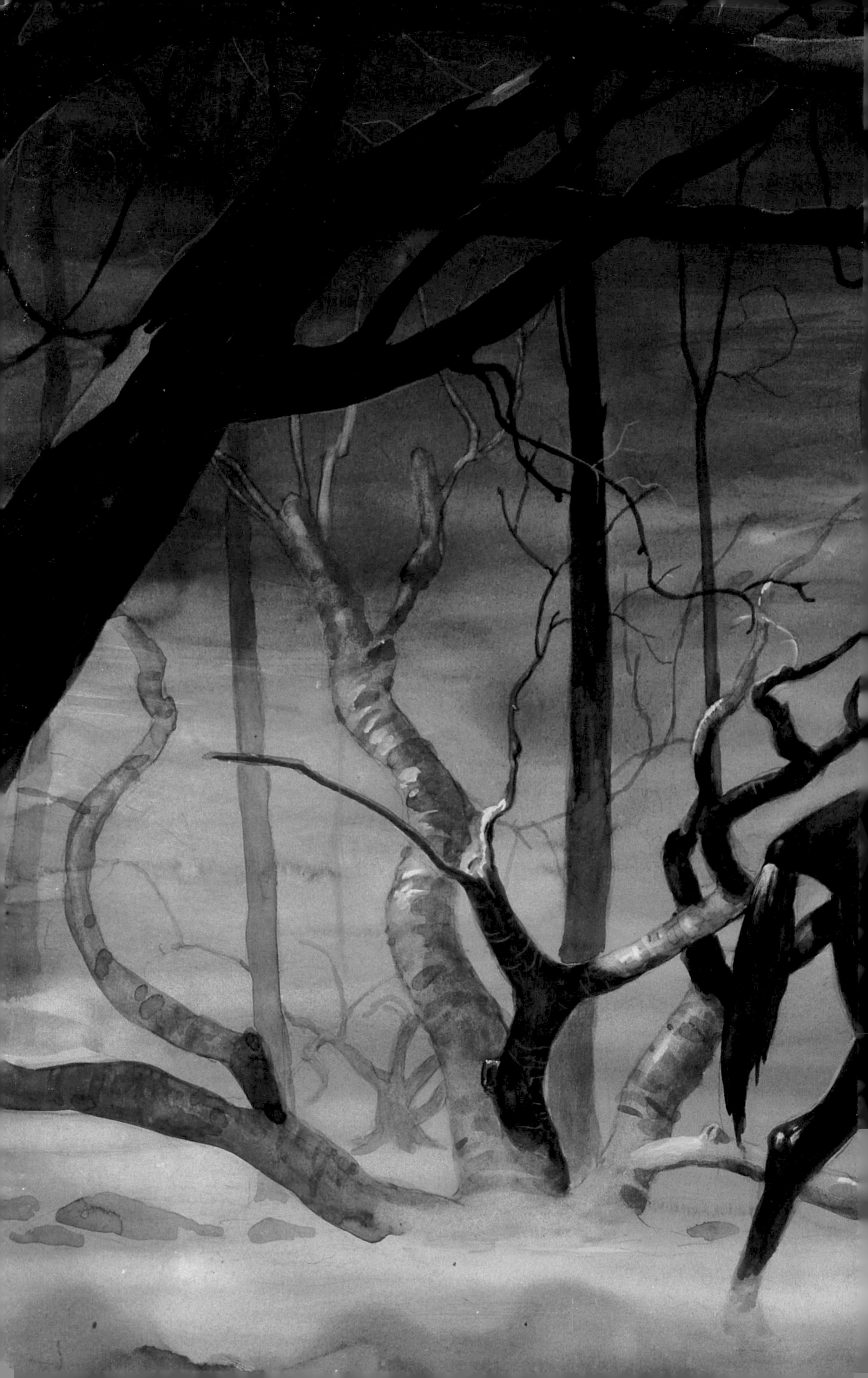

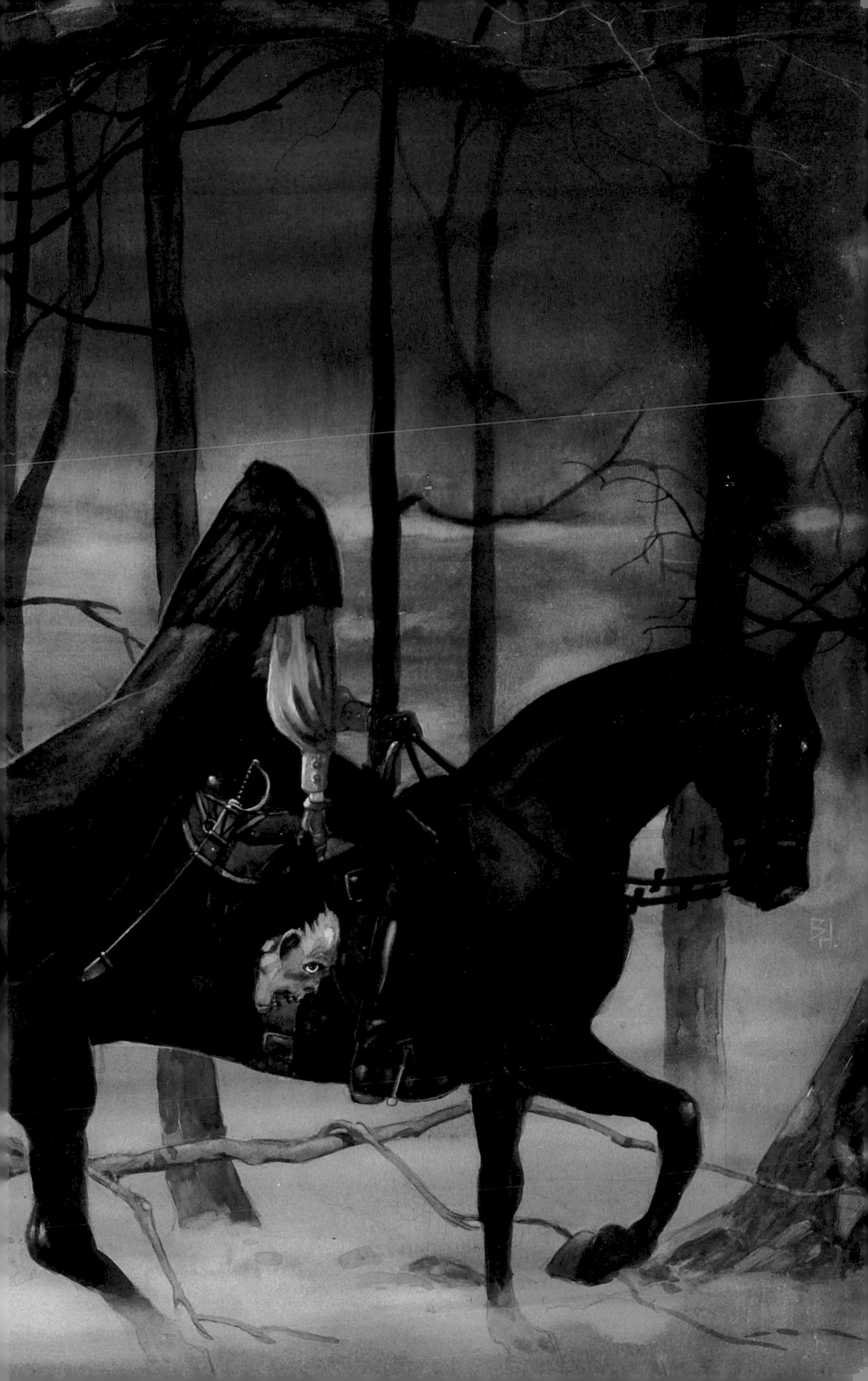

FOR
BUZ MARTIN

IMAGE COMICS, INC.
Erik Larsen - *Publisher*
Todd McFarlane - *President*
Marc Silvestri - *CEO*
Jim Valentino - *Vice-President*
Eric Stephenson - *Executive Director*
Brett Evans - *Production Manager*
Cindie Espinoza - *Controller*
B. Clay Moore - *PR & Marketing Coordinator*
Allen Hui - *Web Developer*
Jon Malin - *Production Assistant*
Tim Hegarty - *Booktrade/International Rights*
www.imagecomics.com

THE LEGEND OF SLEEPY HOLLOW. October, 2004. First Printing. Published by Image Comics, Inc. Office of publication: 1071 N. Batavia St. Suite A, Orange, CA 92867. Image and its logos are ® and © 2004 Image Comics, Inc. All rights reserved. Originally published by Tundra Publishing LTD. The Legend of Sleepy Hollow is ™ and © 2004 Bo Hampton. All rights reserved. The characters, events and stories in this publication are entirely fictional. No portion of this publication may be reproduced by any means without the expressed written permission of the copyright holder except for artwork used for review purposes. Printed in Canada

★ INTRODUCTION ★

This version of Washington Irving's classic was originally slated to be published by First Comics back in '92 as part of their "Classics Illustrated" line of Graphic Novels. A young editor agreed to do it and asked me to do pencil breakdowns of all the pages and submit them, as part of their editorial policy. I didn't mind since I had to do the drawing anyway. Two weeks later I submitted the pages and was promptly informed that the young editor [Wayne-something, as I recall] was not actually authorized to "greenlight" books! Who knew?

I was, at that juncture, out on a shaking limb, with considerable time invested and no contract, other than "verbal" [translate as "useless"]. Once the steam blowing out of my ears subsided I started looking for other options.

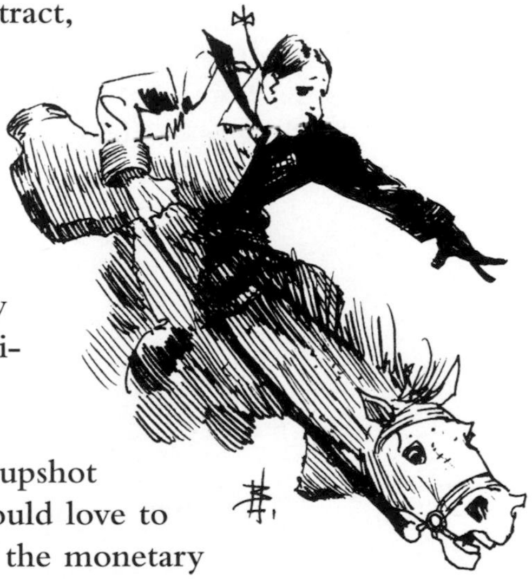

After a frantic week of failed attempts it was Kevin Eastman, who happily agreed to publish the book—with one proviso. It would be incumbent upon me to be paid nearly TWICE the amount of money offered at First Comics.... I relented. The upshot of which was that I now had a project I would love to adapt and draw and paint... and because of the monetary increase I was in a position to give it the time it deserved!

It came out in October '93 and was nominated for Best Graphic Novel with the Harvey Awards that year. My brother and colleague, Scott Hampton, was also up for the award for his book, *The Upturned Stone.* Fortunately, Will Eisner—my former teacher and employer—had the diplomatic aplomb to step in and win it. If ya gotta lose...

My wife, Teresa and I and our daughter, Caitlin lived in Milford New Hampshire at the time the book was being created and that "Mayberry" of the Far North, its churches, farms, graveyards, dead trees and old Georgian-style architecture provided the visual inspiration for the story's setting. The only models used were; my face for a couple of Ichabod close-ups [we were separated-at-birth] and my father-in-law, Russel Mcleod, who played Ichabod, singing in the choir. I can still fondly recall Russell's glorious vocal stylings reverberating through the church as he got "into" the character.

What I loved about Irving's story was the prose, which could be at times wonderfully moody and atmospheric and, when required, completely hilarious. And his ability to set a scene was extraordinary. This is what I call drawing "in the womb"—completely secure with the material and inspired by it on a very basic level.

Because Sleepy Hollow was actually more of a lengthy short story as opposed to a novel, I was able to retain nearly all of the main text and character interactions, which means it is a true adaptation of the work and not an "abridged" or condensed version. While considering the project, I attended the San Diego Comics Convention and another artist in attendance warned me off it! He maintained the "classics" should be left alone, intact and not corrupted by a comic artist's interpretation!!

I'm glad I didn't listen to him.

And for those of you who think that Disney was an overriding influence on my book, remember this: The object adorning the pommel of the Headless Hessian's saddle was his own dessicated head and that is what gets hurled at Ichabod in the story's climax—not a laughing Jack-o-Lantern...

Finally... I want to thank my agent but I don't have one.

So instead, hugs and hearty hand-clasps go out to the following: Gloria, Wade, Scott, Bunny, Robin, Tracy, [my favorite letterer] Toby, Teresa, Caitlin, Callie, Tickets and Lionel ...Hampton.

And help was much appreciated from: Jeff Parker, Alex Saviuk and Bob Tinnell.

And... oh yeah—thanks to Wayne Something.

Bo Hampton
September 17, 2004

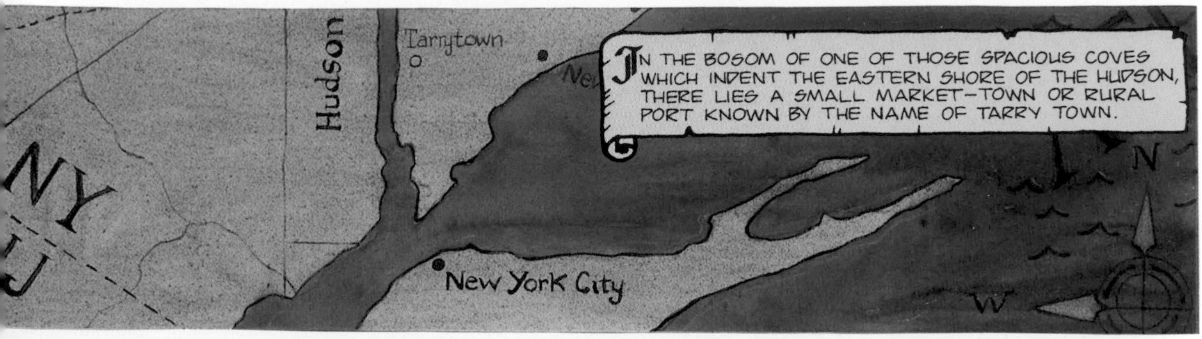
Hudson
Tarrytown
NY
NJ
New York City
W
N
IN THE BOSOM OF ONE OF THOSE SPACIOUS COVES WHICH INDENT THE EASTERN SHORE OF THE HUDSON, THERE LIES A SMALL MARKET-TOWN OR RURAL PORT KNOWN BY THE NAME OF TARRY TOWN.

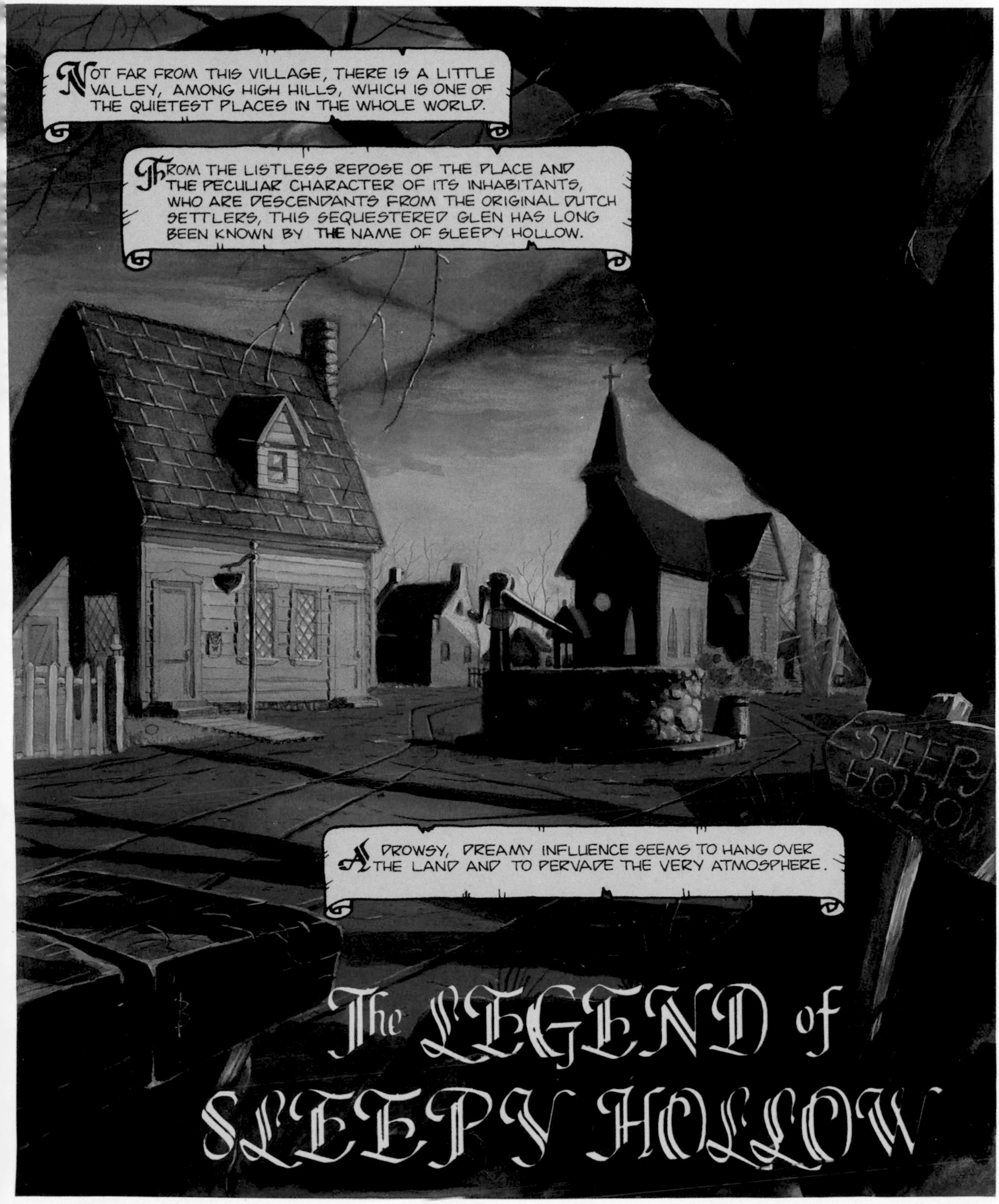
NOT FAR FROM THIS VILLAGE, THERE IS A LITTLE VALLEY, AMONG HIGH HILLS, WHICH IS ONE OF THE QUIETEST PLACES IN THE WHOLE WORLD.
FROM THE LISTLESS REPOSE OF THE PLACE AND THE PECULIAR CHARACTER OF ITS INHABITANTS, WHO ARE DESCENDANTS FROM THE ORIGINAL DUTCH SETTLERS, THIS SEQUESTERED GLEN HAS LONG BEEN KNOWN BY THE NAME OF SLEEPY HOLLOW.
SLEEPY HOLLOW
A DROWSY, DREAMY INFLUENCE SEEMS TO HANG OVER THE LAND AND TO PERVADE THE VERY ATMOSPHERE.
The LEGEND of SLEEPY HOLLOW

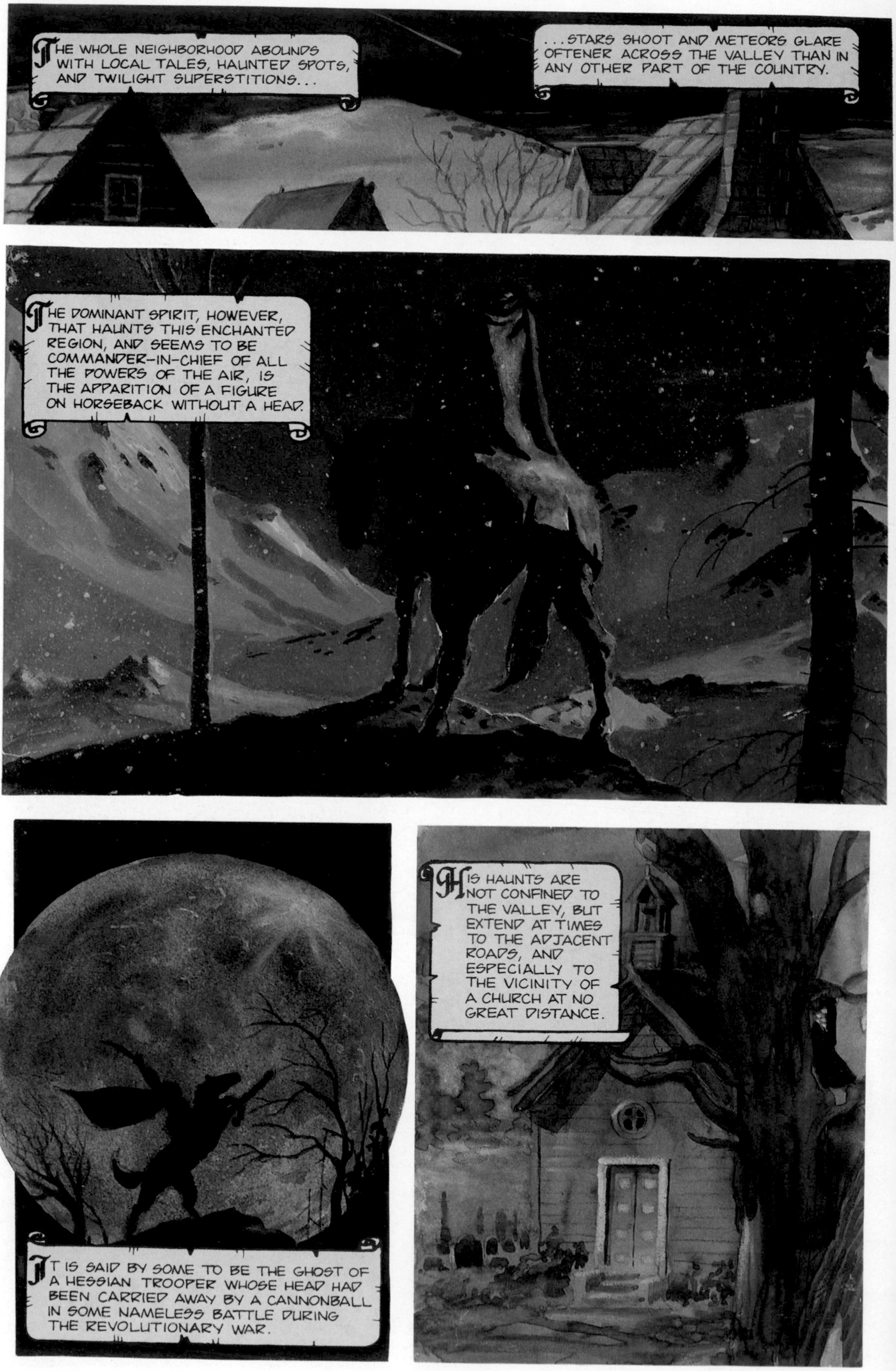
THE WHOLE NEIGHBORHOOD ABOUNDS WITH LOCAL TALES, HAUNTED SPOTS, AND TWILIGHT SUPERSTITIONS...
...STARS SHOOT AND METEORS GLARE OFTENER ACROSS THE VALLEY THAN IN ANY OTHER PART OF THE COUNTRY.
THE DOMINANT SPIRIT, HOWEVER, THAT HAUNTS THIS ENCHANTED REGION, AND SEEMS TO BE COMMANDER-IN-CHIEF OF ALL THE POWERS OF THE AIR, IS THE APPARITION OF A FIGURE ON HORSEBACK WITHOUT A HEAD.
IT IS SAID BY SOME TO BE THE GHOST OF A HESSIAN TROOPER WHOSE HEAD HAD BEEN CARRIED AWAY BY A CANNONBALL IN SOME NAMELESS BATTLE DURING THE REVOLUTIONARY WAR.
HIS HAUNTS ARE NOT CONFINED TO THE VALLEY, BUT EXTEND AT TIMES TO THE ADJACENT ROADS, AND ESPECIALLY TO THE VICINITY OF A CHURCH AT NO GREAT DISTANCE.

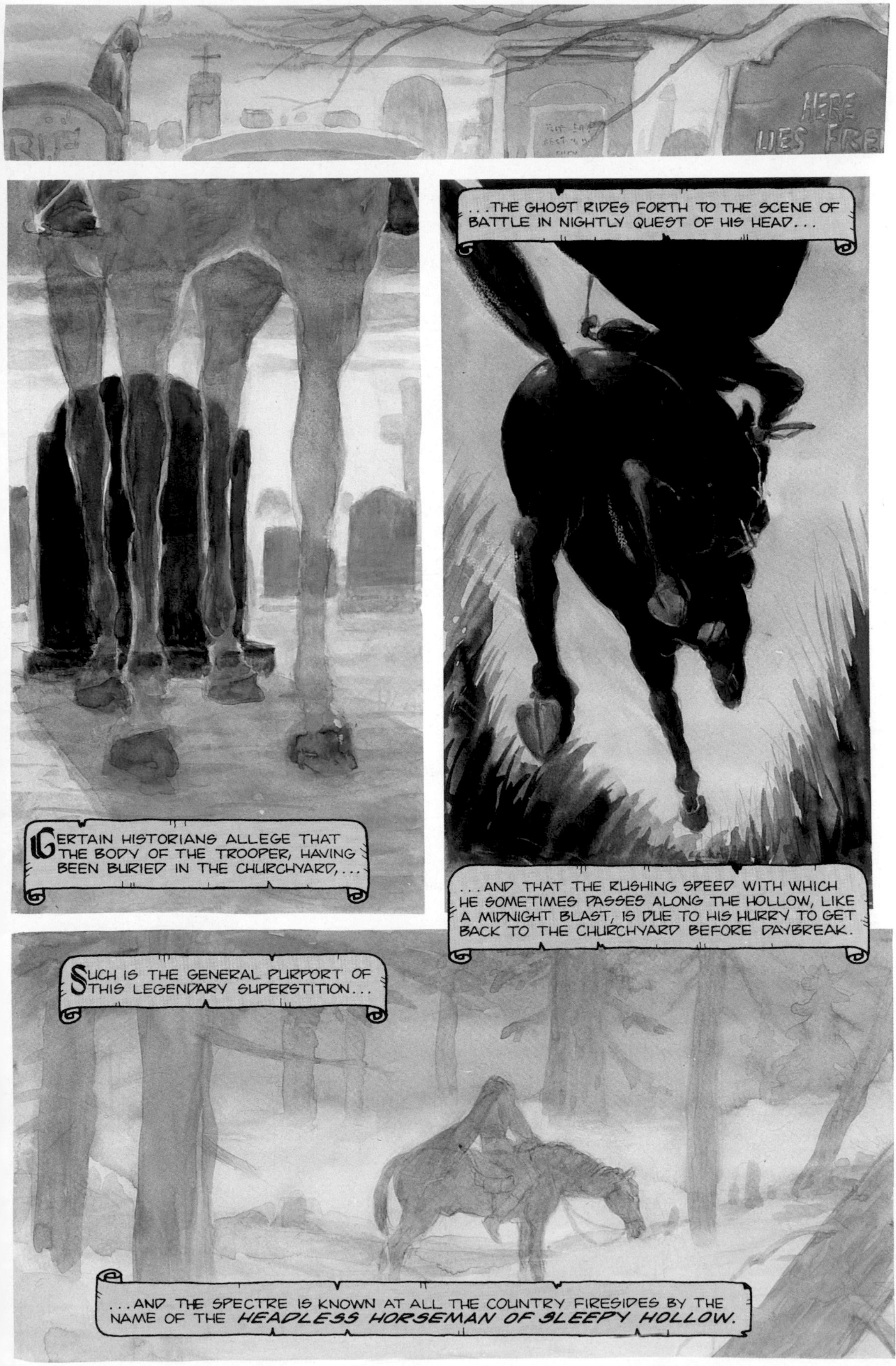
HERE LIES FRE
CERTAIN HISTORIANS ALLEGE THAT THE BODY OF THE TROOPER, HAVING BEEN BURIED IN THE CHURCHYARD, . . .
. . . THE GHOST RIDES FORTH TO THE SCENE OF BATTLE IN NIGHTLY QUEST OF HIS HEAD . . .
. . . AND THAT THE RUSHING SPEED WITH WHICH HE SOMETIMES PASSES ALONG THE HOLLOW, LIKE A MIDNIGHT BLAST, IS DUE TO HIS HURRY TO GET BACK TO THE CHURCHYARD BEFORE DAYBREAK.
SUCH IS THE GENERAL PURPORT OF THIS LEGENDARY SUPERSTITION . . .
. . . AND THE SPECTRE IS KNOWN AT ALL THE COUNTRY FIRESIDES BY THE NAME OF THE *HEADLESS HORSEMAN OF SLEEPY HOLLOW*.

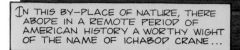

IN THIS BY-PLACE OF NATURE, THERE ABODE IN A REMOTE PERIOD OF AMERICAN HISTORY A WORTHY WIGHT OF THE NAME OF ICHABOD CRANE...

...WHO SOJOURNED IN SLEEPY HOLLOW FOR THE PURPOSE OF INSTRUCTING THE CHILDREN OF THE VICINITY.

HE WAS A NATIVE OF CONNECTICUT, A STATE WHICH SUPPLIES THE UNION WITH PIONEERS FOR THE MIND AS WELL AS FOR THE FOREST.

THE COGNOMEN OF CRANE WAS NOT INAPPLICABLE TO HIS PERSON.

HE WAS TALL, BUT EXCEEDINGLY LANK, WITH NARROW SHOULDERS, LONG ARMS AND LEGS, AND HIS WHOLE FRAME MOST LOOSELY HUNG TOGETHER.

TO SEE HIM STRIDING ALONG THE PROFILE OF A HILL ON A WINDY DAY, WITH HIS CLOTHES BAGGING AND FLUTTERING ABOUT HIM...

...ONE MIGHT HAVE MISTAKEN HIM FOR SOME SCARECROW ELOPED FROM A CORNFIELD.

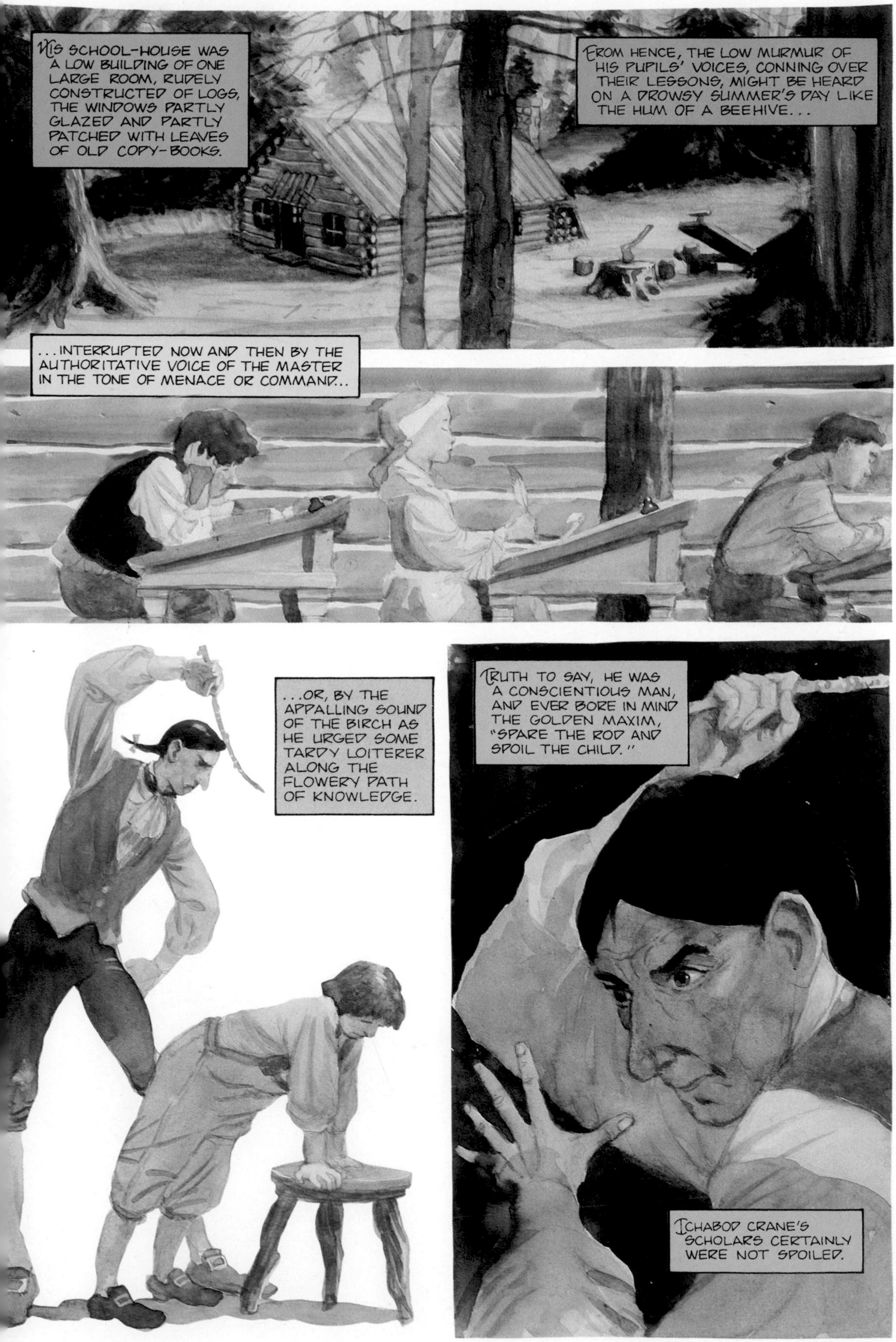
HIS SCHOOL-HOUSE WAS A LOW BUILDING OF ONE LARGE ROOM, RUDELY CONSTRUCTED OF LOGS, THE WINDOWS PARTLY GLAZED AND PARTLY PATCHED WITH LEAVES OF OLD COPY-BOOKS.
FROM HENCE, THE LOW MURMUR OF HIS PUPILS' VOICES, CONNING OVER THEIR LESSONS, MIGHT BE HEARD ON A DROWSY SUMMER'S DAY LIKE THE HUM OF A BEEHIVE...
...INTERRUPTED NOW AND THEN BY THE AUTHORITATIVE VOICE OF THE MASTER IN THE TONE OF MENACE OR COMMAND...
...OR, BY THE APPALLING SOUND OF THE BIRCH AS HE URGED SOME TARDY LOITERER ALONG THE FLOWERY PATH OF KNOWLEDGE.
TRUTH TO SAY, HE WAS A CONSCIENTIOUS MAN, AND EVER BORE IN MIND THE GOLDEN MAXIM, "SPARE THE ROD AND SPOIL THE CHILD."
ICHABOD CRANE'S SCHOLARS CERTAINLY WERE NOT SPOILED.

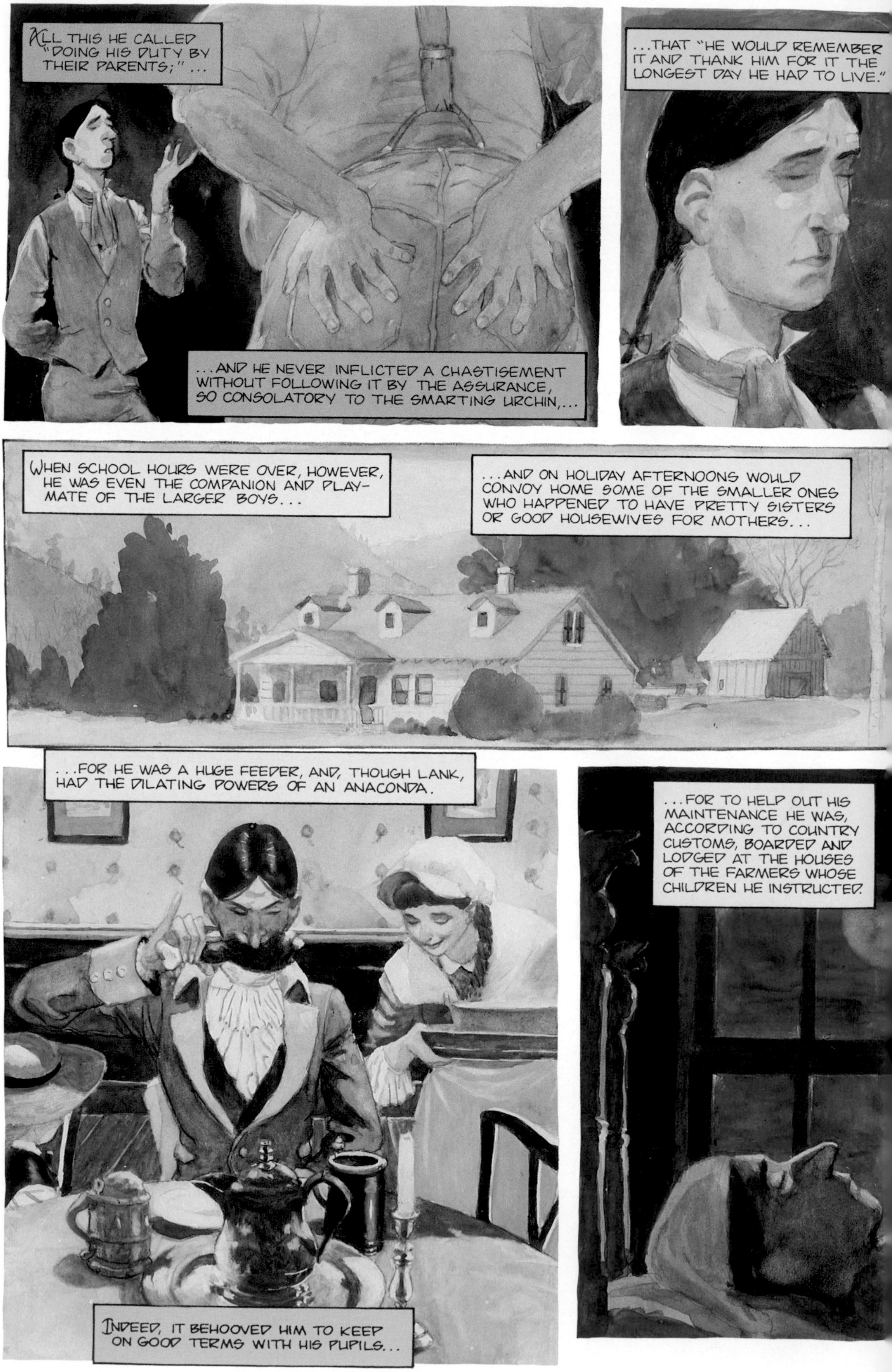
ALL THIS HE CALLED "DOING HIS DUTY BY THEIR PARENTS;" ...
...AND HE NEVER INFLICTED A CHASTISEMENT WITHOUT FOLLOWING IT BY THE ASSURANCE, SO CONSOLATORY TO THE SMARTING URCHIN,...
...THAT "HE WOULD REMEMBER IT AND THANK HIM FOR IT THE LONGEST DAY HE HAD TO LIVE."
WHEN SCHOOL HOURS WERE OVER, HOWEVER, HE WAS EVEN THE COMPANION AND PLAY-MATE OF THE LARGER BOYS...
...AND ON HOLIDAY AFTERNOONS WOULD CONVOY HOME SOME OF THE SMALLER ONES WHO HAPPENED TO HAVE PRETTY SISTERS OR GOOD HOUSEWIVES FOR MOTHERS...
...FOR HE WAS A HUGE FEEDER, AND, THOUGH LANK, HAD THE DILATING POWERS OF AN ANACONDA.
INDEED, IT BEHOOVED HIM TO KEEP ON GOOD TERMS WITH HIS PUPILS...
...FOR TO HELP OUT HIS MAINTENANCE HE WAS, ACCORDING TO COUNTRY CUSTOMS, BOARDED AND LODGED AT THE HOUSES OF THE FARMERS WHOSE CHILDREN HE INSTRUCTED.

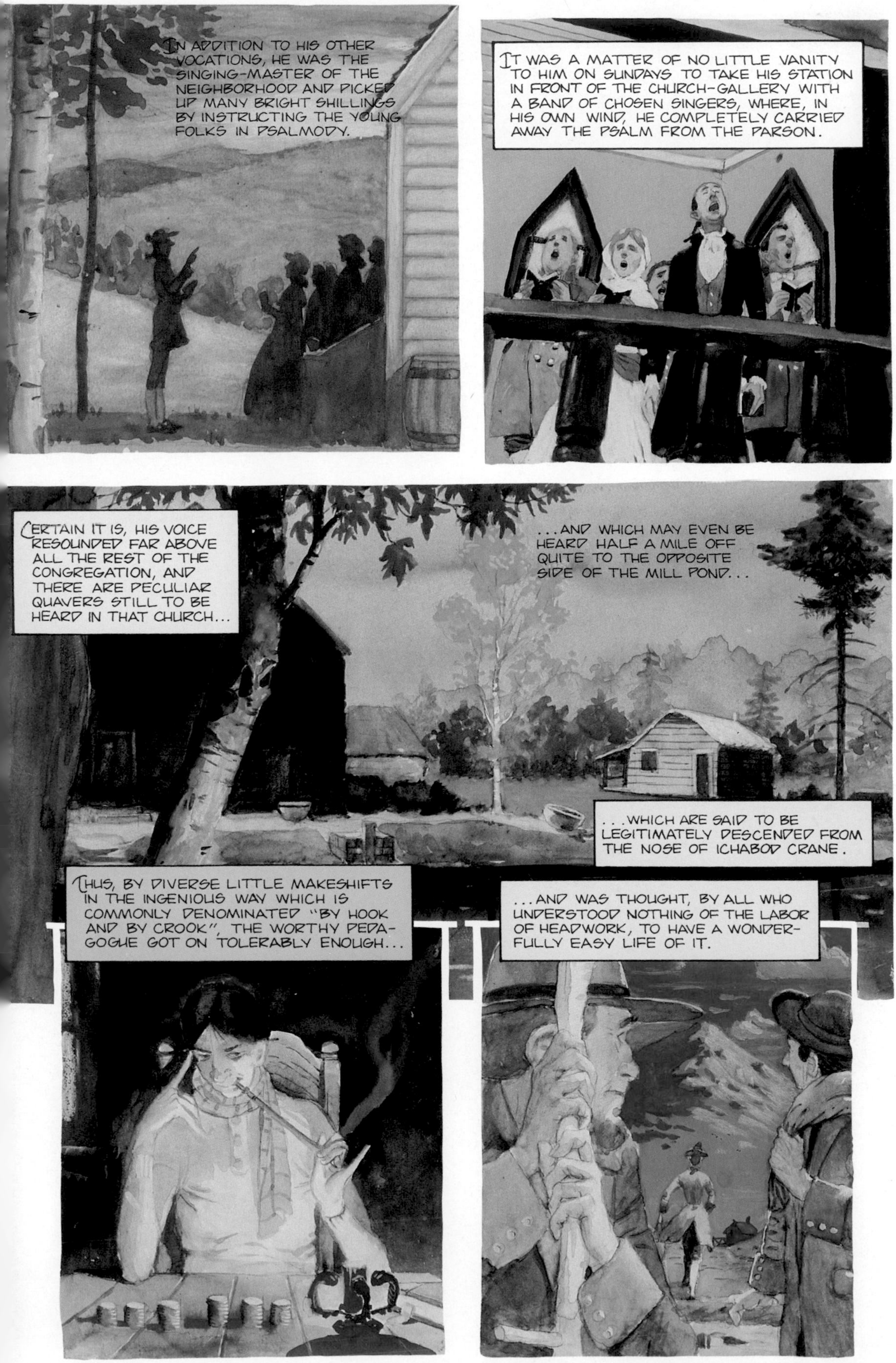
IN ADDITION TO HIS OTHER VOCATIONS, HE WAS THE SINGING-MASTER OF THE NEIGHBORHOOD AND PICKED UP MANY BRIGHT SHILLINGS BY INSTRUCTING THE YOUNG FOLKS IN PSALMODY.
IT WAS A MATTER OF NO LITTLE VANITY TO HIM ON SUNDAYS TO TAKE HIS STATION IN FRONT OF THE CHURCH-GALLERY WITH A BAND OF CHOSEN SINGERS, WHERE, IN HIS OWN WIND, HE COMPLETELY CARRIED AWAY THE PSALM FROM THE PARSON.
CERTAIN IT IS, HIS VOICE RESOUNDED FAR ABOVE ALL THE REST OF THE CONGREGATION, AND THERE ARE PECULIAR QUAVERS STILL TO BE HEARD IN THAT CHURCH...
...AND WHICH MAY EVEN BE HEARD HALF A MILE OFF QUITE TO THE OPPOSITE SIDE OF THE MILL POND...
...WHICH ARE SAID TO BE LEGITIMATELY DESCENDED FROM THE NOSE OF ICHABOD CRANE.
THUS, BY DIVERSE LITTLE MAKESHIFTS IN THE INGENIOUS WAY WHICH IS COMMONLY DENOMINATED "BY HOOK AND BY CROOK", THE WORTHY PEDAGOGUE GOT ON TOLERABLY ENOUGH...
...AND WAS THOUGHT, BY ALL WHO UNDERSTOOD NOTHING OF THE LABOR OF HEADWORK, TO HAVE A WONDERFULLY EASY LIFE OF IT.

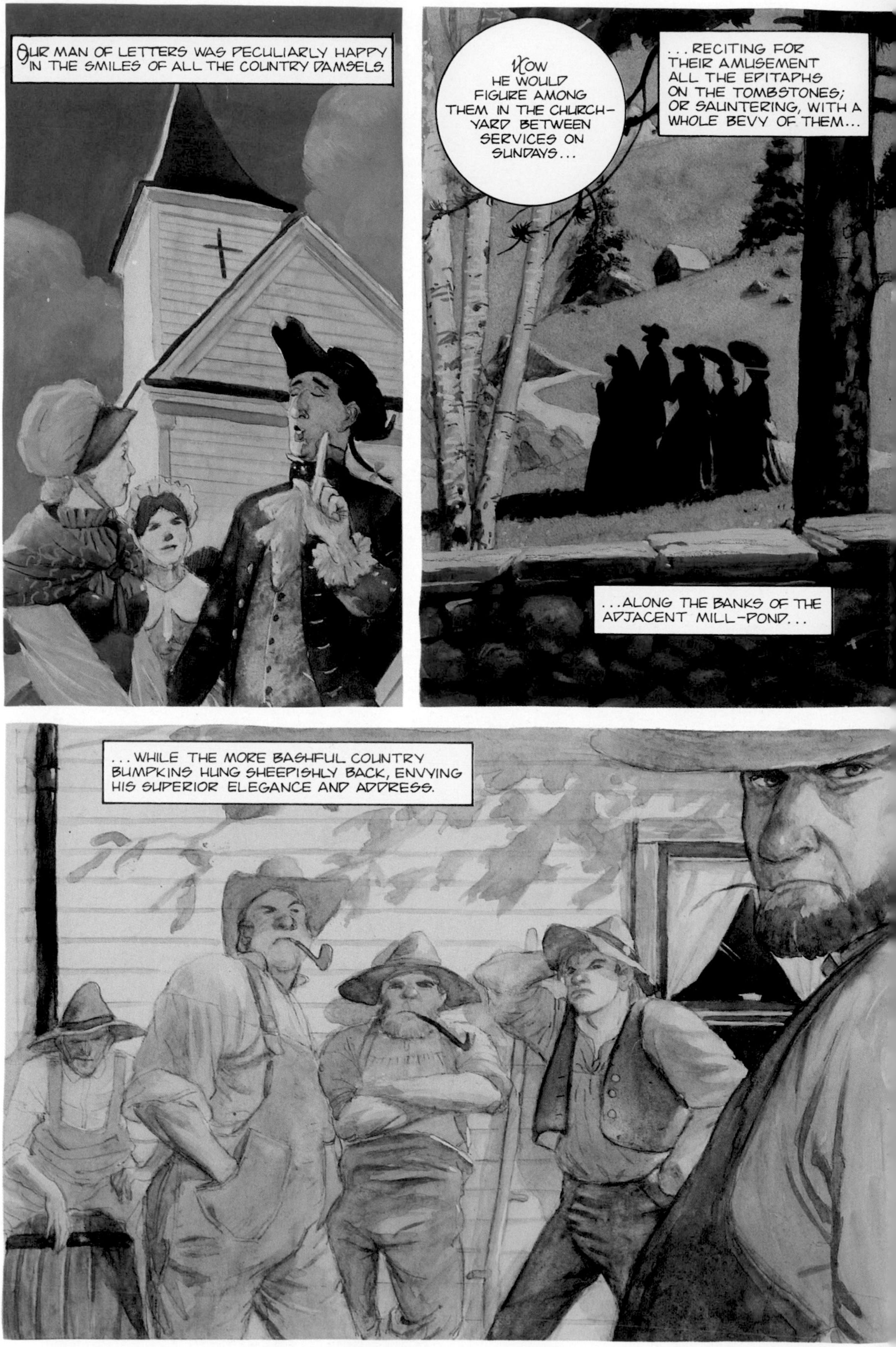
OUR MAN OF LETTERS WAS PECULIARLY HAPPY IN THE SMILES OF ALL THE COUNTRY DAMSELS.
HOW HE WOULD FIGURE AMONG THEM IN THE CHURCH-YARD BETWEEN SERVICES ON SUNDAYS...
...RECITING FOR THEIR AMUSEMENT ALL THE EPITAPHS ON THE TOMBSTONES; OR SAUNTERING, WITH A WHOLE BEVY OF THEM...
...ALONG THE BANKS OF THE ADJACENT MILL-POND...
...WHILE THE MORE BASHFUL COUNTRY BUMPKINS HUNG SHEEPISHLY BACK, ENVYING HIS SUPERIOR ELEGANCE AND ADDRESS.

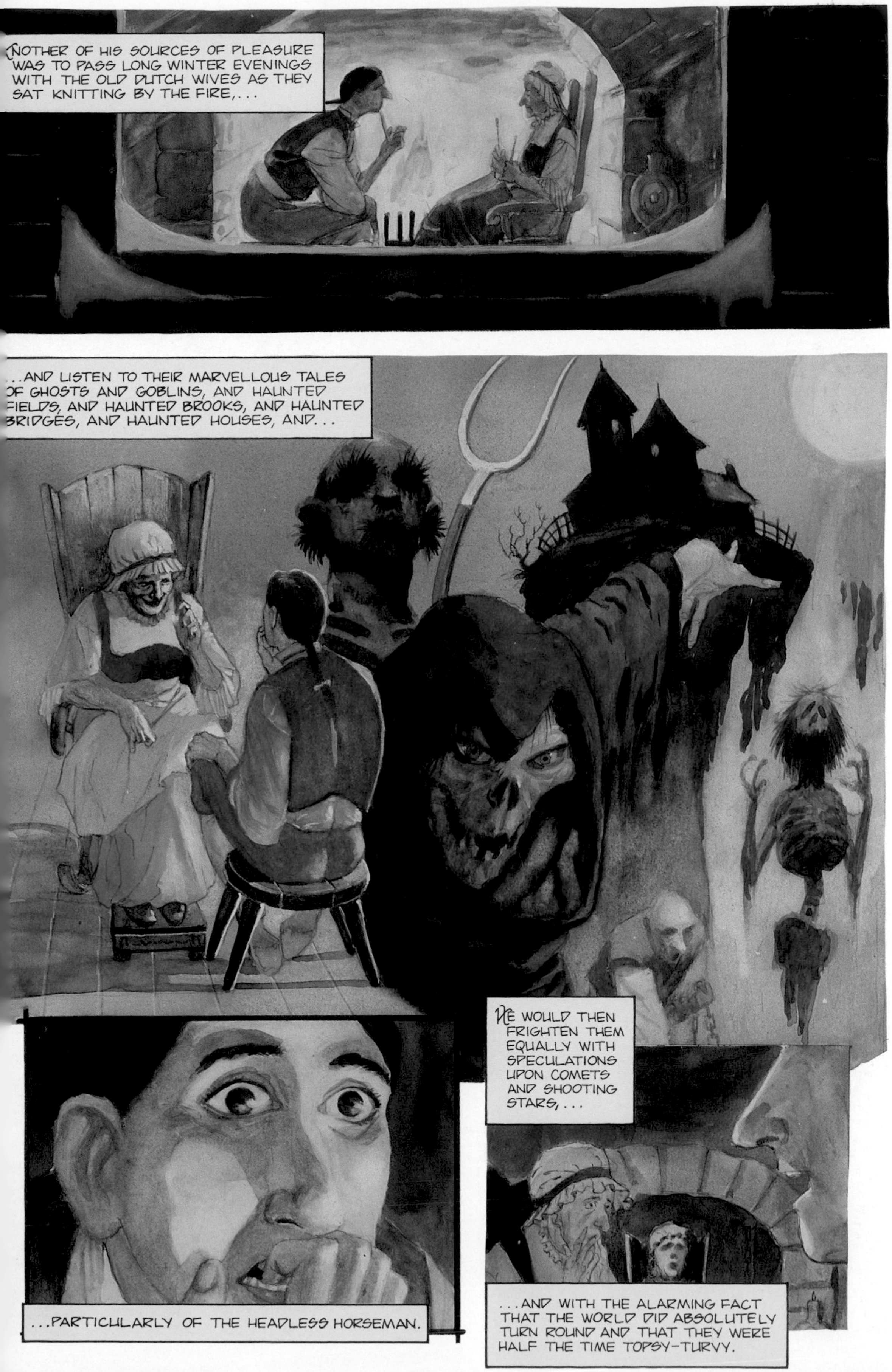
ANOTHER OF HIS SOURCES OF PLEASURE WAS TO PASS LONG WINTER EVENINGS WITH THE OLD DUTCH WIVES AS THEY SAT KNITTING BY THE FIRE,...
...AND LISTEN TO THEIR MARVELLOUS TALES OF GHOSTS AND GOBLINS, AND HAUNTED FIELDS, AND HAUNTED BROOKS, AND HAUNTED BRIDGES, AND HAUNTED HOUSES, AND...
...PARTICULARLY OF THE HEADLESS HORSEMAN.
HE WOULD THEN FRIGHTEN THEM EQUALLY WITH SPECULATIONS UPON COMETS AND SHOOTING STARS,...
...AND WITH THE ALARMING FACT THAT THE WORLD DID ABSOLUTELY TURN ROUND AND THAT THEY WERE HALF THE TIME TOPSY-TURVY.

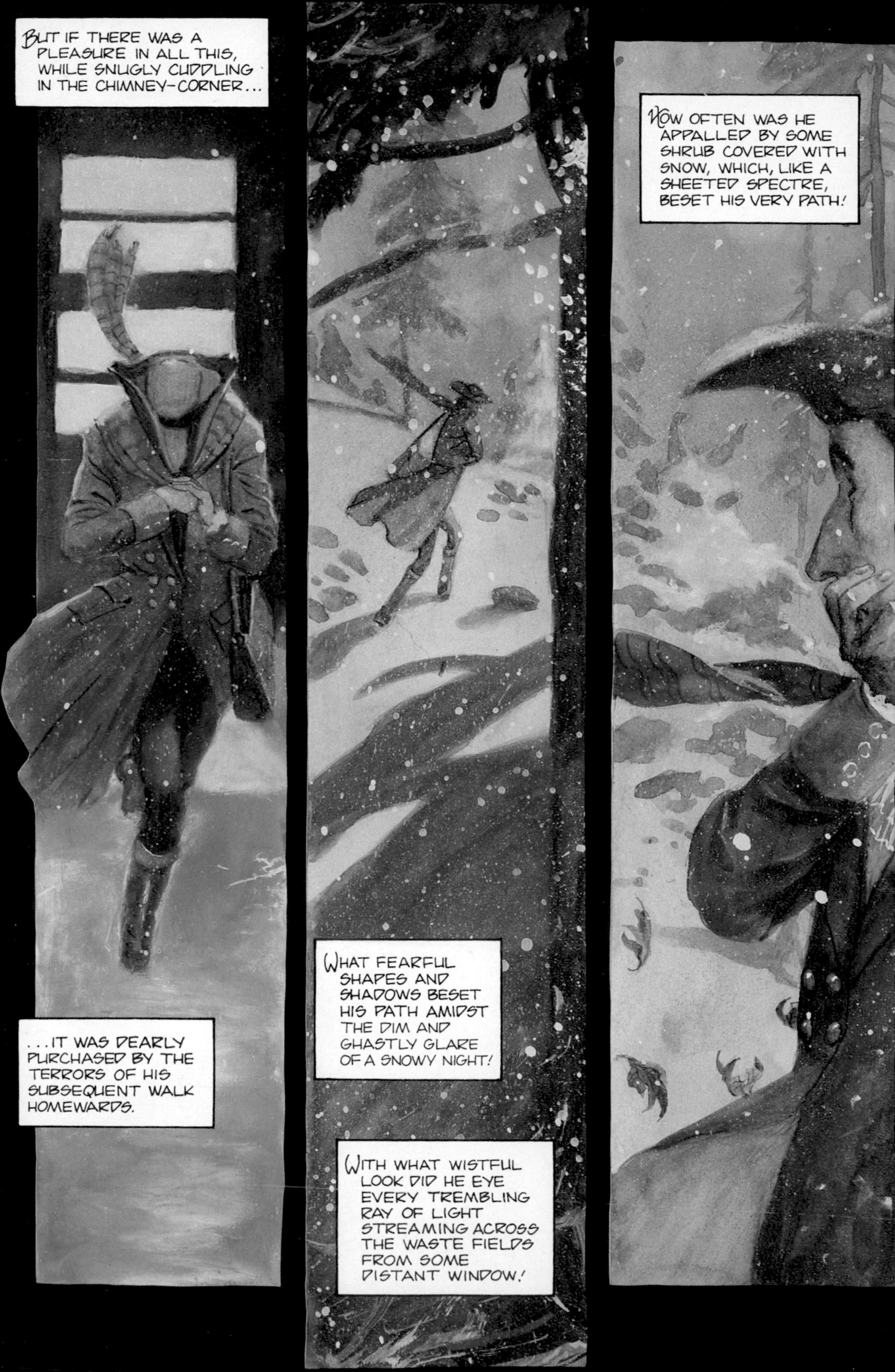
BUT IF THERE WAS A PLEASURE IN ALL THIS, WHILE SNUGLY CUDDLING IN THE CHIMNEY-CORNER...
...IT WAS DEARLY PURCHASED BY THE TERRORS OF HIS SUBSEQUENT WALK HOMEWARDS.
WHAT FEARFUL SHAPES AND SHADOWS BESET HIS PATH AMIDST THE DIM AND GHASTLY GLARE OF A SNOWY NIGHT!
WITH WHAT WISTFUL LOOK DID HE EYE EVERY TREMBLING RAY OF LIGHT STREAMING ACROSS THE WASTE FIELDS FROM SOME DISTANT WINDOW!
HOW OFTEN WAS HE APPALLED BY SOME SHRUB COVERED WITH SNOW, WHICH, LIKE A SHEETED SPECTRE, BESET HIS VERY PATH!

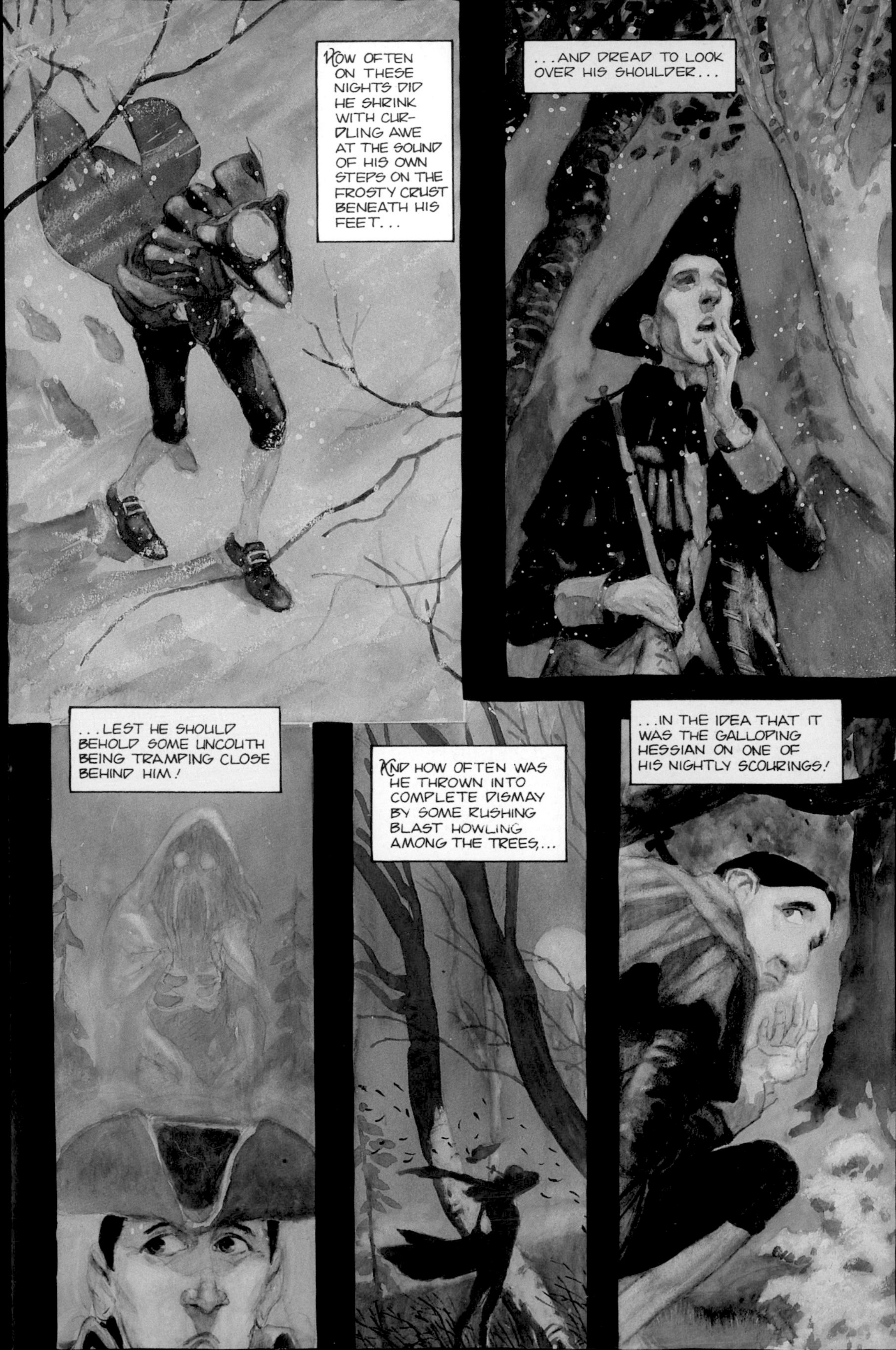
HOW OFTEN ON THESE NIGHTS DID HE SHRINK WITH CURDLING AWE AT THE SOUND OF HIS OWN STEPS ON THE FROSTY CRUST BENEATH HIS FEET...
...AND DREAD TO LOOK OVER HIS SHOULDER...
...LEST HE SHOULD BEHOLD SOME UNCOUTH BEING TRAMPING CLOSE BEHIND HIM!
AND HOW OFTEN WAS HE THROWN INTO COMPLETE DISMAY BY SOME RUSHING BLAST HOWLING AMONG THE TREES,...
...IN THE IDEA THAT IT WAS THE GALLOPING HESSIAN ON ONE OF HIS NIGHTLY SCOURINGS!

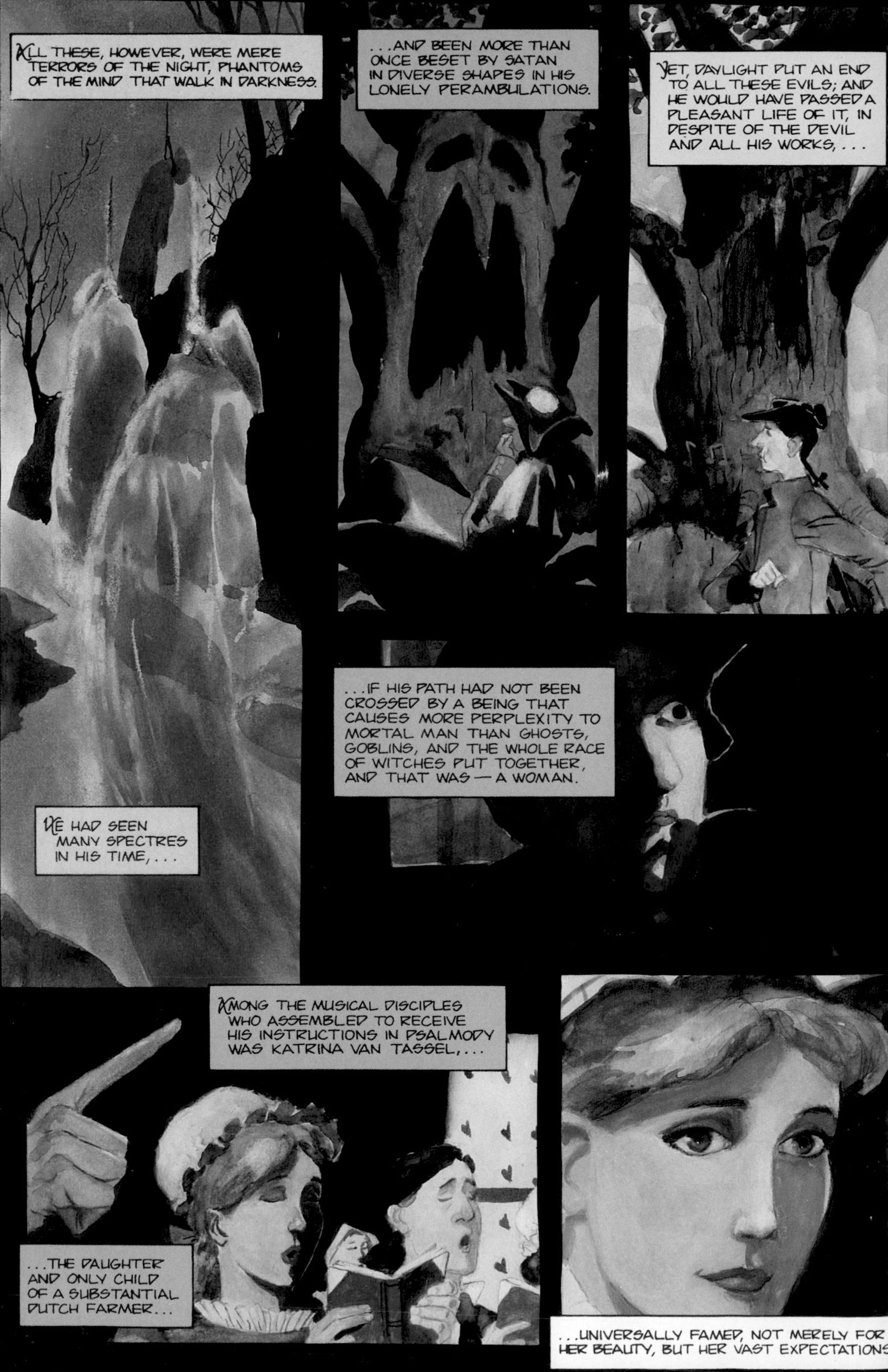
ALL THESE, HOWEVER, WERE MERE TERRORS OF THE NIGHT, PHANTOMS OF THE MIND THAT WALK IN DARKNESS.
HE HAD SEEN MANY SPECTRES IN HIS TIME, . . .
. . .AND BEEN MORE THAN ONCE BESET BY SATAN IN DIVERSE SHAPES IN HIS LONELY PERAMBULATIONS.
YET, DAYLIGHT PUT AN END TO ALL THESE EVILS; AND HE WOULD HAVE PASSED A PLEASANT LIFE OF IT, IN DESPITE OF THE DEVIL AND ALL HIS WORKS, . . .
. . .IF HIS PATH HAD NOT BEEN CROSSED BY A BEING THAT CAUSES MORE PERPLEXITY TO MORTAL MAN THAN GHOSTS, GOBLINS, AND THE WHOLE RACE OF WITCHES PUT TOGETHER, AND THAT WAS — A WOMAN.
AMONG THE MUSICAL DISCIPLES WHO ASSEMBLED TO RECEIVE HIS INSTRUCTIONS IN PSALMODY WAS KATRINA VAN TASSEL, . . .
. . .THE DAUGHTER AND ONLY CHILD OF A SUBSTANTIAL DUTCH FARMER . . .
. . .UNIVERSALLY FAMED, NOT MERELY FOR HER BEAUTY, BUT HER VAST EXPECTATIONS.

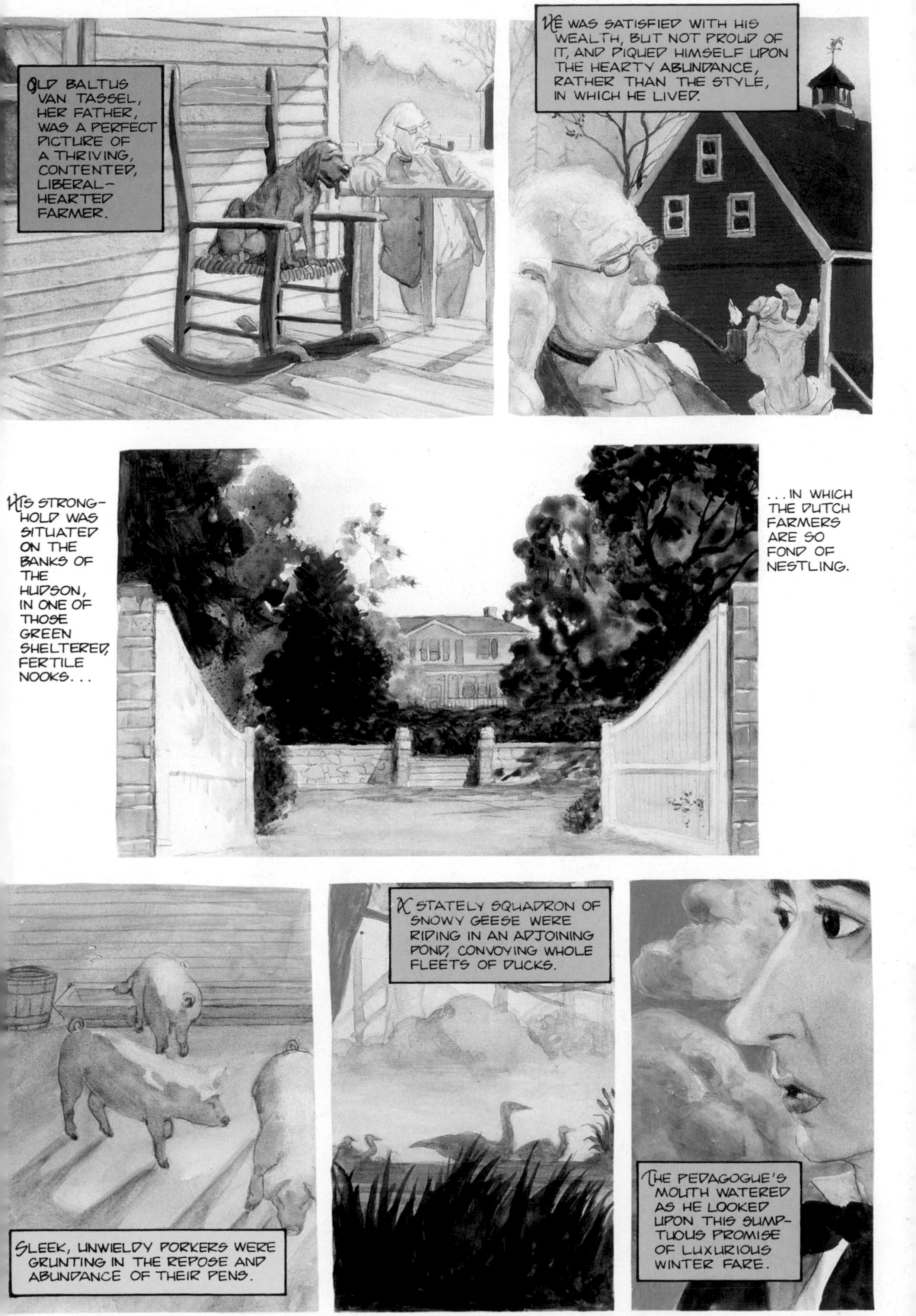
OLD BALTUS VAN TASSEL, HER FATHER, WAS A PERFECT PICTURE OF A THRIVING, CONTENTED, LIBERAL-HEARTED FARMER.
HE WAS SATISFIED WITH HIS WEALTH, BUT NOT PROUD OF IT, AND PIQUED HIMSELF UPON THE HEARTY ABUNDANCE, RATHER THAN THE STYLE, IN WHICH HE LIVED.
HIS STRONG-HOLD WAS SITUATED ON THE BANKS OF THE HUDSON, IN ONE OF THOSE GREEN SHELTERED, FERTILE NOOKS...
...IN WHICH THE DUTCH FARMERS ARE SO FOND OF NESTLING.
SLEEK, UNWIELDY PORKERS WERE GRUNTING IN THE REPOSE AND ABUNDANCE OF THEIR PENS.
A STATELY SQUADRON OF SNOWY GEESE WERE RIDING IN AN ADJOINING POND, CONVOYING WHOLE FLEETS OF DUCKS.
THE PEDAGOGUE'S MOUTH WATERED AS HE LOOKED UPON THIS SUMPTUOUS PROMISE OF LUXURIOUS WINTER FARE.

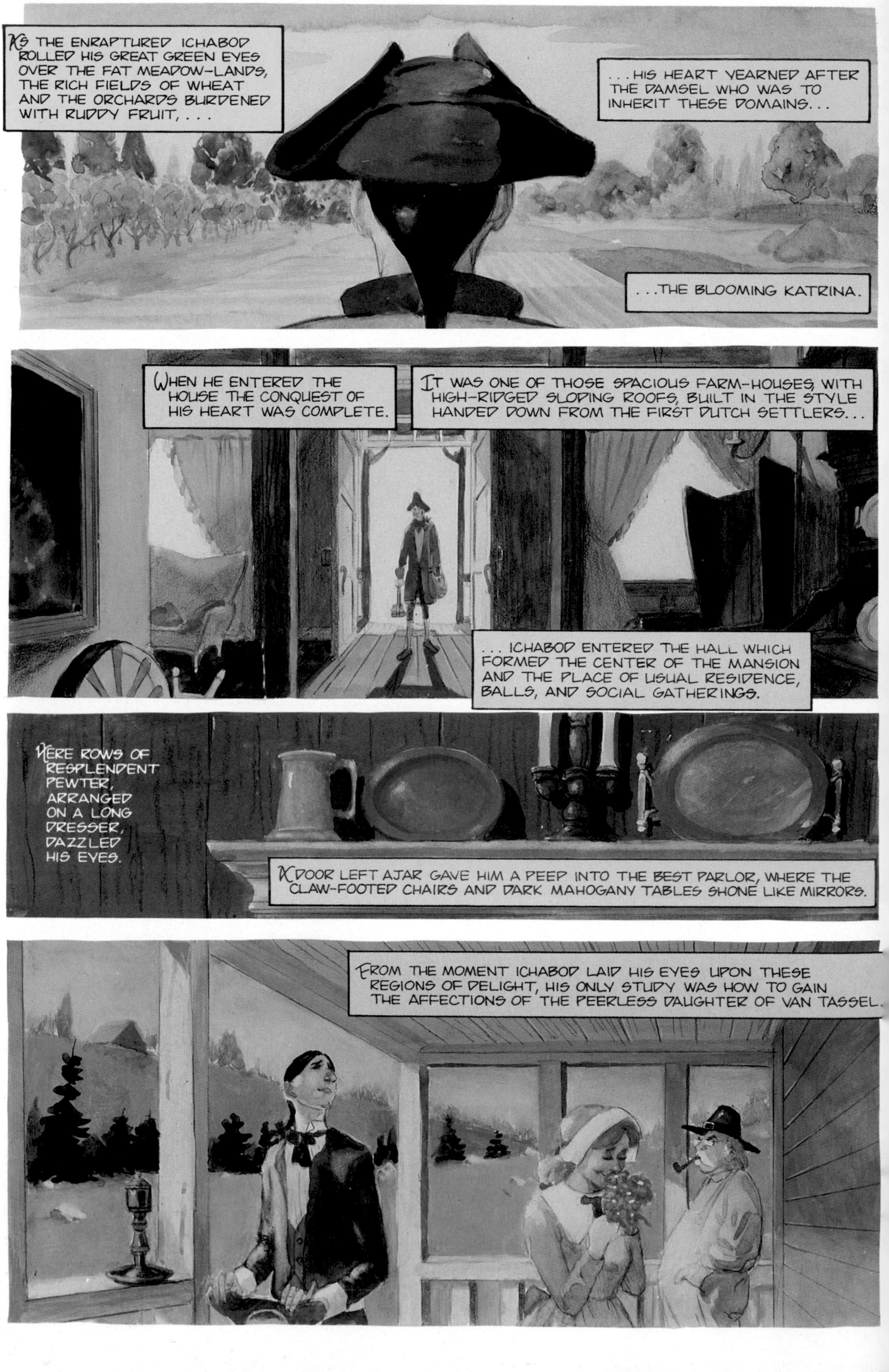
AS THE ENRAPTURED ICHABOD ROLLED HIS GREAT GREEN EYES OVER THE FAT MEADOW-LANDS, THE RICH FIELDS OF WHEAT AND THE ORCHARDS BURDENED WITH RUDDY FRUIT, . . .
. . . HIS HEART YEARNED AFTER THE DAMSEL WHO WAS TO INHERIT THESE DOMAINS. . .
. . . THE BLOOMING KATRINA.
WHEN HE ENTERED THE HOUSE THE CONQUEST OF HIS HEART WAS COMPLETE.
IT WAS ONE OF THOSE SPACIOUS FARM-HOUSES, WITH HIGH-RIDGED SLOPING ROOFS, BUILT IN THE STYLE HANDED DOWN FROM THE FIRST DUTCH SETTLERS. . .
. . . ICHABOD ENTERED THE HALL WHICH FORMED THE CENTER OF THE MANSION AND THE PLACE OF USUAL RESIDENCE, BALLS, AND SOCIAL GATHERINGS.
HERE ROWS OF RESPLENDENT PEWTER, ARRANGED ON A LONG DRESSER, DAZZLED HIS EYES.
A DOOR LEFT AJAR GAVE HIM A PEEP INTO THE BEST PARLOR, WHERE THE CLAW-FOOTED CHAIRS AND DARK MAHOGANY TABLES SHONE LIKE MIRRORS.
FROM THE MOMENT ICHABOD LAID HIS EYES UPON THESE REGIONS OF DELIGHT, HIS ONLY STUDY WAS HOW TO GAIN THE AFFECTIONS OF THE PEERLESS DAUGHTER OF VAN TASSEL.

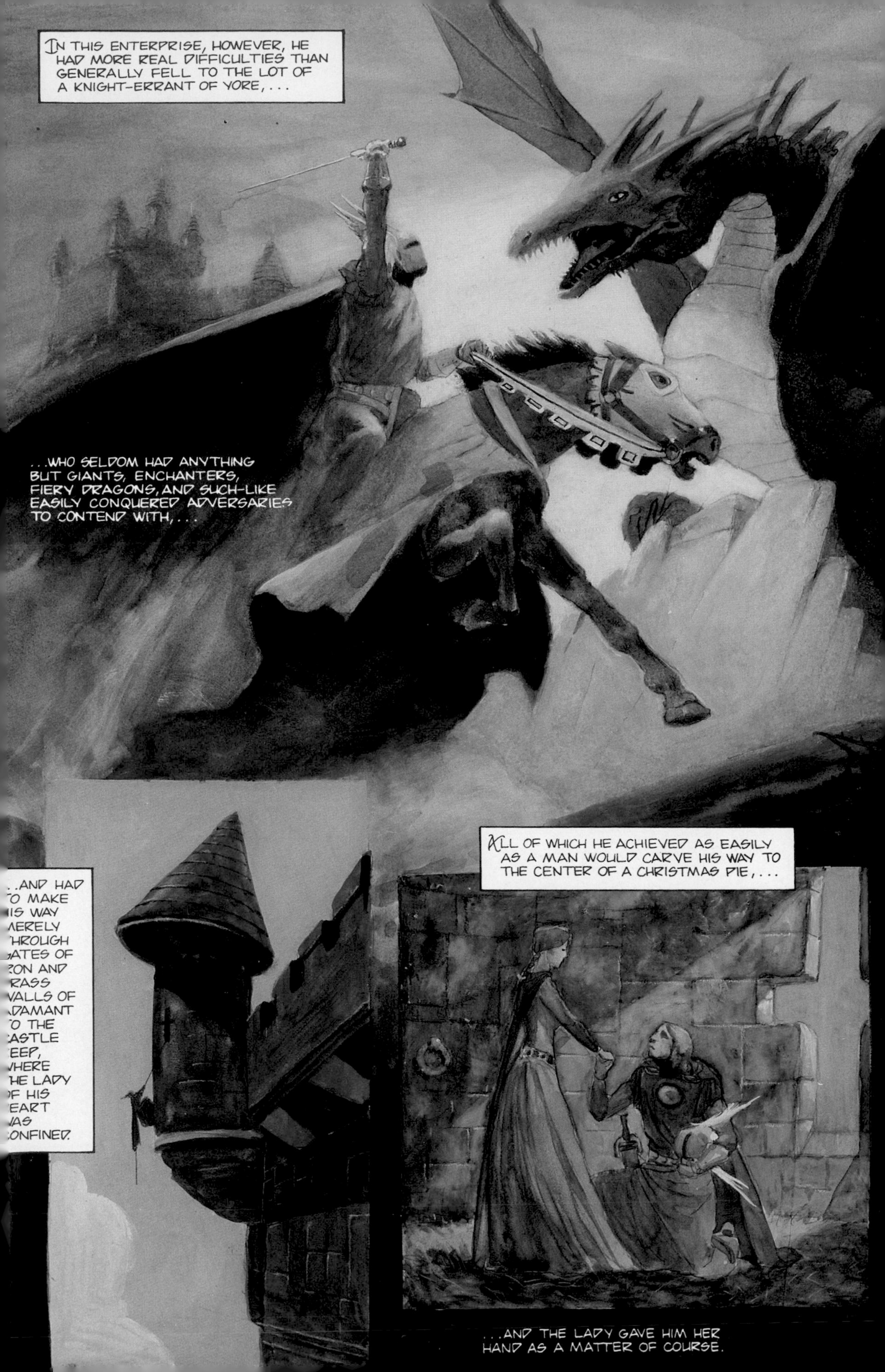
IN THIS ENTERPRISE, HOWEVER, HE HAD MORE REAL DIFFICULTIES THAN GENERALLY FELL TO THE LOT OF A KNIGHT-ERRANT OF YORE, . . .
. . .WHO SELDOM HAD ANYTHING BUT GIANTS, ENCHANTERS, FIERY DRAGONS, AND SUCH-LIKE EASILY CONQUERED ADVERSARIES TO CONTEND WITH, . . .
. .AND HAD O MAKE IS WAY MERELY THROUGH GATES OF RON AND RASS WALLS OF ADAMANT TO THE ASTLE EEP, WHERE THE LADY OF HIS EART WAS ONFINED.
ALL OF WHICH HE ACHIEVED AS EASILY AS A MAN WOULD CARVE HIS WAY TO THE CENTER OF A CHRISTMAS PIE, . . .
. . .AND THE LADY GAVE HIM HER HAND AS A MATTER OF COURSE.

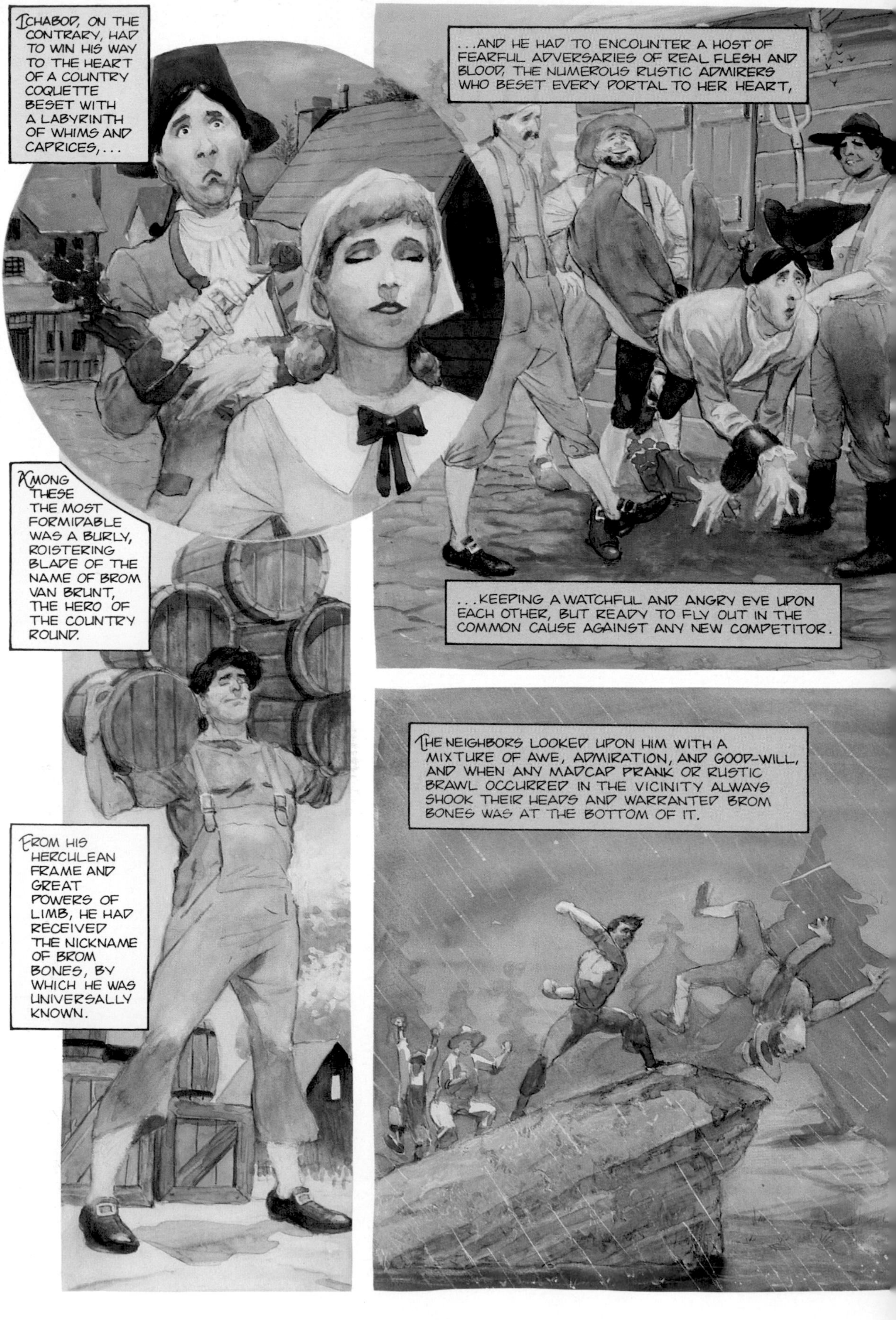
ICHABOD, ON THE CONTRARY, HAD TO WIN HIS WAY TO THE HEART OF A COUNTRY COQUETTE BESET WITH A LABYRINTH OF WHIMS AND CAPRICES, . . .
. . . AND HE HAD TO ENCOUNTER A HOST OF FEARFUL ADVERSARIES OF REAL FLESH AND BLOOD, THE NUMEROUS RUSTIC ADMIRERS WHO BESET EVERY PORTAL TO HER HEART,
. . . KEEPING A WATCHFUL AND ANGRY EYE UPON EACH OTHER, BUT READY TO FLY OUT IN THE COMMON CAUSE AGAINST ANY NEW COMPETITOR.
AMONG THESE THE MOST FORMIDABLE WAS A BURLY, ROISTERING BLADE OF THE NAME OF BROM VAN BRUNT, THE HERO OF THE COUNTRY ROUND.
FROM HIS HERCULEAN FRAME AND GREAT POWERS OF LIMB, HE HAD RECEIVED THE NICKNAME OF BROM BONES, BY WHICH HE WAS UNIVERSALLY KNOWN.
THE NEIGHBORS LOOKED UPON HIM WITH A MIXTURE OF AWE, ADMIRATION, AND GOOD-WILL, AND WHEN ANY MADCAP PRANK OR RUSTIC BRAWL OCCURRED IN THE VICINITY ALWAYS SHOOK THEIR HEADS AND WARRANTED BROM BONES WAS AT THE BOTTOM OF IT.

WHEN HIS HORSE WAS SEEN TIED TO VAN TASSEL'S PALING ON A SUNDAY NIGHT, IT WAS A SURE SIGN THAT HIS MASTER WAS COURTING—OR, AS IT IS TERMED, "SPARKING"—WITHIN, AND ALL OTHER SUITORS PASSED BY IN DESPAIR.

SUCH WAS THE FORMIDABLE RIVAL WITH WHOM ICHABOD CRANE HAD TO CONTEND...

ICHABOD HAD, HOWEVER, A HAPPY MIXTURE OF PLIABILITY AND PERSEVERANCE IN HIS NATURE—YIELDING, BUT TOUGH.

THOUGH HE BENT, HE NEVER BROKE; AND THOUGH HE BOWED BENEATH THE SLIGHTEST PRESSURE,...

...YET THE MOMENT IT WAS AWAY, JERK! HE WAS AS ERECT AND CARRIED HIS HEAD AS HIGH AS EVER.

ICHABOD, THEREFORE, MADE HIS ADVANCES IN A QUIET AND GENTLY INSINUATING MANNER.

UNDER COVER OF H... CHAR... OF S... MAST... HE MADE FREQUENT VISITS AT THE FARM—HOUSE.

ICHABOD WOULD CARRY ON HIS SUIT WITH THE DAUGHTER BY THE SIDE OF THE SPRING UNDER THE GREAT ELM OR SAUNTERING ALONG IN THE TWILIGHT.

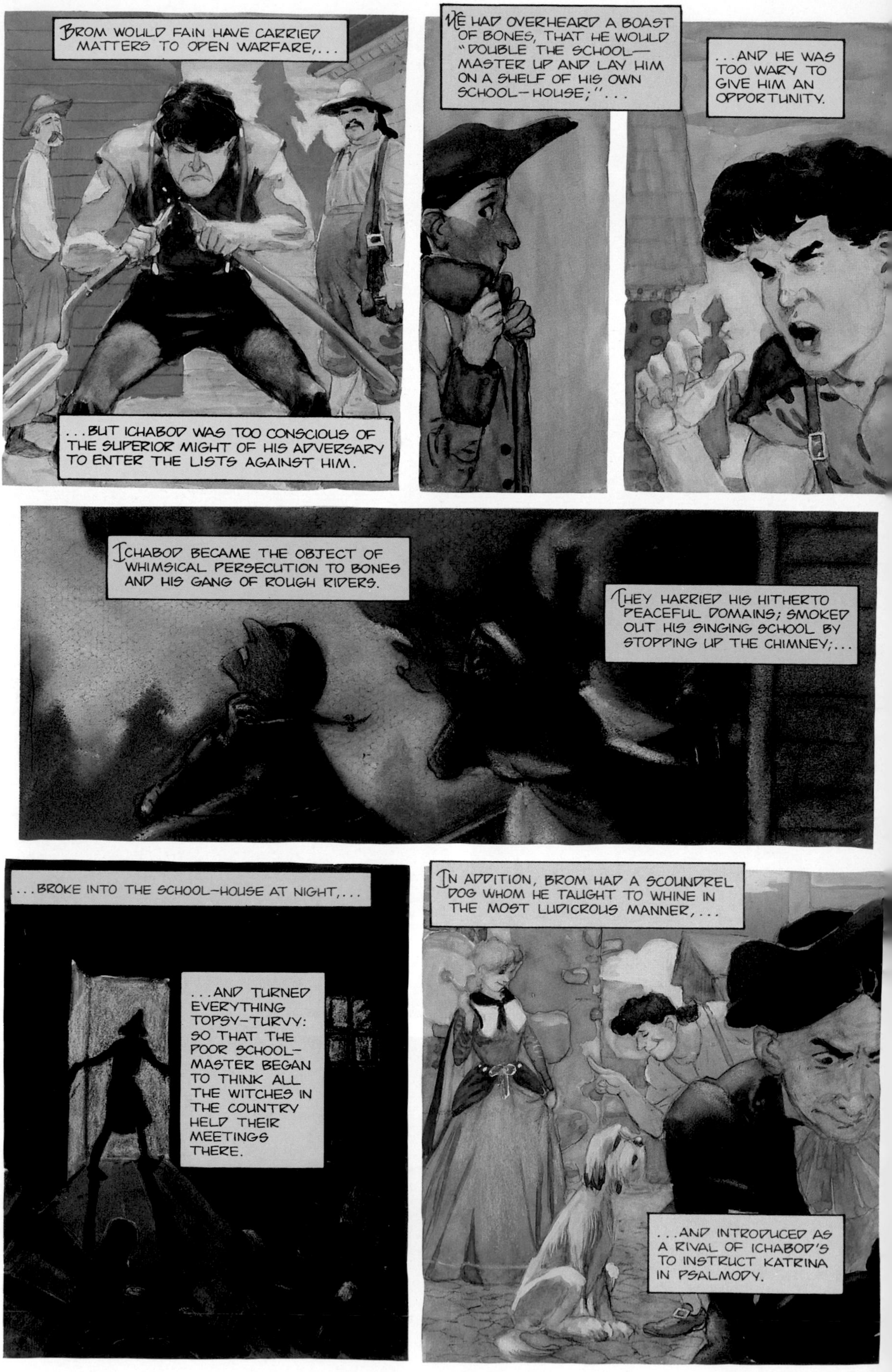
BROM WOULD FAIN HAVE CARRIED MATTERS TO OPEN WARFARE,...
...BUT ICHABOD WAS TOO CONSCIOUS OF THE SUPERIOR MIGHT OF HIS ADVERSARY TO ENTER THE LISTS AGAINST HIM.
HE HAD OVERHEARD A BOAST OF BONES, THAT HE WOULD "DOUBLE THE SCHOOL-MASTER UP AND LAY HIM ON A SHELF OF HIS OWN SCHOOL-HOUSE;"...
...AND HE WAS TOO WARY TO GIVE HIM AN OPPORTUNITY.
ICHABOD BECAME THE OBJECT OF WHIMSICAL PERSECUTION TO BONES AND HIS GANG OF ROUGH RIDERS.
THEY HARRIED HIS HITHERTO PEACEFUL DOMAINS; SMOKED OUT HIS SINGING SCHOOL BY STOPPING UP THE CHIMNEY;...
...BROKE INTO THE SCHOOL-HOUSE AT NIGHT,...
...AND TURNED EVERYTHING TOPSY-TURVY: SO THAT THE POOR SCHOOL-MASTER BEGAN TO THINK ALL THE WITCHES IN THE COUNTRY HELD THEIR MEETINGS THERE.
IN ADDITION, BROM HAD A SCOUNDREL DOG WHOM HE TAUGHT TO WHINE IN THE MOST LUDICROUS MANNER,...
...AND INTRODUCED AS A RIVAL OF ICHABOD'S TO INSTRUCT KATRINA IN PSALMODY.

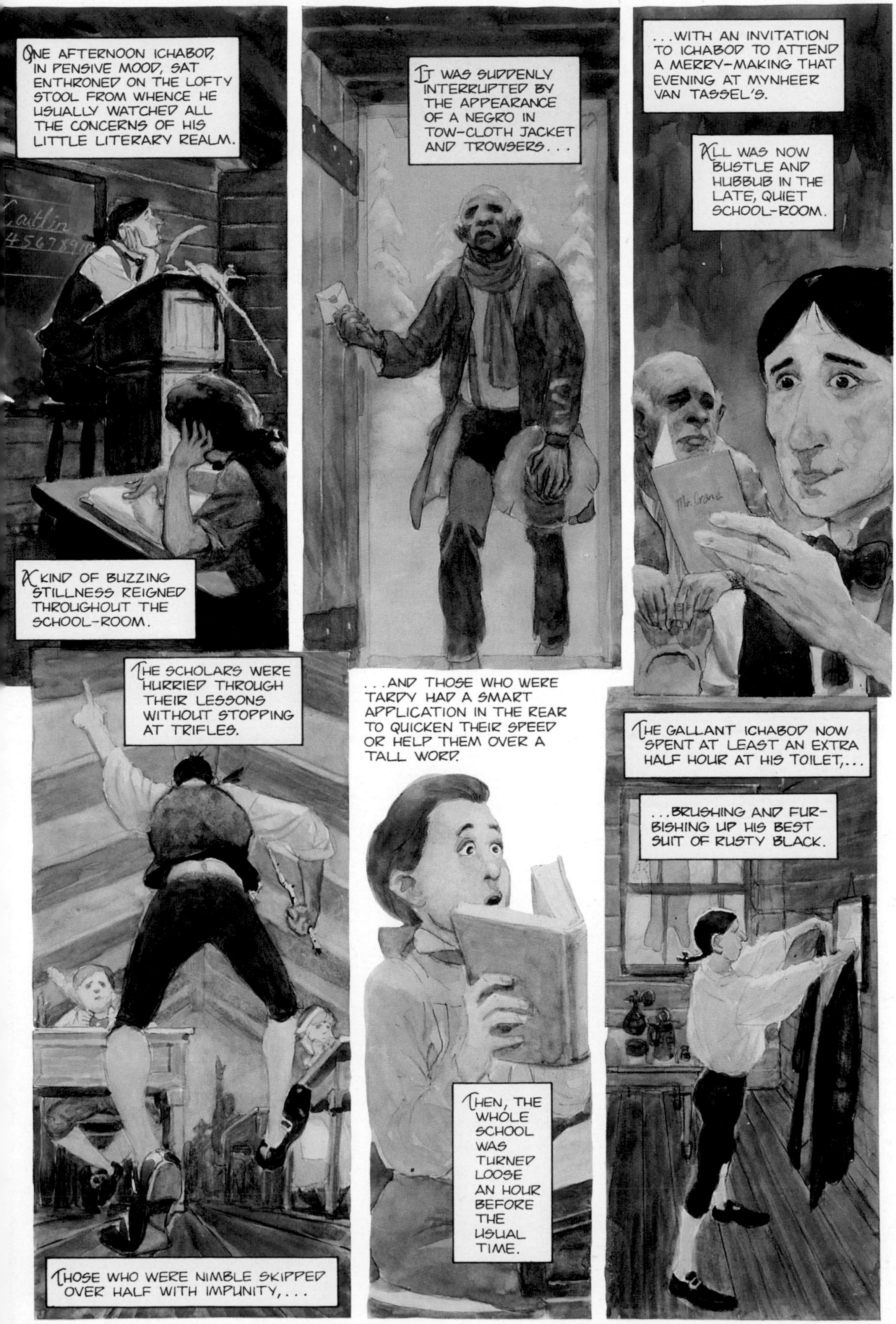
ONE AFTERNOON ICHABOD, IN PENSIVE MOOD, SAT ENTHRONED ON THE LOFTY STOOL FROM WHENCE HE USUALLY WATCHED ALL THE CONCERNS OF HIS LITTLE LITERARY REALM.
A KIND OF BUZZING STILLNESS REIGNED THROUGHOUT THE SCHOOL-ROOM.
IT WAS SUDDENLY INTERRUPTED BY THE APPEARANCE OF A NEGRO IN TOW-CLOTH JACKET AND TROWSERS . . .
. . . WITH AN INVITATION TO ICHABOD TO ATTEND A MERRY-MAKING THAT EVENING AT MYNHEER VAN TASSEL'S.
ALL WAS NOW BUSTLE AND HUBBUB IN THE LATE, QUIET SCHOOL-ROOM.
THE SCHOLARS WERE HURRIED THROUGH THEIR LESSONS WITHOUT STOPPING AT TRIFLES.
THOSE WHO WERE NIMBLE SKIPPED OVER HALF WITH IMPUNITY, . . .
. . . AND THOSE WHO WERE TARDY HAD A SMART APPLICATION IN THE REAR TO QUICKEN THEIR SPEED OR HELP THEM OVER A TALL WORD.
THEN, THE WHOLE SCHOOL WAS TURNED LOOSE AN HOUR BEFORE THE USUAL TIME.
THE GALLANT ICHABOD NOW SPENT AT LEAST AN EXTRA HALF HOUR AT HIS TOILET, . . .
. . . BRUSHING AND FUR-BISHING UP HIS BEST SUIT OF RUSTY BLACK.

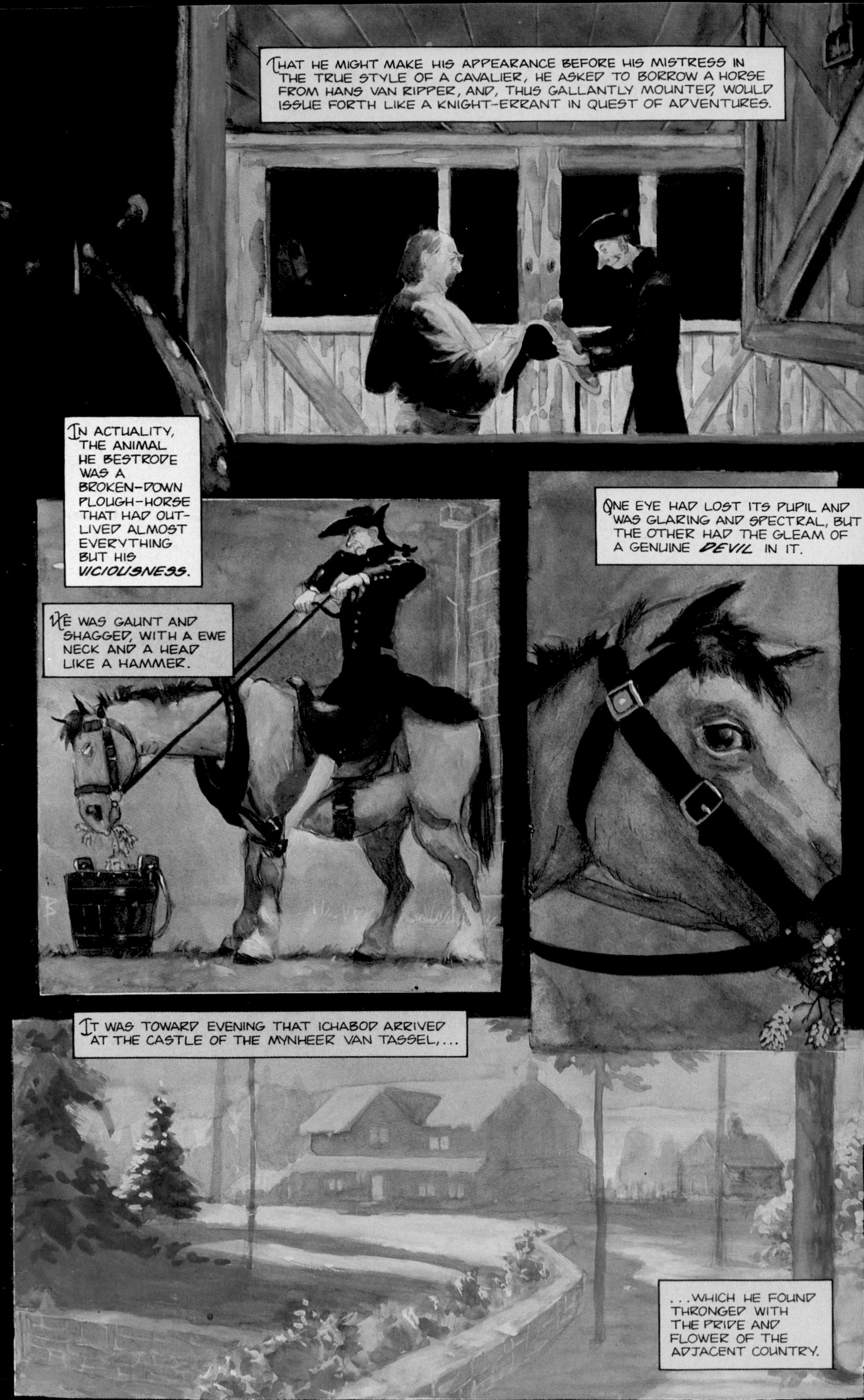
THAT HE MIGHT MAKE HIS APPEARANCE BEFORE HIS MISTRESS IN THE TRUE STYLE OF A CAVALIER, HE ASKED TO BORROW A HORSE FROM HANS VAN RIPPER, AND, THUS GALLANTLY MOUNTED, WOULD ISSUE FORTH LIKE A KNIGHT-ERRANT IN QUEST OF ADVENTURES.
IN ACTUALITY, THE ANIMAL HE BESTRODE WAS A BROKEN-DOWN PLOUGH-HORSE THAT HAD OUT-LIVED ALMOST EVERYTHING BUT HIS VICIOUSNESS.
HE WAS GAUNT AND SHAGGED, WITH A EWE NECK AND A HEAD LIKE A HAMMER.
ONE EYE HAD LOST ITS PUPIL AND WAS GLARING AND SPECTRAL, BUT THE OTHER HAD THE GLEAM OF A GENUINE DEVIL IN IT.
IT WAS TOWARD EVENING THAT ICHABOD ARRIVED AT THE CASTLE OF THE MYNHEER VAN TASSEL,...
...WHICH HE FOUND THRONGED WITH THE PRIDE AND FLOWER OF THE ADJACENT COUNTRY.

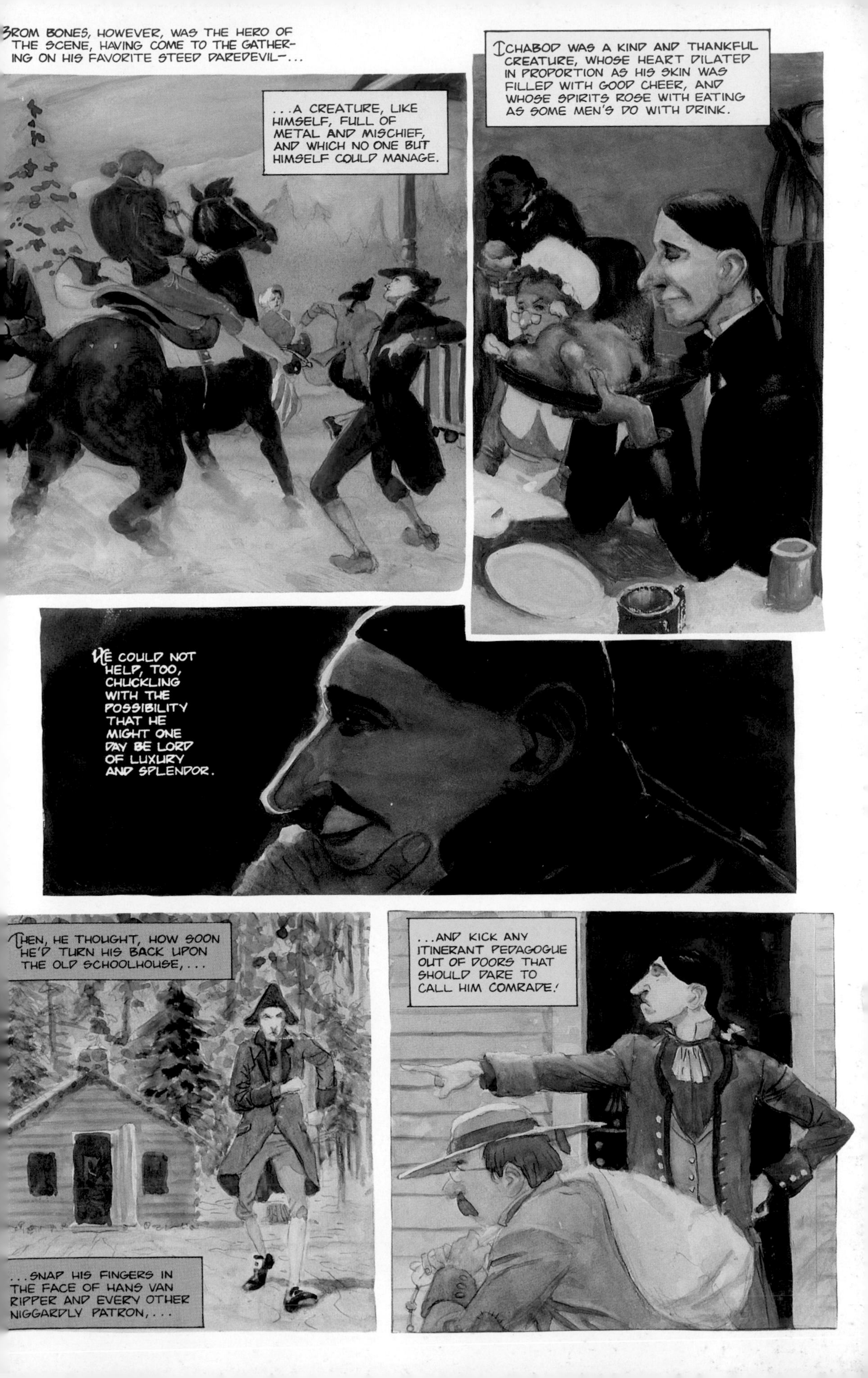
BROM BONES, HOWEVER, WAS THE HERO OF THE SCENE, HAVING COME TO THE GATHERING ON HIS FAVORITE STEED DAREDEVIL–...
...A CREATURE, LIKE HIMSELF, FULL OF METAL AND MISCHIEF, AND WHICH NO ONE BUT HIMSELF COULD MANAGE.
ICHABOD WAS A KIND AND THANKFUL CREATURE, WHOSE HEART DILATED IN PROPORTION AS HIS SKIN WAS FILLED WITH GOOD CHEER, AND WHOSE SPIRITS ROSE WITH EATING AS SOME MEN'S DO WITH DRINK.
HE COULD NOT HELP, TOO, CHUCKLING WITH THE POSSIBILITY THAT HE MIGHT ONE DAY BE LORD OF LUXURY AND SPLENDOR.
THEN, HE THOUGHT, HOW SOON HE'D TURN HIS BACK UPON THE OLD SCHOOLHOUSE,...
...SNAP HIS FINGERS IN THE FACE OF HANS VAN RIPPER AND EVERY OTHER NIGGARDLY PATRON,...
...AND KICK ANY ITINERANT PEDAGOGUE OUT OF DOORS THAT SHOULD DARE TO CALL HIM COMRADE!

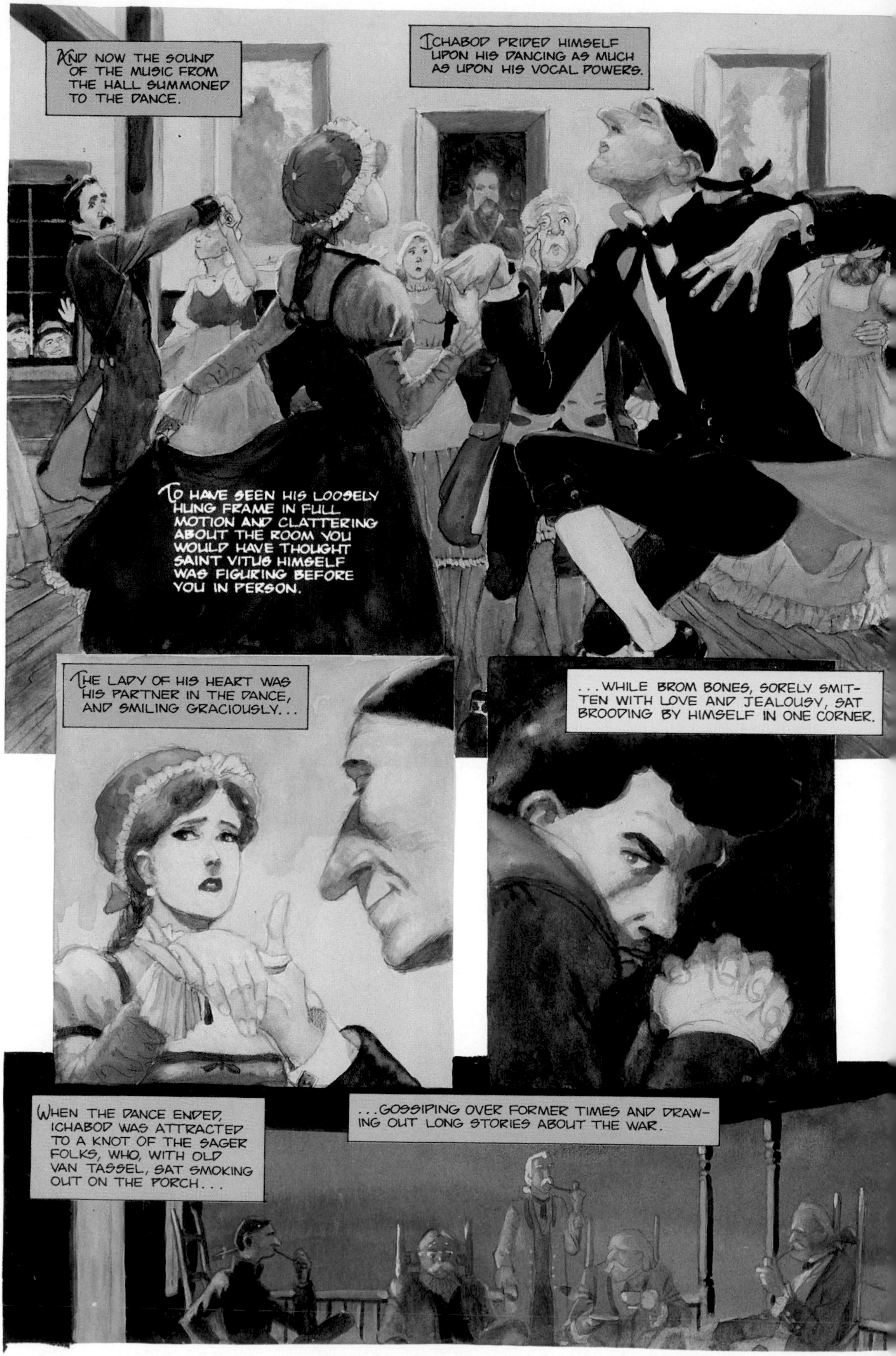
AND NOW THE SOUND OF THE MUSIC FROM THE HALL SUMMONED TO THE DANCE.
ICHABOD PRIDED HIMSELF UPON HIS DANCING AS MUCH AS UPON HIS VOCAL POWERS.
TO HAVE SEEN HIS LOOSELY HUNG FRAME IN FULL MOTION AND CLATTERING ABOUT THE ROOM YOU WOULD HAVE THOUGHT SAINT VITUS HIMSELF WAS FIGURING BEFORE YOU IN PERSON.
THE LADY OF HIS HEART WAS HIS PARTNER IN THE DANCE, AND SMILING GRACIOUSLY...
...WHILE BROM BONES, SORELY SMITTEN WITH LOVE AND JEALOUSY, SAT BROODING BY HIMSELF IN ONE CORNER.
WHEN THE DANCE ENDED, ICHABOD WAS ATTRACTED TO A KNOT OF THE SAGER FOLKS, WHO, WITH OLD VAN TASSEL, SAT SMOKING OUT ON THE PORCH...
...GOSSIPING OVER FORMER TIMES AND DRAWING OUT LONG STORIES ABOUT THE WAR.

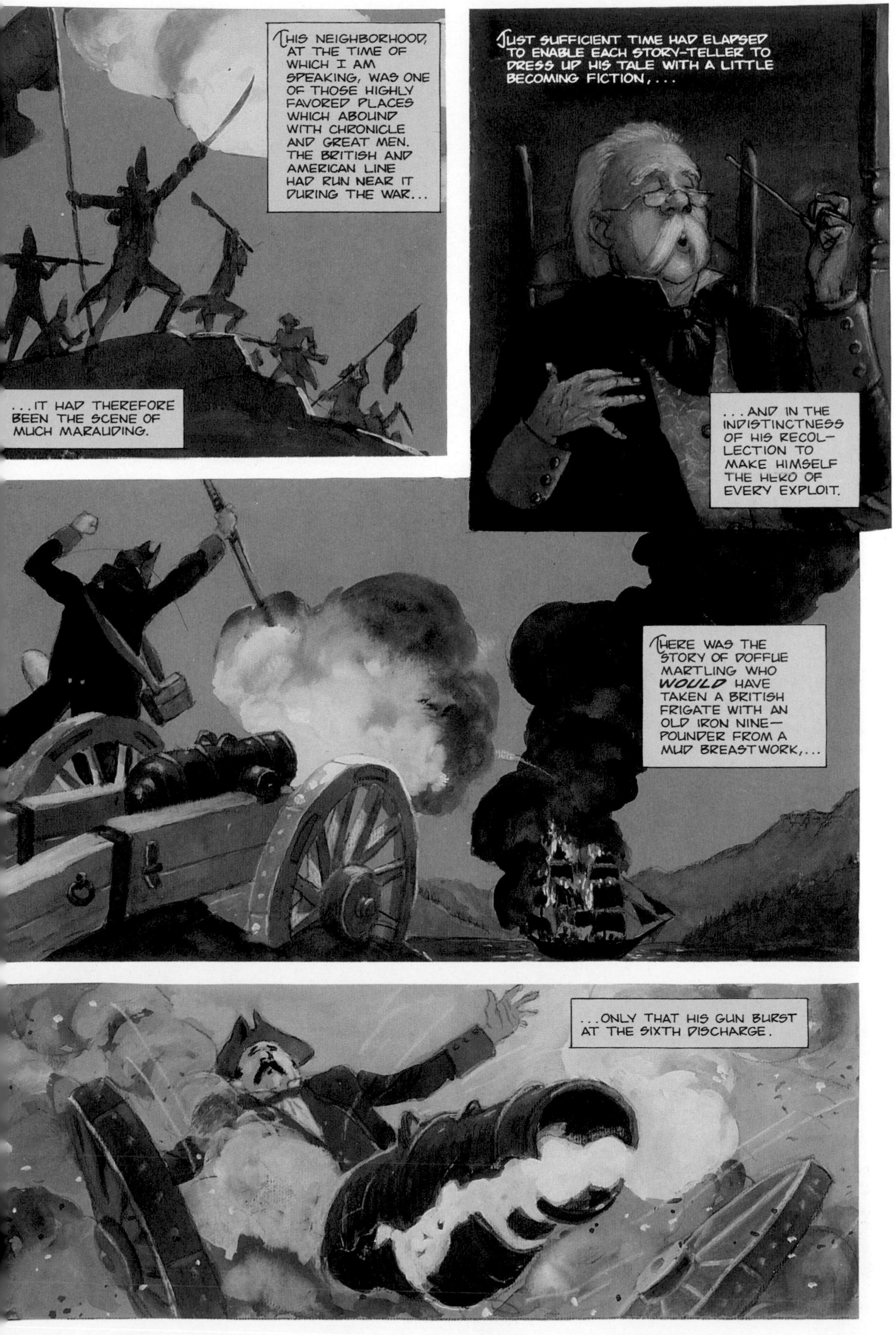
THIS NEIGHBORHOOD, AT THE TIME OF WHICH I AM SPEAKING, WAS ONE OF THOSE HIGHLY FAVORED PLACES WHICH ABOUND WITH CHRONICLE AND GREAT MEN. THE BRITISH AND AMERICAN LINE HAD RUN NEAR IT DURING THE WAR...
...IT HAD THEREFORE BEEN THE SCENE OF MUCH MARAUDING.
JUST SUFFICIENT TIME HAD ELAPSED TO ENABLE EACH STORY-TELLER TO DRESS UP HIS TALE WITH A LITTLE BECOMING FICTION,...
...AND IN THE INDISTINCTNESS OF HIS RECOL-LECTION TO MAKE HIMSELF THE HERO OF EVERY EXPLOIT.
THERE WAS THE STORY OF DOFFUE MARTLING WHO ***WOULD*** HAVE TAKEN A BRITISH FRIGATE WITH AN OLD IRON NINE-POUNDER FROM A MUD BREASTWORK,...
...ONLY THAT HIS GUN BURST AT THE SIXTH DISCHARGE.

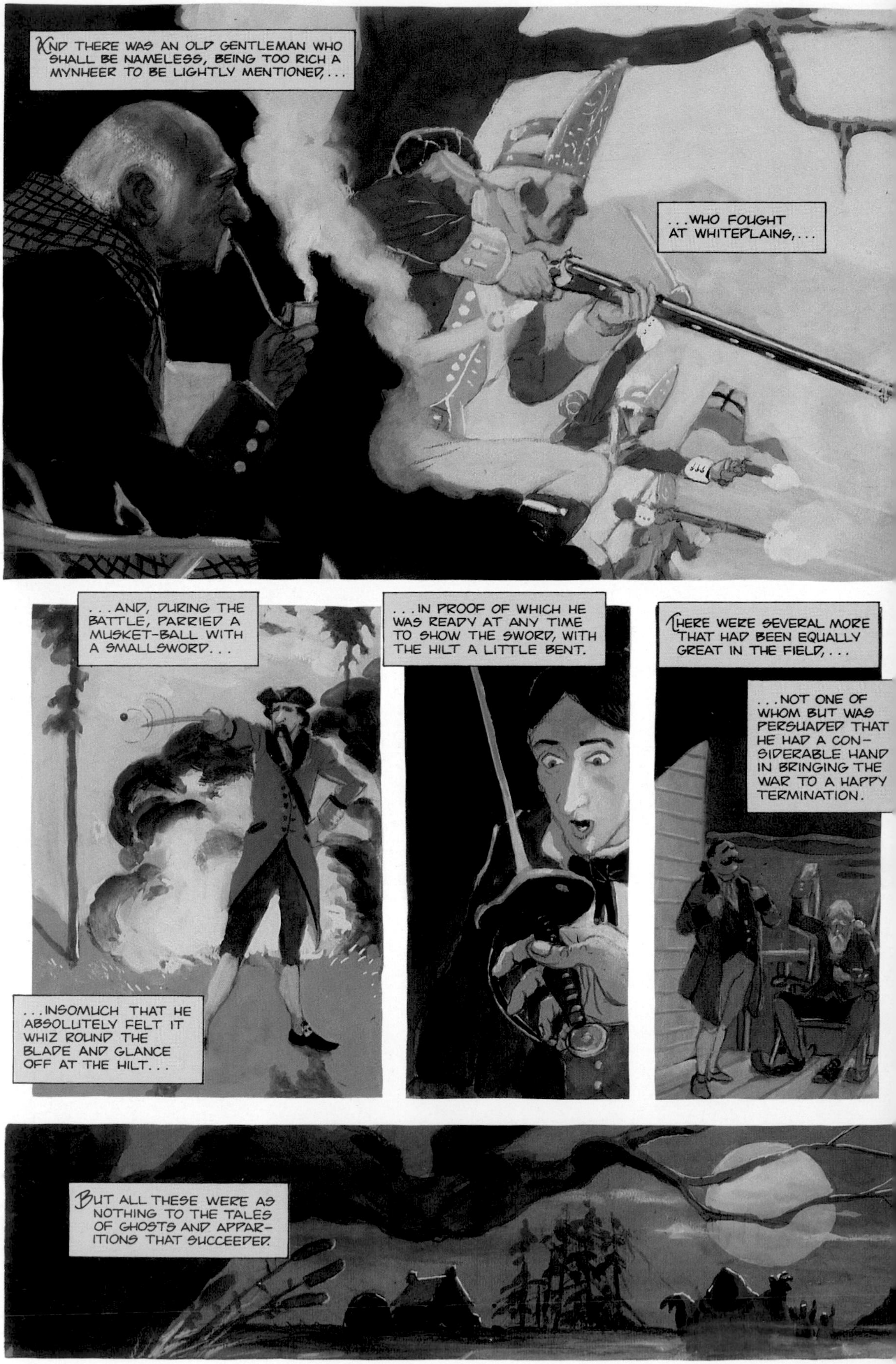
AND THERE WAS AN OLD GENTLEMAN WHO SHALL BE NAMELESS, BEING TOO RICH A MYNHEER TO BE LIGHTLY MENTIONED, . . .
. . . WHO FOUGHT AT WHITEPLAINS, . . .
. . . AND, DURING THE BATTLE, PARRIED A MUSKET-BALL WITH A SMALLSWORD . . .
. . . INSOMUCH THAT HE ABSOLUTELY FELT IT WHIZ ROUND THE BLADE AND GLANCE OFF AT THE HILT . . .
. . . IN PROOF OF WHICH HE WAS READY AT ANY TIME TO SHOW THE SWORD, WITH THE HILT A LITTLE BENT.
THERE WERE SEVERAL MORE THAT HAD BEEN EQUALLY GREAT IN THE FIELD, . . .
. . . NOT ONE OF WHOM BUT WAS PERSUADED THAT HE HAD A CONSIDERABLE HAND IN BRINGING THE WAR TO A HAPPY TERMINATION.
BUT ALL THESE WERE AS NOTHING TO THE TALES OF GHOSTS AND APPARITIONS THAT SUCCEEDED.

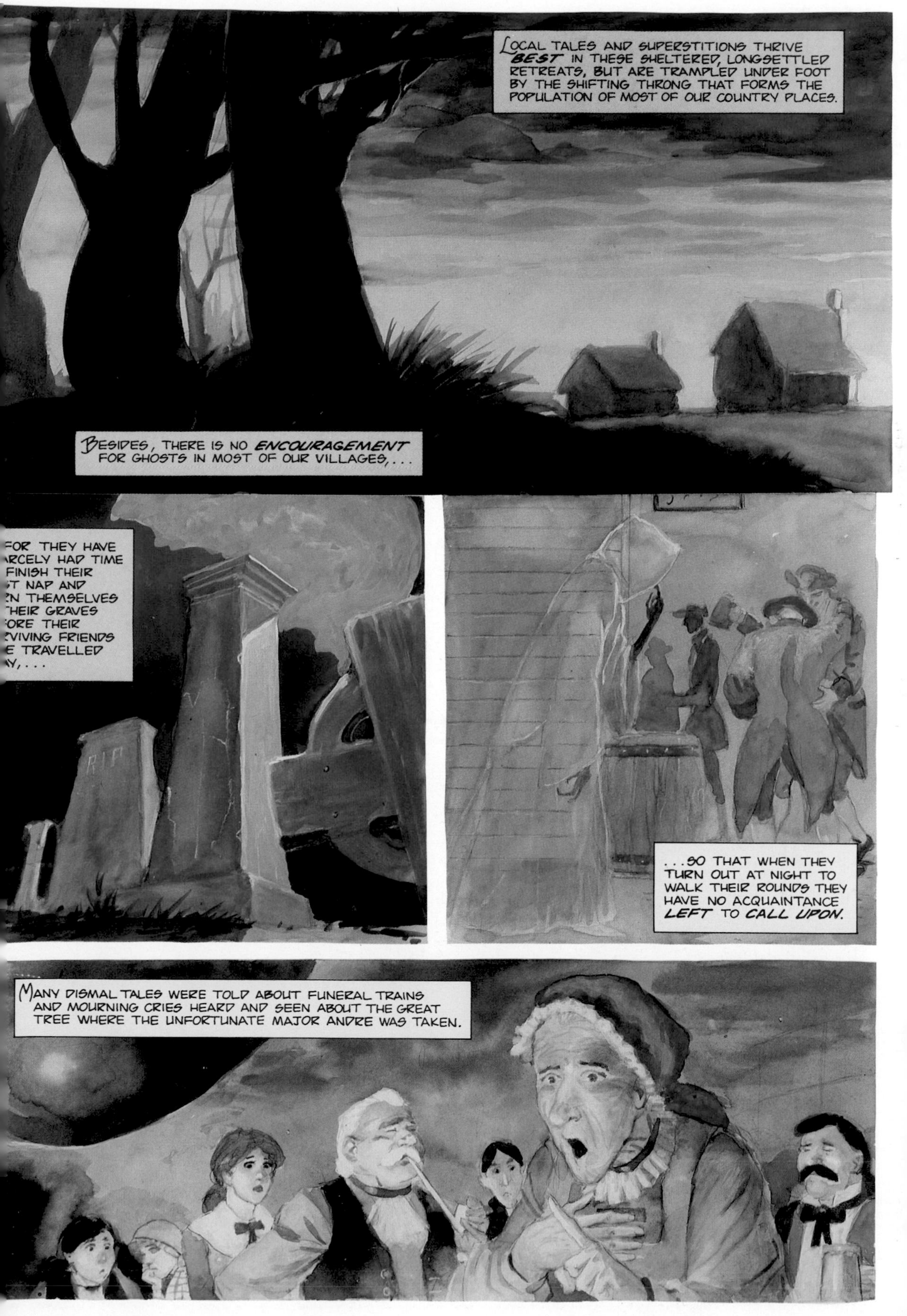
LOCAL TALES AND SUPERSTITIONS THRIVE BEST IN THESE SHELTERED, LONGSETTLED RETREATS, BUT ARE TRAMPLED UNDER FOOT BY THE SHIFTING THRONG THAT FORMS THE POPULATION OF MOST OF OUR COUNTRY PLACES.
BESIDES, THERE IS NO ENCOURAGEMENT FOR GHOSTS IN MOST OF OUR VILLAGES, . . .
FOR THEY HAVE ARCELY HAD TIME FINISH THEIR ST NAP AND EN THEMSELVES THEIR GRAVES FORE THEIR RVIVING FRIENDS E TRAVELLED AY, . . .
. . . SO THAT WHEN THEY TURN OUT AT NIGHT TO WALK THEIR ROUNDS THEY HAVE NO ACQUAINTANCE LEFT TO CALL UPON.
MANY DISMAL TALES WERE TOLD ABOUT FUNERAL TRAINS AND MOURNING CRIES HEARD AND SEEN ABOUT THE GREAT TREE WHERE THE UNFORTUNATE MAJOR ANDRE WAS TAKEN.

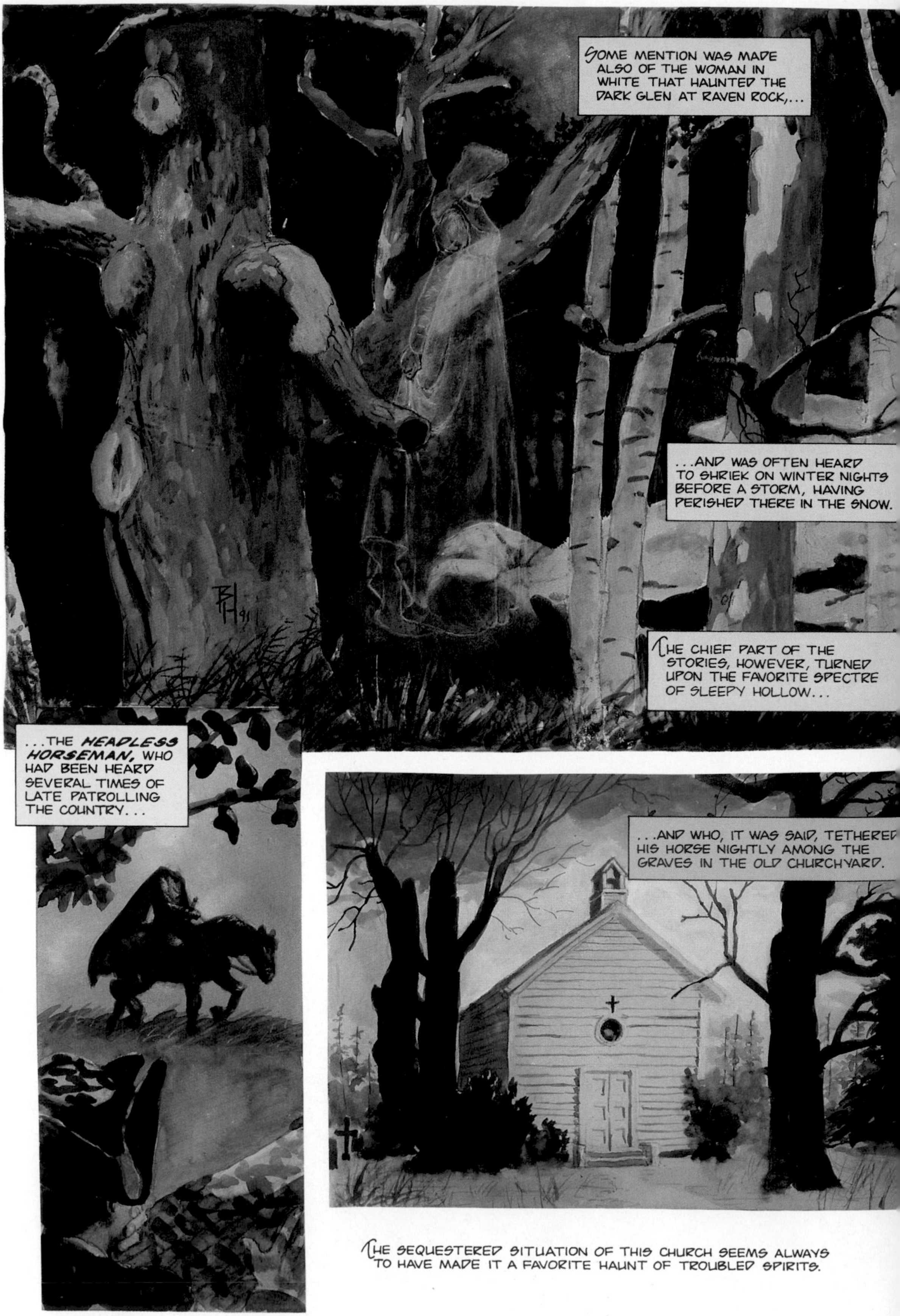
SOME MENTION WAS MADE ALSO OF THE WOMAN IN WHITE THAT HAUNTED THE DARK GLEN AT RAVEN ROCK,...
...AND WAS OFTEN HEARD TO SHRIEK ON WINTER NIGHTS BEFORE A STORM, HAVING PERISHED THERE IN THE SNOW.
THE CHIEF PART OF THE STORIES, HOWEVER, TURNED UPON THE FAVORITE SPECTRE OF SLEEPY HOLLOW...
...THE *HEADLESS HORSEMAN,* WHO HAD BEEN HEARD SEVERAL TIMES OF LATE PATROLLING THE COUNTRY...
...AND WHO, IT WAS SAID, TETHERED HIS HORSE NIGHTLY AMONG THE GRAVES IN THE OLD CHURCHYARD.
THE SEQUESTERED SITUATION OF THIS CHURCH SEEMS ALWAYS TO HAVE MADE IT A FAVORITE HAUNT OF TROUBLED SPIRITS.

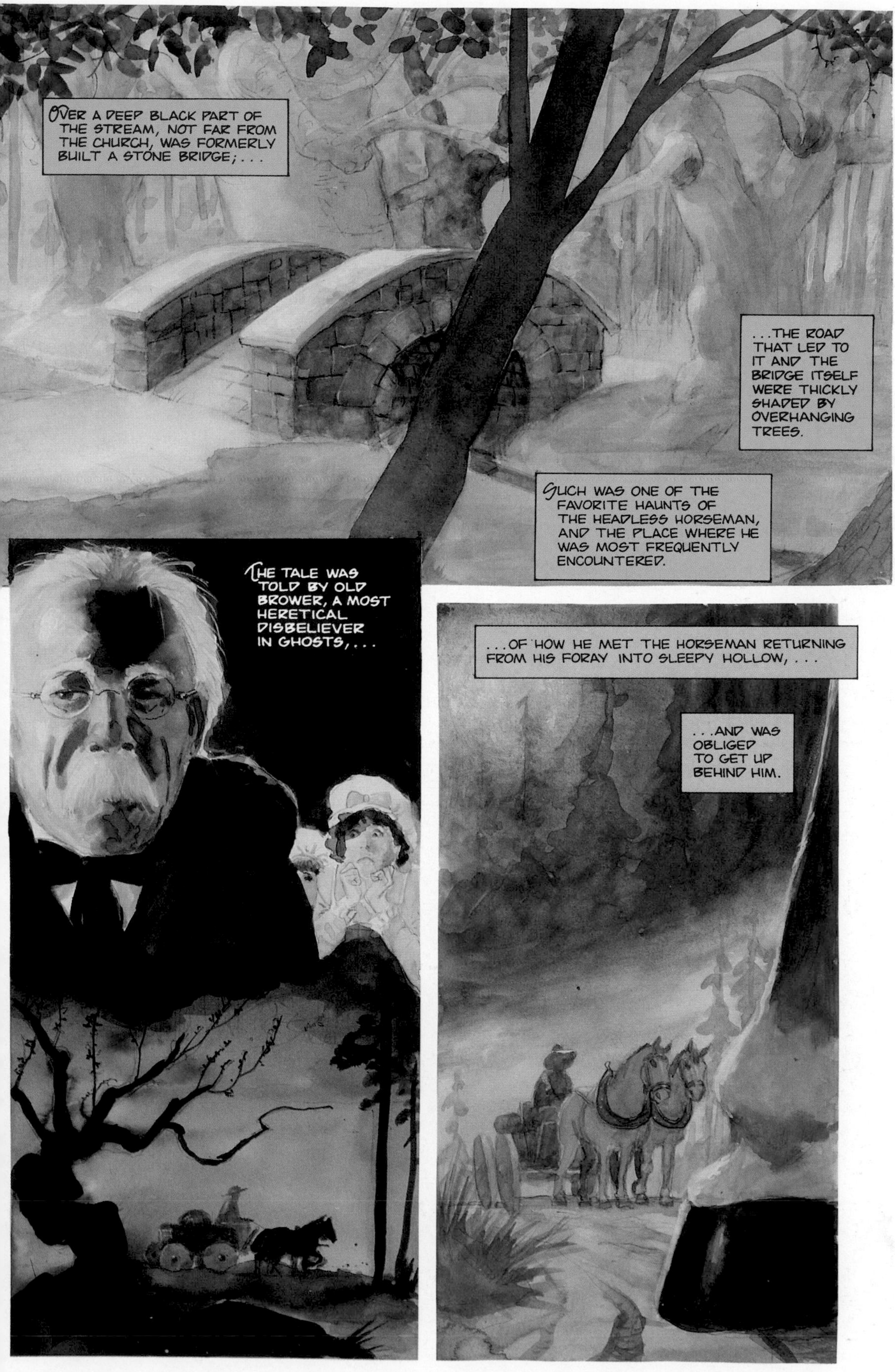
OVER A DEEP BLACK PART OF THE STREAM, NOT FAR FROM THE CHURCH, WAS FORMERLY BUILT A STONE BRIDGE; . . .
. . .THE ROAD THAT LED TO IT AND THE BRIDGE ITSELF WERE THICKLY SHADED BY OVERHANGING TREES.
SUCH WAS ONE OF THE FAVORITE HAUNTS OF THE HEADLESS HORSEMAN, AND THE PLACE WHERE HE WAS MOST FREQUENTLY ENCOUNTERED.
THE TALE WAS TOLD BY OLD BROWER, A MOST HERETICAL DISBELIEVER IN GHOSTS, . . .
. . .OF HOW HE MET THE HORSEMAN RETURNING FROM HIS FORAY INTO SLEEPY HOLLOW, . . .
. . .AND WAS OBLIGED TO GET UP BEHIND HIM.

NOW THEY GALLOPED OVER BUSH AND BRAKE, OVER HILL AND SWAMP, UNTIL THEY REACHED THE BRIDGE, . . .

. . .WHEN THE HORSEMAN SUDDENLY TURNED INTO A SKELETON, . . .

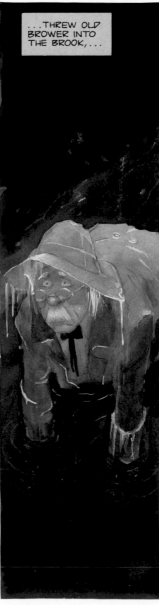

. . .THREW OLD BROWER INTO THE BROOK, . . .

. . .AND SPRANG AWAY OVER THE TREE-TOPS WITH A CLAP OF THUNDER.

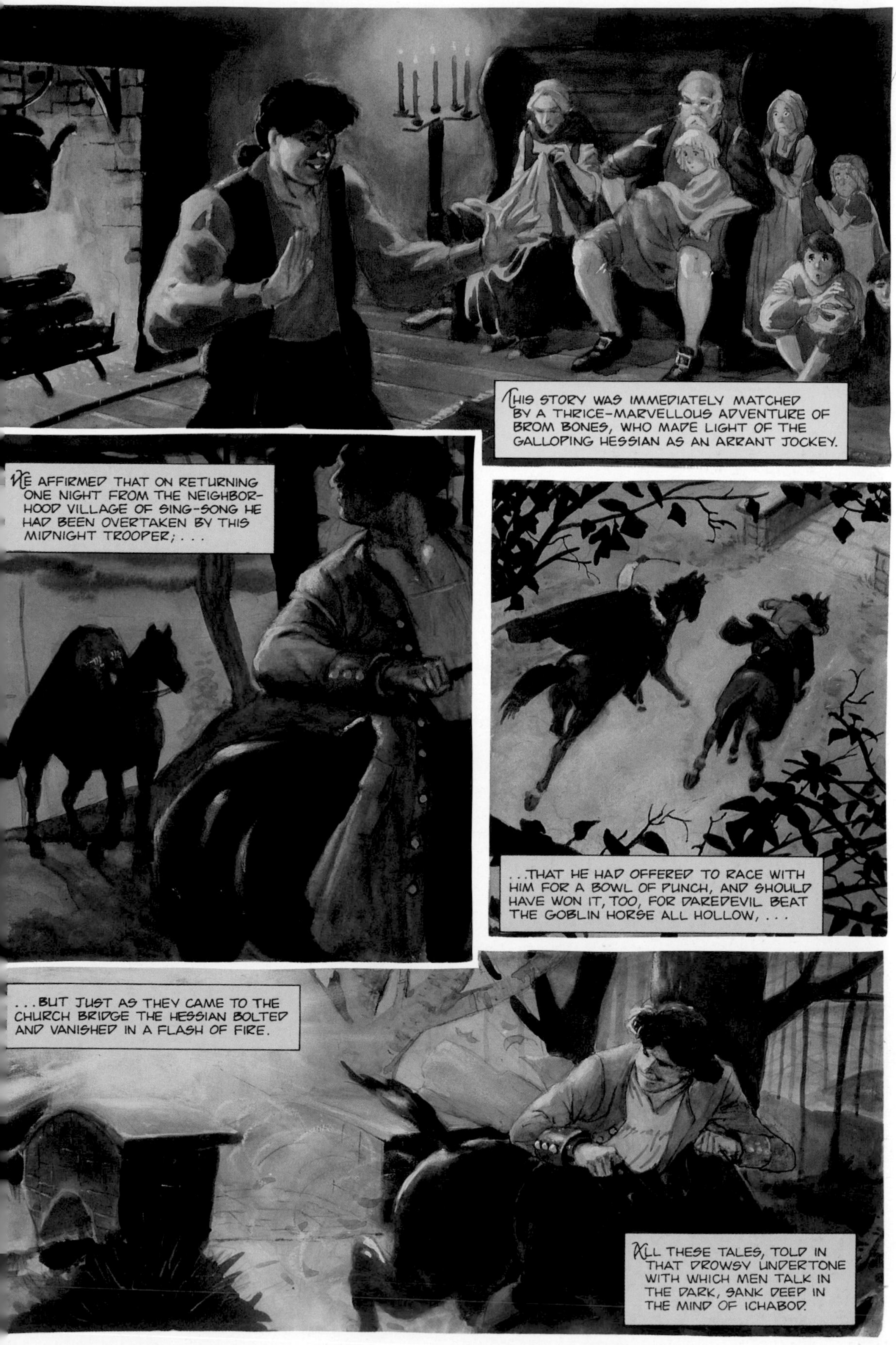
THIS STORY WAS IMMEDIATELY MATCHED BY A THRICE-MARVELLOUS ADVENTURE OF BROM BONES, WHO MADE LIGHT OF THE GALLOPING HESSIAN AS AN ARRANT JOCKEY.
HE AFFIRMED THAT ON RETURNING ONE NIGHT FROM THE NEIGHBORHOOD VILLAGE OF SING-SONG HE HAD BEEN OVERTAKEN BY THIS MIDNIGHT TROOPER; . . .
. . .THAT HE HAD OFFERED TO RACE WITH HIM FOR A BOWL OF PUNCH, AND SHOULD HAVE WON IT, TOO, FOR DAREDEVIL BEAT THE GOBLIN HORSE ALL HOLLOW, . . .
. . . BUT JUST AS THEY CAME TO THE CHURCH BRIDGE THE HESSIAN BOLTED AND VANISHED IN A FLASH OF FIRE.
ALL THESE TALES, TOLD IN THAT DROWSY UNDERTONE WITH WHICH MEN TALK IN THE DARK, SANK DEEP IN THE MIND OF ICHABOD.

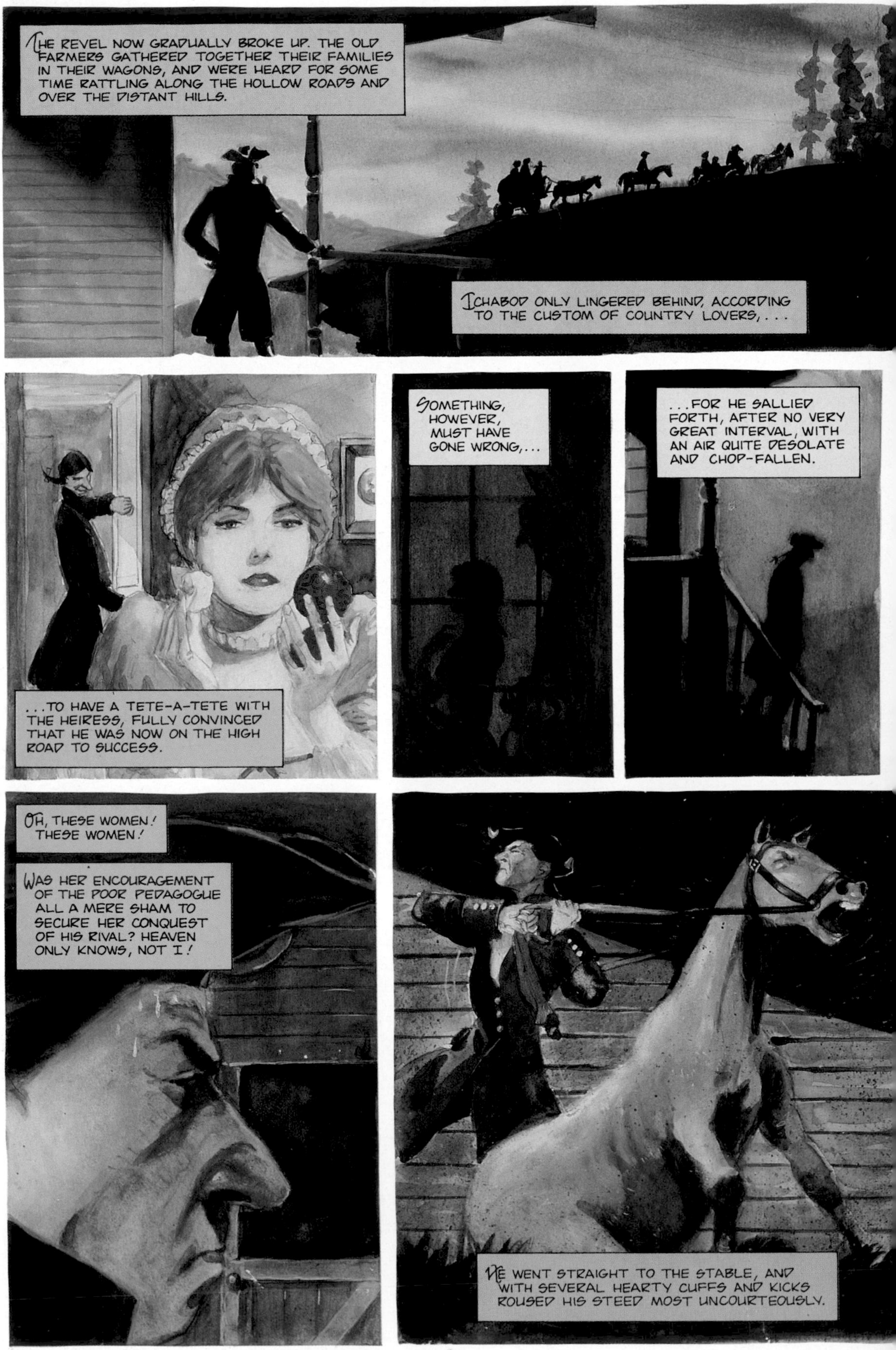
THE REVEL NOW GRADUALLY BROKE UP. THE OLD FARMERS GATHERED TOGETHER THEIR FAMILIES IN THEIR WAGONS, AND WERE HEARD FOR SOME TIME RATTLING ALONG THE HOLLOW ROADS AND OVER THE DISTANT HILLS.
ICHABOD ONLY LINGERED BEHIND, ACCORDING TO THE CUSTOM OF COUNTRY LOVERS, . . .
. . .TO HAVE A TETE-A-TETE WITH THE HEIRESS, FULLY CONVINCED THAT HE WAS NOW ON THE HIGH ROAD TO SUCCESS.
SOMETHING, HOWEVER, MUST HAVE GONE WRONG,. . .
. . .FOR HE SALLIED FORTH, AFTER NO VERY GREAT INTERVAL, WITH AN AIR QUITE DESOLATE AND CHOP-FALLEN.
OH, THESE WOMEN! THESE WOMEN!
WAS HER ENCOURAGEMENT OF THE POOR PEDAGOGUE ALL A MERE SHAM TO SECURE HER CONQUEST OF HIS RIVAL? HEAVEN ONLY KNOWS, NOT I!
HE WENT STRAIGHT TO THE STABLE, AND WITH SEVERAL HEARTY CUFFS AND KICKS ROUSED HIS STEED MOST UNCOURTEOUSLY.

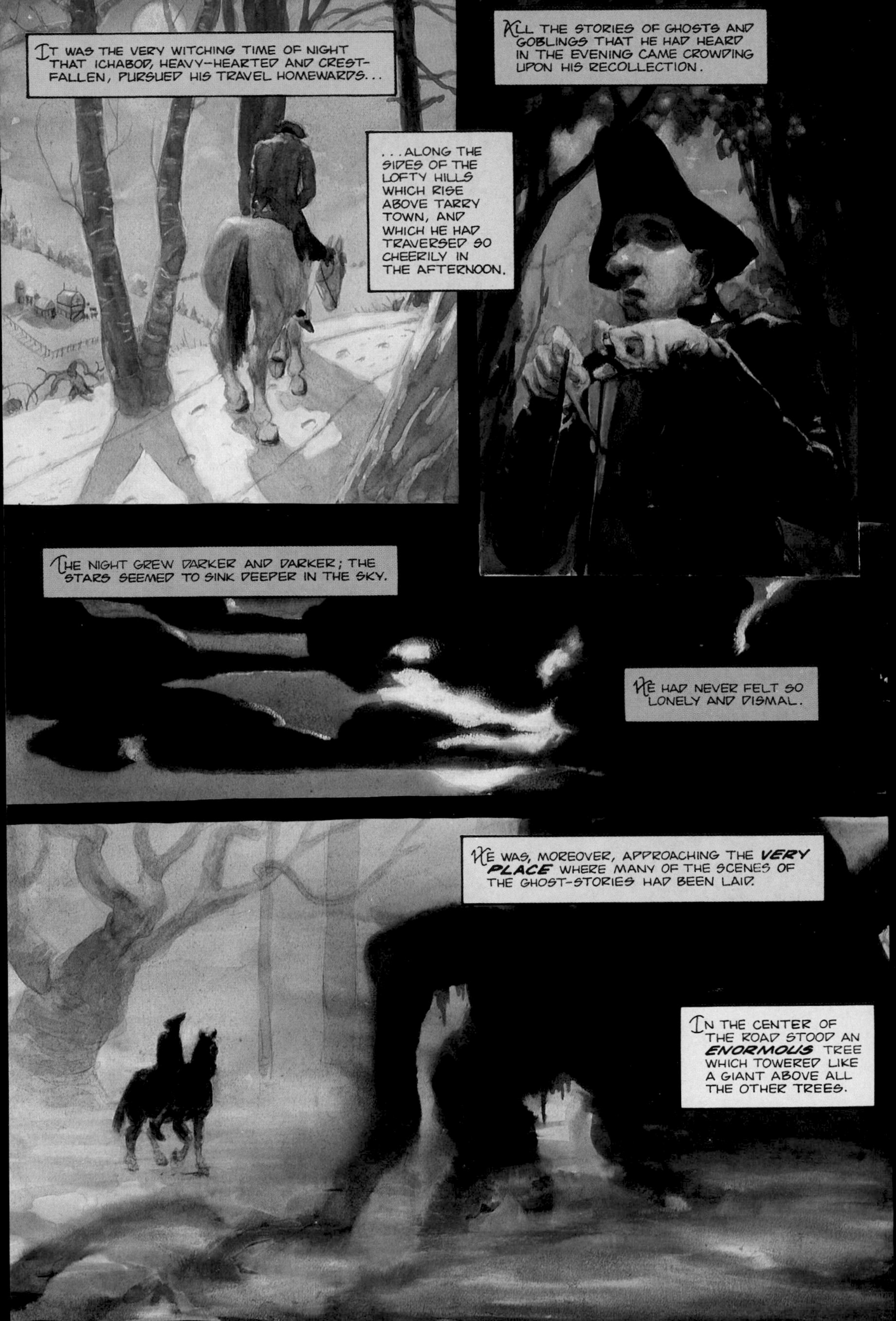
IT WAS THE VERY WITCHING TIME OF NIGHT THAT ICHABOD, HEAVY-HEARTED AND CREST-FALLEN, PURSUED HIS TRAVEL HOMEWARDS...
...ALONG THE SIDES OF THE LOFTY HILLS WHICH RISE ABOVE TARRY TOWN, AND WHICH HE HAD TRAVERSED SO CHEERILY IN THE AFTERNOON.
ALL THE STORIES OF GHOSTS AND GOBLINGS THAT HE HAD HEARD IN THE EVENING CAME CROWDING UPON HIS RECOLLECTION.
THE NIGHT GREW DARKER AND DARKER; THE STARS SEEMED TO SINK DEEPER IN THE SKY.
HE HAD NEVER FELT SO LONELY AND DISMAL.
HE WAS, MOREOVER, APPROACHING THE VERY PLACE WHERE MANY OF THE SCENES OF THE GHOST-STORIES HAD BEEN LAID.
IN THE CENTER OF THE ROAD STOOD AN ENORMOUS TREE WHICH TOWERED LIKE A GIANT ABOVE ALL THE OTHER TREES.

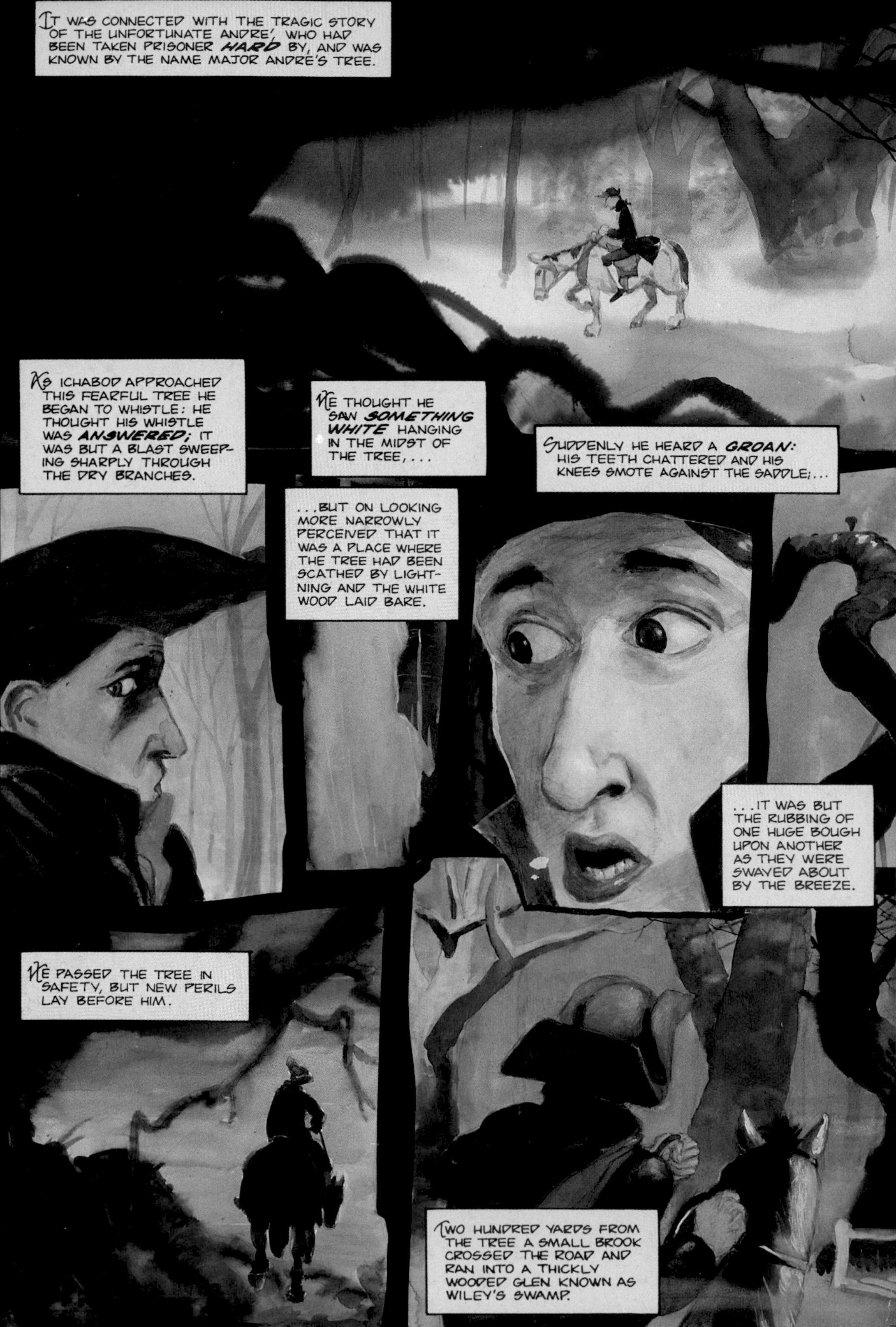
IT WAS CONNECTED WITH THE TRAGIC STORY OF THE UNFORTUNATE ANDRE', WHO HAD BEEN TAKEN PRISONER HARD BY, AND WAS KNOWN BY THE NAME MAJOR ANDRE'S TREE.
AS ICHABOD APPROACHED THIS FEARFUL TREE HE BEGAN TO WHISTLE: HE THOUGHT HIS WHISTLE WAS ANSWERED; IT WAS BUT A BLAST SWEEPING SHARPLY THROUGH THE DRY BRANCHES.
HE THOUGHT HE SAW SOMETHING WHITE HANGING IN THE MIDST OF THE TREE, ...
...BUT ON LOOKING MORE NARROWLY PERCEIVED THAT IT WAS A PLACE WHERE THE TREE HAD BEEN SCATHED BY LIGHTNING AND THE WHITE WOOD LAID BARE.
SUDDENLY HE HEARD A GROAN: HIS TEETH CHATTERED AND HIS KNEES SMOTE AGAINST THE SADDLE; ...
...IT WAS BUT THE RUBBING OF ONE HUGE BOUGH UPON ANOTHER AS THEY WERE SWAYED ABOUT BY THE BREEZE.
HE PASSED THE TREE IN SAFETY, BUT NEW PERILS LAY BEFORE HIM.
TWO HUNDRED YARDS FROM THE TREE A SMALL BROOK CROSSED THE ROAD AND RAN INTO A THICKLY WOODED GLEN KNOWN AS WILEY'S SWAMP.

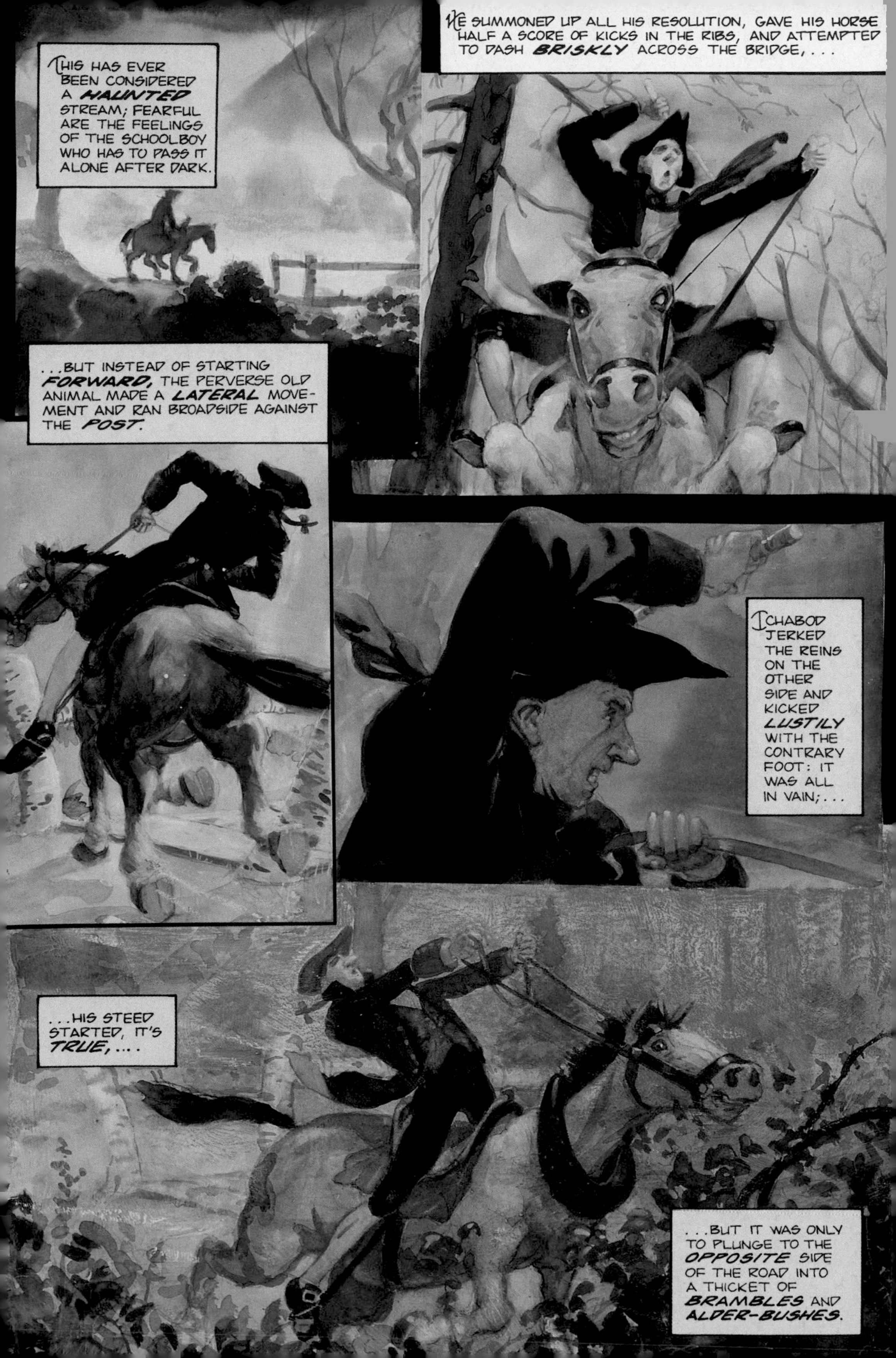
THIS HAS EVER BEEN CONSIDERED A HAUNTED STREAM; FEARFUL ARE THE FEELINGS OF THE SCHOOLBOY WHO HAS TO PASS IT ALONE AFTER DARK.
HE SUMMONED UP ALL HIS RESOLUTION, GAVE HIS HORSE HALF A SCORE OF KICKS IN THE RIBS, AND ATTEMPTED TO DASH BRISKLY ACROSS THE BRIDGE, . . .
. . .BUT INSTEAD OF STARTING FORWARD, THE PERVERSE OLD ANIMAL MADE A LATERAL MOVEMENT AND RAN BROADSIDE AGAINST THE POST.
ICHABOD JERKED THE REINS ON THE OTHER SIDE AND KICKED LUSTILY WITH THE CONTRARY FOOT: IT WAS ALL IN VAIN; . . .
. . .HIS STEED STARTED, IT'S TRUE, ...
. . .BUT IT WAS ONLY TO PLUNGE TO THE OPPOSITE SIDE OF THE ROAD INTO A THICKET OF BRAMBLES AND ALDER-BUSHES.

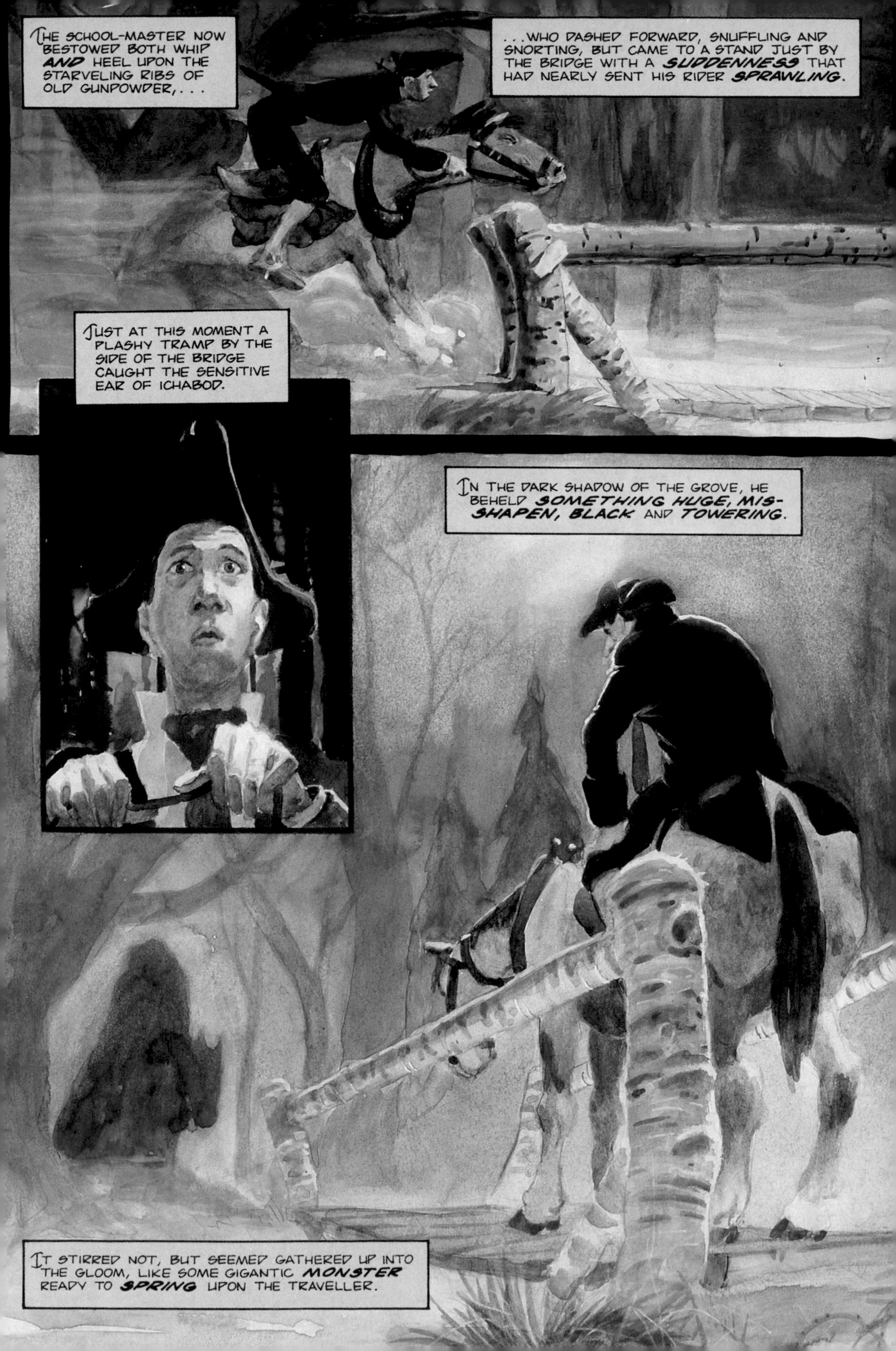
THE SCHOOL-MASTER NOW BESTOWED BOTH WHIP AND HEEL UPON THE STARVELING RIBS OF OLD GUNPOWDER, . . .
. . . WHO DASHED FORWARD, SNUFFLING AND SNORTING, BUT CAME TO A STAND JUST BY THE BRIDGE WITH A SUDDENNESS THAT HAD NEARLY SENT HIS RIDER SPRAWLING.
JUST AT THIS MOMENT A PLASHY TRAMP BY THE SIDE OF THE BRIDGE CAUGHT THE SENSITIVE EAR OF ICHABOD.
IN THE DARK SHADOW OF THE GROVE, HE BEHELD SOMETHING HUGE, MIS-SHAPEN, BLACK AND TOWERING.
IT STIRRED NOT, BUT SEEMED GATHERED UP INTO THE GLOOM, LIKE SOME GIGANTIC MONSTER READY TO SPRING UPON THE TRAVELLER.

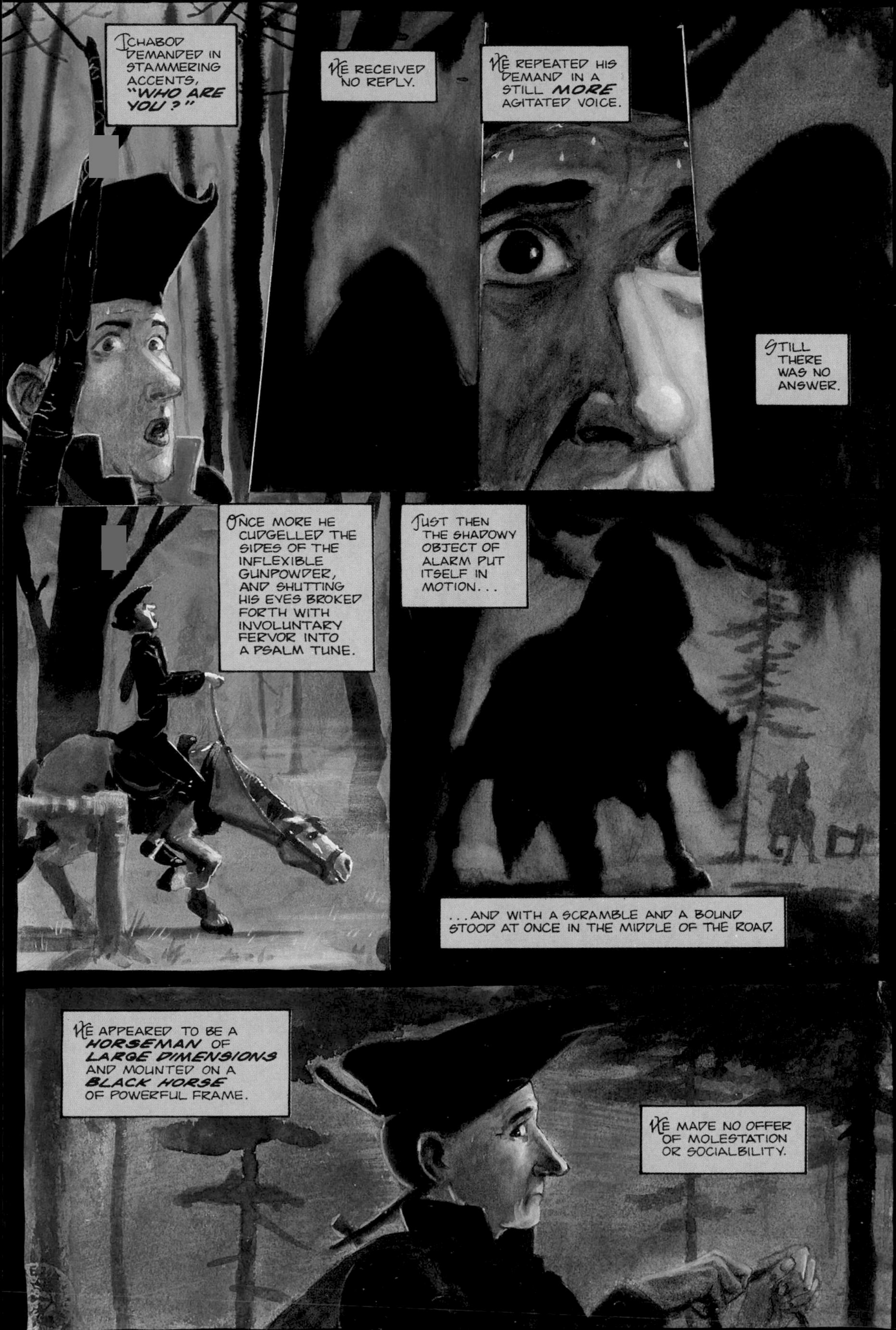
ICHABOD DEMANDED IN STAMMERING ACCENTS, "WHO ARE YOU?"
HE RECEIVED NO REPLY.
HE REPEATED HIS DEMAND IN A STILL MORE AGITATED VOICE.
STILL THERE WAS NO ANSWER.
ONCE MORE HE CUDGELLED THE SIDES OF THE INFLEXIBLE GUNPOWDER, AND SHUTTING HIS EYES BROKED FORTH WITH INVOLUNTARY FERVOR INTO A PSALM TUNE.
JUST THEN THE SHADOWY OBJECT OF ALARM PUT ITSELF IN MOTION...
...AND WITH A SCRAMBLE AND A BOUND STOOD AT ONCE IN THE MIDDLE OF THE ROAD.
HE APPEARED TO BE A HORSEMAN OF LARGE DIMENSIONS AND MOUNTED ON A BLACK HORSE OF POWERFUL FRAME.
HE MADE NO OFFER OF MOLESTATION OR SOCIALBILITY.

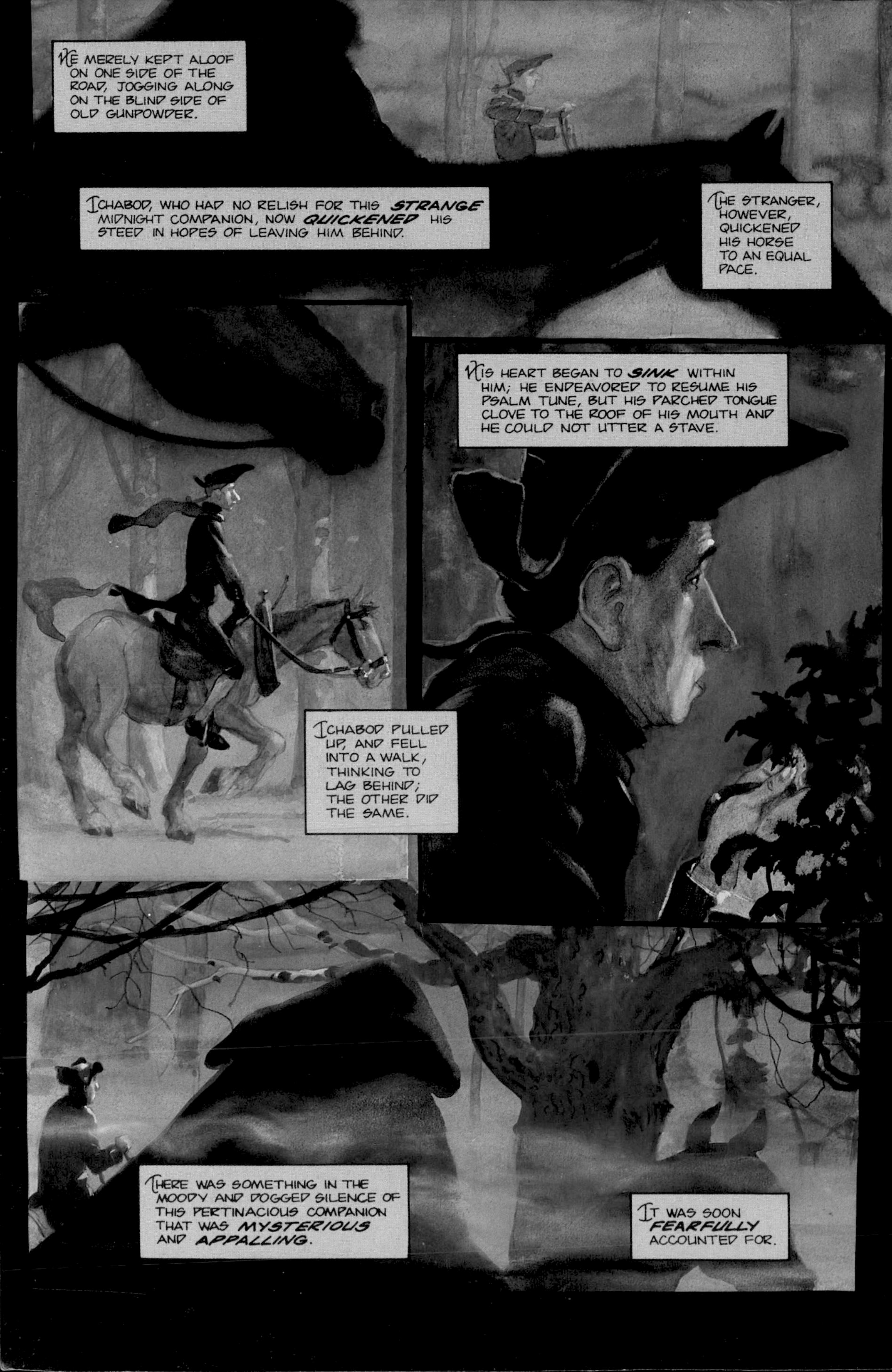
He merely kept aloof on one side of the road, jogging along on the blind side of old Gunpowder.
Ichabod, who had no relish for this strange midnight companion, now quickened his steed in hopes of leaving him behind.
The stranger, however, quickened his horse to an equal pace.
Ichabod pulled up, and fell into a walk, thinking to lag behind; the other did the same.
His heart began to sink within him; he endeavored to resume his psalm tune, but his parched tongue clove to the roof of his mouth and he could not utter a stave.
There was something in the moody and dogged silence of this pertinacious companion that was mysterious and appalling.
It was soon fearfully accounted for.

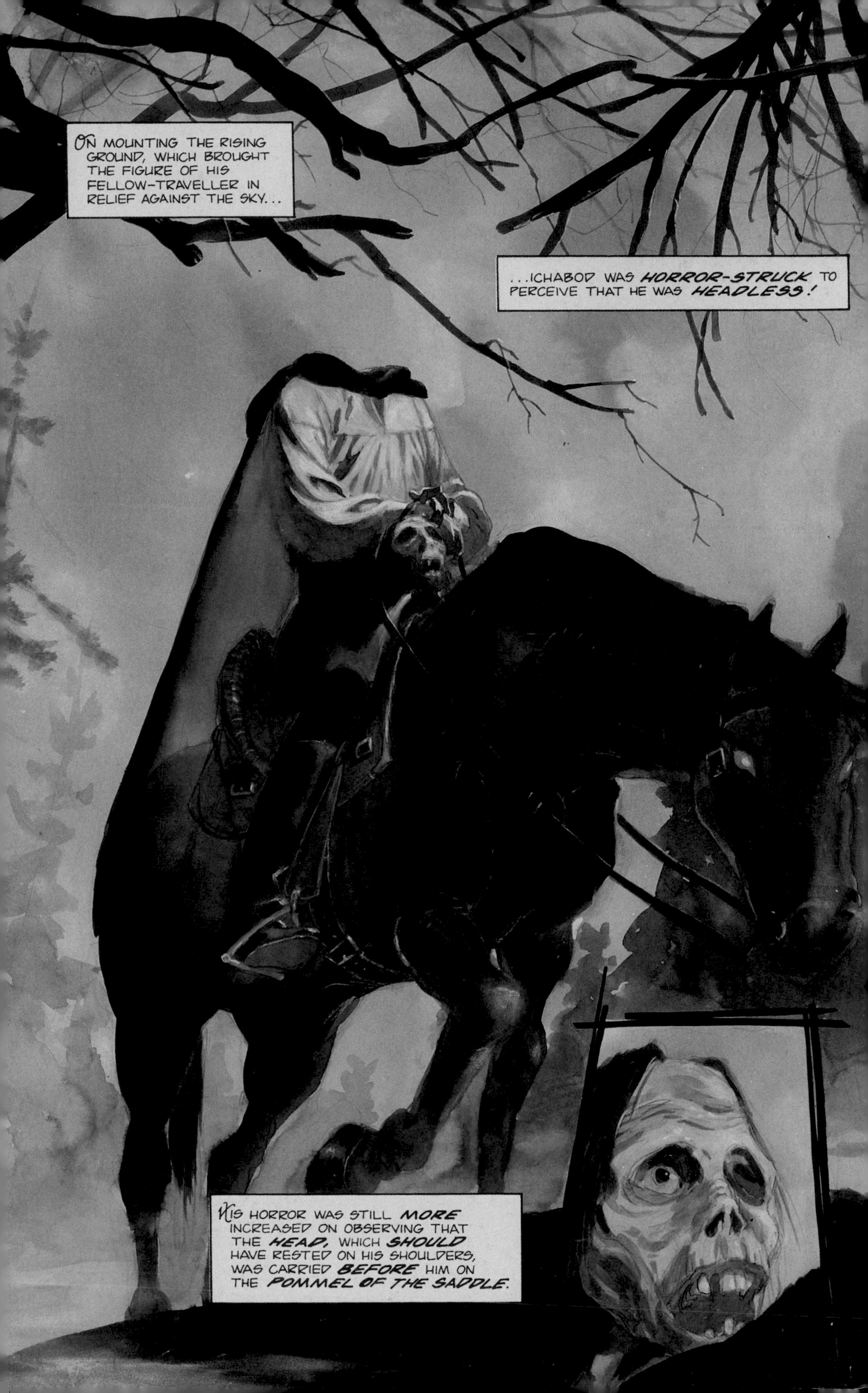
ON MOUNTING THE RISING GROUND, WHICH BROUGHT THE FIGURE OF HIS FELLOW-TRAVELLER IN RELIEF AGAINST THE SKY...
...ICHABOD WAS HORROR-STRUCK TO PERCEIVE THAT HE WAS HEADLESS!
HIS HORROR WAS STILL MORE INCREASED ON OBSERVING THAT THE HEAD, WHICH SHOULD HAVE RESTED ON HIS SHOULDERS, WAS CARRIED BEFORE HIM ON THE POMMEL OF THE SADDLE.

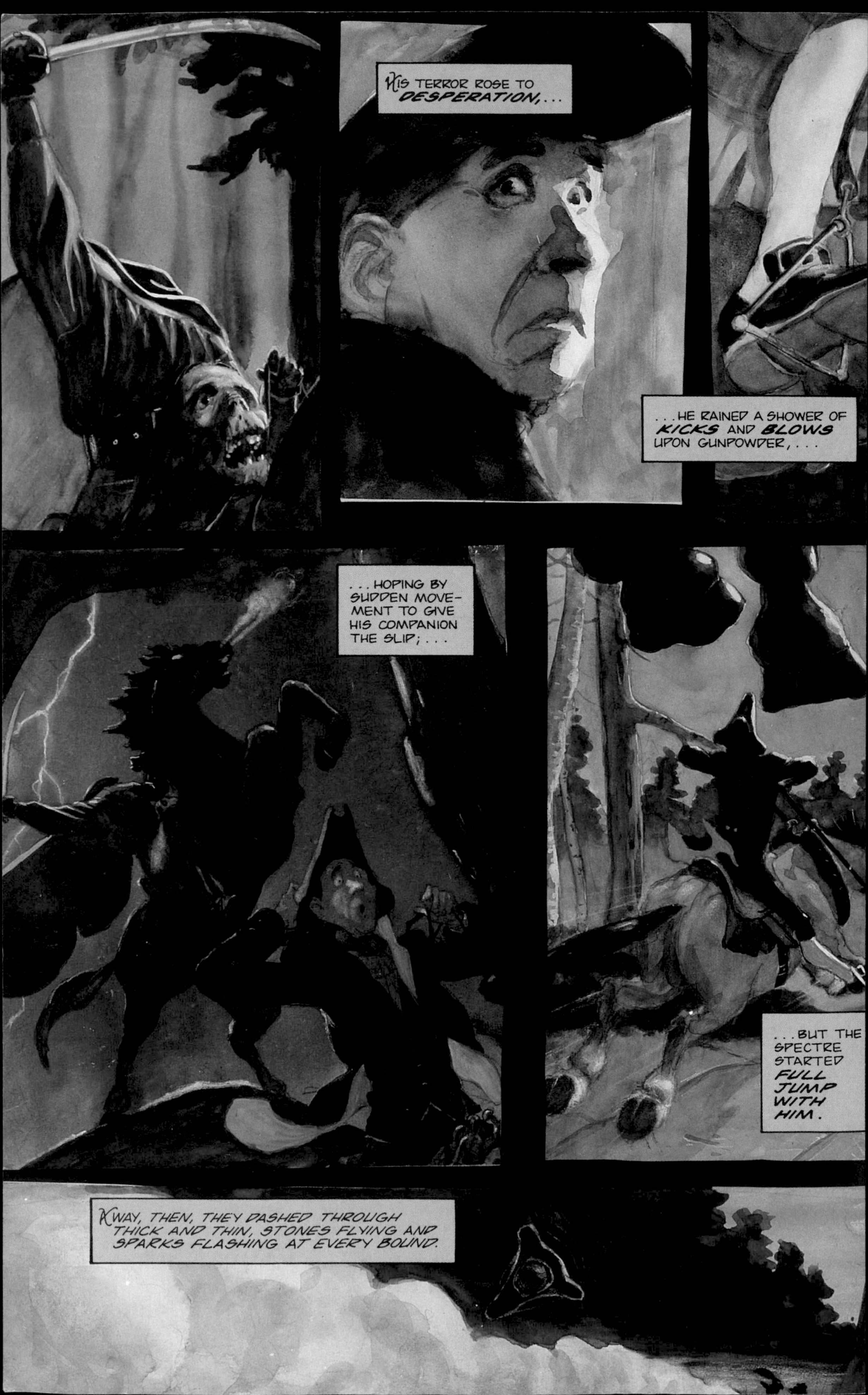
His terror rose to DESPERATION, . . .
. . . HE RAINED A SHOWER OF KICKS AND BLOWS UPON GUNPOWDER, . . .
. . . HOPING BY SUDDEN MOVE-MENT TO GIVE HIS COMPANION THE SLIP; . . .
. . . BUT THE SPECTRE STARTED FULL JUMP WITH HIM.
AWAY, THEN, THEY DASHED THROUGH THICK AND THIN, STONES FLYING AND SPARKS FLASHING AT EVERY BOUND.

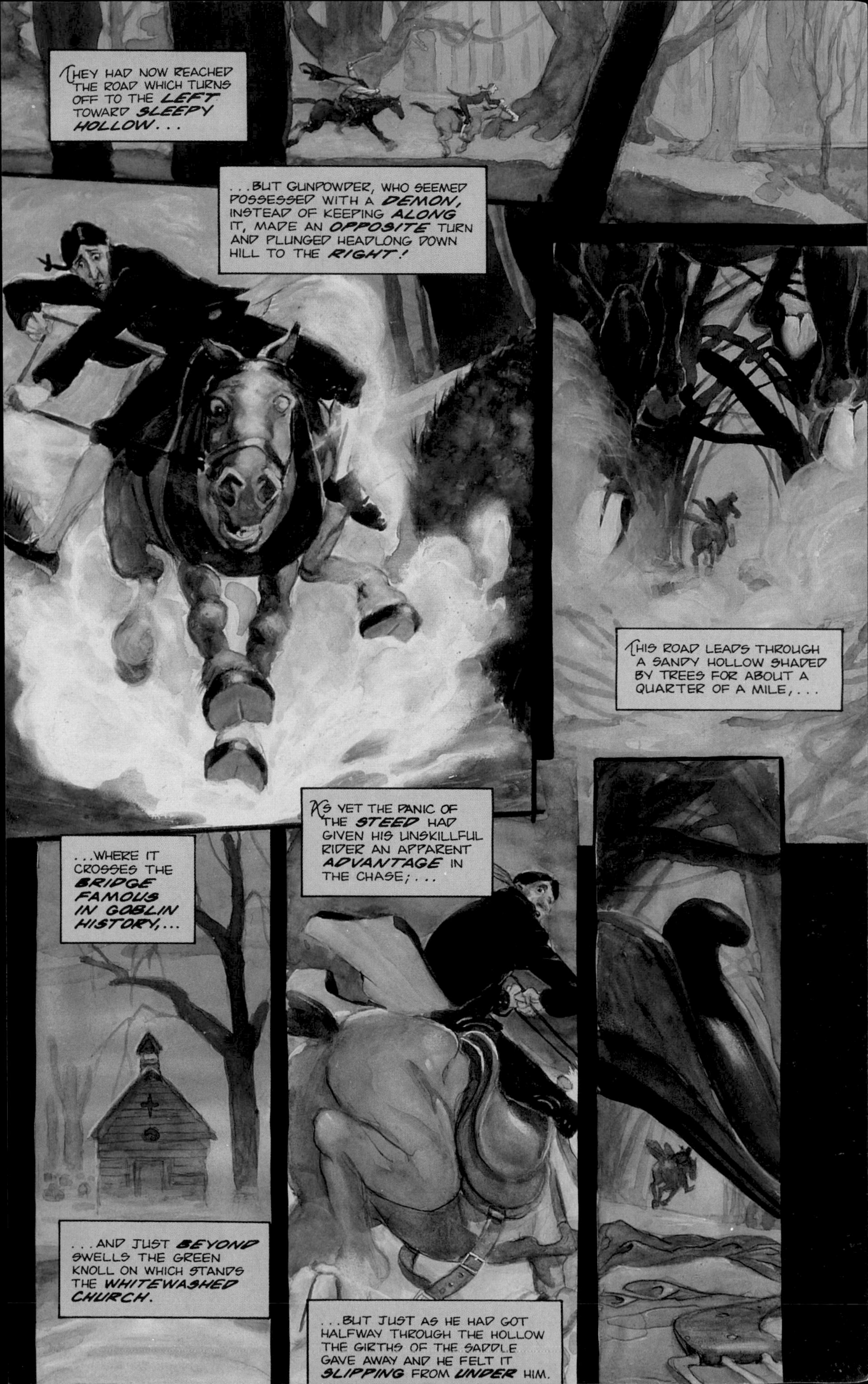
THEY HAD NOW REACHED THE ROAD WHICH TURNS OFF TO THE LEFT TOWARD SLEEPY HOLLOW...
...BUT GUNPOWDER, WHO SEEMED POSSESSED WITH A DEMON, INSTEAD OF KEEPING ALONG IT, MADE AN OPPOSITE TURN AND PLUNGED HEADLONG DOWN HILL TO THE RIGHT!
THIS ROAD LEADS THROUGH A SANDY HOLLOW SHADED BY TREES FOR ABOUT A QUARTER OF A MILE,...
...WHERE IT CROSSES THE BRIDGE FAMOUS IN GOBLIN HISTORY,...
...AND JUST BEYOND SWELLS THE GREEN KNOLL ON WHICH STANDS THE WHITEWASHED CHURCH.
AS YET THE PANIC OF THE STEED HAD GIVEN HIS UNSKILLFUL RIDER AN APPARENT ADVANTAGE IN THE CHASE;...
...BUT JUST AS HE HAD GOT HALFWAY THROUGH THE HOLLOW THE GIRTHS OF THE SADDLE GAVE AWAY AND HE FELT IT SLIPPING FROM UNDER HIM.

HE HAD JUST TIME TO *SAVE* HIMSELF BY CLASPING OLD GUNPOWDER ROUND THE *NECK*.

FOR A MOMENT THE TERROR OF HANS VAN RIPPER'S *WRATH* PASSED ACROSS HIS MIND, FOR IT WAS HIS SUNDAY SADDLE; ...

...BUT THIS WAS NO TIME FOR PETTY FEARS, ...

...THE GOBLIN WAS HARD ON HIS *HAUNCHES*.

AN OPENING IN THE TREES NOW *CHEERED* HIM AS HE SAW THE CHURCH BRIDGE WAS AT HAND.

"IF I CAN BUT REACH THAT BRIDGE," THOUGHT ICHABOD, "I AM *SAFE*."

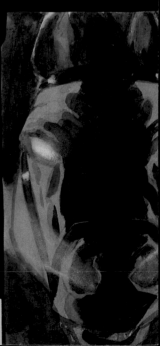

JUST THEN HE HEARD THE BLACK STEED *PANTING* AND *BLOWING* CLOSE BEHIND HIM; HE EVEN FANCIED THAT HE FELT HIS *HOT BREATH*.

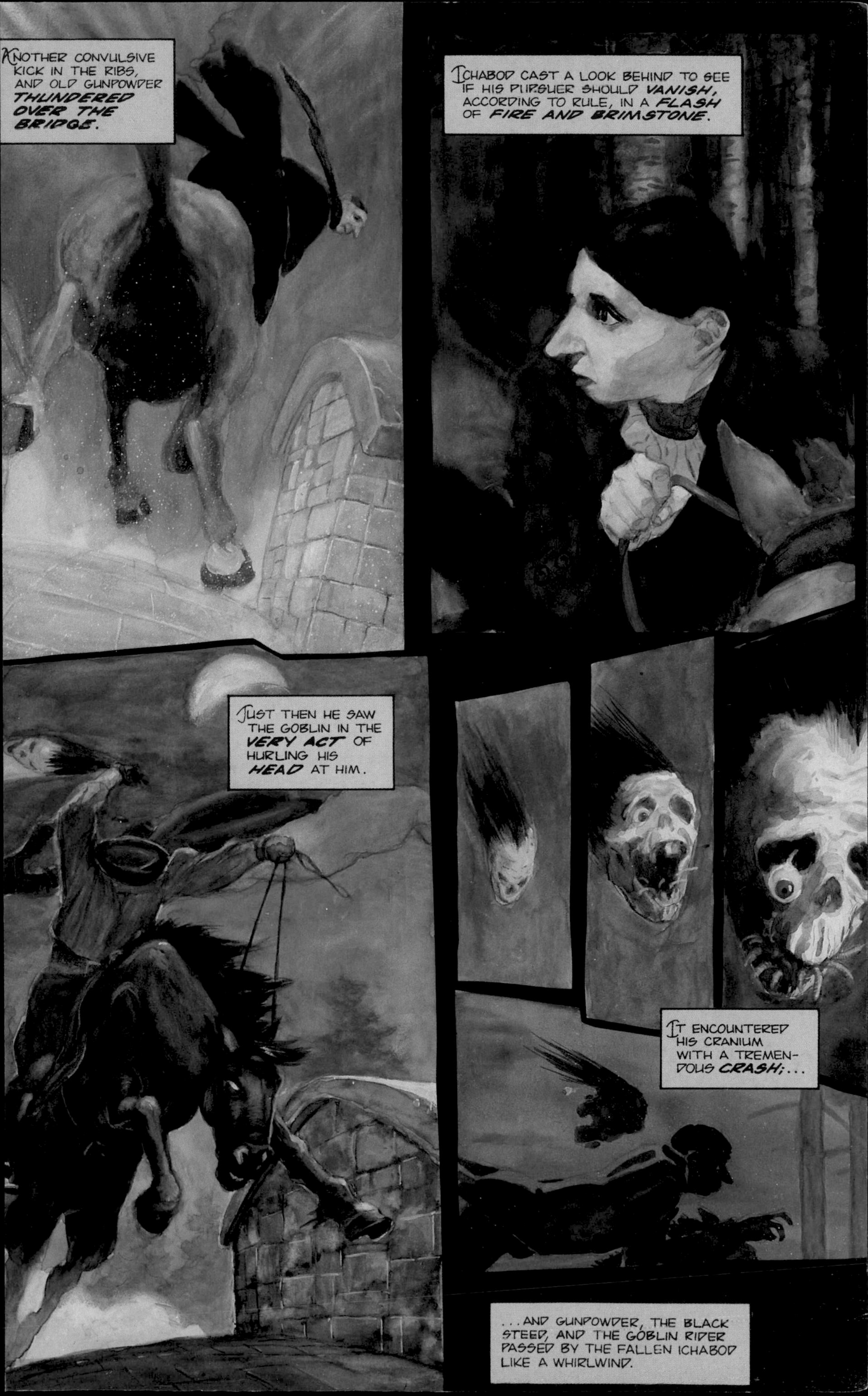
ANOTHER CONVULSIVE KICK IN THE RIBS, AND OLD GUNPOWDER THUNDERED OVER THE BRIDGE.
ICHABOD CAST A LOOK BEHIND TO SEE IF HIS PURSUER SHOULD VANISH, ACCORDING TO RULE, IN A FLASH OF FIRE AND BRIMSTONE.
JUST THEN HE SAW THE GOBLIN IN THE VERY ACT OF HURLING HIS HEAD AT HIM.
IT ENCOUNTERED HIS CRANIUM WITH A TREMENDOUS CRASH;...
...AND GUNPOWDER, THE BLACK STEED, AND THE GOBLIN RIDER PASSED BY THE FALLEN ICHABOD LIKE A WHIRLWIND.

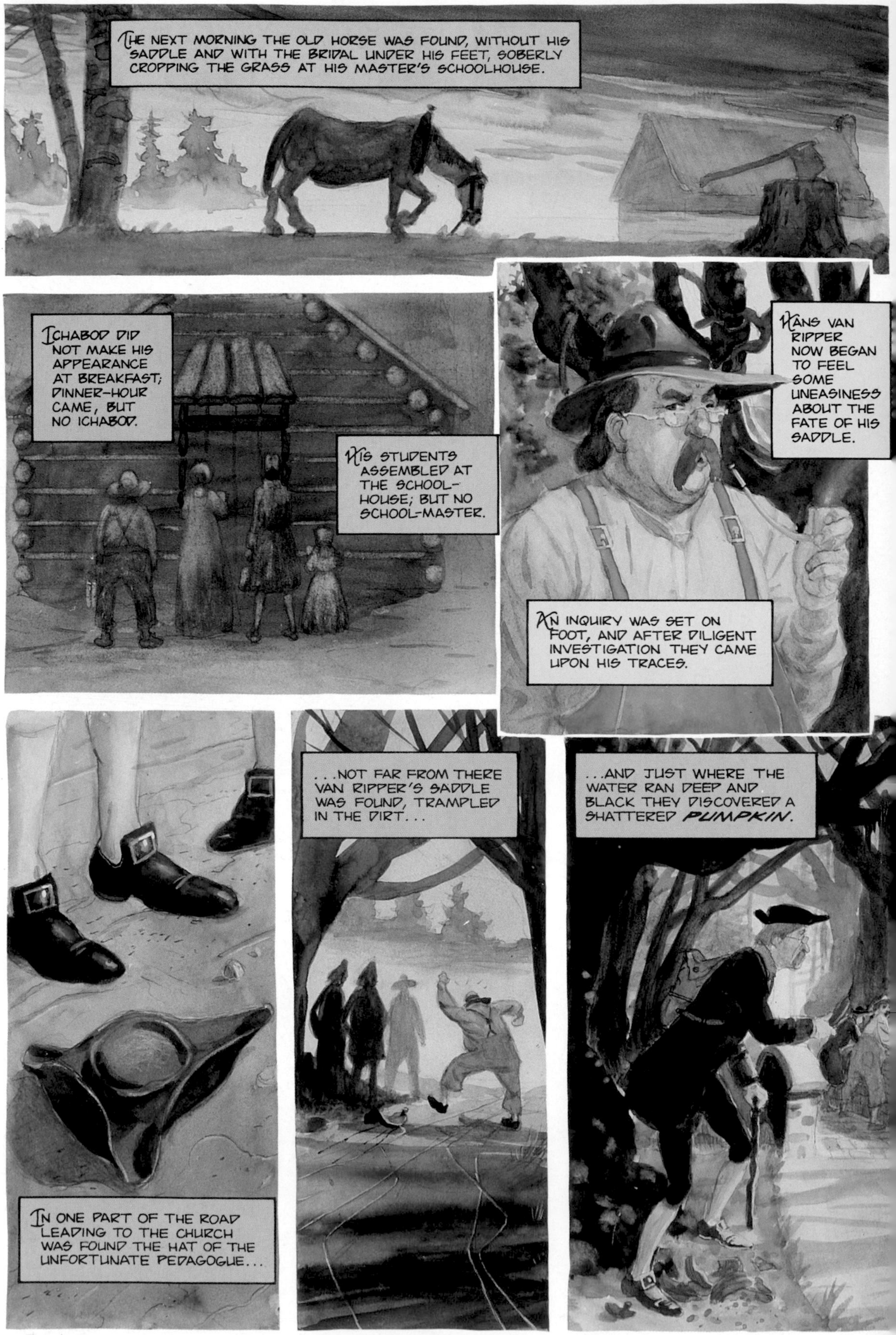
THE NEXT MORNING THE OLD HORSE WAS FOUND, WITHOUT HIS SADDLE AND WITH THE BRIDAL UNDER HIS FEET, SOBERLY CROPPING THE GRASS AT HIS MASTER'S SCHOOLHOUSE.
ICHABOD DID NOT MAKE HIS APPEARANCE AT BREAKFAST; DINNER-HOUR CAME, BUT NO ICHABOD.
HIS STUDENTS ASSEMBLED AT THE SCHOOL-HOUSE; BUT NO SCHOOL-MASTER.
HANS VAN RIPPER NOW BEGAN TO FEEL SOME UNEASINESS ABOUT THE FATE OF HIS SADDLE.
AN INQUIRY WAS SET ON FOOT, AND AFTER DILIGENT INVESTIGATION THEY CAME UPON HIS TRACES.
IN ONE PART OF THE ROAD LEADING TO THE CHURCH WAS FOUND THE HAT OF THE UNFORTUNATE PEDAGOGUE...
...NOT FAR FROM THERE VAN RIPPER'S SADDLE WAS FOUND, TRAMPLED IN THE DIRT...
...AND JUST WHERE THE WATER RAN DEEP AND BLACK THEY DISCOVERED A SHATTERED PUMPKIN.

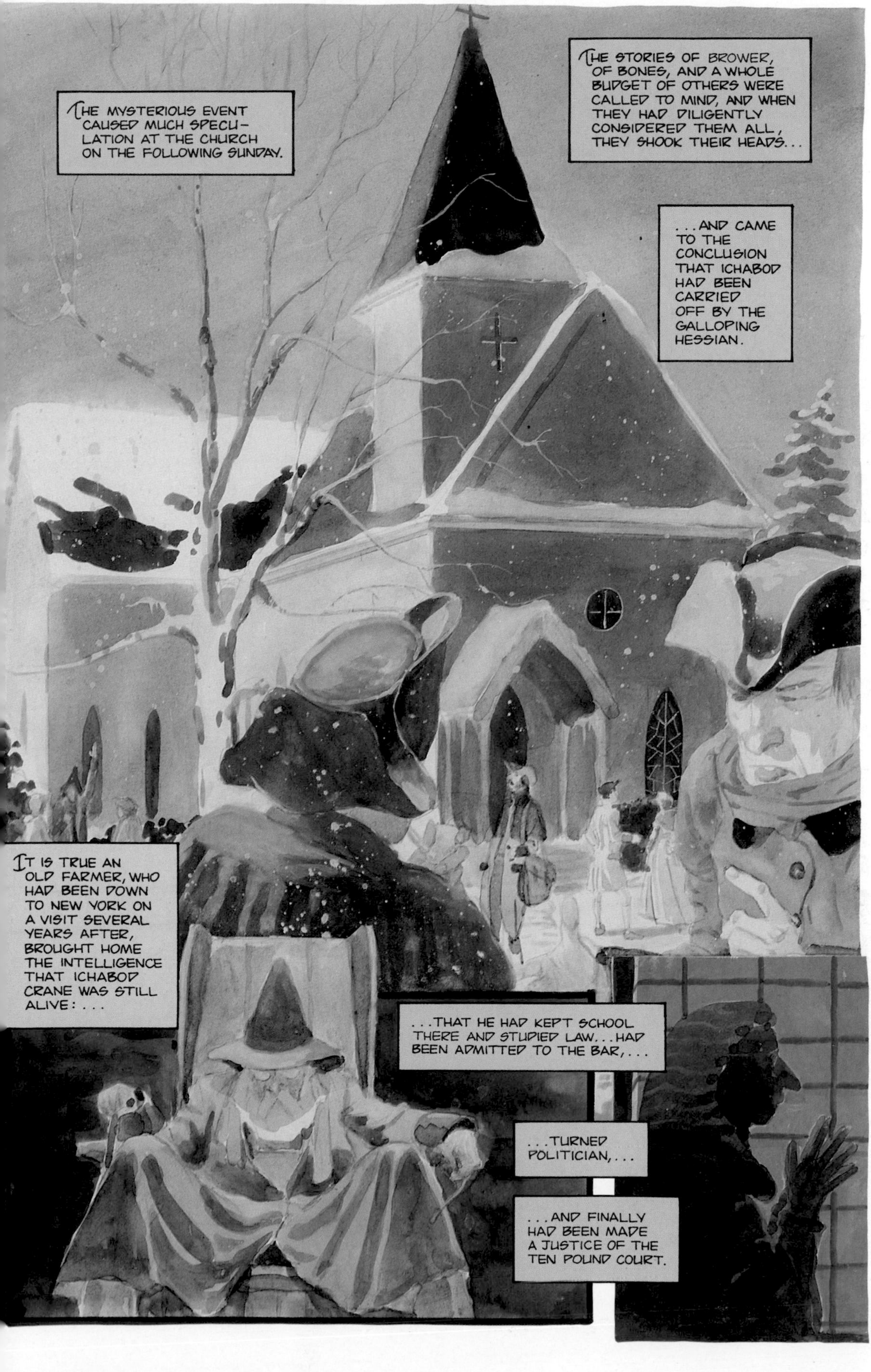
THE MYSTERIOUS EVENT CAUSED MUCH SPECU-LATION AT THE CHURCH ON THE FOLLOWING SUNDAY.
THE STORIES OF BROWER, OF BONES, AND A WHOLE BUDGET OF OTHERS WERE CALLED TO MIND, AND WHEN THEY HAD DILIGENTLY CONSIDERED THEM ALL, THEY SHOOK THEIR HEADS...
...AND CAME TO THE CONCLUSION THAT ICHABOD HAD BEEN CARRIED OFF BY THE GALLOPING HESSIAN.
IT IS TRUE AN OLD FARMER, WHO HAD BEEN DOWN TO NEW YORK ON A VISIT SEVERAL YEARS AFTER, BROUGHT HOME THE INTELLIGENCE THAT ICHABOD CRANE WAS STILL ALIVE:...
...THAT HE HAD KEPT SCHOOL THERE AND STUDIED LAW...HAD BEEN ADMITTED TO THE BAR,...
...TURNED POLITICIAN,...
...AND FINALLY HAD BEEN MADE A JUSTICE OF THE TEN POUND COURT.

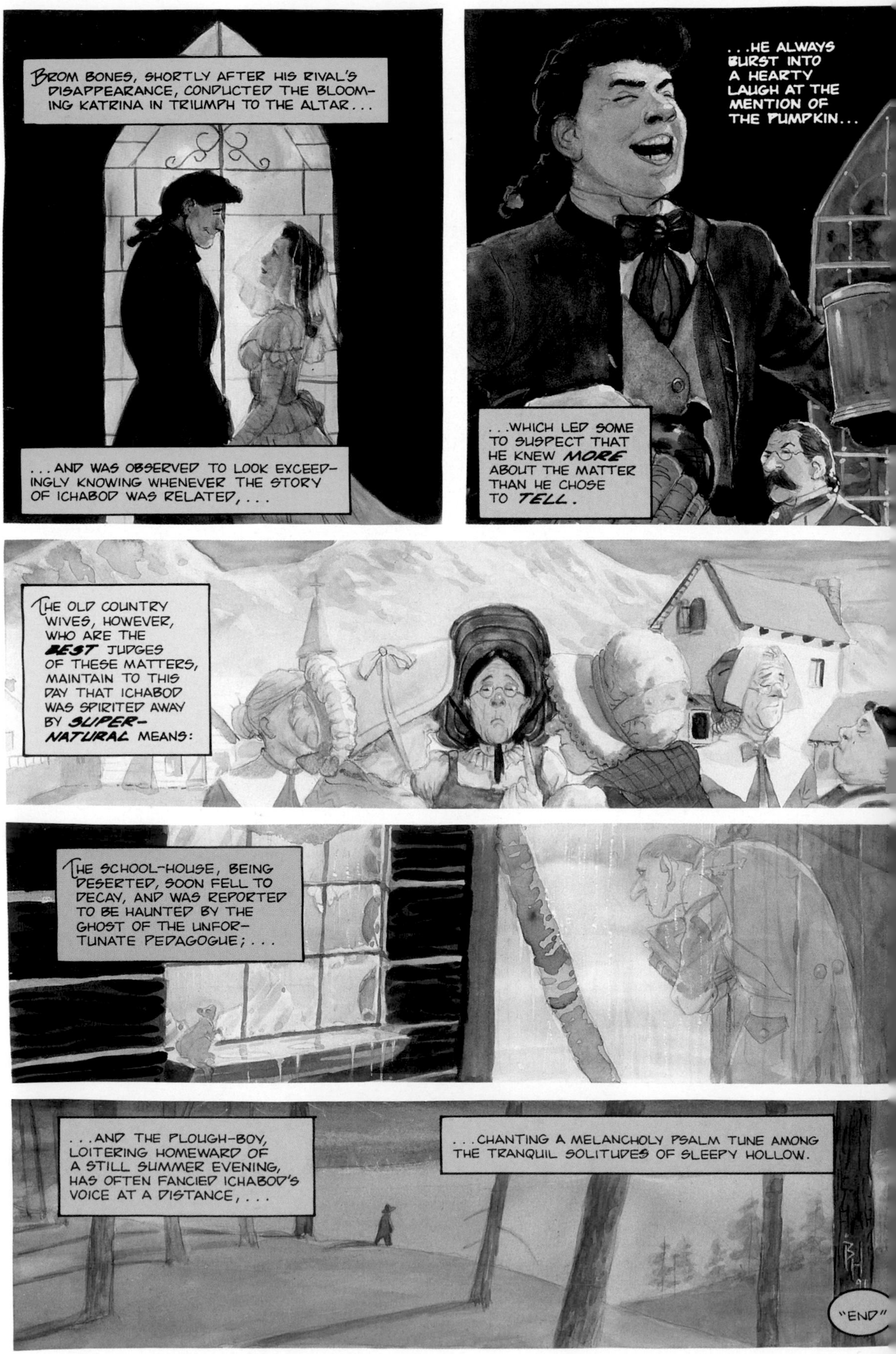
BROM BONES, SHORTLY AFTER HIS RIVAL'S DISAPPEARANCE, CONDUCTED THE BLOOMING KATRINA IN TRIUMPH TO THE ALTAR...
...AND WAS OBSERVED TO LOOK EXCEEDINGLY KNOWING WHENEVER THE STORY OF ICHABOD WAS RELATED, ...
...HE ALWAYS BURST INTO A HEARTY LAUGH AT THE MENTION OF THE PUMPKIN...
...WHICH LED SOME TO SUSPECT THAT HE KNEW MORE ABOUT THE MATTER THAN HE CHOSE TO TELL.
THE OLD COUNTRY WIVES, HOWEVER, WHO ARE THE BEST JUDGES OF THESE MATTERS, MAINTAIN TO THIS DAY THAT ICHABOD WAS SPIRITED AWAY BY SUPER-NATURAL MEANS:
THE SCHOOL-HOUSE, BEING DESERTED, SOON FELL TO DECAY, AND WAS REPORTED TO BE HAUNTED BY THE GHOST OF THE UNFORTUNATE PEDAGOGUE; ...
...AND THE PLOUGH-BOY, LOITERING HOMEWARD OF A STILL SUMMER EVENING, HAS OFTEN FANCIED ICHABOD'S VOICE AT A DISTANCE, ...
...CHANTING A MELANCHOLY PSALM TUNE AMONG THE TRANQUIL SOLITUDES OF SLEEPY HOLLOW.
"END"

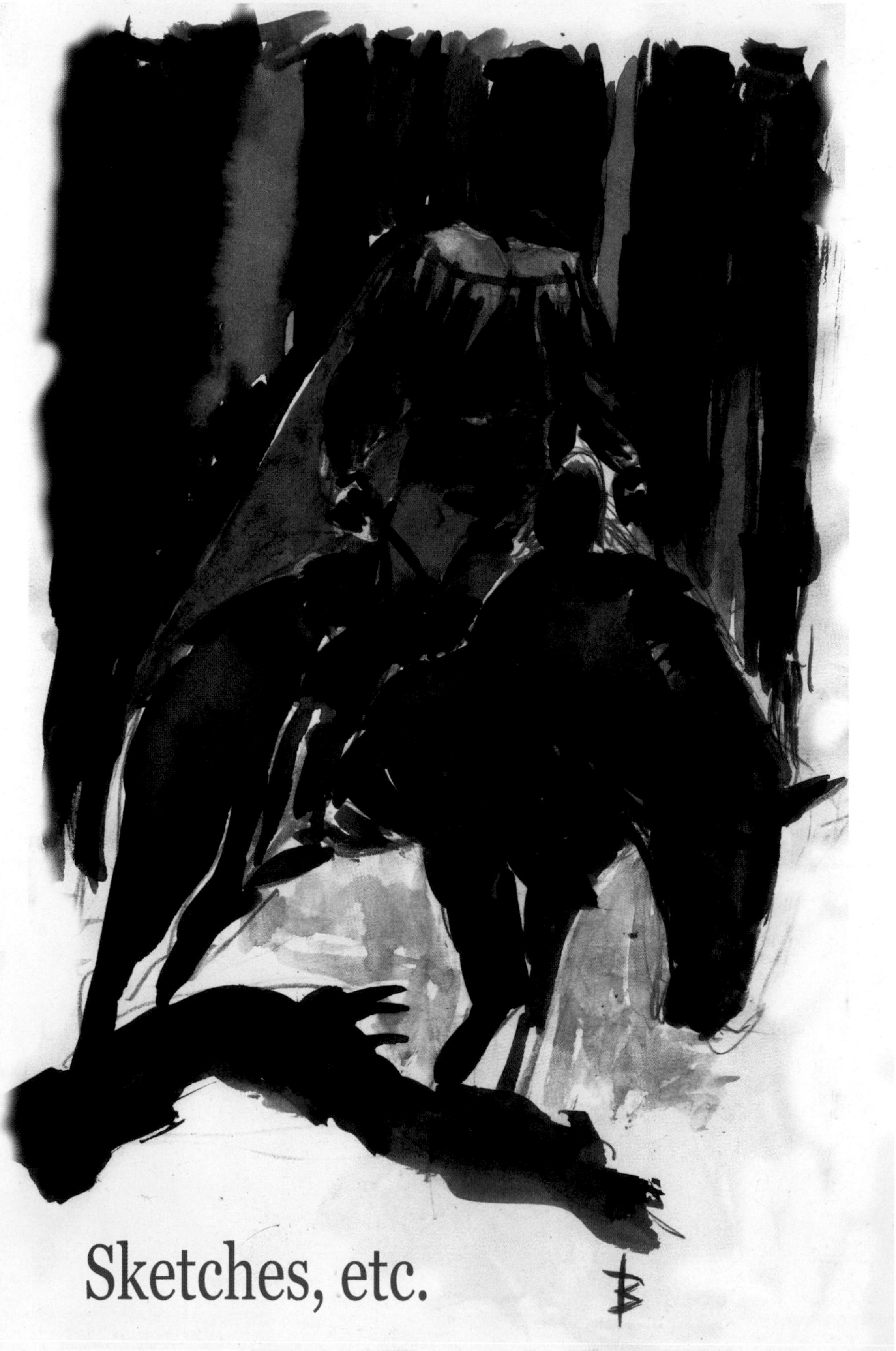

Sketches, etc.

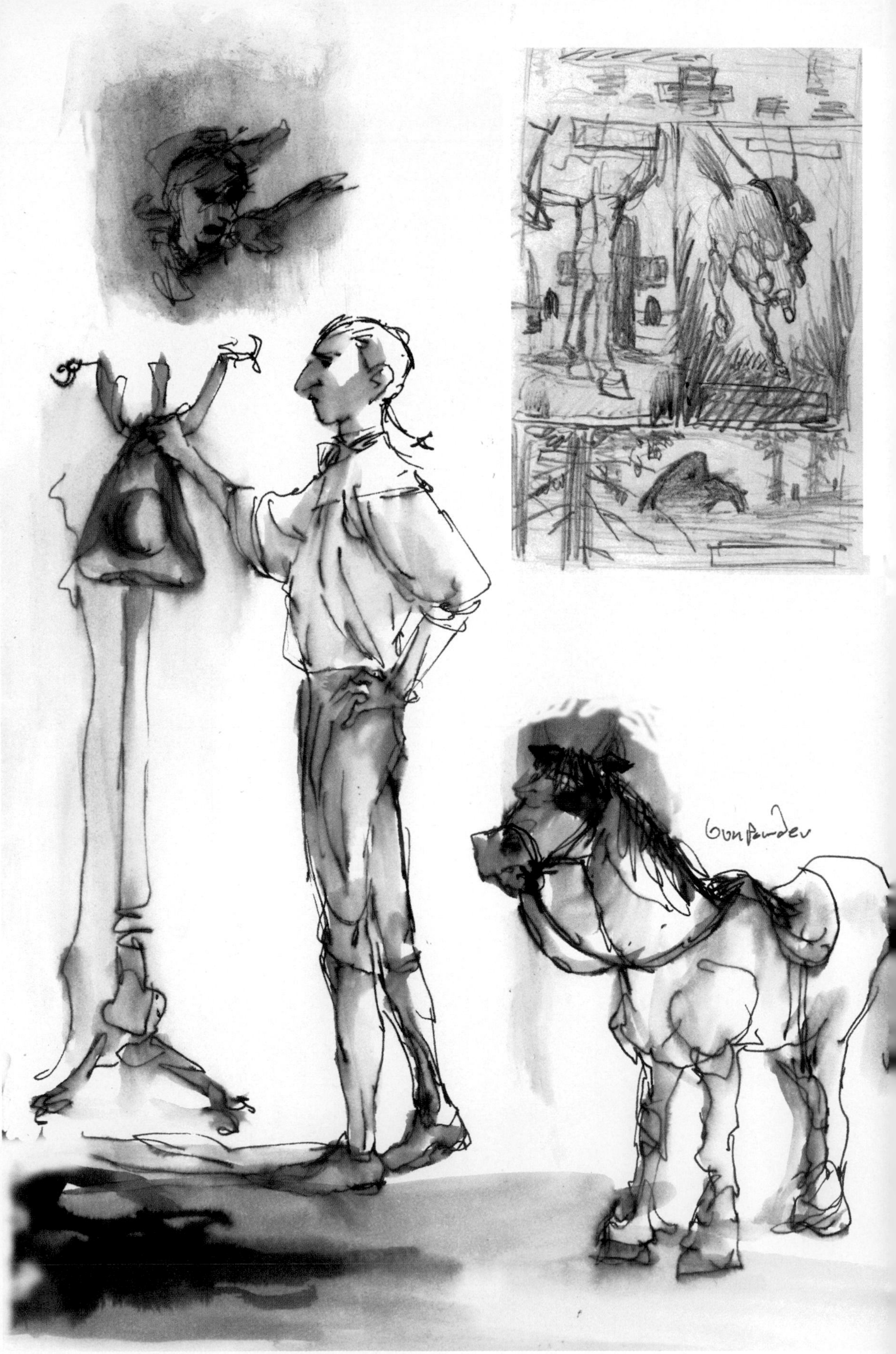
Gunpowder

PORT, J

4407

Thursday, November 16, 2023

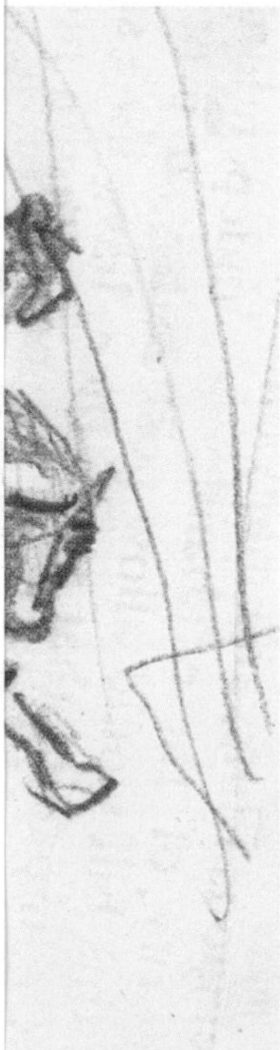

All sketches and paintings were done in pencil, ink and watercolor...

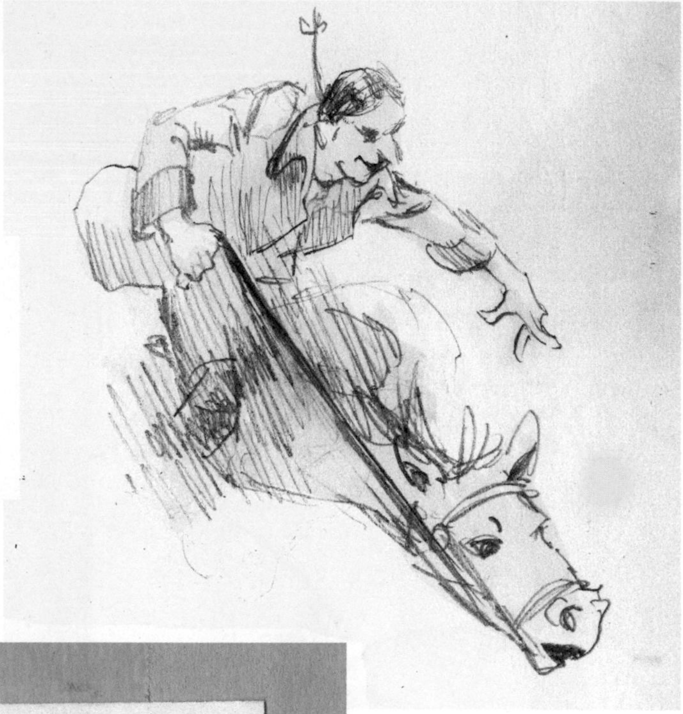

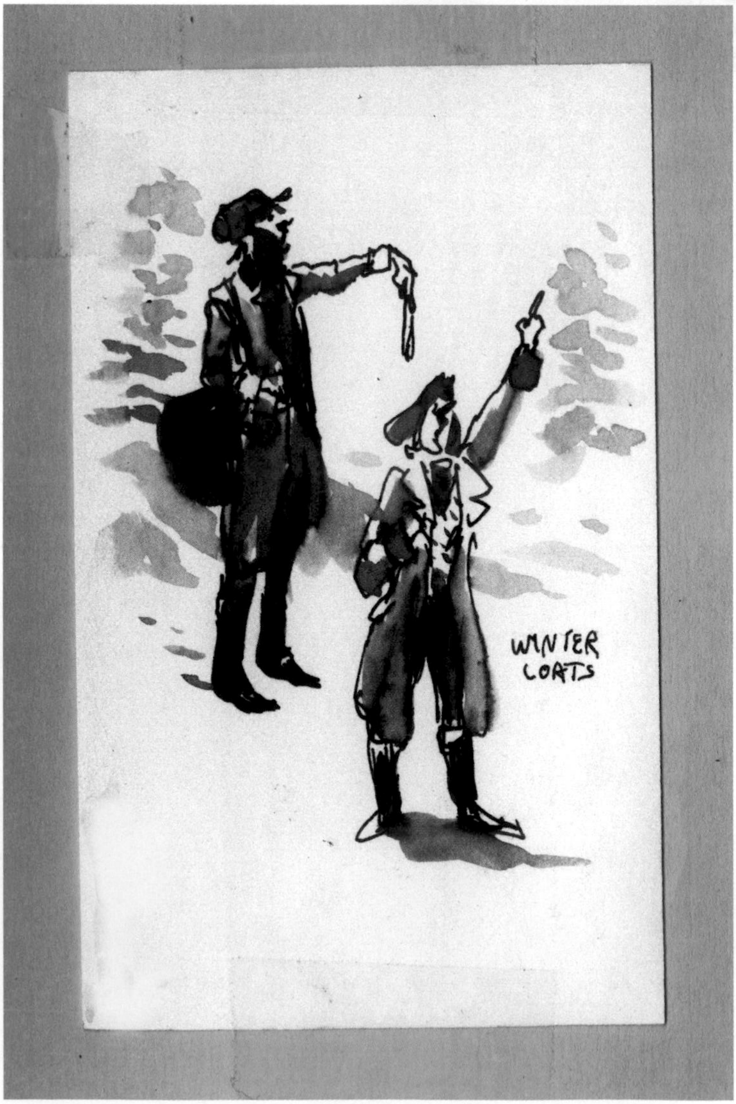
WINTER
COATS

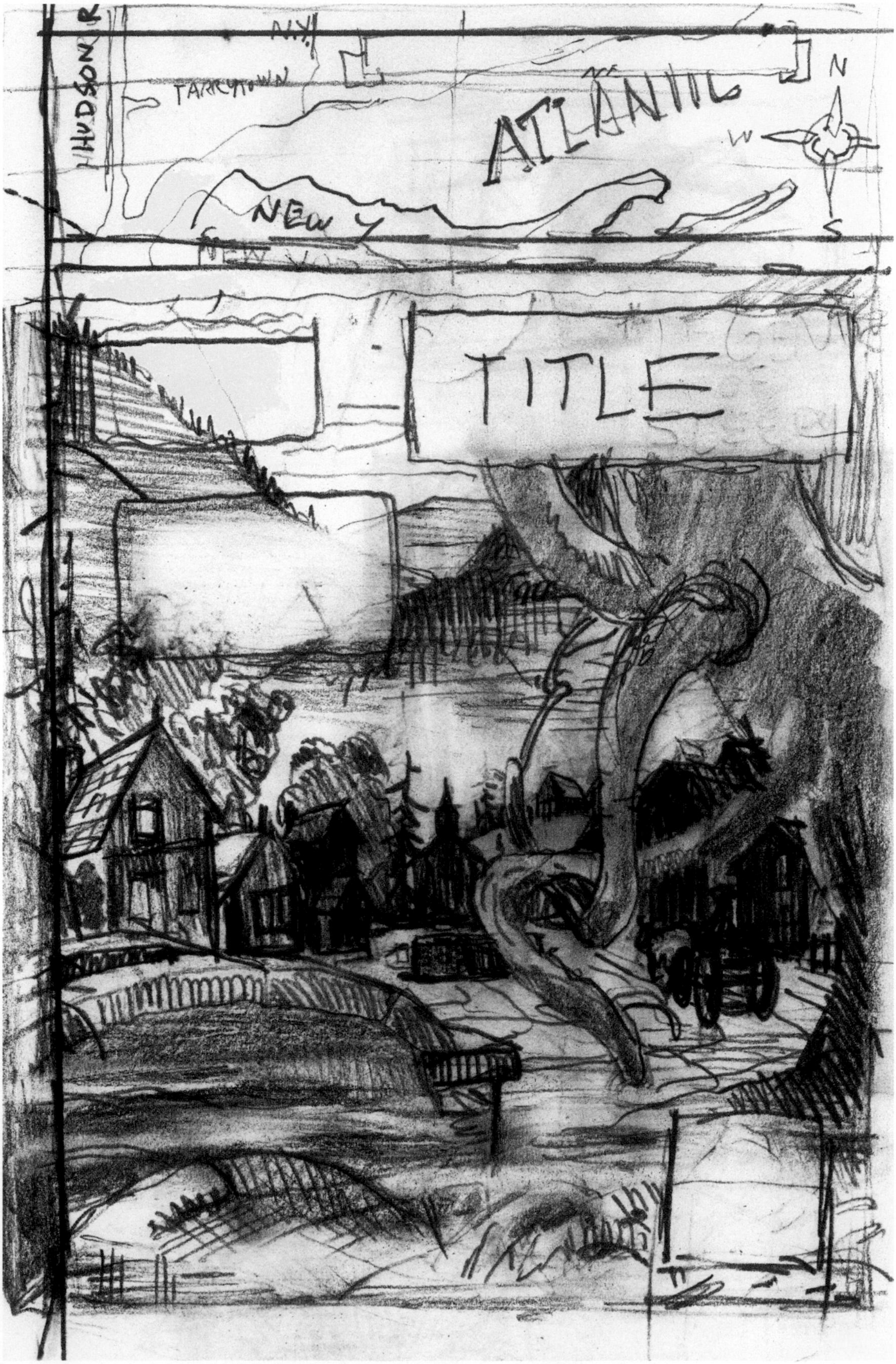
HUDSON R
N.Y.
TARRYTOWN
ATLANTIC
NEW Y
N
W
S
TITLE

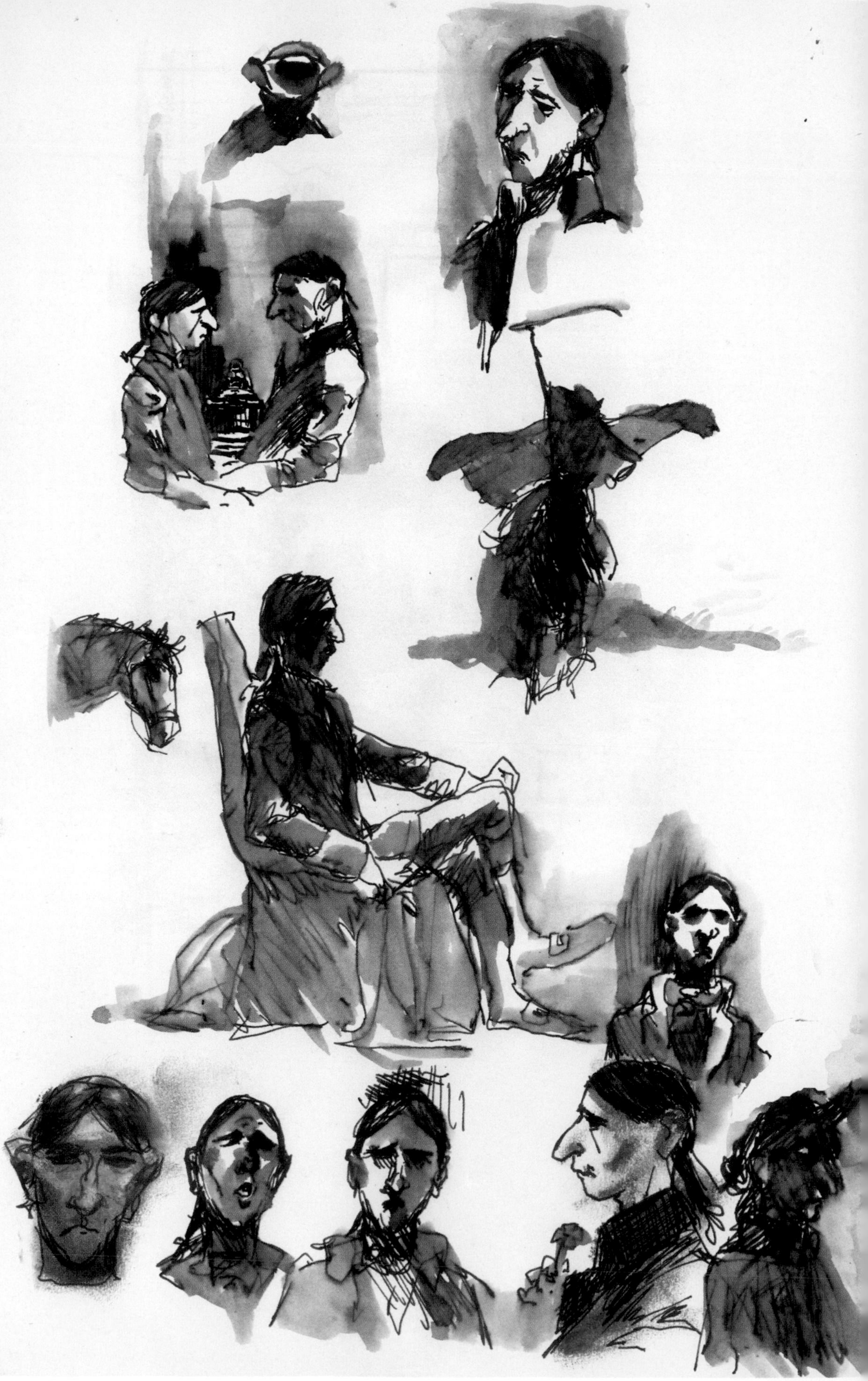

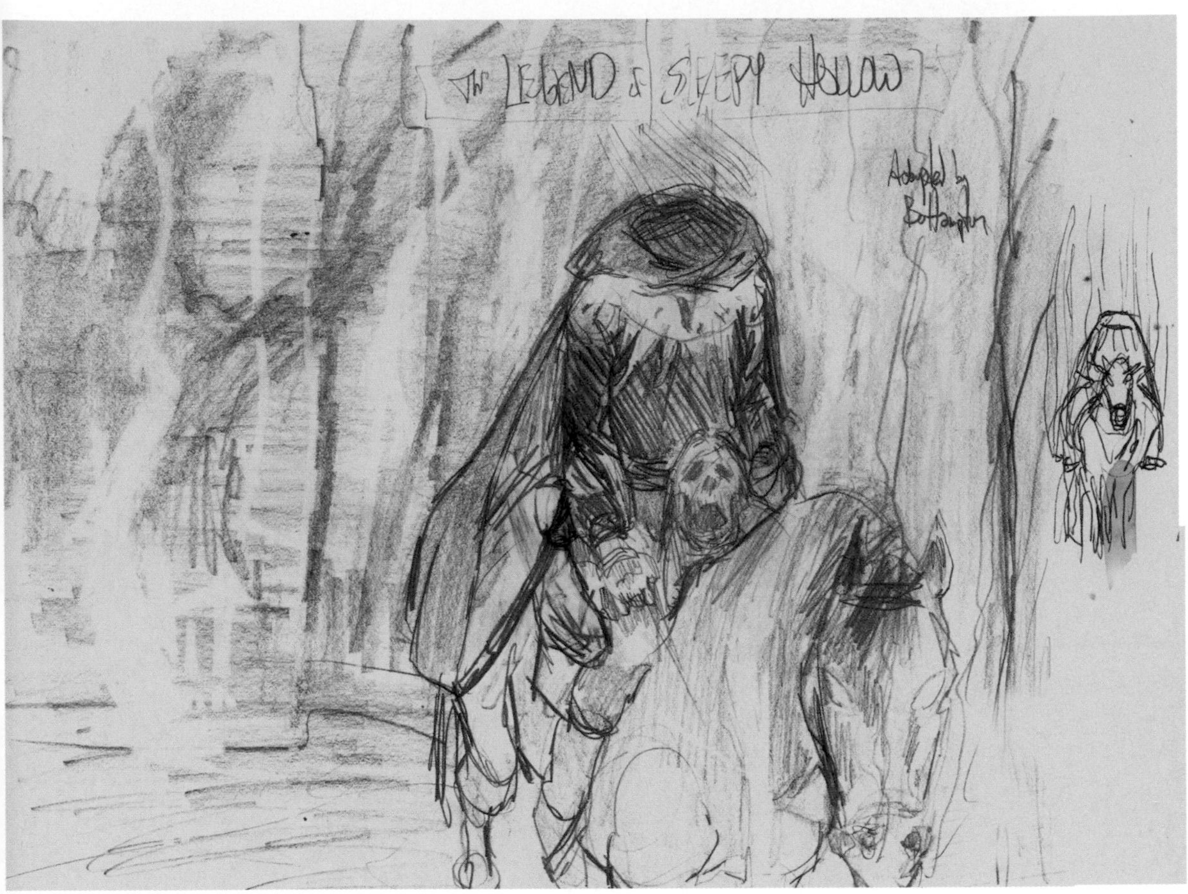
THE LEGEND OF SLEEPY HOLLOW
Adapted by
Bo Hampton

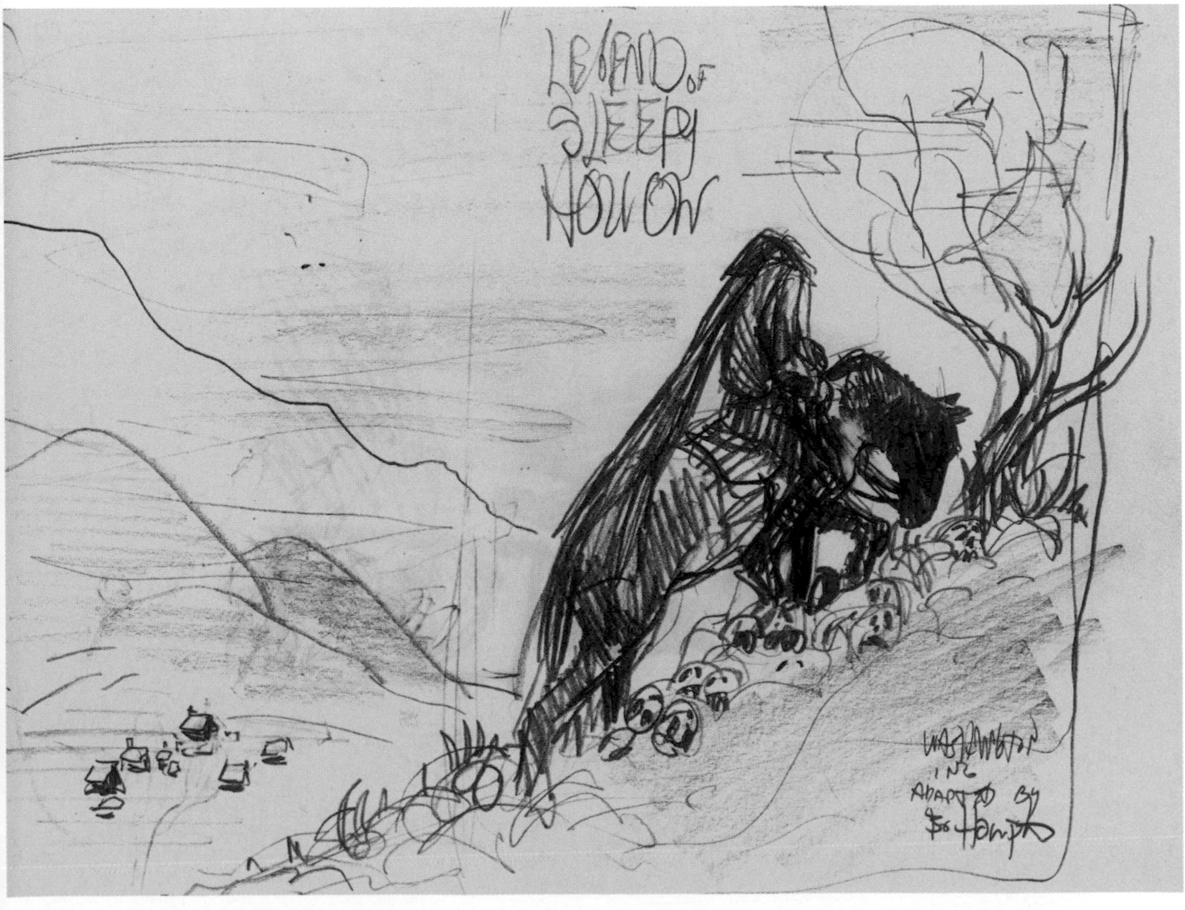
LEGEND OF SLEEPY HOLLOW
ADAPTED BY
Bo Hampton

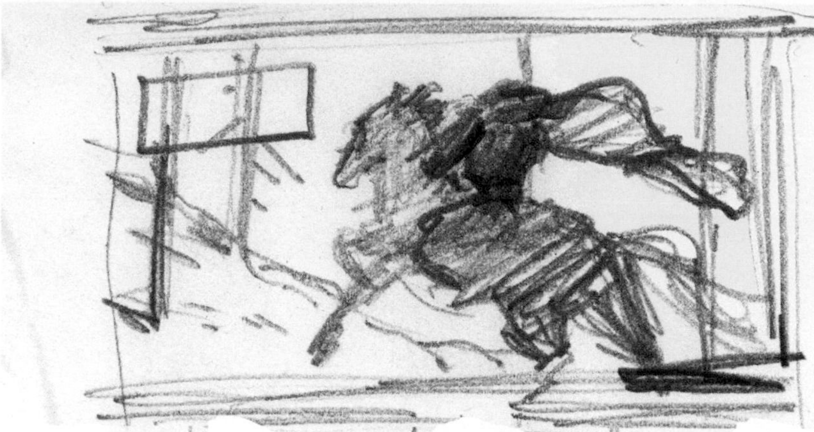

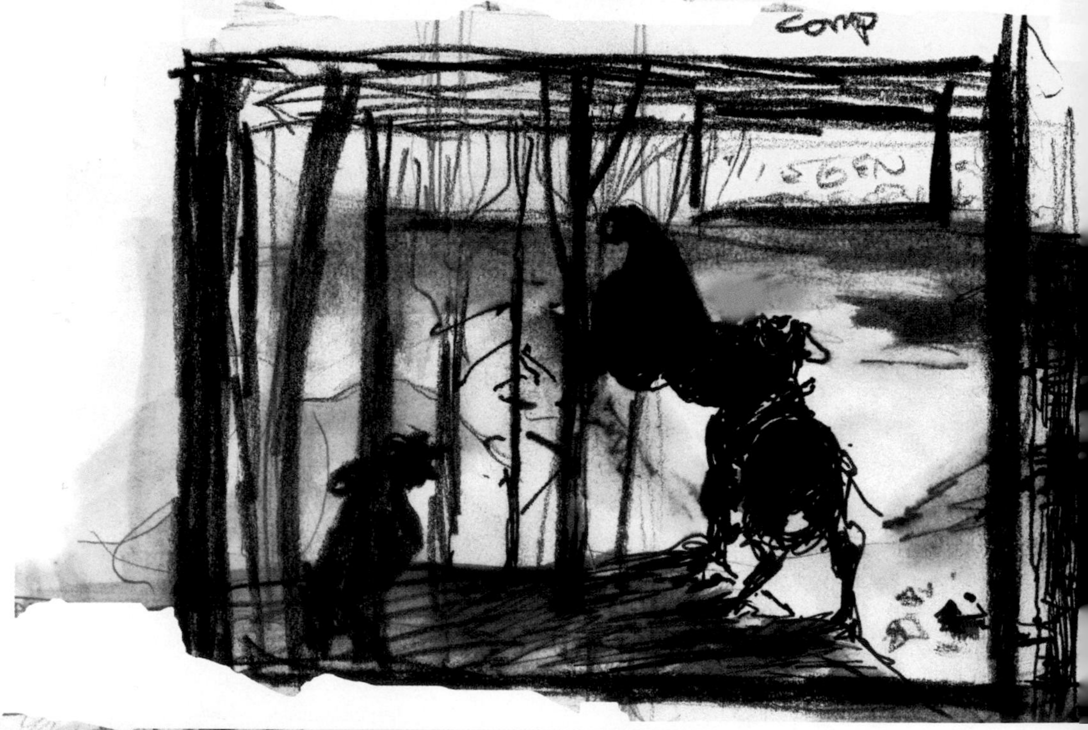
comp

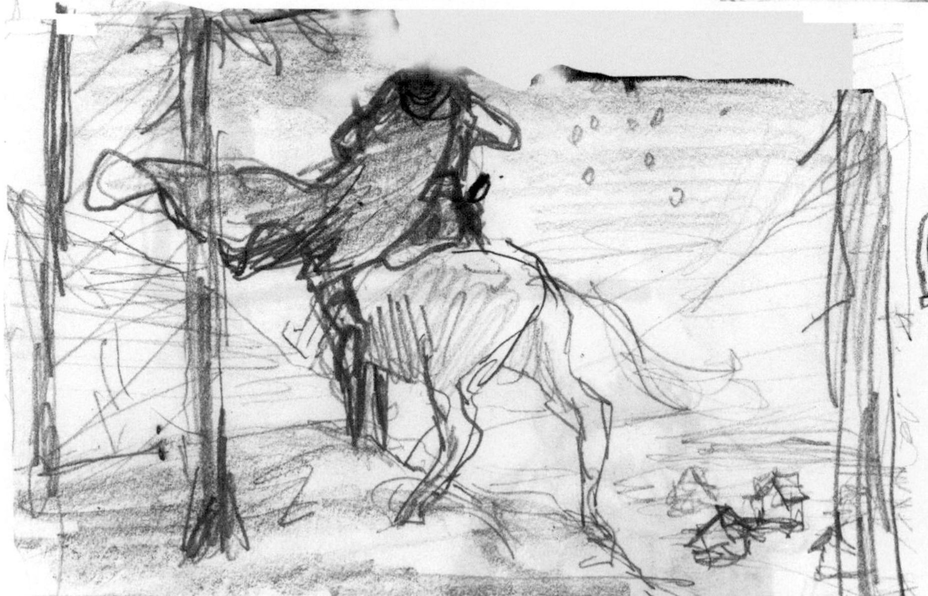

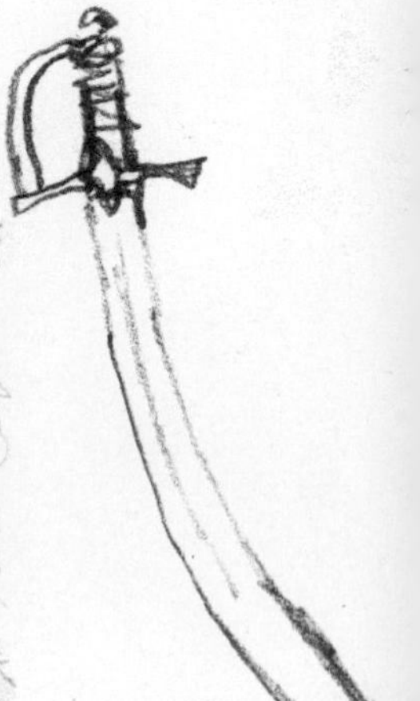

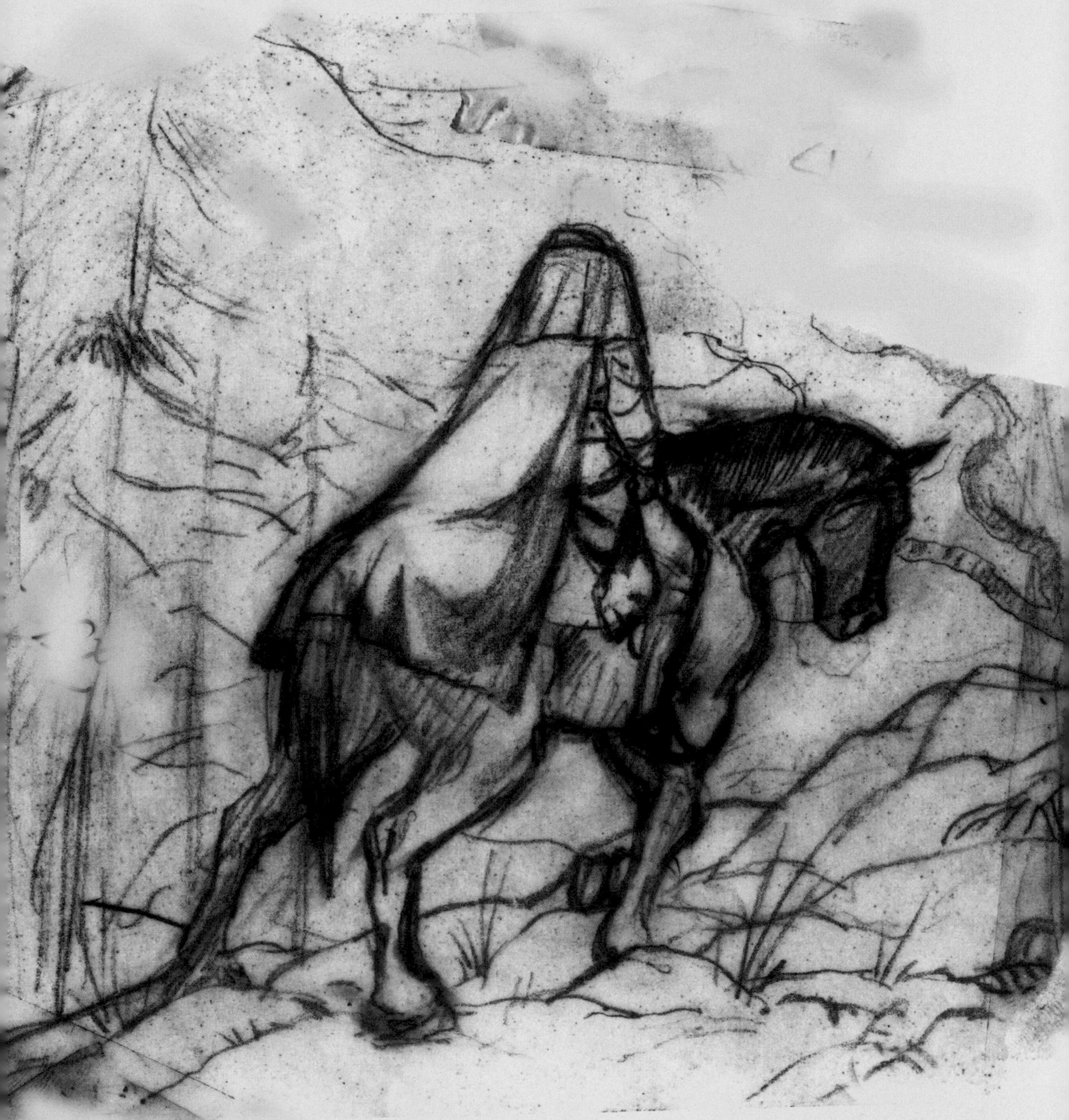

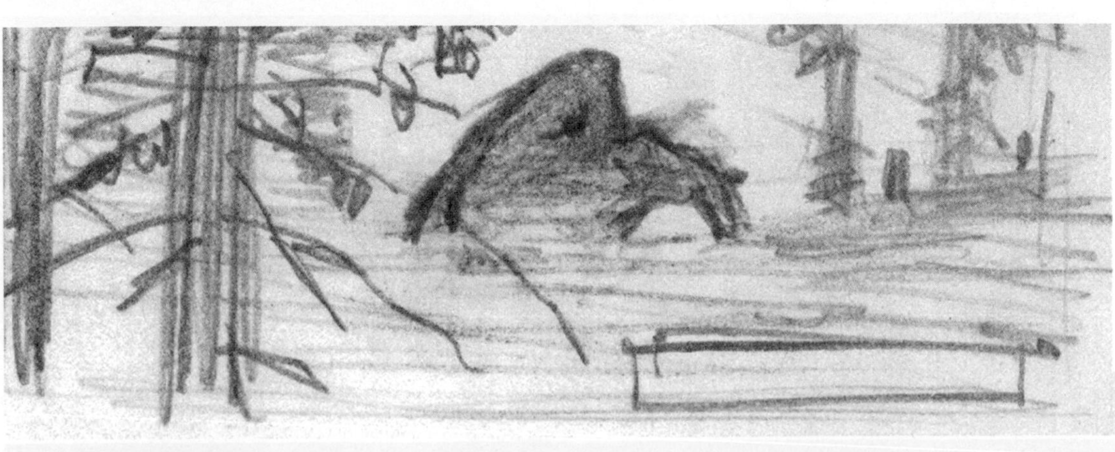

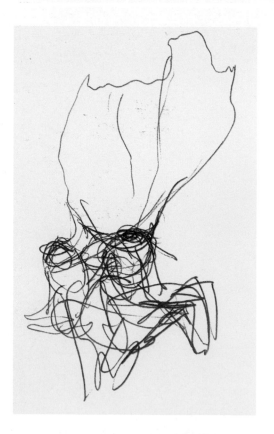

VIRMILLION
&
PAYNES G

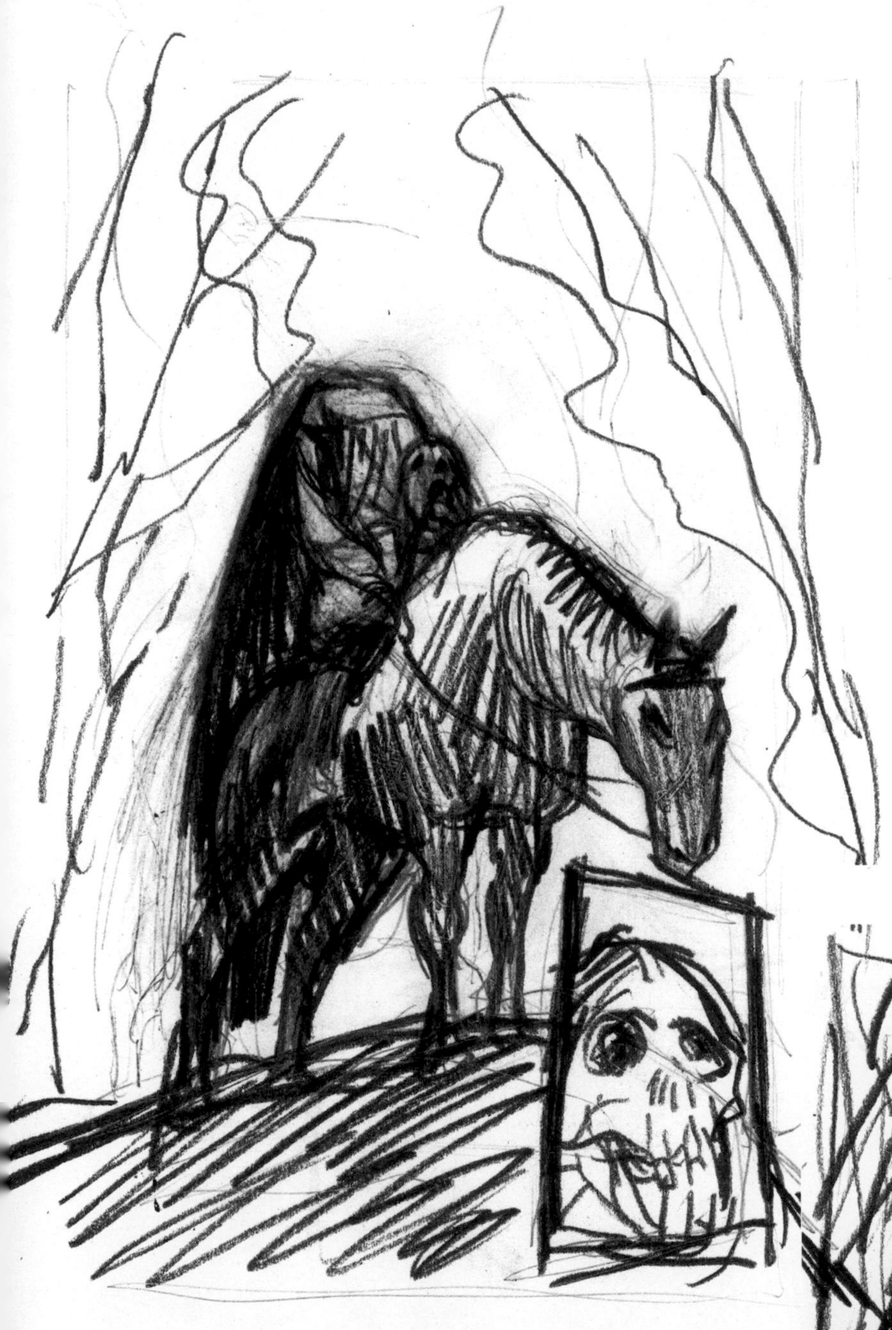
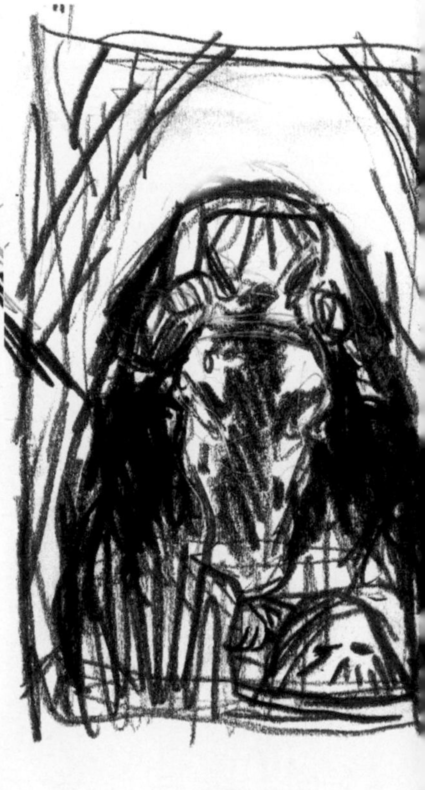
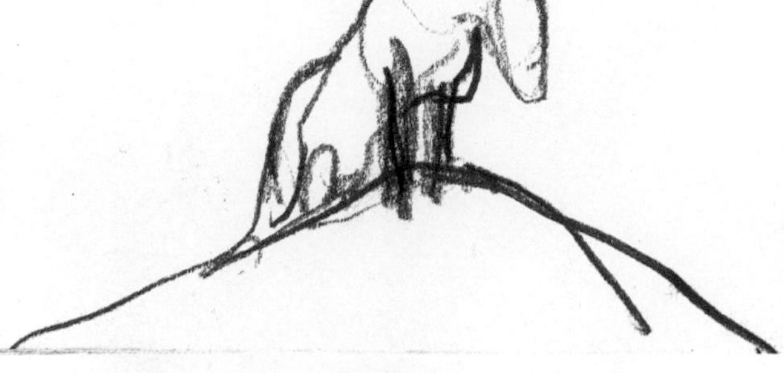

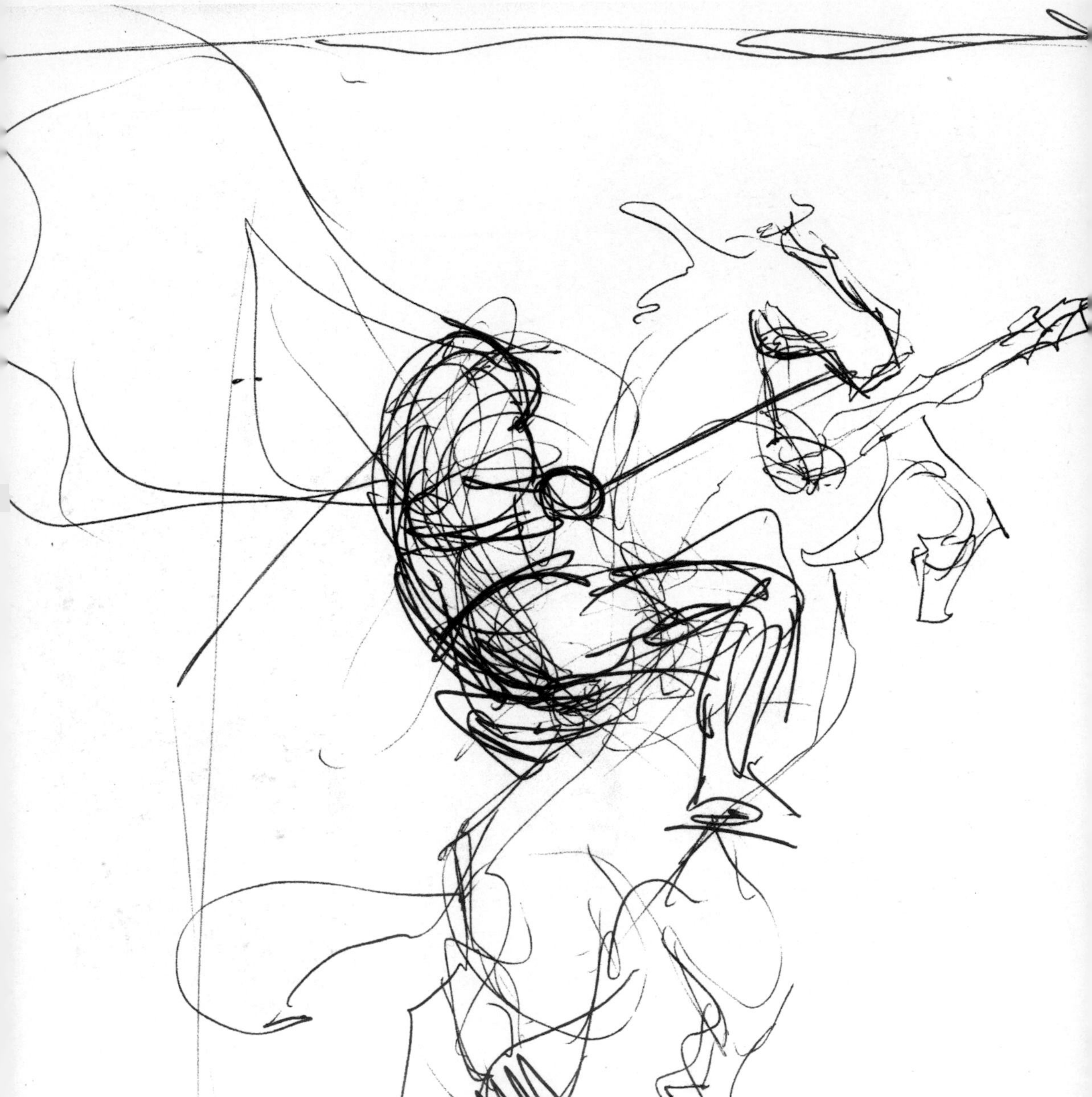
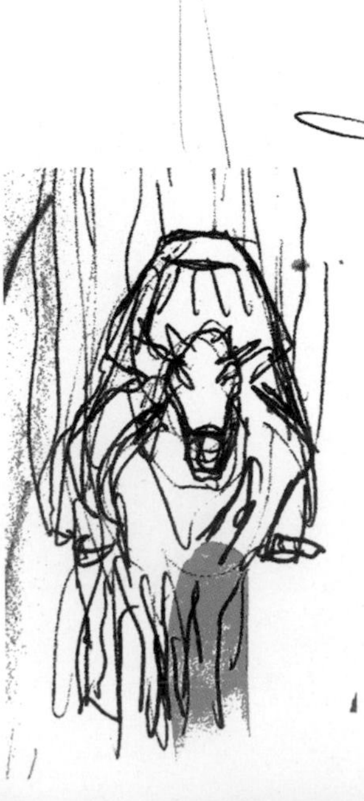
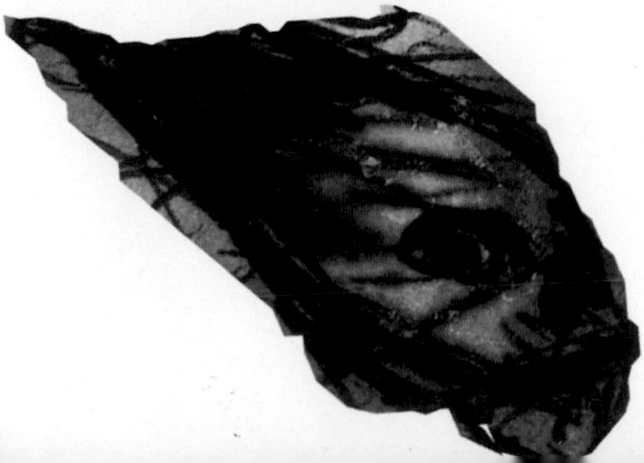

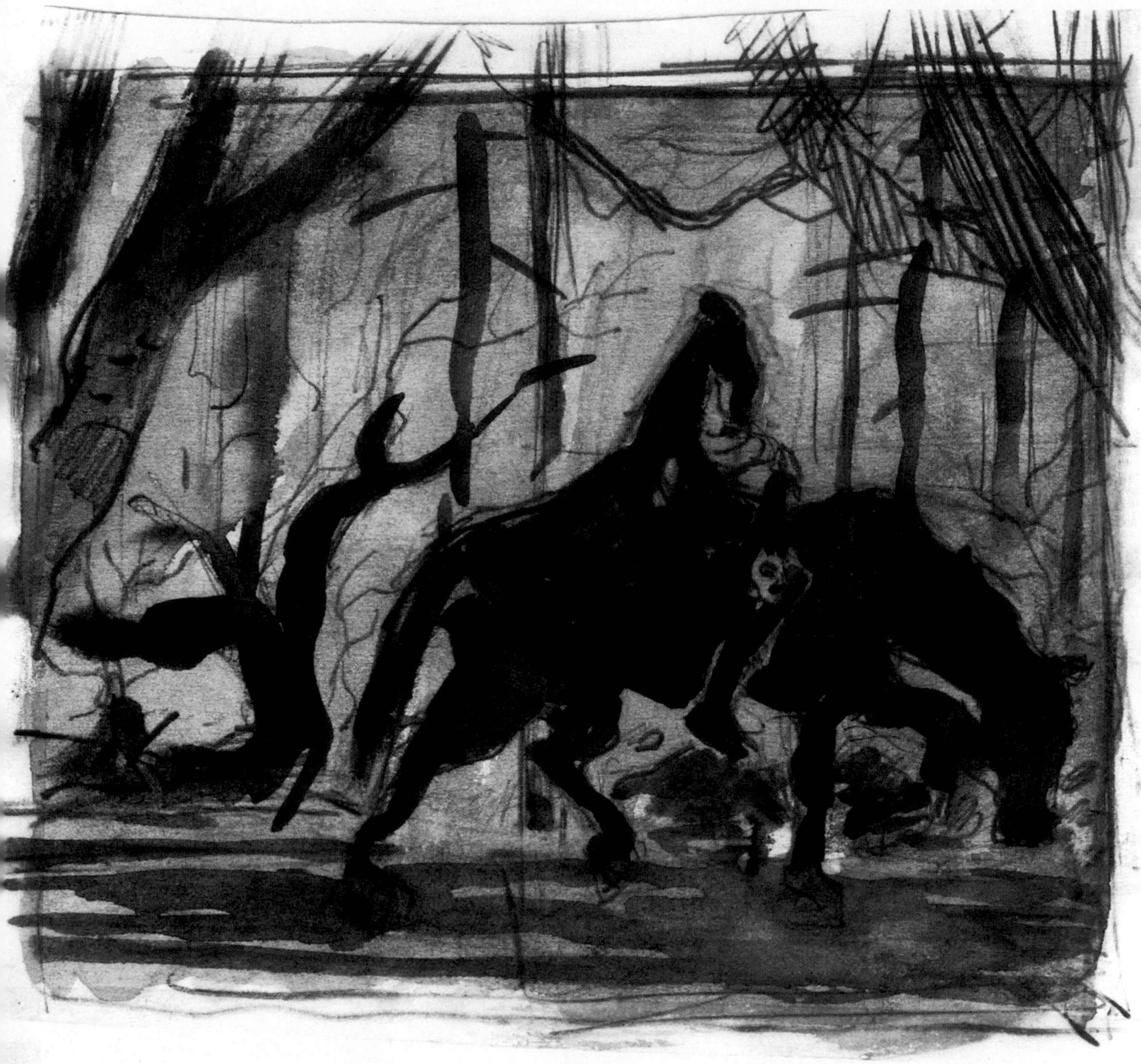

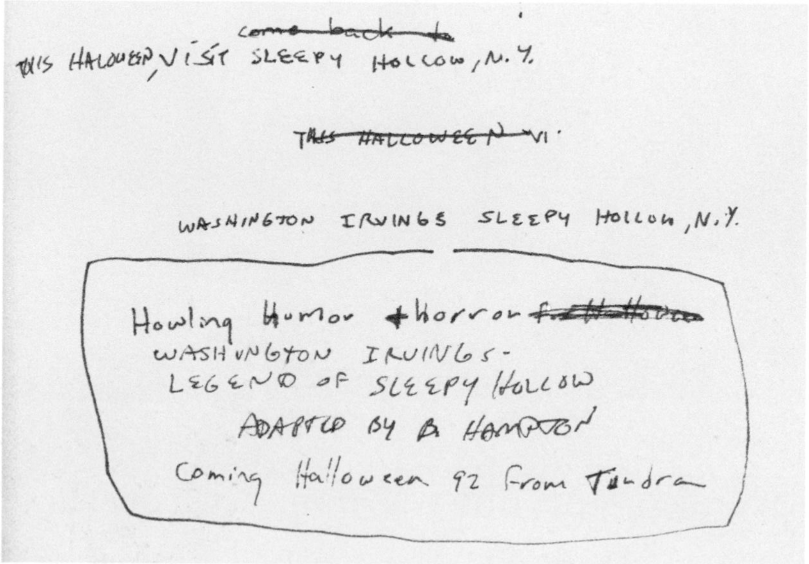

~~come back to~~
THIS HALOWEEN, VISIT SLEEPY HOLLOW, N.Y.

~~THIS HALLOWEEN~~ VI

WASHINGTON IRVINGS SLEEPY HOLLOW, N.Y.

Howling Humor + horror ~~for Halloween~~
WASHINGTON IRVINGS-
LEGEND OF SLEEPY HOLLOW
ADAPTED BY B HAMPTON
Coming Halloween 92 from Tundra

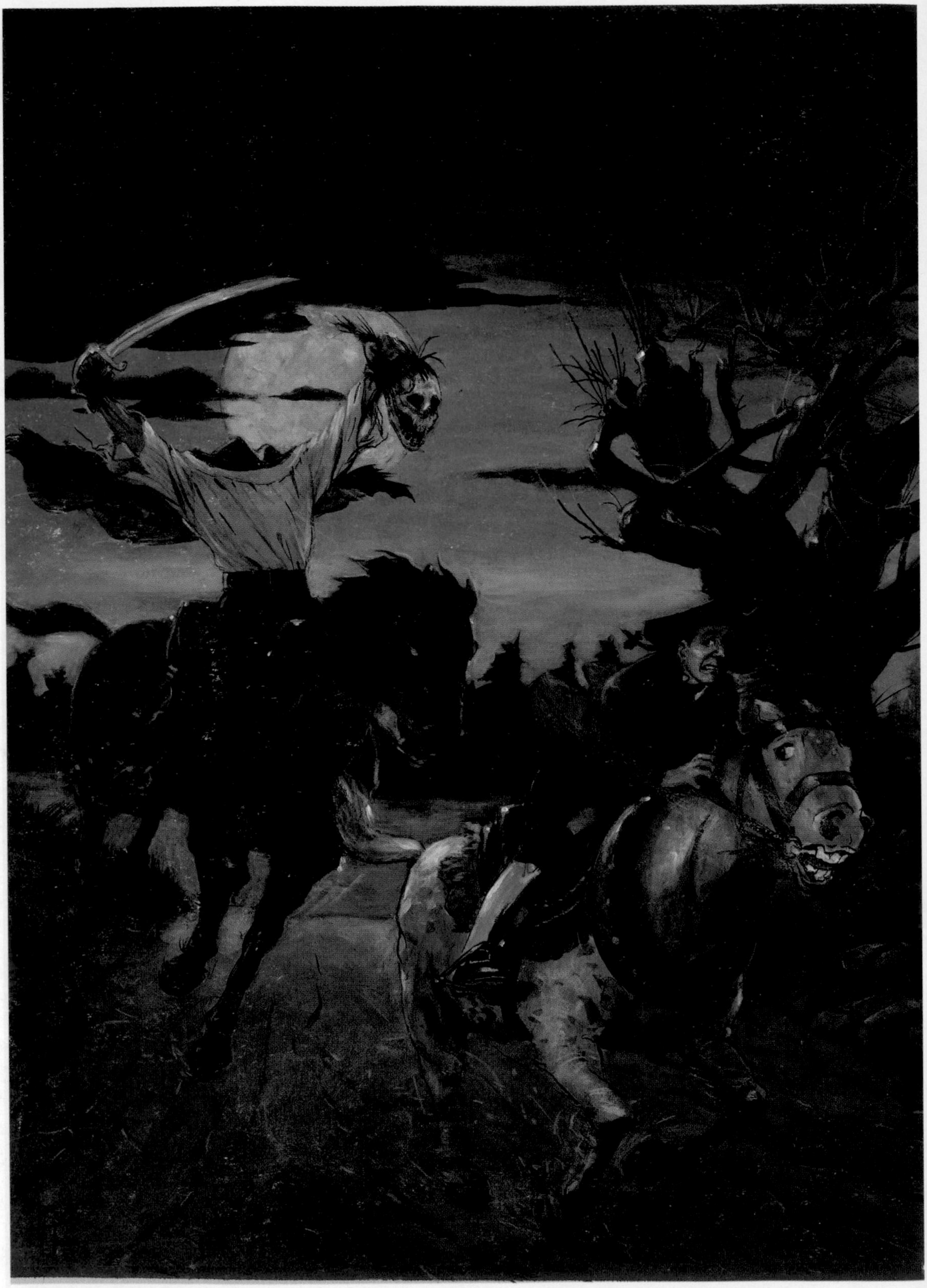

...Okay, I lied--this one was done with acrylics.

Happy Halloween!

BOOK

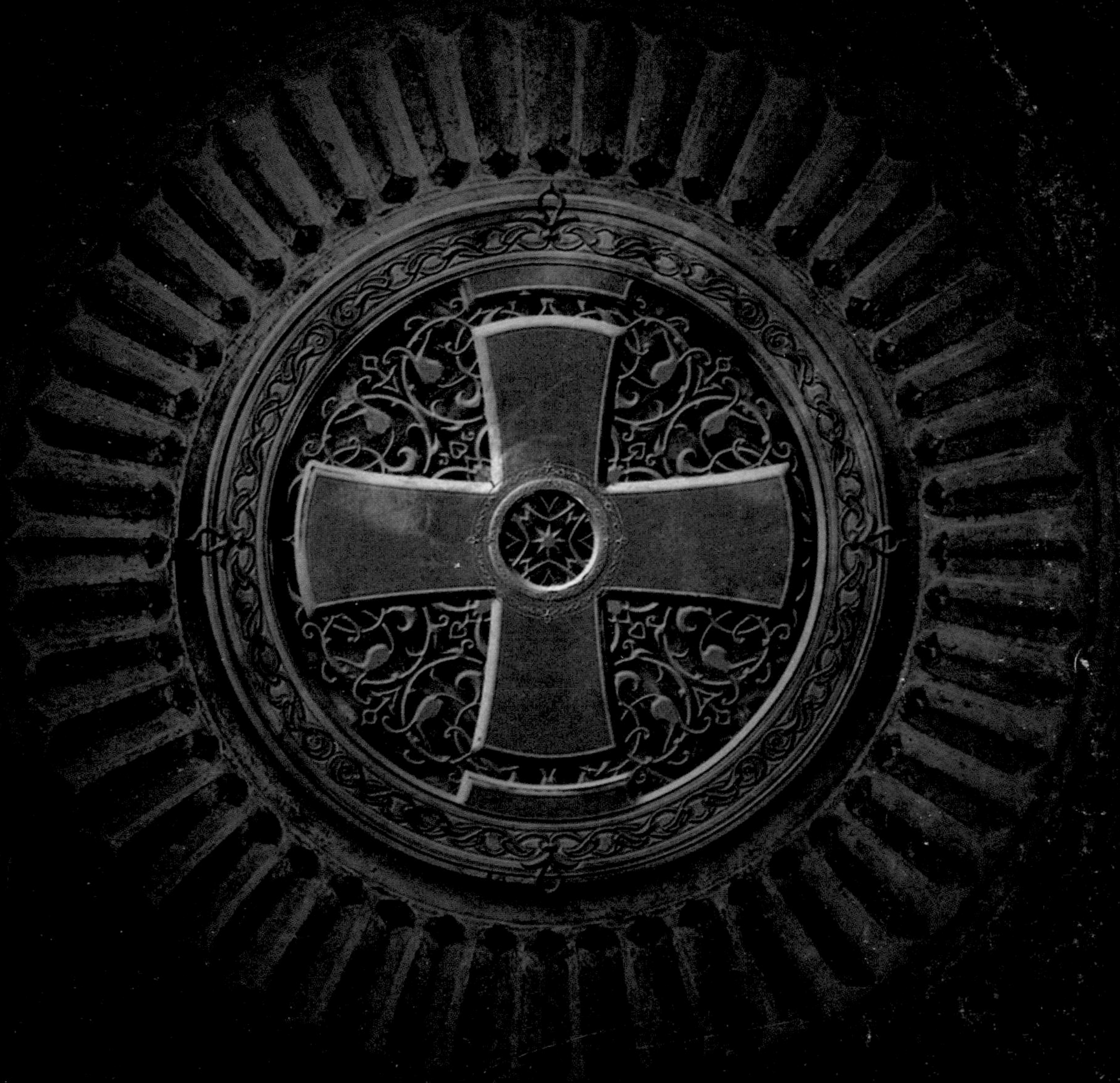

THE
CIRCLE
TRILOGY

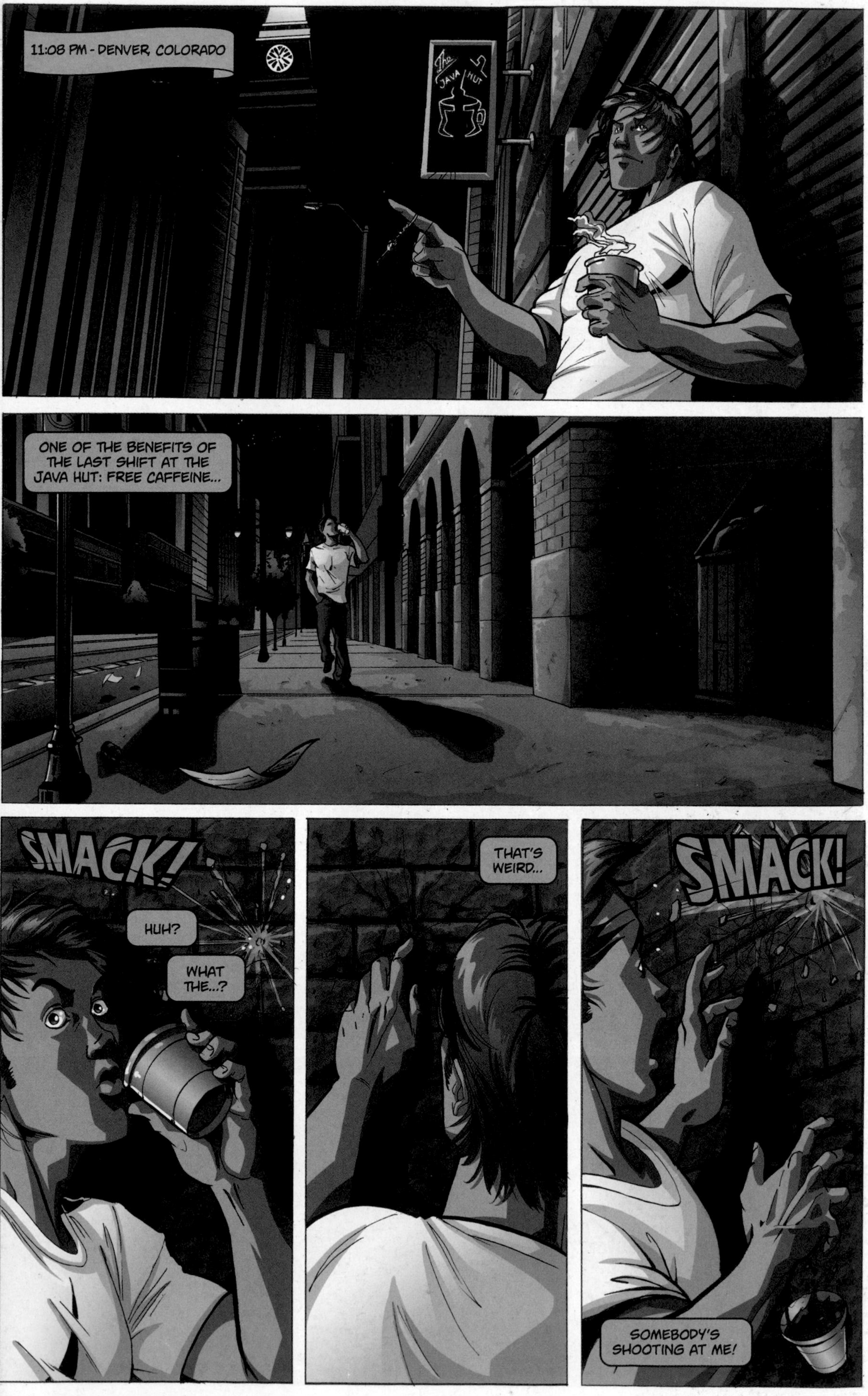
11:08 PM - DENVER, COLORADO
THE JAVA HUT
ONE OF THE BENEFITS OF THE LAST SHIFT AT THE JAVA HUT: FREE CAFFEINE...
SMACK!
HUH?
WHAT THE...?
THAT'S WEIRD...
SMACK!
SOMEBODY'S SHOOTING AT ME!

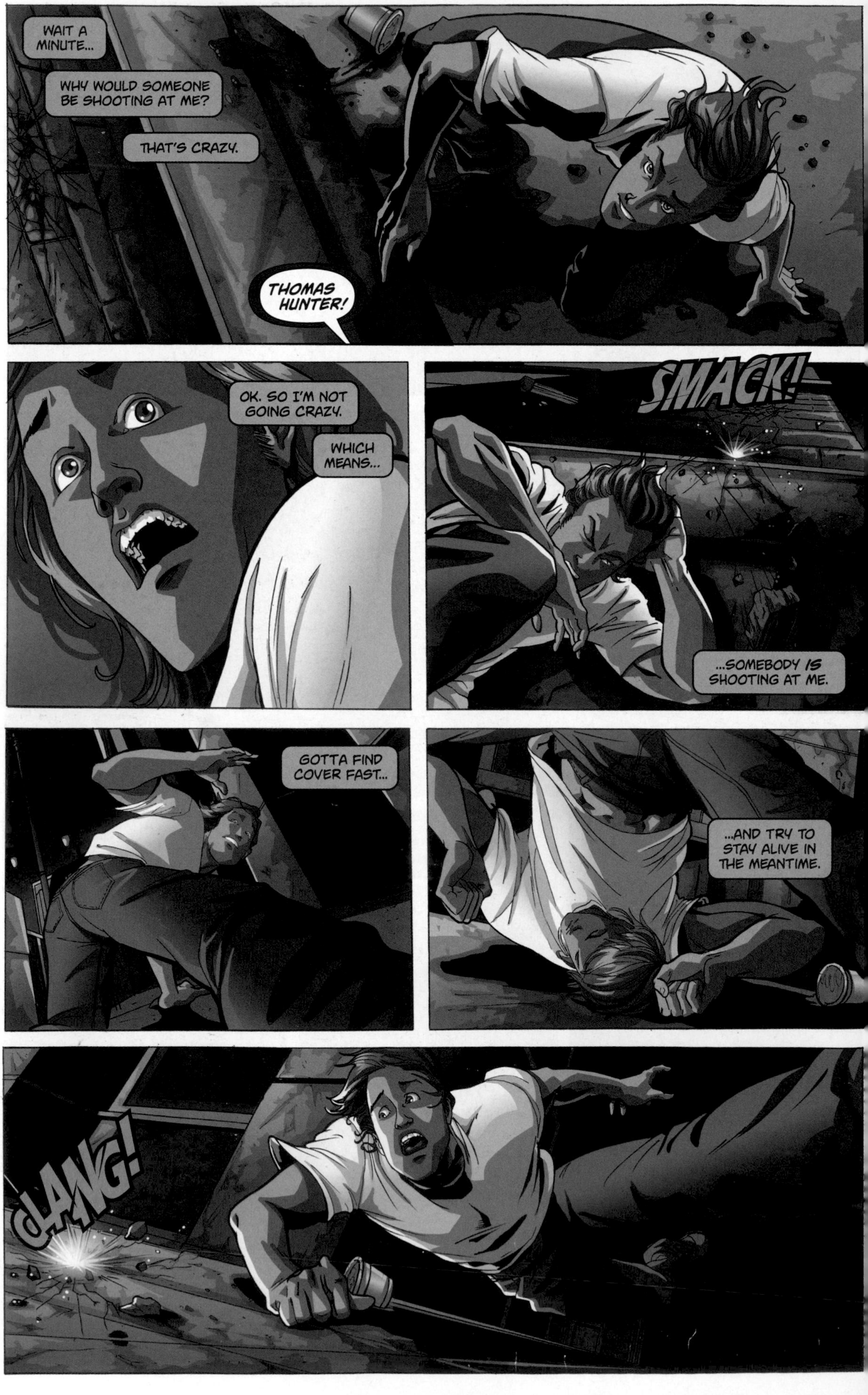
WAIT A MINUTE...
WHY WOULD SOMEONE BE SHOOTING AT ME?
THAT'S CRAZY.
THOMAS HUNTER!
OK. SO I'M NOT GOING CRAZY.
WHICH MEANS...
SMACK!
...SOMEBODY IS SHOOTING AT ME.
GOTTA FIND COVER FAST...
...AND TRY TO STAY ALIVE IN THE MEANTIME.
CLANG!

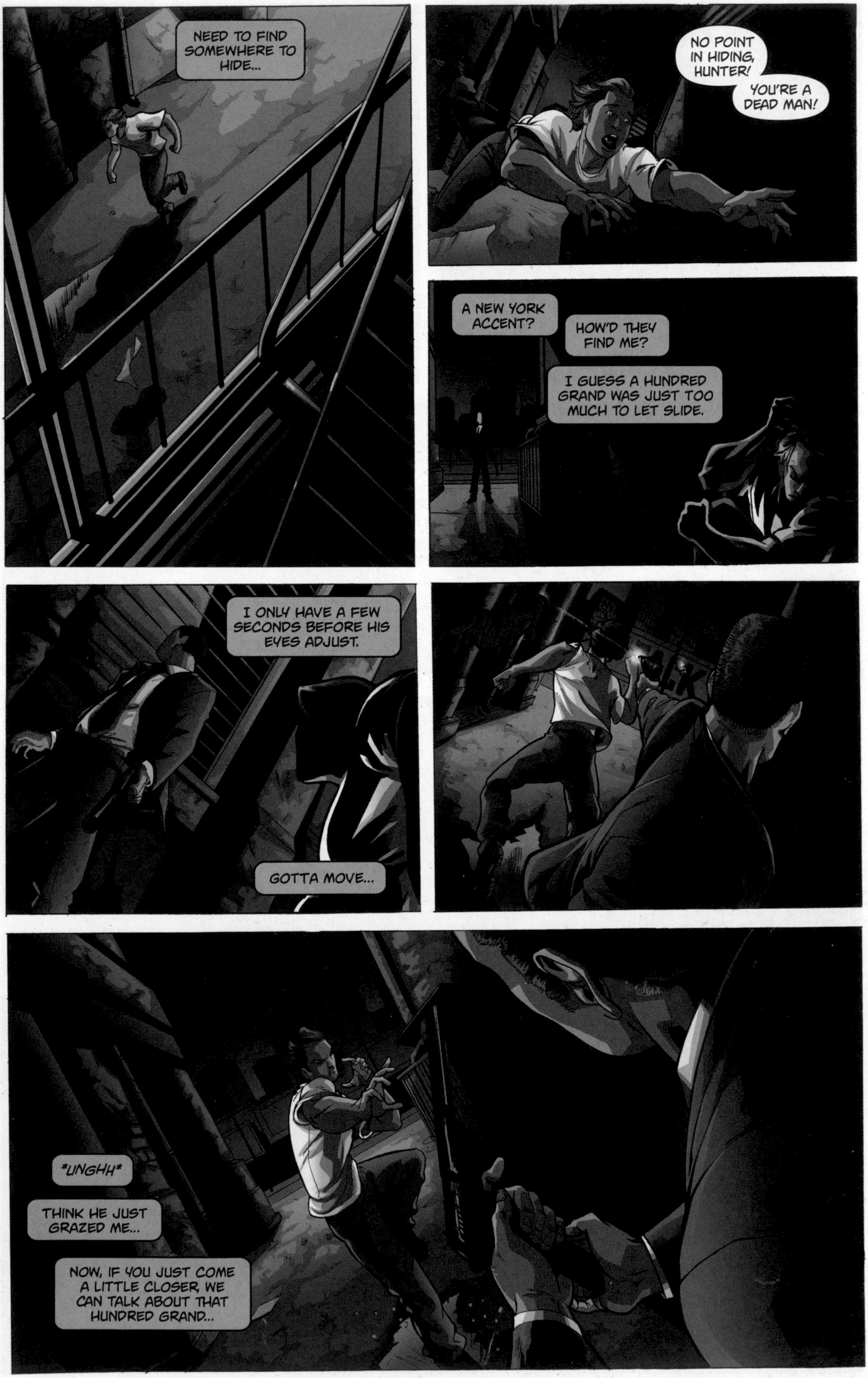
NEED TO FIND SOMEWHERE TO HIDE...
NO POINT IN HIDING, HUNTER!
YOU'RE A DEAD MAN!
A NEW YORK ACCENT?
HOW'D THEY FIND ME?
I GUESS A HUNDRED GRAND WAS JUST TOO MUCH TO LET SLIDE.
I ONLY HAVE A FEW SECONDS BEFORE HIS EYES ADJUST.
GOTTA MOVE...
UNGHH
THINK HE JUST GRAZED ME...
NOW, IF YOU JUST COME A LITTLE CLOSER, WE CAN TALK ABOUT THAT HUNDRED GRAND...

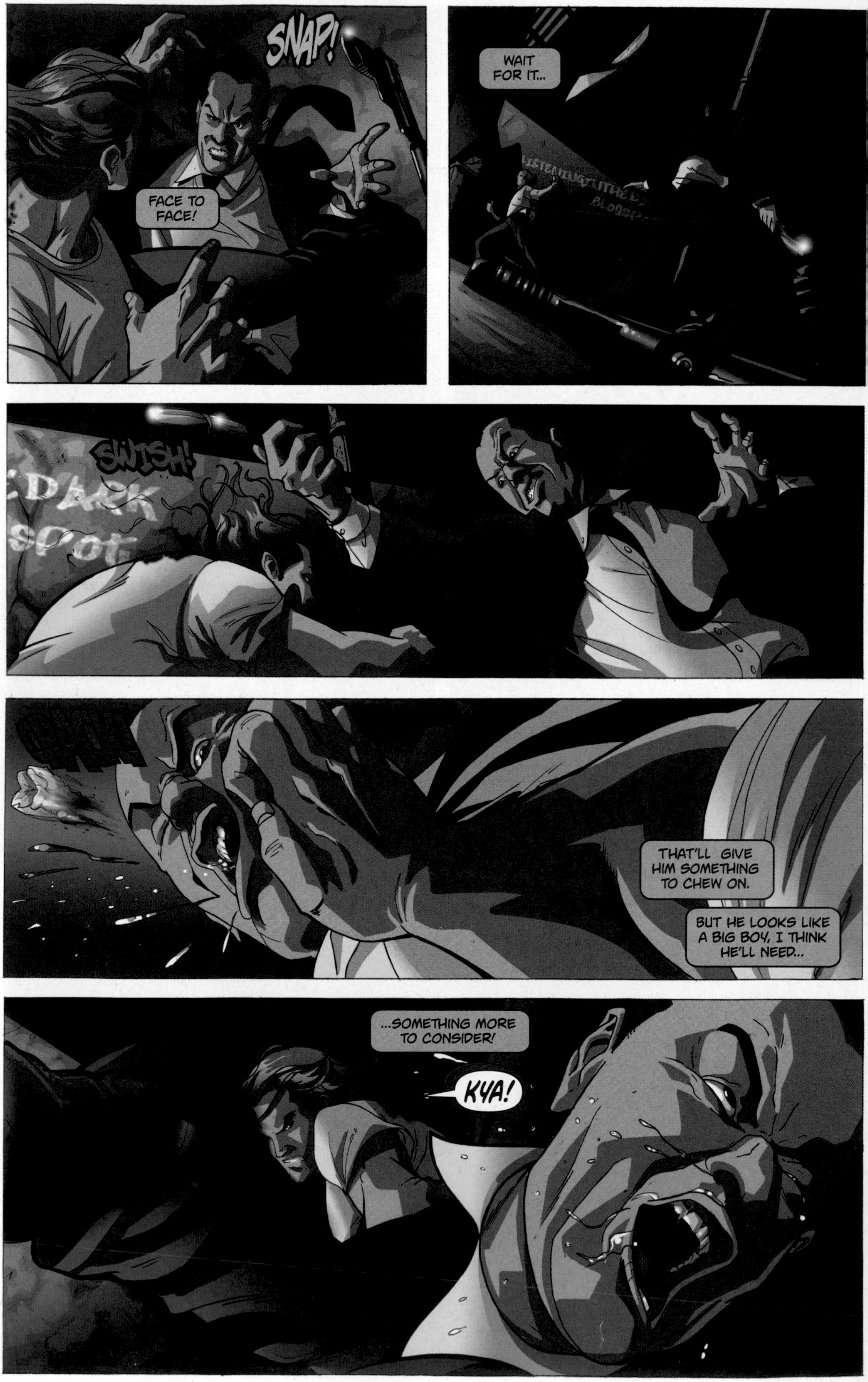

SNAP!
FACE TO FACE!
WAIT FOR IT...
SWISH!
THAT'LL GIVE HIM SOMETHING TO CHEW ON.
BUT HE LOOKS LIKE A BIG BOY, I THINK HE'LL NEED...
...SOMETHING MORE TO CONSIDER!
KYA!

NOT BAD FOR AN OUT OF SHAPE BLUE BELT.

IF THEY FOUND OUT WHERE I WORK THEN THEY KNOW WHERE I LIVE.

UNGHHH

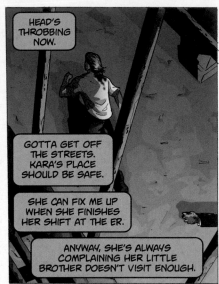

HEAD'S THROBBING NOW.

GOTTA GET OFF THE STREETS. KARA'S PLACE SHOULD BE SAFE.

SHE CAN FIX ME UP WHEN SHE FINISHES HER SHIFT AT THE ER.

ANYWAY, SHE'S ALWAYS COMPLAINING HER LITTLE BROTHER DOESN'T VISIT ENOUGH.

LOOKS ALL CLEAR. THINK I'M SAFE. FOR THE MOMENT AT LEAST.

GOOD THING I KNOW WHERE SHE KEEPS HER SPARE KEY.

MAYBE I SHOULD LIE DOWN... JUST FOR A MINUTE.

KARA WILL BE HOME SOON...

... SHE CAN TELL ME...

...IF IT'S SERIOUS...

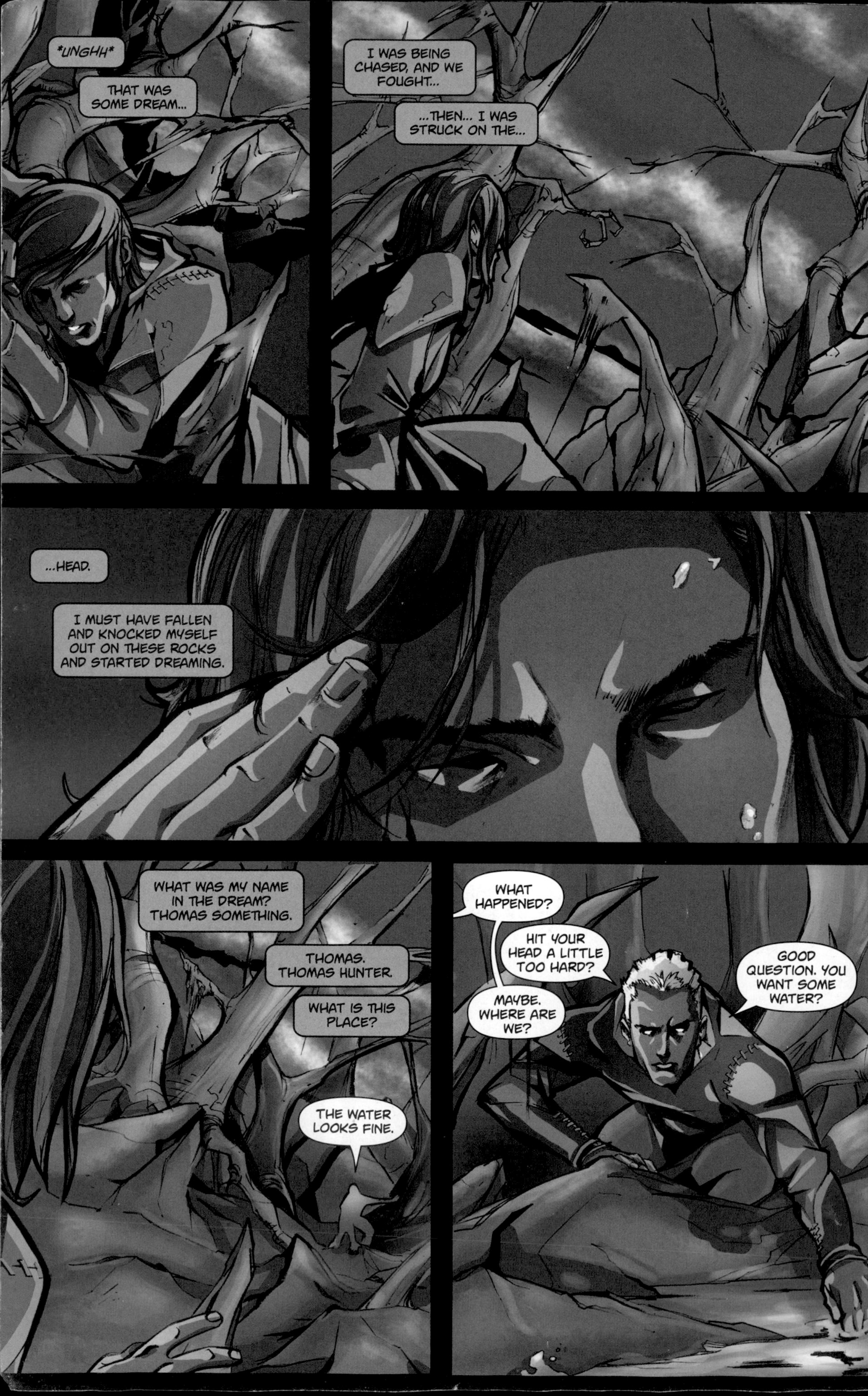
UNGHH
THAT WAS SOME DREAM...
I WAS BEING CHASED, AND WE FOUGHT...
...THEN... I WAS STRUCK ON THE...
...HEAD.
I MUST HAVE FALLEN AND KNOCKED MYSELF OUT ON THESE ROCKS AND STARTED DREAMING.
WHAT WAS MY NAME IN THE DREAM? THOMAS SOMETHING.
THOMAS. THOMAS HUNTER.
WHAT IS THIS PLACE?
THE WATER LOOKS FINE.
WHAT HAPPENED?
HIT YOUR HEAD A LITTLE TOO HARD?
MAYBE. WHERE ARE WE?
GOOD QUESTION. YOU WANT SOME WATER?

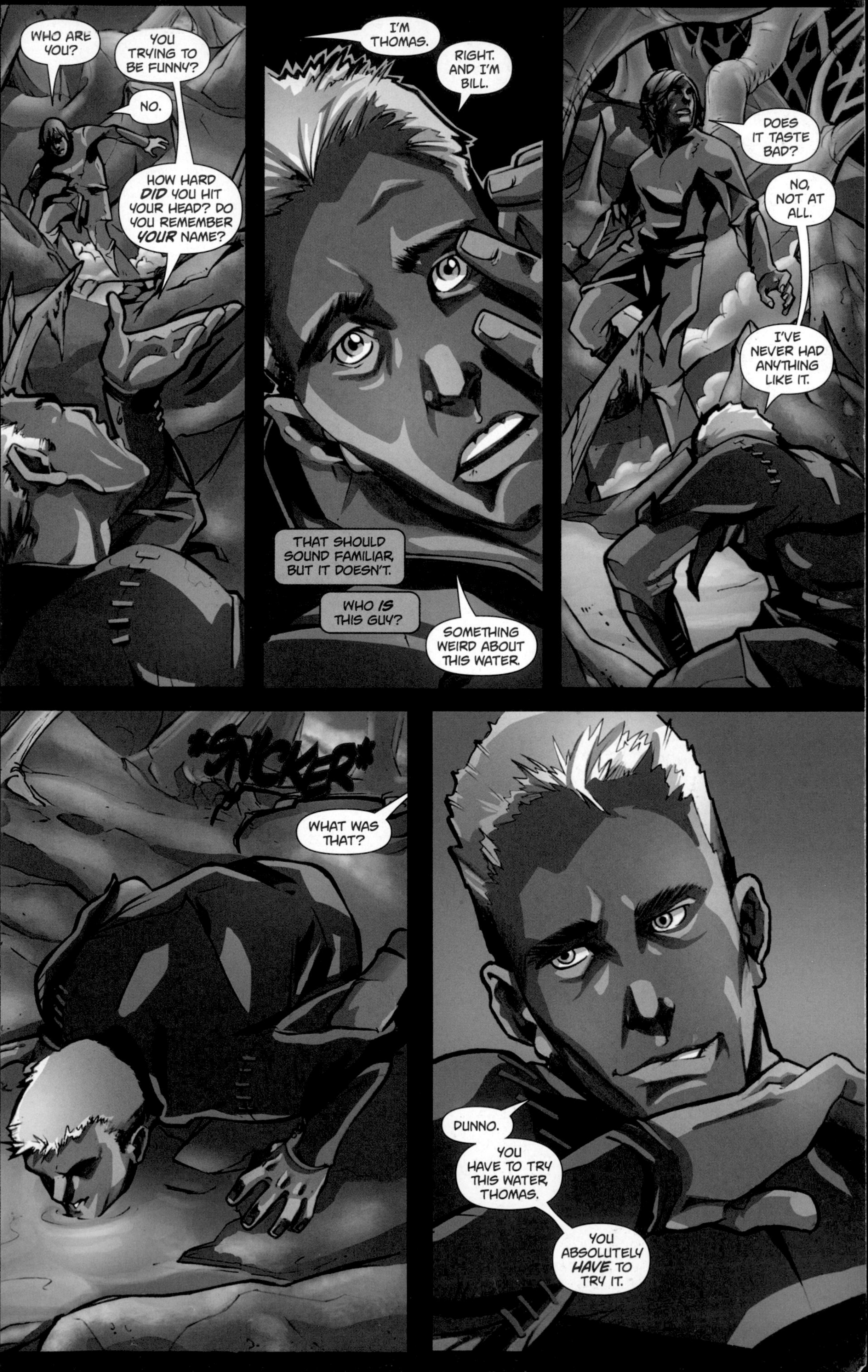
WHO ARE YOU?
YOU TRYING TO BE FUNNY?
NO.
HOW HARD DID YOU HIT YOUR HEAD? DO YOU REMEMBER YOUR NAME?
I'M THOMAS.
RIGHT. AND I'M BILL.
THAT SHOULD SOUND FAMILIAR, BUT IT DOESN'T.
WHO IS THIS GUY?
SOMETHING WEIRD ABOUT THIS WATER.
DOES IT TASTE BAD?
NO, NOT AT ALL.
I'VE NEVER HAD ANYTHING LIKE IT.
SNICKER
WHAT WAS THAT?
DUNNO.
YOU HAVE TO TRY THIS WATER, THOMAS.
YOU ABSOLUTELY HAVE TO TRY IT.

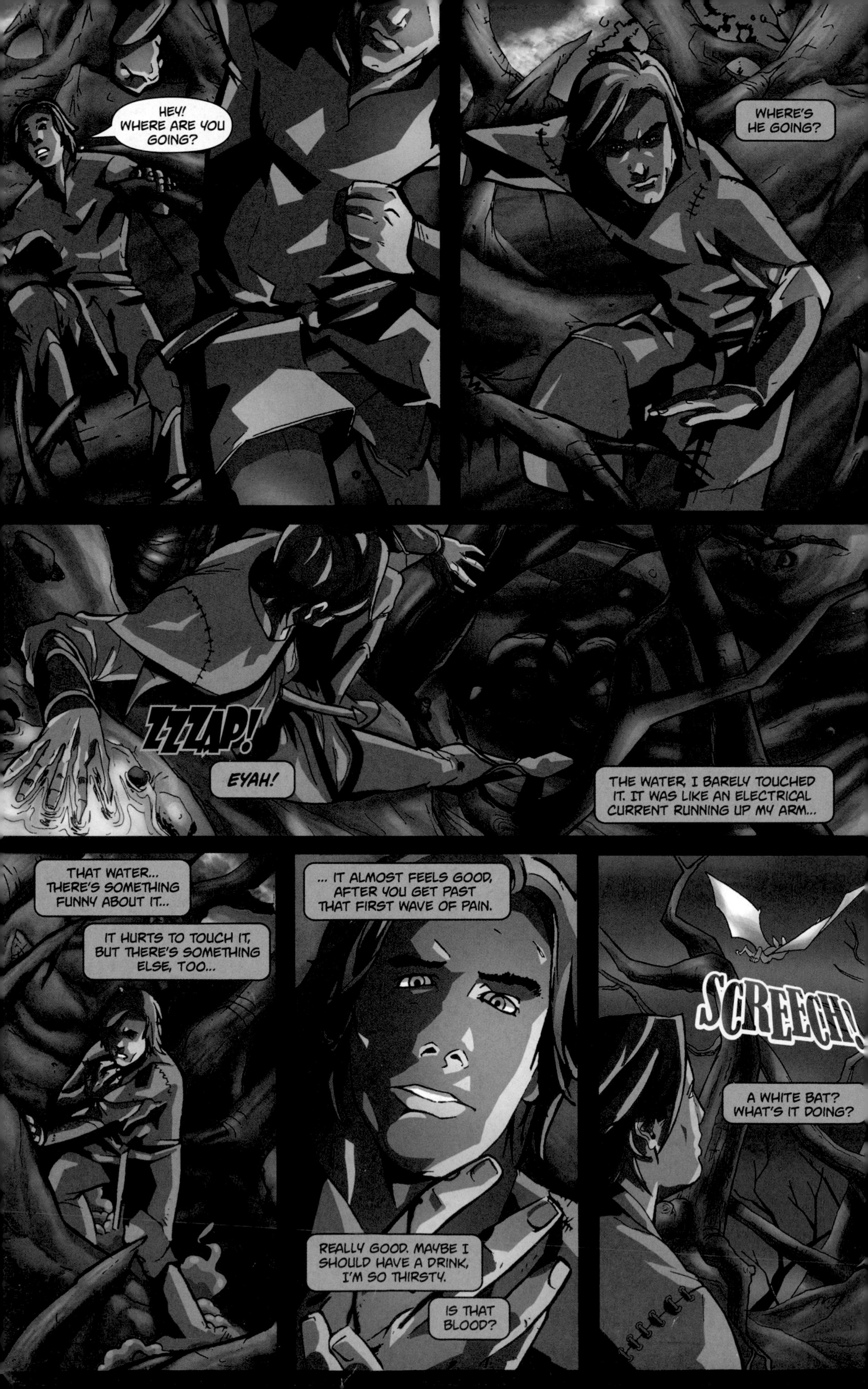
HEY! WHERE ARE YOU GOING?
WHERE'S HE GOING?
ZZZAP!
EYAH!
THE WATER, I BARELY TOUCHED IT. IT WAS LIKE AN ELECTRICAL CURRENT RUNNING UP MY ARM...
THAT WATER... THERE'S SOMETHING FUNNY ABOUT IT...
IT HURTS TO TOUCH IT, BUT THERE'S SOMETHING ELSE, TOO...
... IT ALMOST FEELS GOOD, AFTER YOU GET PAST THAT FIRST WAVE OF PAIN.
REALLY GOOD. MAYBE I SHOULD HAVE A DRINK, I'M SO THIRSTY.
IS THAT BLOOD?
SCREECH!
A WHITE BAT? WHAT'S IT DOING?

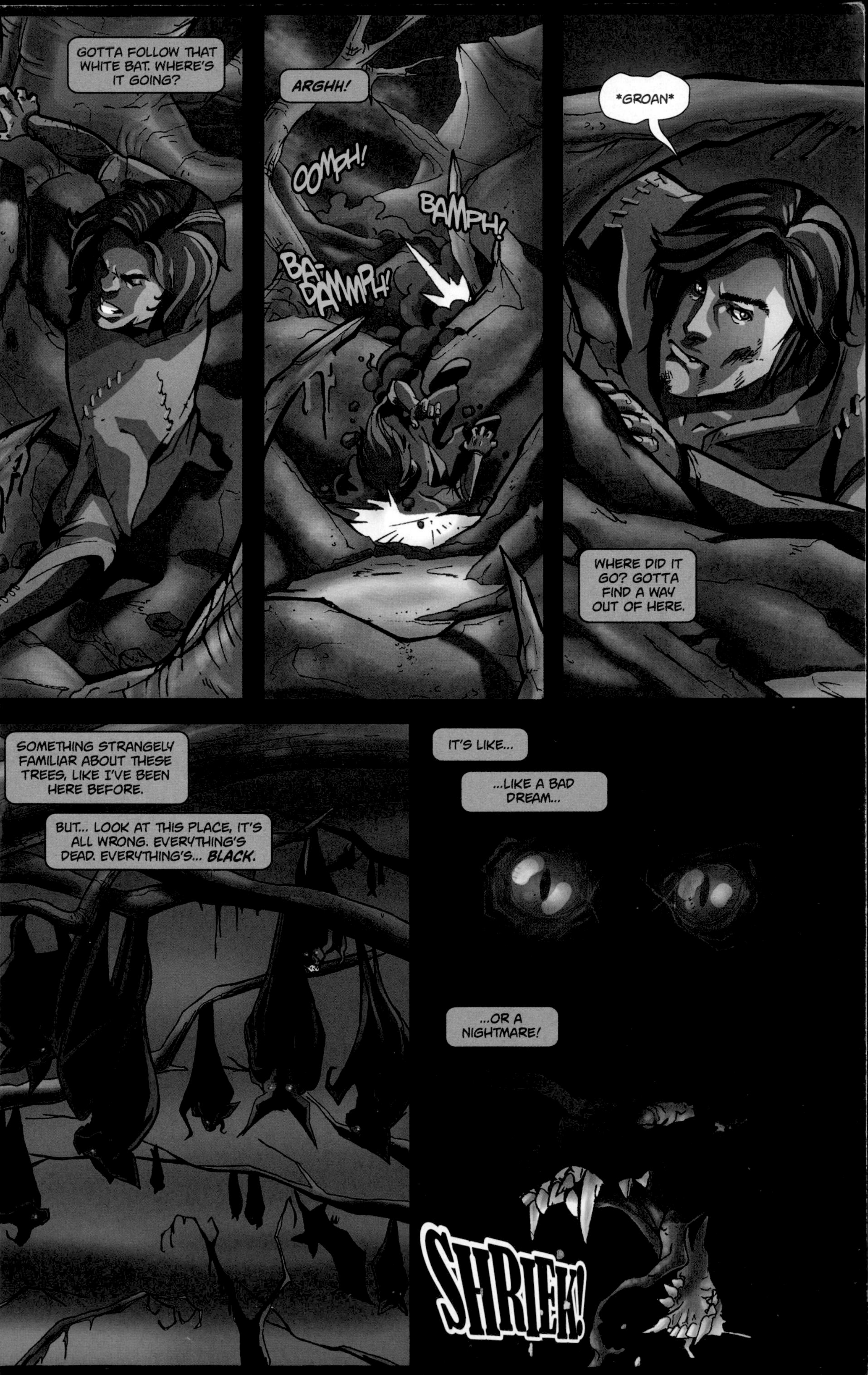
GOTTA FOLLOW THAT WHITE BAT. WHERE'S IT GOING?
ARGHH!
OOMPH!
BAMPH!
BA-DAMMPH!
GROAN
WHERE DID IT GO? GOTTA FIND A WAY OUT OF HERE.
SOMETHING STRANGELY FAMILIAR ABOUT THESE TREES, LIKE I'VE BEEN HERE BEFORE.
BUT... LOOK AT THIS PLACE, IT'S ALL WRONG. EVERYTHING'S DEAD. EVERYTHING'S... BLACK.
IT'S LIKE...
...LIKE A BAD DREAM...
...OR A NIGHTMARE!
SHRIEK!

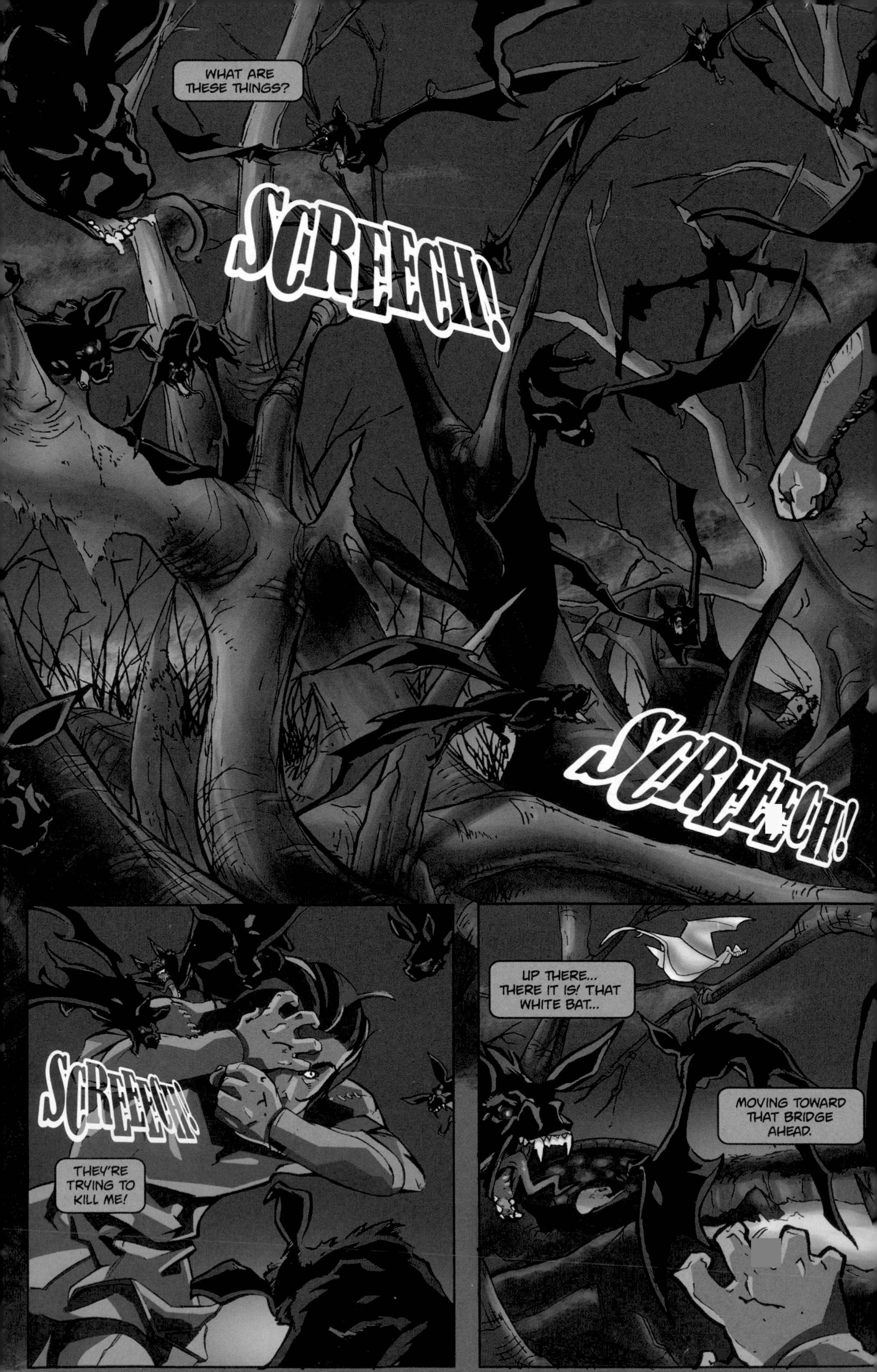
WHAT ARE THESE THINGS?
SCREECH!
SCREECH!
SCREECH!
THEY'RE TRYING TO KILL ME!
UP THERE... THERE IT IS! THAT WHITE BAT...
MOVING TOWARD THAT BRIDGE AHEAD.

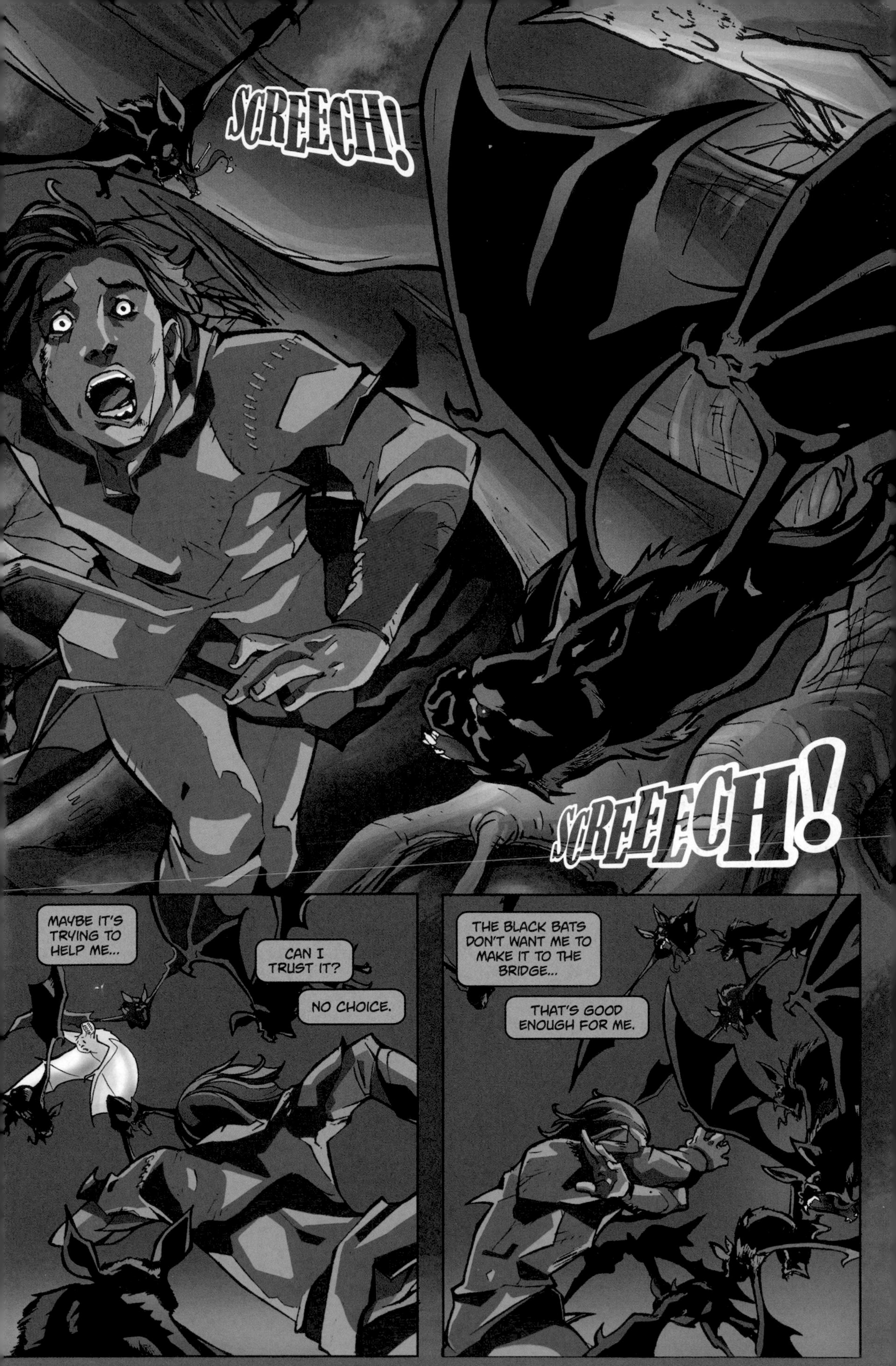
SCREECH!
SCREECH!
MAYBE IT'S TRYING TO HELP ME...
CAN I TRUST IT?
NO CHOICE.
THE BLACK BATS DON'T WANT ME TO MAKE IT TO THE BRIDGE...
THAT'S GOOD ENOUGH FOR ME.

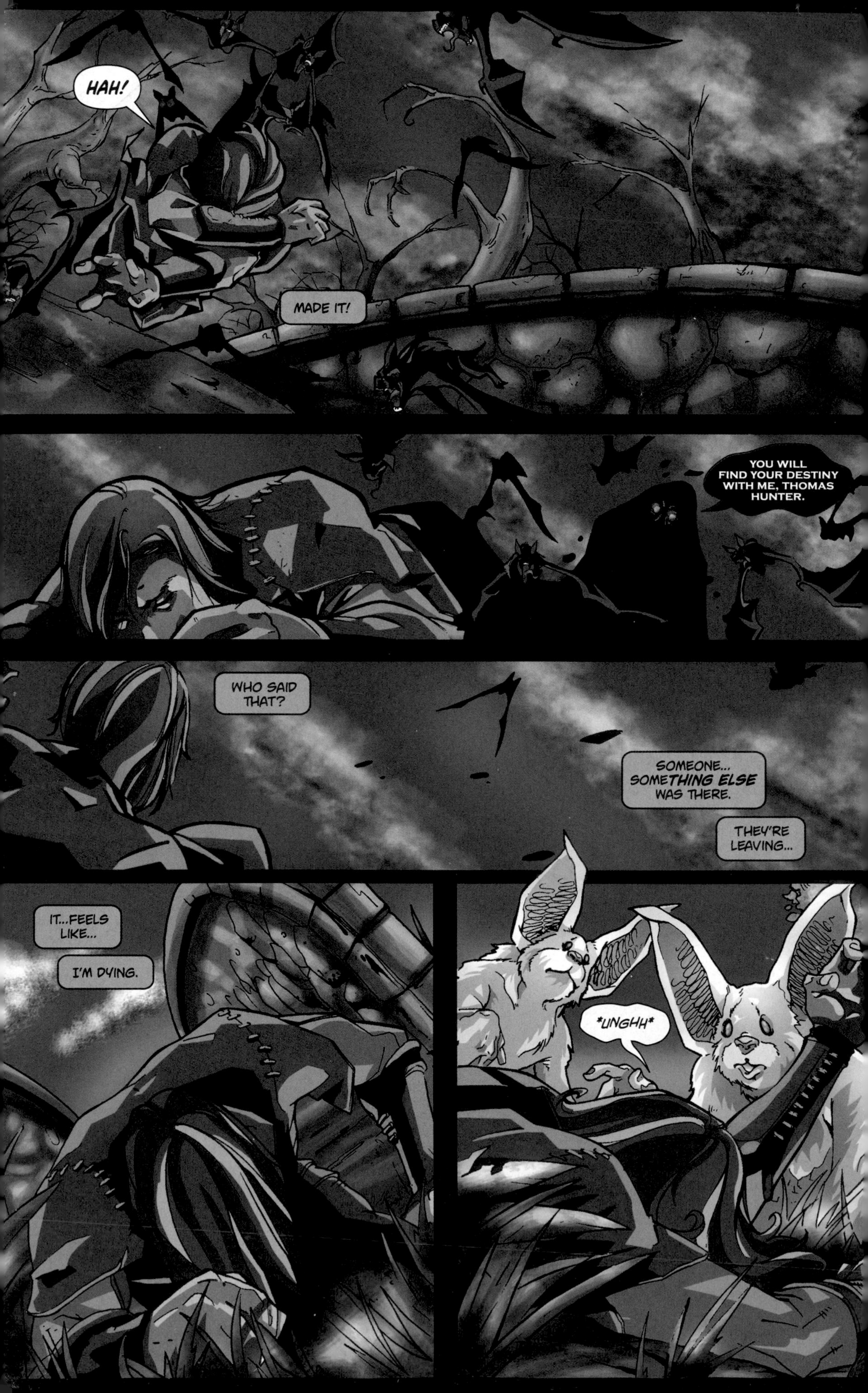
HAH!
MADE IT!
YOU WILL FIND YOUR DESTINY WITH ME, THOMAS HUNTER.
WHO SAID THAT?
SOMEONE... SOMETHING ELSE WAS THERE.
THEY'RE LEAVING...
IT...FEELS LIKE...
I'M DYING.
UNGHH

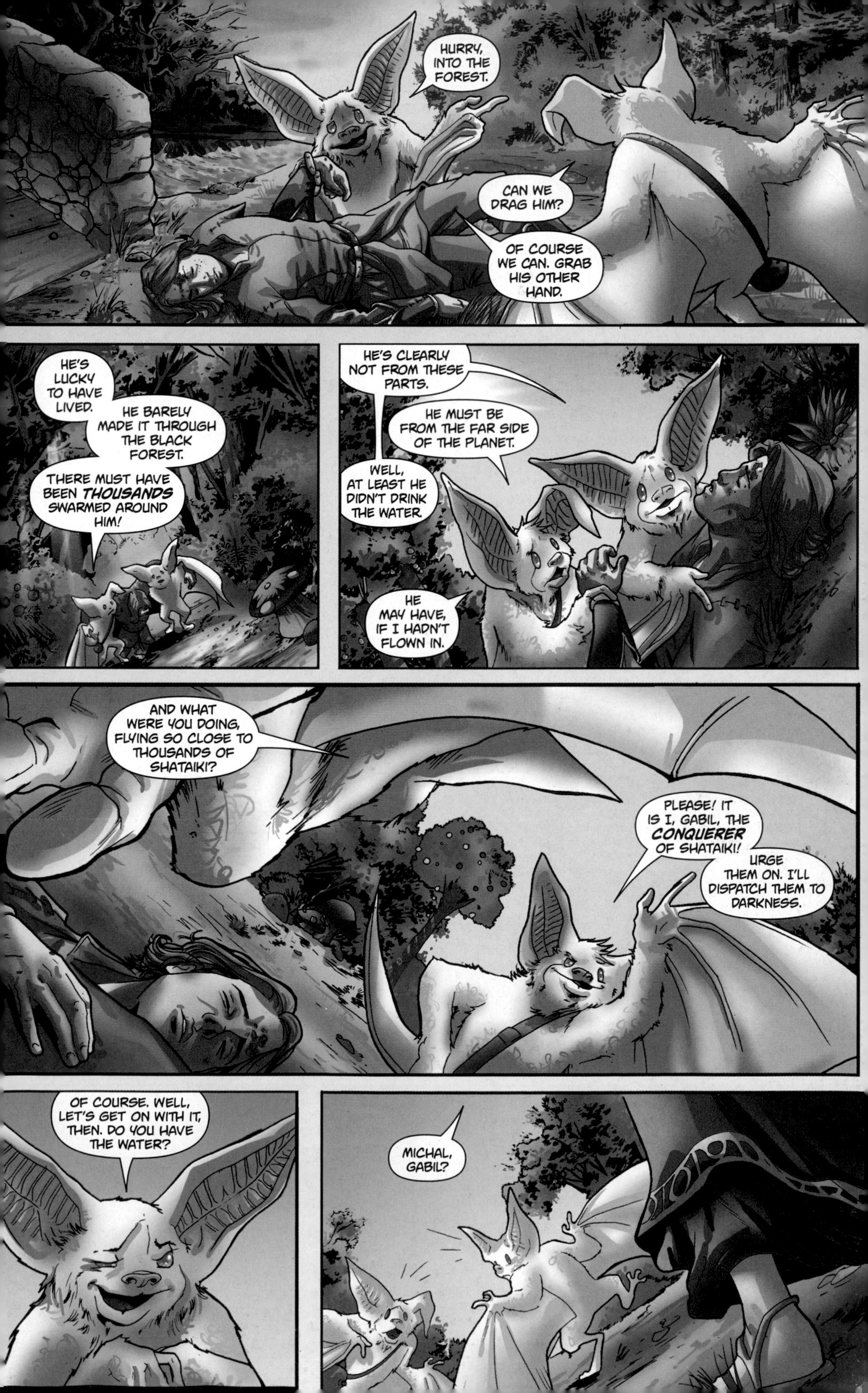
HURRY, INTO THE FOREST.
CAN WE DRAG HIM?
OF COURSE WE CAN. GRAB HIS OTHER HAND.
HE'S LUCKY TO HAVE LIVED.
HE BARELY MADE IT THROUGH THE BLACK FOREST.
THERE MUST HAVE BEEN THOUSANDS SWARMED AROUND HIM!
HE'S CLEARLY NOT FROM THESE PARTS.
HE MUST BE FROM THE FAR SIDE OF THE PLANET.
WELL, AT LEAST HE DIDN'T DRINK THE WATER.
HE MAY HAVE, IF I HADN'T FLOWN IN.
AND WHAT WERE YOU DOING, FLYING SO CLOSE TO THOUSANDS OF SHATAIKI?
PLEASE! IT IS I, GABIL, THE CONQUERER OF SHATAIKI!
URGE THEM ON. I'LL DISPATCH THEM TO DARKNESS.
OF COURSE. WELL, LET'S GET ON WITH IT, THEN. DO YOU HAVE THE WATER?
MICHAL, GABIL?

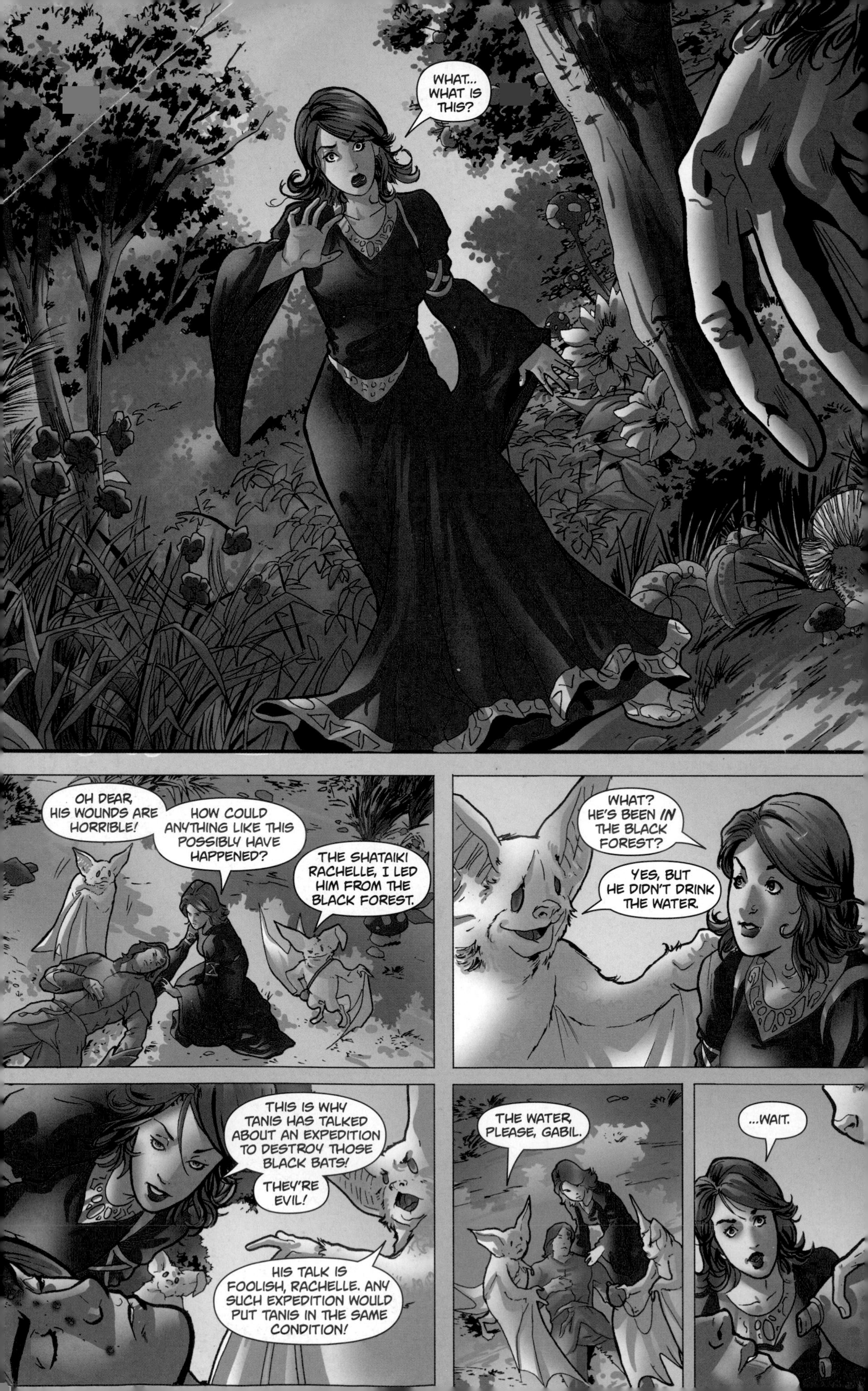
WHAT... WHAT IS THIS?
OH DEAR, HIS WOUNDS ARE HORRIBLE!
HOW COULD ANYTHING LIKE THIS POSSIBLY HAVE HAPPENED?
THE SHATAIKI RACHELLE, I LED HIM FROM THE BLACK FOREST.
WHAT? HE'S BEEN *IN* THE BLACK FOREST?
YES, BUT HE DIDN'T DRINK THE WATER.
THIS IS WHY TANIS HAS TALKED ABOUT AN EXPEDITION TO DESTROY THOSE BLACK BATS!
THEY'RE EVIL!
HIS TALK IS FOOLISH, RACHELLE. ANY SUCH EXPEDITION WOULD PUT TANIS IN THE SAME CONDITION!
THE WATER, PLEASE, GABIL.
...WAIT.

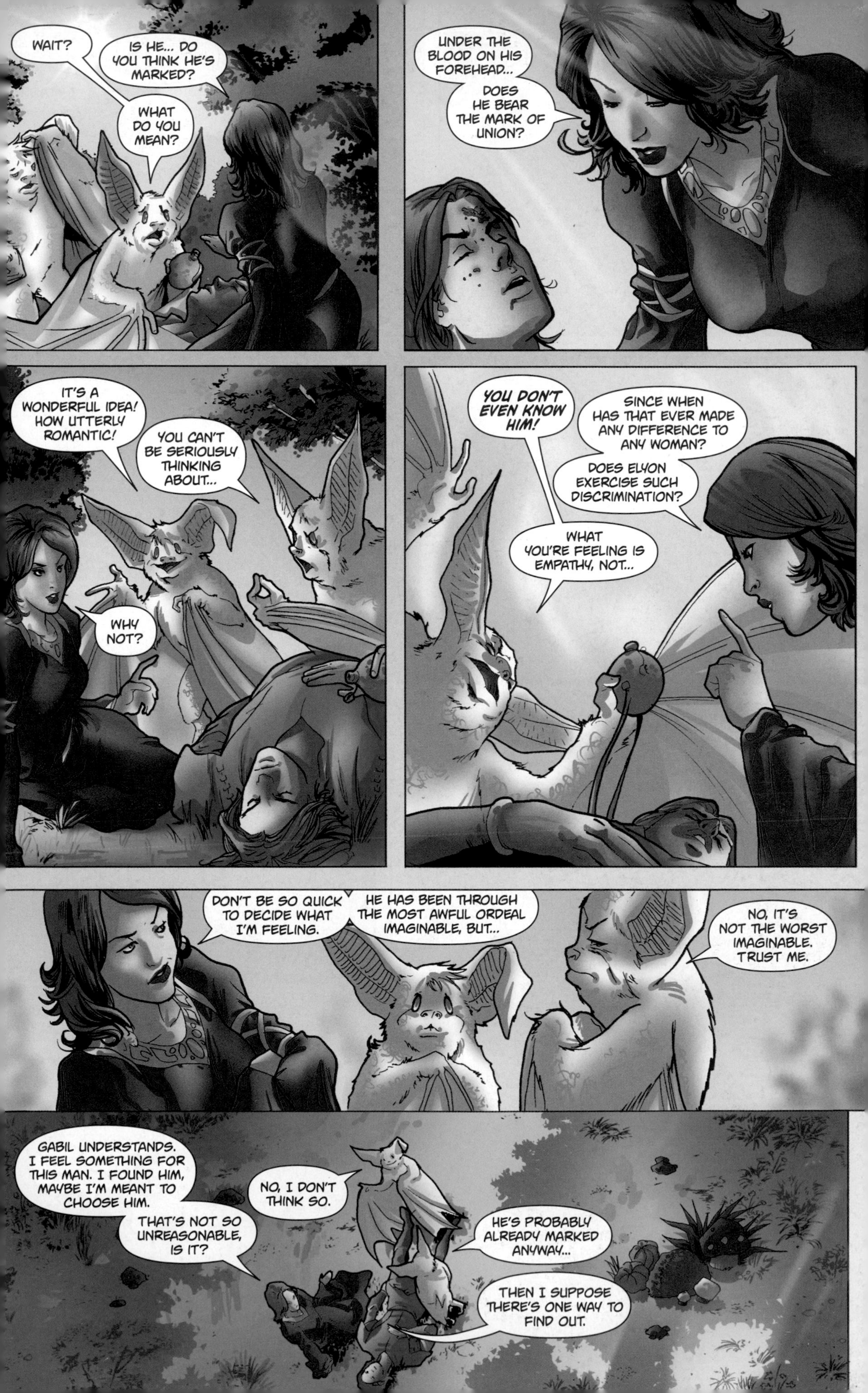
WAIT?
IS HE... DO YOU THINK HE'S MARKED?
WHAT DO YOU MEAN?
UNDER THE BLOOD ON HIS FOREHEAD...
DOES HE BEAR THE MARK OF UNION?
IT'S A WONDERFUL IDEA! HOW UTTERLY ROMANTIC!
YOU CAN'T BE SERIOUSLY THINKING ABOUT...
WHY NOT?
YOU DON'T EVEN KNOW HIM!
SINCE WHEN HAS THAT EVER MADE ANY DIFFERENCE TO ANY WOMAN?
DOES ELYON EXERCISE SUCH DISCRIMINATION?
WHAT YOU'RE FEELING IS EMPATHY, NOT...
DON'T BE SO QUICK TO DECIDE WHAT I'M FEELING.
HE HAS BEEN THROUGH THE MOST AWFUL ORDEAL IMAGINABLE, BUT...
NO, IT'S NOT THE WORST IMAGINABLE. TRUST ME.
GABIL UNDERSTANDS. I FEEL SOMETHING FOR THIS MAN. I FOUND HIM, MAYBE I'M MEANT TO CHOOSE HIM.
THAT'S NOT SO UNREASONABLE, IS IT?
NO, I DON'T THINK SO.
HE'S PROBABLY ALREADY MARKED ANYWAY...
THEN I SUPPOSE THERE'S ONE WAY TO FIND OUT.

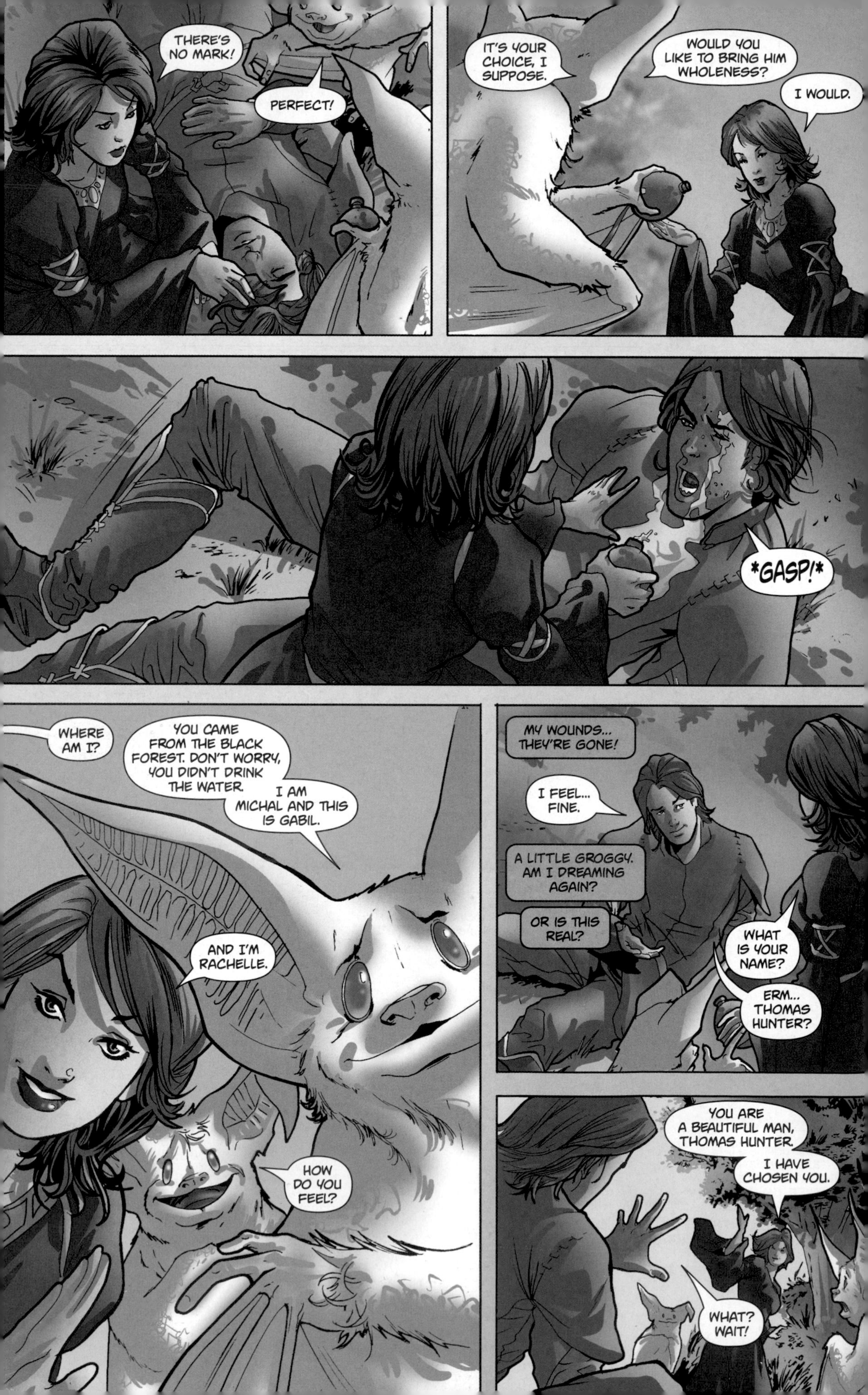
THERE'S NO MARK!
PERFECT!
IT'S YOUR CHOICE, I SUPPOSE.
WOULD YOU LIKE TO BRING HIM WHOLENESS?
I WOULD.
GASP!
WHERE AM I?
YOU CAME FROM THE BLACK FOREST. DON'T WORRY, YOU DIDN'T DRINK THE WATER.
I AM MICHAL AND THIS IS GABIL.
AND I'M RACHELLE.
HOW DO YOU FEEL?
MY WOUNDS... THEY'RE GONE!
I FEEL... FINE.
A LITTLE GROGGY. AM I DREAMING AGAIN?
OR IS THIS REAL?
WHAT IS YOUR NAME?
ERM... THOMAS HUNTER?
YOU ARE A BEAUTIFUL MAN, THOMAS HUNTER.
I HAVE CHOSEN YOU.
WHAT? WAIT!

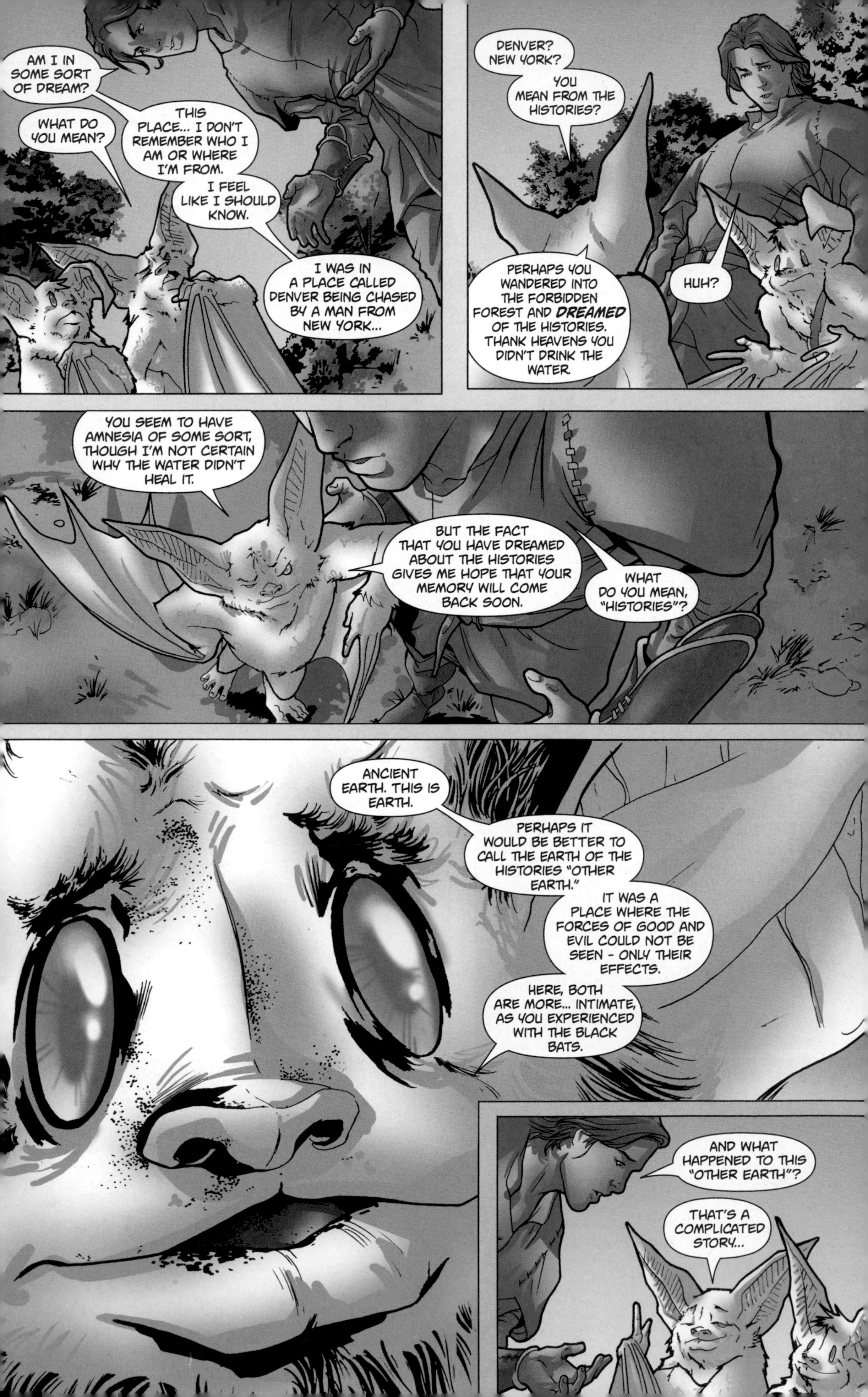
AM I IN SOME SORT OF DREAM?
WHAT DO YOU MEAN?
THIS PLACE... I DON'T REMEMBER WHO I AM OR WHERE I'M FROM.
I FEEL LIKE I SHOULD KNOW.
I WAS IN A PLACE CALLED DENVER BEING CHASED BY A MAN FROM NEW YORK...
DENVER? NEW YORK?
YOU MEAN FROM THE HISTORIES?
PERHAPS YOU WANDERED INTO THE FORBIDDEN FOREST AND DREAMED OF THE HISTORIES. THANK HEAVENS YOU DIDN'T DRINK THE WATER.
HUH?
YOU SEEM TO HAVE AMNESIA OF SOME SORT, THOUGH I'M NOT CERTAIN WHY THE WATER DIDN'T HEAL IT.
BUT THE FACT THAT YOU HAVE DREAMED ABOUT THE HISTORIES GIVES ME HOPE THAT YOUR MEMORY WILL COME BACK SOON.
WHAT DO YOU MEAN, "HISTORIES"?
ANCIENT EARTH. THIS IS EARTH.
PERHAPS IT WOULD BE BETTER TO CALL THE EARTH OF THE HISTORIES "OTHER EARTH."
IT WAS A PLACE WHERE THE FORCES OF GOOD AND EVIL COULD NOT BE SEEN - ONLY THEIR EFFECTS.
HERE, BOTH ARE MORE... INTIMATE, AS YOU EXPERIENCED WITH THE BLACK BATS.
AND WHAT HAPPENED TO THIS "OTHER EARTH"?
THAT'S A COMPLICATED STORY...

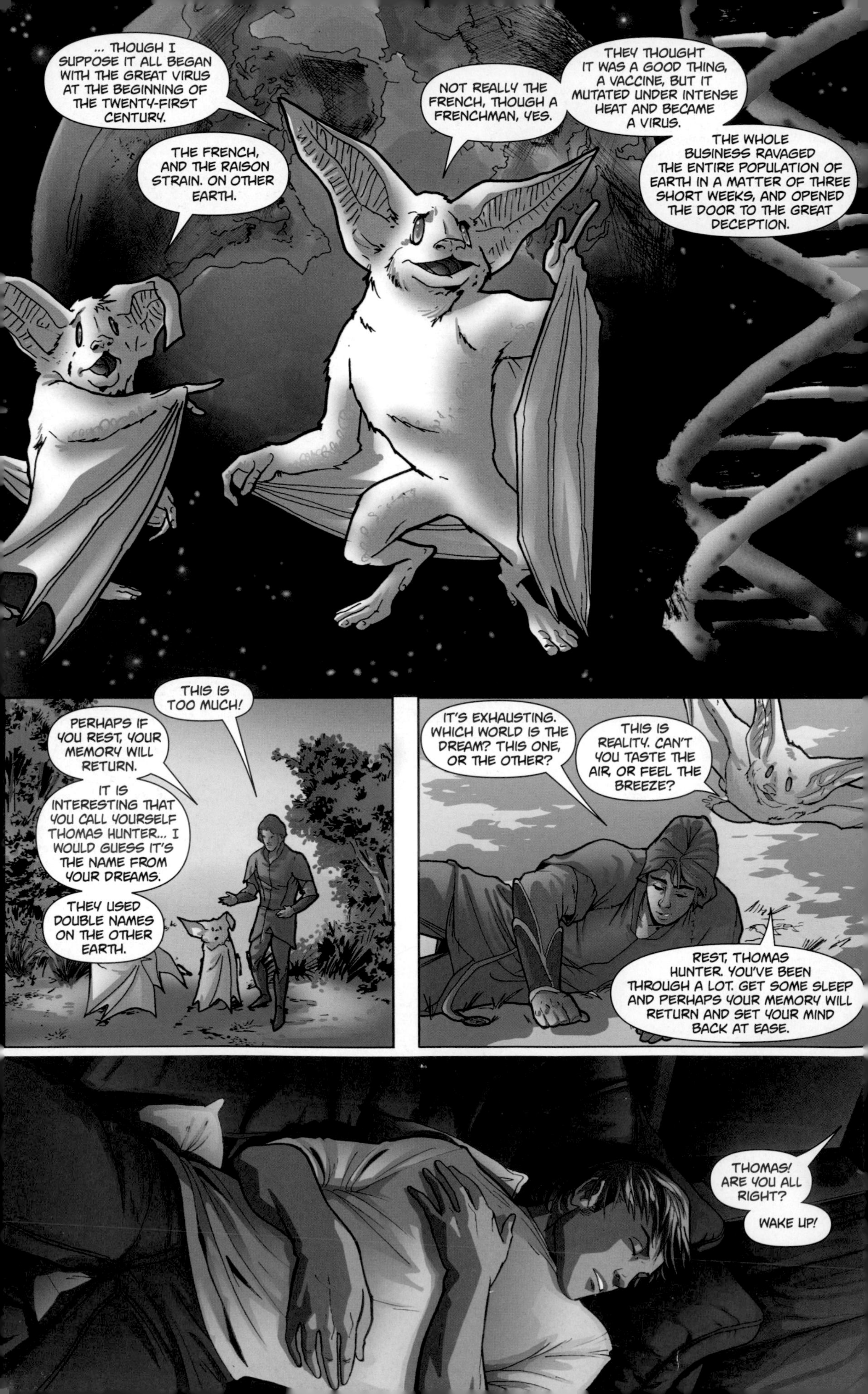
... THOUGH I SUPPOSE IT ALL BEGAN WITH THE GREAT VIRUS AT THE BEGINNING OF THE TWENTY-FIRST CENTURY.
THE FRENCH, AND THE RAISON STRAIN. ON OTHER EARTH.
NOT REALLY THE FRENCH, THOUGH A FRENCHMAN, YES.
THEY THOUGHT IT WAS A GOOD THING, A VACCINE, BUT IT MUTATED UNDER INTENSE HEAT AND BECAME A VIRUS.
THE WHOLE BUSINESS RAVAGED THE ENTIRE POPULATION OF EARTH IN A MATTER OF THREE SHORT WEEKS, AND OPENED THE DOOR TO THE GREAT DECEPTION.
PERHAPS IF YOU REST, YOUR MEMORY WILL RETURN.
THIS IS TOO MUCH!
IT IS INTERESTING THAT YOU CALL YOURSELF THOMAS HUNTER... I WOULD GUESS IT'S THE NAME FROM YOUR DREAMS.
THEY USED DOUBLE NAMES ON THE OTHER EARTH.
IT'S EXHAUSTING. WHICH WORLD IS THE DREAM? THIS ONE, OR THE OTHER?
THIS IS REALITY. CAN'T YOU TASTE THE AIR, OR FEEL THE BREEZE?
REST, THOMAS HUNTER. YOU'VE BEEN THROUGH A LOT. GET SOME SLEEP AND PERHAPS YOUR MEMORY WILL RETURN AND SET YOUR MIND BACK AT EASE.
THOMAS! ARE YOU ALL RIGHT?
WAKE UP!

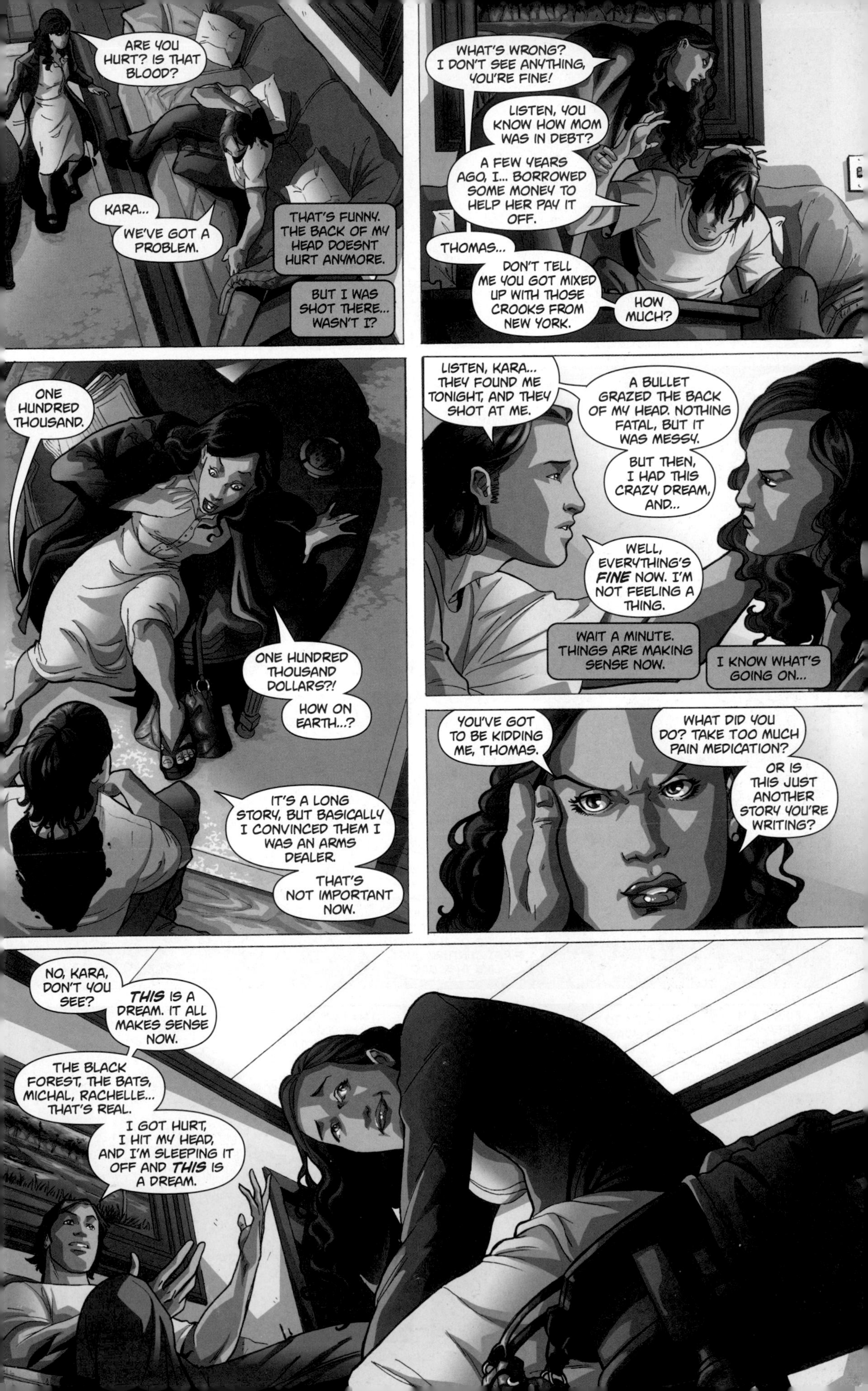
ARE YOU HURT? IS THAT BLOOD?
KARA...
WE'VE GOT A PROBLEM.
THAT'S FUNNY. THE BACK OF MY HEAD DOESNT HURT ANYMORE.
BUT I WAS SHOT THERE... WASN'T I?
WHAT'S WRONG? I DON'T SEE ANYTHING, YOU'RE FINE!
LISTEN, YOU KNOW HOW MOM WAS IN DEBT?
A FEW YEARS AGO, I... BORROWED SOME MONEY TO HELP HER PAY IT OFF.
THOMAS...
DON'T TELL ME YOU GOT MIXED UP WITH THOSE CROOKS FROM NEW YORK.
HOW MUCH?
ONE HUNDRED THOUSAND.
ONE HUNDRED THOUSAND DOLLARS?!
HOW ON EARTH...?
IT'S A LONG STORY, BUT BASICALLY I CONVINCED THEM I WAS AN ARMS DEALER.
THAT'S NOT IMPORTANT NOW.
LISTEN, KARA... THEY FOUND ME TONIGHT, AND THEY SHOT AT ME.
A BULLET GRAZED THE BACK OF MY HEAD. NOTHING FATAL, BUT IT WAS MESSY.
BUT THEN, I HAD THIS CRAZY DREAM, AND...
WELL, EVERYTHING'S *FINE* NOW. I'M NOT FEELING A THING.
WAIT A MINUTE. THINGS ARE MAKING SENSE NOW.
I KNOW WHAT'S GOING ON...
YOU'VE GOT TO BE KIDDING ME, THOMAS.
WHAT DID YOU DO? TAKE TOO MUCH PAIN MEDICATION?
OR IS THIS JUST ANOTHER STORY YOU'RE WRITING?
NO, KARA, DON'T YOU SEE?
THIS IS A DREAM. IT ALL MAKES SENSE NOW.
THE BLACK FOREST, THE BATS, MICHAL, RACHELLE... THAT'S REAL.
I GOT HURT, I HIT MY HEAD, AND I'M SLEEPING IT OFF AND *THIS* IS A DREAM.

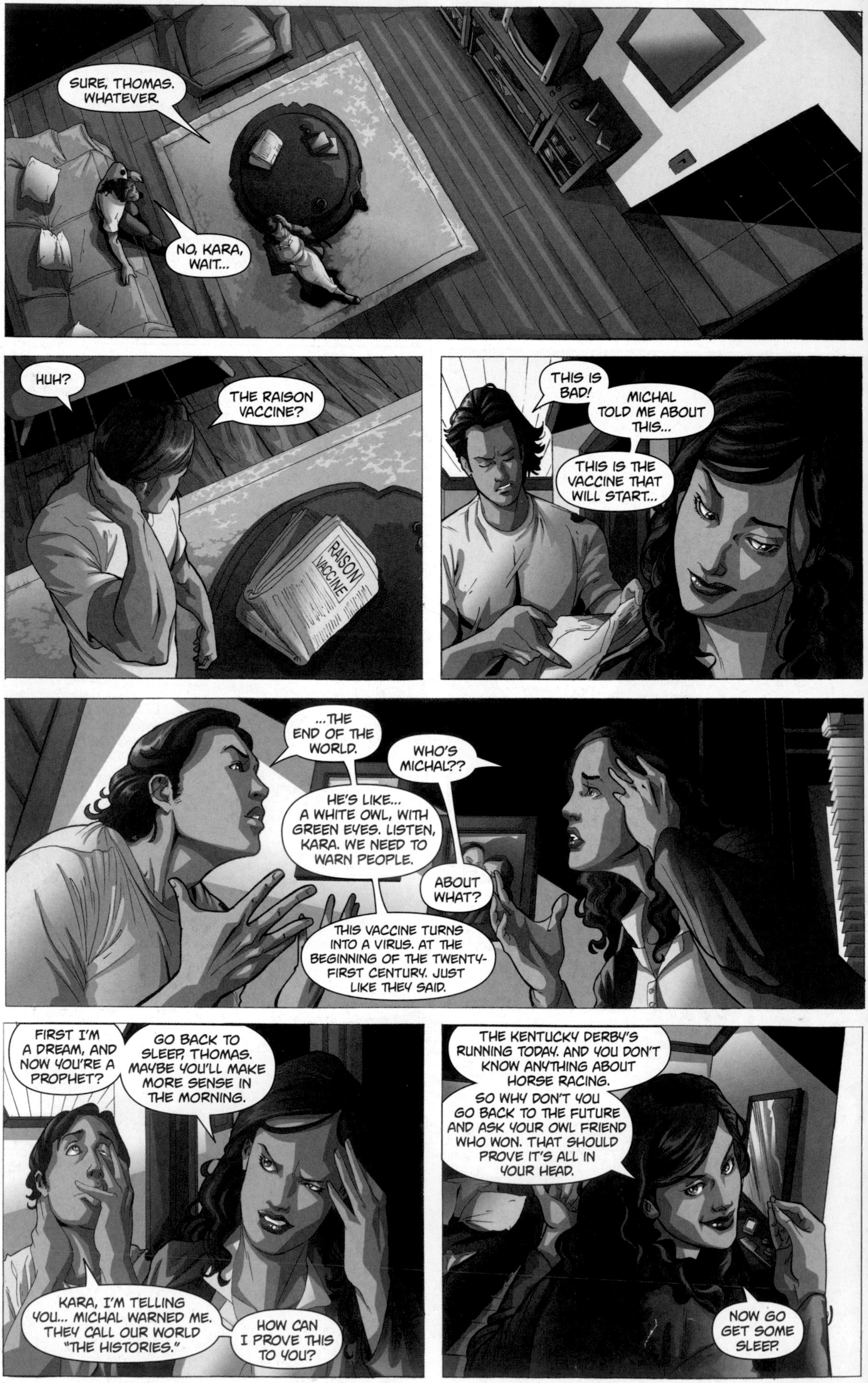
SURE, THOMAS. WHATEVER.
NO, KARA, WAIT...
HUH?
THE RAISON VACCINE?
RAISON VACCINE
THIS IS BAD!
MICHAL TOLD ME ABOUT THIS...
THIS IS THE VACCINE THAT WILL START...
...THE END OF THE WORLD.
WHO'S MICHAL??
HE'S LIKE... A WHITE OWL, WITH GREEN EYES. LISTEN, KARA. WE NEED TO WARN PEOPLE.
ABOUT WHAT?
THIS VACCINE TURNS INTO A VIRUS. AT THE BEGINNING OF THE TWENTY-FIRST CENTURY. JUST LIKE THEY SAID.
FIRST I'M A DREAM, AND NOW YOU'RE A PROPHET?
GO BACK TO SLEEP, THOMAS. MAYBE YOU'LL MAKE MORE SENSE IN THE MORNING.
KARA, I'M TELLING YOU... MICHAL WARNED ME. THEY CALL OUR WORLD "THE HISTORIES."
HOW CAN I PROVE THIS TO YOU?
THE KENTUCKY DERBY'S RUNNING TODAY. AND YOU DON'T KNOW ANYTHING ABOUT HORSE RACING.
SO WHY DON'T YOU GO BACK TO THE FUTURE AND ASK YOUR OWL FRIEND WHO WON. THAT SHOULD PROVE IT'S ALL IN YOUR HEAD.
NOW GO GET SOME SLEEP.

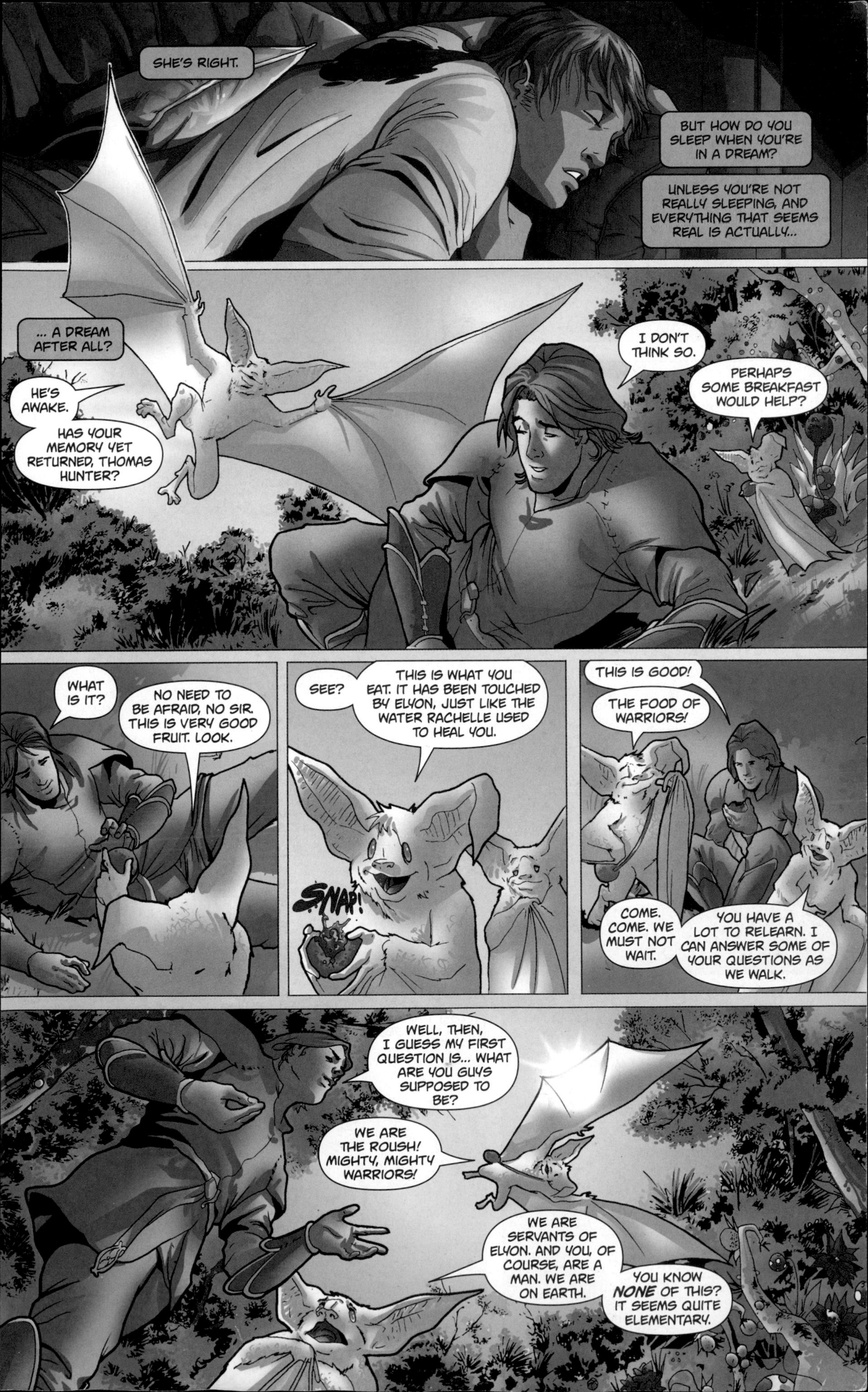
SHE'S RIGHT.
BUT HOW DO YOU SLEEP WHEN YOU'RE IN A DREAM?
UNLESS YOU'RE NOT REALLY SLEEPING, AND EVERYTHING THAT SEEMS REAL IS ACTUALLY...
... A DREAM AFTER ALL?
HE'S AWAKE.
HAS YOUR MEMORY YET RETURNED, THOMAS HUNTER?
I DON'T THINK SO.
PERHAPS SOME BREAKFAST WOULD HELP?
WHAT IS IT?
NO NEED TO BE AFRAID, NO SIR. THIS IS VERY GOOD FRUIT. LOOK.
SEE?
THIS IS WHAT YOU EAT. IT HAS BEEN TOUCHED BY ELYON, JUST LIKE THE WATER RACHELLE USED TO HEAL YOU.
SNAP!
THIS IS GOOD!
THE FOOD OF WARRIORS!
COME. COME. WE MUST NOT WAIT.
YOU HAVE A LOT TO RELEARN. I CAN ANSWER SOME OF YOUR QUESTIONS AS WE WALK.
WELL, THEN, I GUESS MY FIRST QUESTION IS... WHAT ARE YOU GUYS SUPPOSED TO BE?
WE ARE THE ROUSH! MIGHTY, MIGHTY WARRIORS!
WE ARE SERVANTS OF ELYON. AND YOU, OF COURSE, ARE A MAN. WE ARE ON EARTH.
YOU KNOW *NONE* OF THIS? IT SEEMS QUITE ELEMENTARY.

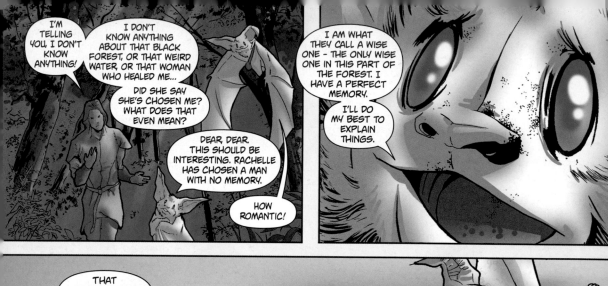

I'M TELLING YOU, I DON'T KNOW ANYTHING!

I DON'T KNOW ANYTHING ABOUT THAT BLACK FOREST, OR THAT WEIRD WATER OR THAT WOMAN WHO HEALED ME...

DID SHE SAY SHE'S CHOSEN ME? WHAT DOES THAT EVEN MEAN?

DEAR, DEAR. THIS SHOULD BE INTERESTING. RACHELLE HAS CHOSEN A MAN WITH NO MEMORY.

HOW ROMANTIC!

I AM WHAT THEY CALL A WISE ONE – THE ONLY WISE ONE IN THIS PART OF THE FOREST. I HAVE A PERFECT MEMORY.

I'LL DO MY BEST TO EXPLAIN THINGS.

THAT IS THE BLACK FOREST. DO YOU REMEMBER IT?

OF COURSE. I WAS IN IT, REMEMBER?

I JUST THOUGHT I WOULD MAKE SURE. THAT FOREST IS WHERE THE SHATAIKI LIVE.

AND THAT RIVER RUNS AROUND THE WHOLE PLANET, DIVIDING THE BLACK FOREST FROM THE GREEN – EVIL FROM GOOD.

THE RIVER RUNS TOO FAST TO SWIM ACROSS – THE ONLY WAY TO CROSS IS ACROSS ONE OF THE BRIDGES.

YOU COULD NOT HAVE COME FROM THIS PART OF THE GREEN FOREST – I WOULD HAVE KNOWN YOU, SINCE THIS AREA IS IN MY CHARGE.

I CAN ONLY ASSUME YOU ENTERED INTO THE BLACK FOREST AT ONE OF THE OTHER CROSSINGS AND MADE YOUR WAY HERE.

THE BLACK FOREST IS WHERE THE EVIL OF THIS WORLD IS CONFINED.

NO ONE IS PERMITTED TO DRINK THE WATER THERE.

IF THEY DO, THE SHATAIKI WILL BE RELEASED TO HAVE THEIR WAY WITH THE COLORED FOREST.

IT WOULD BE A SLAUGHTER

BUT, BILL DRANK THE WATER. HE SEEMED FINE.

I DO NOT KNOW WHO BILL IS, BUT NO MAN HAS YET DRUNK THE WATER OF THE SHATAIKI. IT IS FAR MORE LIKELY THAT THEY DECEIVED YOU.

ELYON INVITES WITH WATER. AND SO THE BLACK SHATAIKI INVITE WITH THEIR WATER. BUT THEY ARE DECEIVERS, AND THEY WILL LIE TO ACHIEVE THEIR OWN ENDS.

THAT IS WHY THE PEOPLE HAVE AGREED NOT TO CROSS THE RIVER AS A MATTER OF PRECAUTION.

VERY WISE, IF YOU ASK ME.

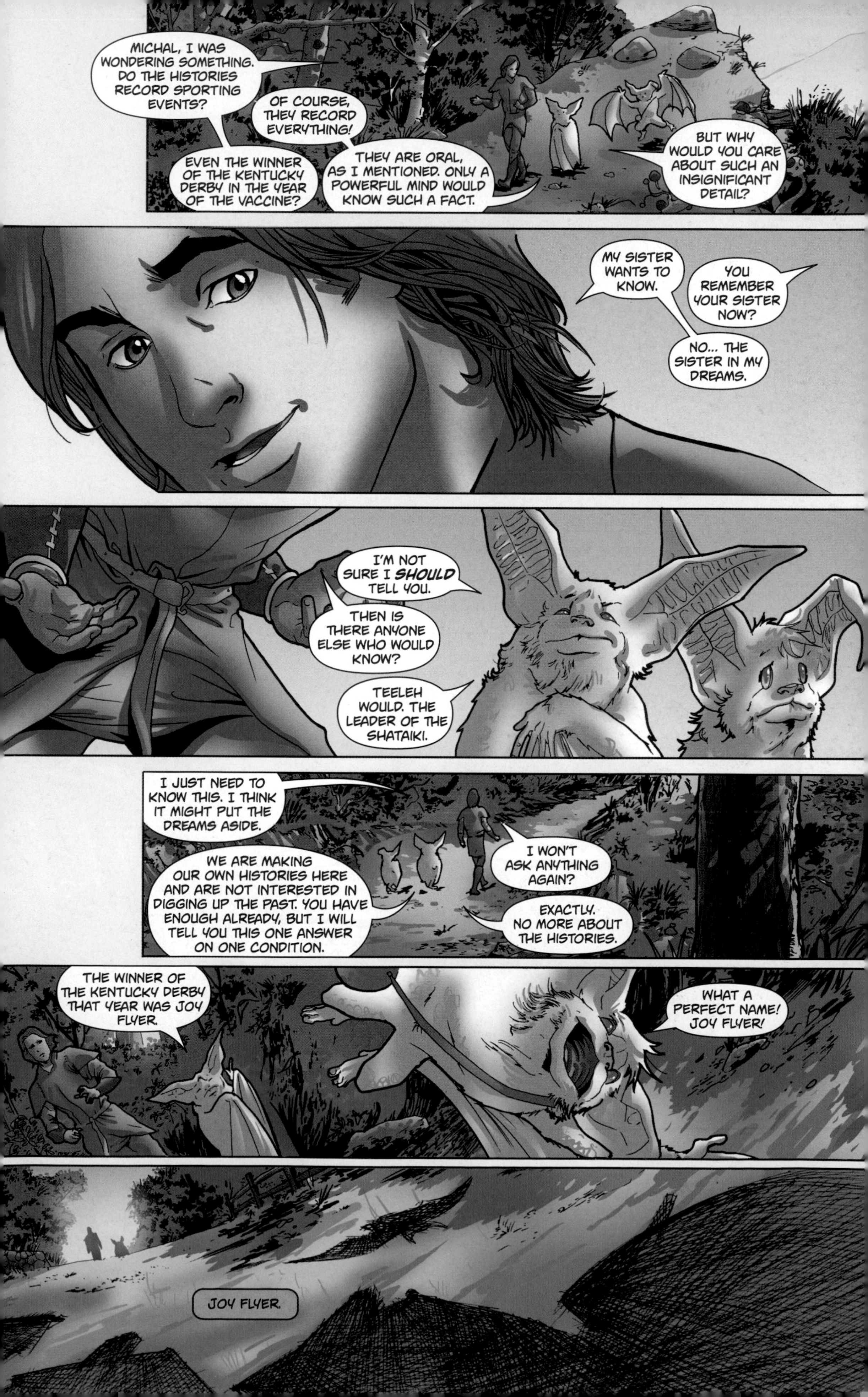
MICHAL, I WAS WONDERING SOMETHING. DO THE HISTORIES RECORD SPORTING EVENTS?
OF COURSE, THEY RECORD EVERYTHING!
EVEN THE WINNER OF THE KENTUCKY DERBY IN THE YEAR OF THE VACCINE?
THEY ARE ORAL, AS I MENTIONED. ONLY A POWERFUL MIND WOULD KNOW SUCH A FACT.
BUT WHY WOULD YOU CARE ABOUT SUCH AN INSIGNIFICANT DETAIL?
MY SISTER WANTS TO KNOW.
YOU REMEMBER YOUR SISTER NOW?
NO... THE SISTER IN MY DREAMS.
I'M NOT SURE I SHOULD TELL YOU.
THEN IS THERE ANYONE ELSE WHO WOULD KNOW?
TEELEH WOULD. THE LEADER OF THE SHATAIKI.
I JUST NEED TO KNOW THIS. I THINK IT MIGHT PUT THE DREAMS ASIDE.
WE ARE MAKING OUR OWN HISTORIES HERE AND ARE NOT INTERESTED IN DIGGING UP THE PAST. YOU HAVE ENOUGH ALREADY, BUT I WILL TELL YOU THIS ONE ANSWER ON ONE CONDITION.
I WON'T ASK ANYTHING AGAIN?
EXACTLY. NO MORE ABOUT THE HISTORIES.
THE WINNER OF THE KENTUCKY DERBY THAT YEAR WAS JOY FLYER.
WHAT A PERFECT NAME! JOY FLYER!
JOY FLYER.

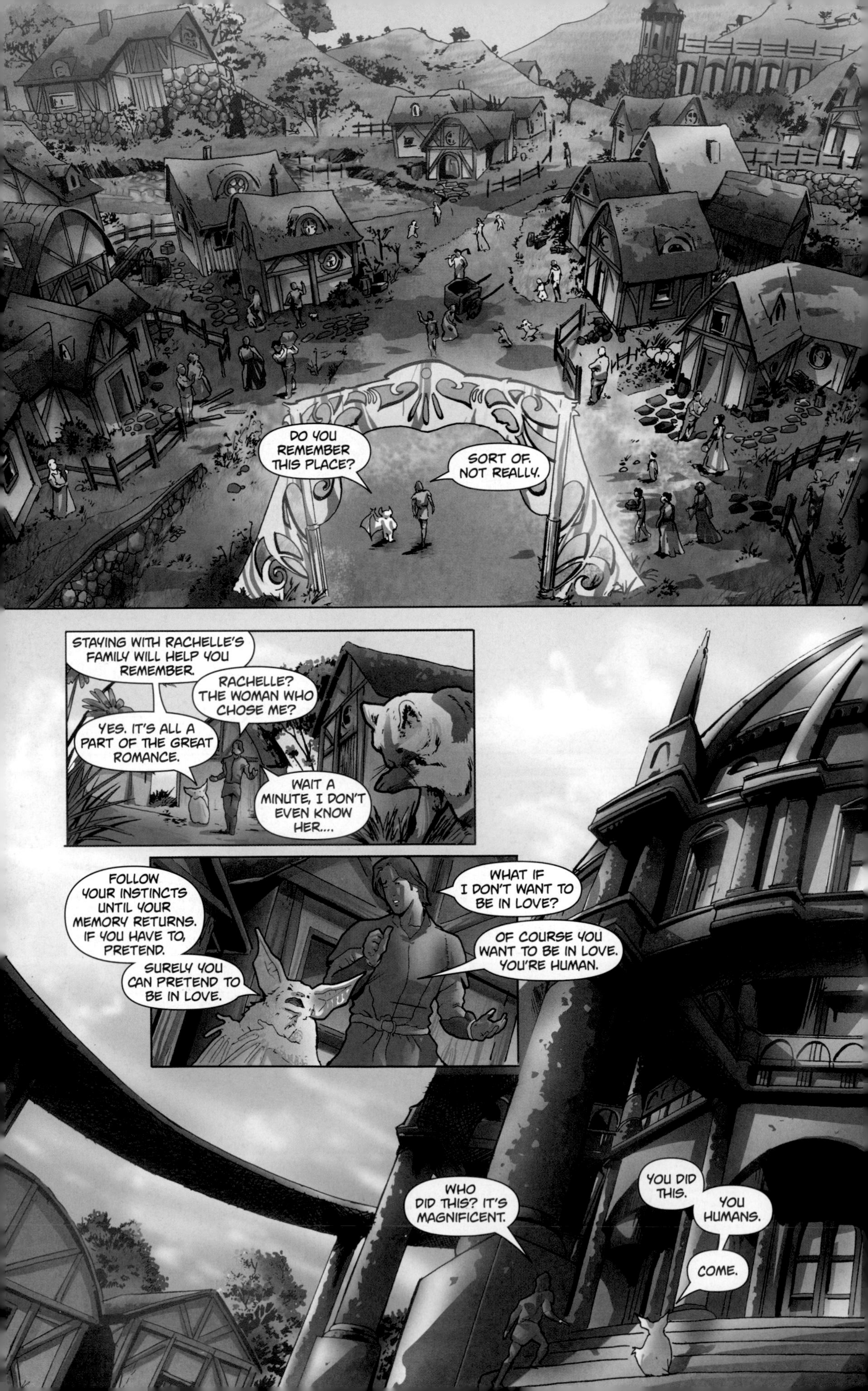
DO YOU REMEMBER THIS PLACE?
SORT OF. NOT REALLY.
STAYING WITH RACHELLE'S FAMILY WILL HELP YOU REMEMBER.
RACHELLE? THE WOMAN WHO CHOSE ME?
YES. IT'S ALL A PART OF THE GREAT ROMANCE.
WAIT A MINUTE, I DON'T EVEN KNOW HER....
FOLLOW YOUR INSTINCTS UNTIL YOUR MEMORY RETURNS. IF YOU HAVE TO, PRETEND.
SURELY YOU CAN PRETEND TO BE IN LOVE.
WHAT IF I DON'T WANT TO BE IN LOVE?
OF COURSE YOU WANT TO BE IN LOVE. YOU'RE HUMAN.
WHO DID THIS? IT'S MAGNIFICENT.
YOU DID THIS.
YOU HUMANS.
COME.

IT'S
AMAZING...

WHA-?

SOMETHING
TINGLING, UP
MY ARM...

IT'S QUITE ALL
RIGHT, MY FRIEND.
MADE FROM A
THOUSAND
GREEN
TREES.

NOT A BLEMISH
TO BE FOUND. IT'S
PERFECT, JUST LIKE
ELYON.

IT'S ..
LIKE THE
WATER?

NO, NO, THE WATER
IS SPECIAL. BUT ELYON IS
THE MAKER OF BOTH.

I MUST BE
OFF NOW, DUTY CALLS.
I WILL LEAVE YOU HERE.
RACHELLE WILL BE HERE
SHORTLY TO PICK YOU UP,
AFTER THE GATHERING.
REMEMBER...WHEN IN
DOUBT—JUST PLAY
ALONG.

RIGHT.

I JUST HOPE
SHE HASN'T BITTEN
OFF MORE THAN
SHE CAN CHEW...

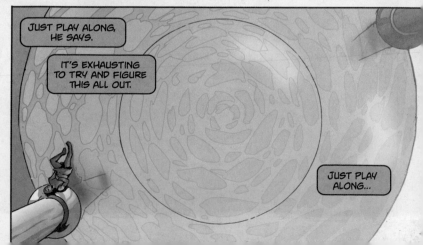

JUST PLAY ALONG,
HE SAYS.

IT'S EXHAUSTING
TO TRY AND FIGURE
THIS ALL OUT.

JUST PLAY
ALONG...

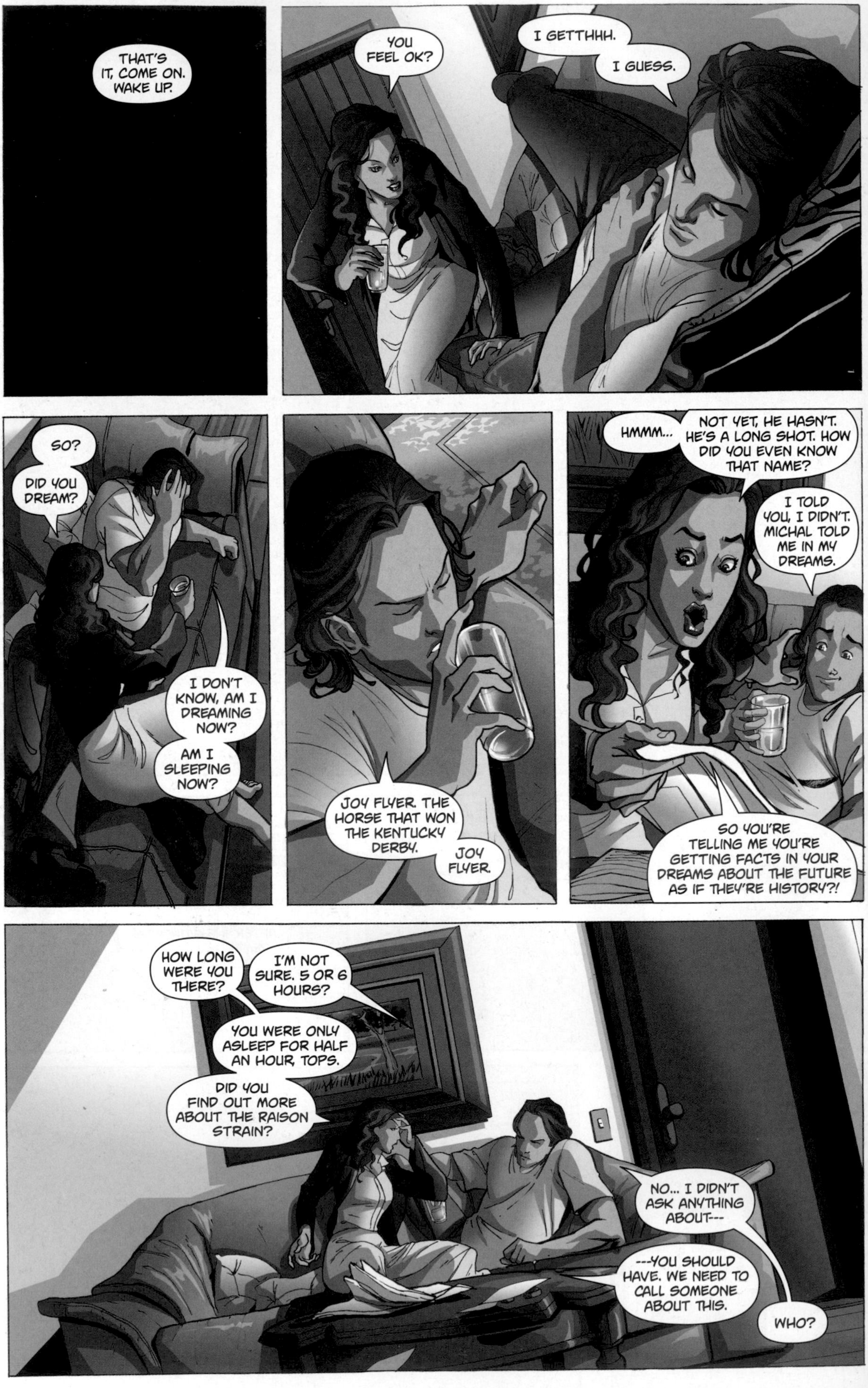
THAT'S IT, COME ON. WAKE UP.
YOU FEEL OK?
I GETTHHH.
I GUESS.
SO?
DID YOU DREAM?
I DON'T KNOW, AM I DREAMING NOW?
AM I SLEEPING NOW?
JOY FLYER. THE HORSE THAT WON THE KENTUCKY DERBY.
JOY FLYER.
HMMM...
NOT YET, HE HASN'T. HE'S A LONG SHOT. HOW DID YOU EVEN KNOW THAT NAME?
I TOLD YOU, I DIDN'T. MICHAL TOLD ME IN MY DREAMS.
SO YOU'RE TELLING ME YOU'RE GETTING FACTS IN YOUR DREAMS ABOUT THE FUTURE AS IF THEY'RE HISTORY?!
HOW LONG WERE YOU THERE?
I'M NOT SURE. 5 OR 6 HOURS?
YOU WERE ONLY ASLEEP FOR HALF AN HOUR, TOPS.
DID YOU FIND OUT MORE ABOUT THE RAISON STRAIN?
NO... I DIDN'T ASK ANYTHING ABOUT---
---YOU SHOULD HAVE. WE NEED TO CALL SOMEONE ABOUT THIS.
WHO?

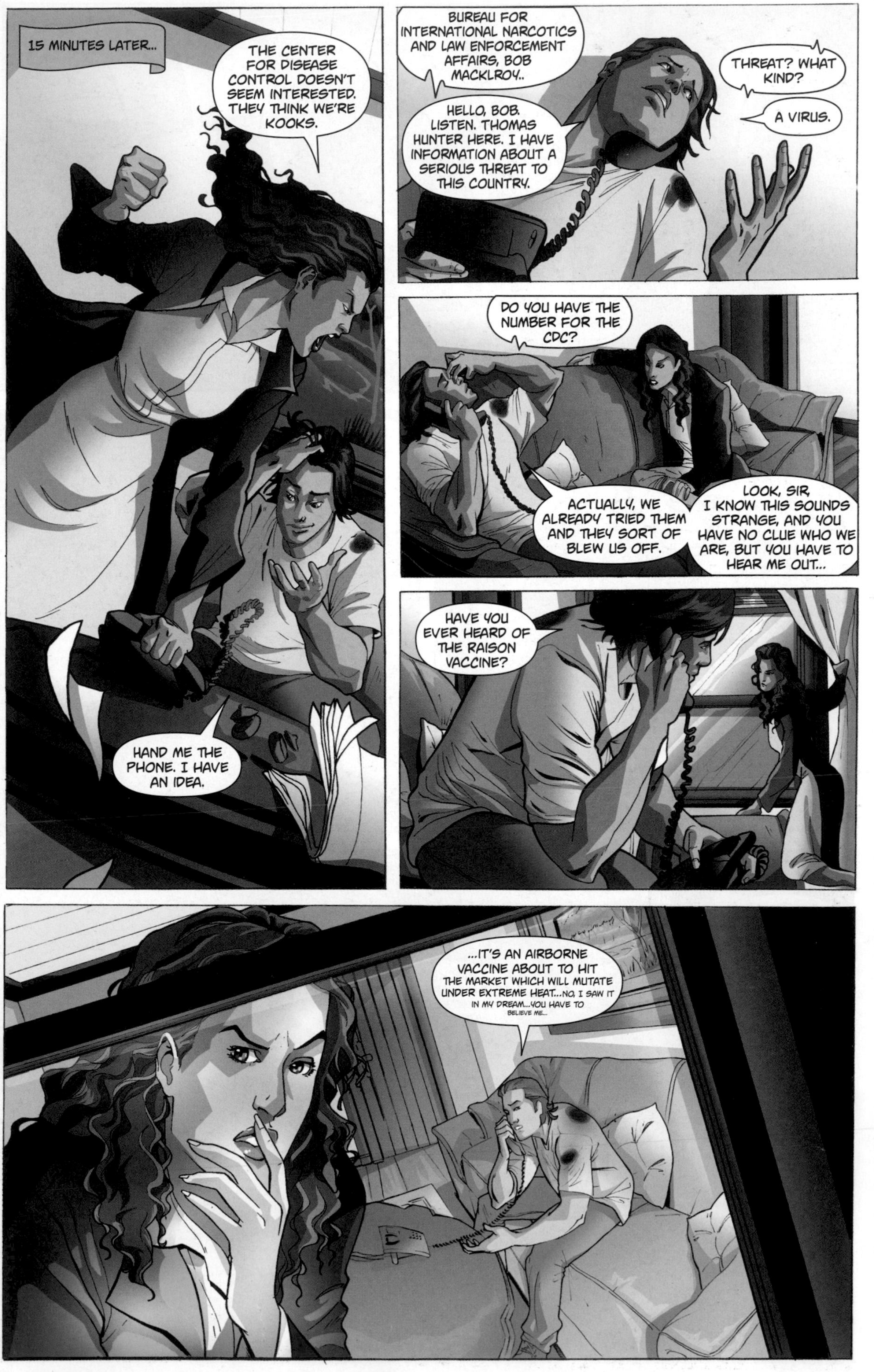
15 MINUTES LATER...
THE CENTER FOR DISEASE CONTROL DOESN'T SEEM INTERESTED. THEY THINK WE'RE KOOKS.
HAND ME THE PHONE. I HAVE AN IDEA.
BUREAU FOR INTERNATIONAL NARCOTICS AND LAW ENFORCEMENT AFFAIRS, BOB MACKLROY..
HELLO, BOB. LISTEN. THOMAS HUNTER HERE. I HAVE INFORMATION ABOUT A SERIOUS THREAT TO THIS COUNTRY.
THREAT? WHAT KIND?
A VIRUS.
DO YOU HAVE THE NUMBER FOR THE CDC?
ACTUALLY, WE ALREADY TRIED THEM AND THEY SORT OF BLEW US OFF.
LOOK, SIR, I KNOW THIS SOUNDS STRANGE, AND YOU HAVE NO CLUE WHO WE ARE, BUT YOU HAVE TO HEAR ME OUT...
HAVE YOU EVER HEARD OF THE RAISON VACCINE?
...IT'S AN AIRBORNE VACCINE ABOUT TO HIT THE MARKET WHICH WILL MUTATE UNDER EXTREME HEAT...NO, I SAW IT IN MY DREAM...YOU HAVE TO BELIEVE ME...

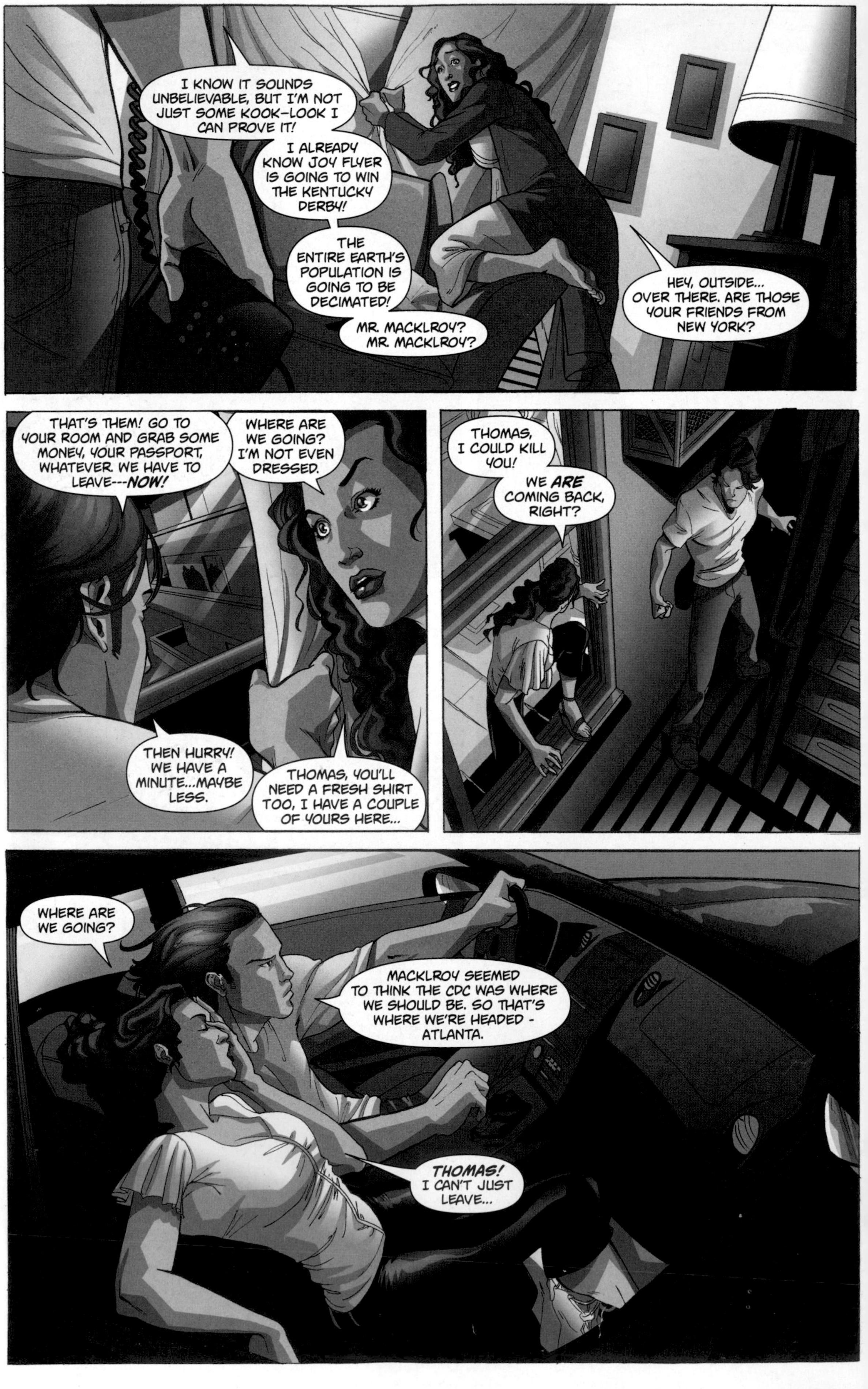
I KNOW IT SOUNDS UNBELIEVABLE, BUT I'M NOT JUST SOME KOOK--LOOK I CAN PROVE IT!
I ALREADY KNOW JOY FLYER IS GOING TO WIN THE KENTUCKY DERBY!
THE ENTIRE EARTH'S POPULATION IS GOING TO BE DECIMATED!
MR. MACKLROY? MR. MACKLROY?
HEY, OUTSIDE... OVER THERE. ARE THOSE YOUR FRIENDS FROM NEW YORK?
THAT'S THEM! GO TO YOUR ROOM AND GRAB SOME MONEY, YOUR PASSPORT, WHATEVER. WE HAVE TO LEAVE---NOW!
WHERE ARE WE GOING? I'M NOT EVEN DRESSED.
THEN HURRY! WE HAVE A MINUTE...MAYBE LESS.
THOMAS, YOU'LL NEED A FRESH SHIRT TOO, I HAVE A COUPLE OF YOURS HERE...
THOMAS, I COULD KILL YOU!
WE ARE COMING BACK, RIGHT?
WHERE ARE WE GOING?
MACKLROY SEEMED TO THINK THE CDC WAS WHERE WE SHOULD BE. SO THAT'S WHERE WE'RE HEADED - ATLANTA.
THOMAS! I CAN'T JUST LEAVE...

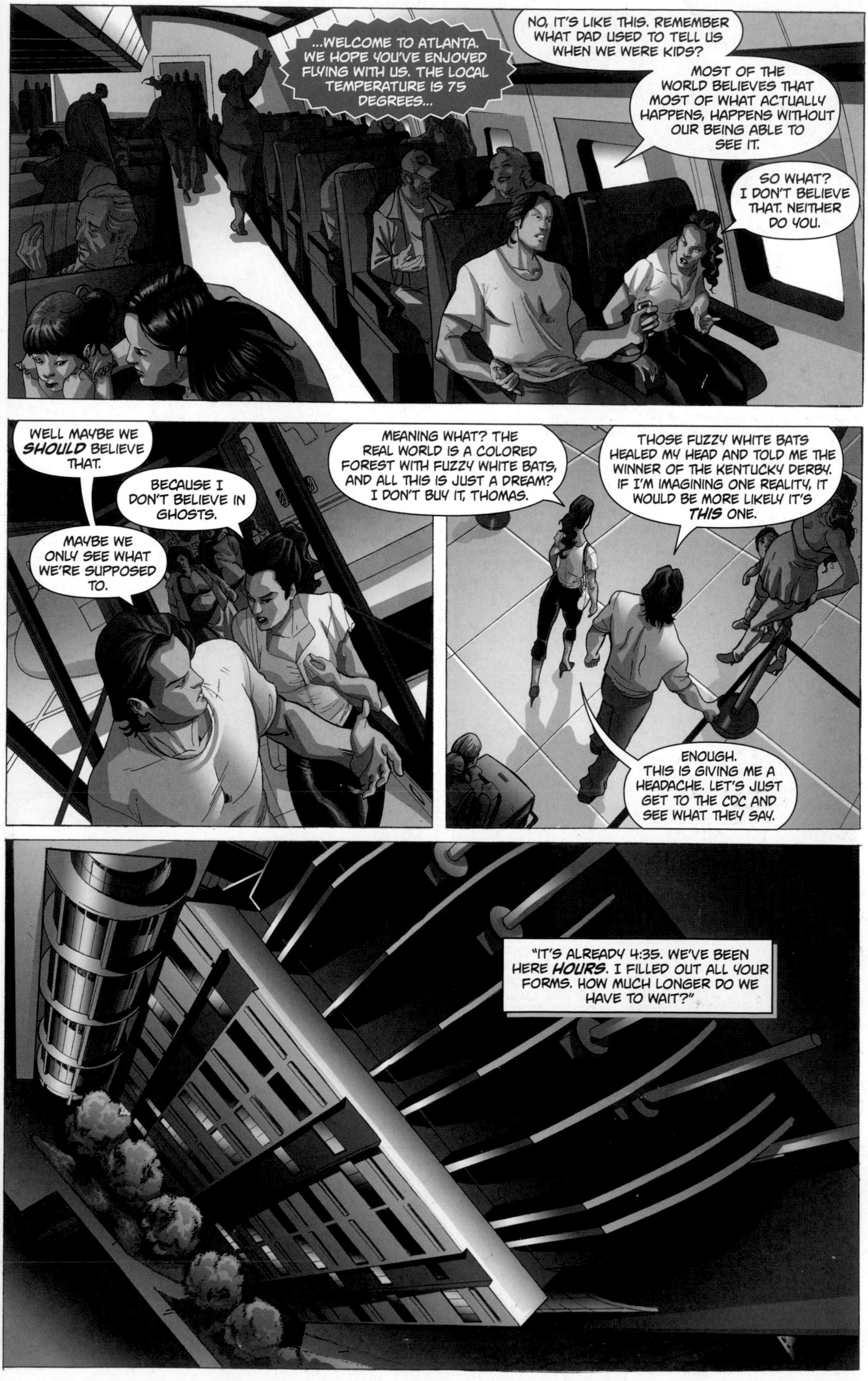
...WELCOME TO ATLANTA. WE HOPE YOU'VE ENJOYED FLYING WITH US. THE LOCAL TEMPERATURE IS 75 DEGREES...
NO, IT'S LIKE THIS. REMEMBER WHAT DAD USED TO TELL US WHEN WE WERE KIDS?
MOST OF THE WORLD BELIEVES THAT MOST OF WHAT ACTUALLY HAPPENS, HAPPENS WITHOUT OUR BEING ABLE TO SEE IT.
SO WHAT? I DON'T BELIEVE THAT. NEITHER DO YOU.
WELL MAYBE WE SHOULD BELIEVE THAT.
BECAUSE I DON'T BELIEVE IN GHOSTS.
MAYBE WE ONLY SEE WHAT WE'RE SUPPOSED TO.
MEANING WHAT? THE REAL WORLD IS A COLORED FOREST WITH FUZZY WHITE BATS, AND ALL THIS IS JUST A DREAM? I DON'T BUY IT, THOMAS.
THOSE FUZZY WHITE BATS HEALED MY HEAD AND TOLD ME THE WINNER OF THE KENTUCKY DERBY. IF I'M IMAGINING ONE REALITY, IT WOULD BE MORE LIKELY IT'S THIS ONE.
ENOUGH. THIS IS GIVING ME A HEADACHE. LET'S JUST GET TO THE CDC AND SEE WHAT THEY SAY.
"IT'S ALREADY 4:35. WE'VE BEEN HERE HOURS. I FILLED OUT ALL YOUR FORMS. HOW MUCH LONGER DO WE HAVE TO WAIT?"

I HAVE TO ADMIT, MR. HUNTER, WHAT YOU'VE JUST TOLD ME IS INDEED... CURIOUS.

I KNOW IT ALL SOUNDS STRANGE. BUT YOU CAN'T IGNORE THIS. THE VACCINE CAN OR WILL MUTATE UNDER EXTREME HEAT AND WIPE OUT... EVERYONE. YOU HAVE TO CONSIDER THE FACTS HERE.

OH, I AM MR. HUNTER, AND THAT'S WHAT'S TROUBLING ME. ARE YOU ACTUALLY TELLING ME THAT ALL THIS INFORMATION CAME...FROM A DREAM?

YOU SAY THAT LIKE IT'S PREPOSTEROUS! DID YOU HEAR A WORD OF WHAT HE JUST TOLD YOU? HE KNOWS ABOUT THE RAISON VACCINE...HE KNEW ABOUT IT BEFORE IT WAS MADE PUBLIC!

WELL...THE RAISON VACCINE HAS BEEN TOUTED IN PRIVATE CIRCLES FOR A FEW MONTHS NOW----

NOT IN *HIS* PRIVATE CIRCLES.

THE WINNER OF THE KENTUCKY DERBY WASN'T PUBLIC TWO HOURS AGO WHEN I PLACED MY BET.

EXPLAIN HOW THOMAS JUST WON ME $345,000 DOLLARS ON A HUNCH FROM THE SAME DREAMS!

YOU WHA--?

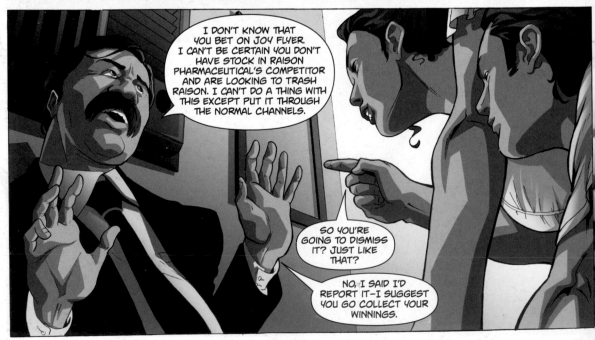

I DON'T KNOW THAT YOU BET ON JOY FLYER. I CAN'T BE CERTAIN YOU DON'T HAVE STOCK IN RAISON PHARMACEUTICAL'S COMPETITOR AND ARE LOOKING TO TRASH RAISON. I CAN'T DO A THING WITH THIS EXCEPT PUT IT THROUGH THE NORMAL CHANNELS.

SO YOU'RE GOING TO DISMISS IT? JUST LIKE THAT?

NO, I SAID I'D REPORT IT--I SUGGEST YOU GO COLLECT YOUR WINNINGS.

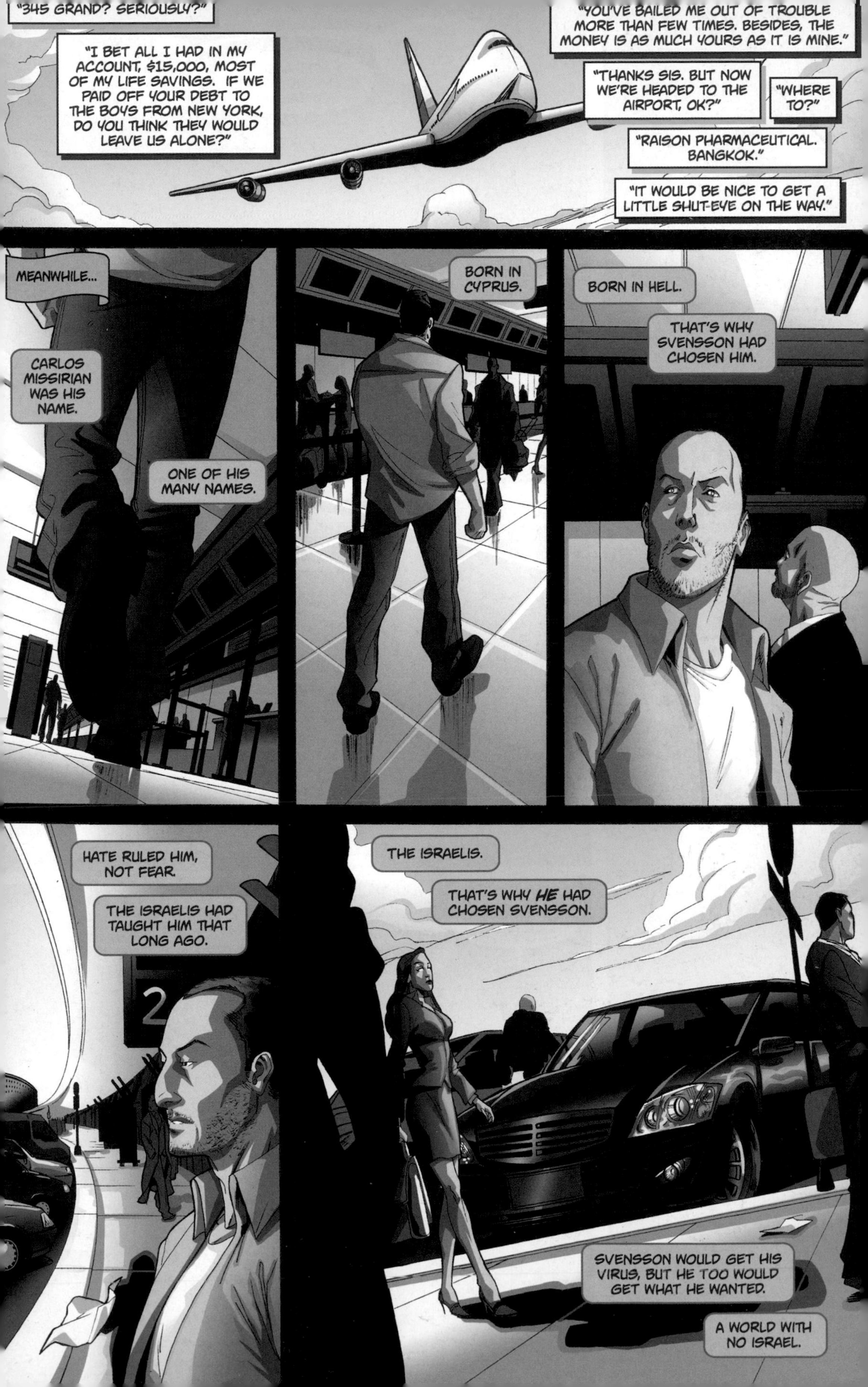
"345 GRAND? SERIOUSLY?"
"I BET ALL I HAD IN MY ACCOUNT, $15,000, MOST OF MY LIFE SAVINGS. IF WE PAID OFF YOUR DEBT TO THE BOYS FROM NEW YORK, DO YOU THINK THEY WOULD LEAVE US ALONE?"
"YOU'VE BAILED ME OUT OF TROUBLE MORE THAN FEW TIMES. BESIDES, THE MONEY IS AS MUCH YOURS AS IT IS MINE."
"THANKS SIS. BUT NOW WE'RE HEADED TO THE AIRPORT, OK?"
"WHERE TO?"
"RAISON PHARMACEUTICAL. BANGKOK."
"IT WOULD BE NICE TO GET A LITTLE SHUT-EYE ON THE WAY."
MEANWHILE...
CARLOS MISSIRIAN WAS HIS NAME.
ONE OF HIS MANY NAMES.
BORN IN CYPRUS.
BORN IN HELL.
THAT'S WHY SVENSSON HAD CHOSEN HIM.
HATE RULED HIM, NOT FEAR.
THE ISRAELIS HAD TAUGHT HIM THAT LONG AGO.
THE ISRAELIS.
THAT'S WHY *HE* HAD CHOSEN SVENSSON.
SVENSSON WOULD GET HIS VIRUS, BUT HE TOO WOULD GET WHAT HE WANTED.
A WORLD WITH NO ISRAEL.

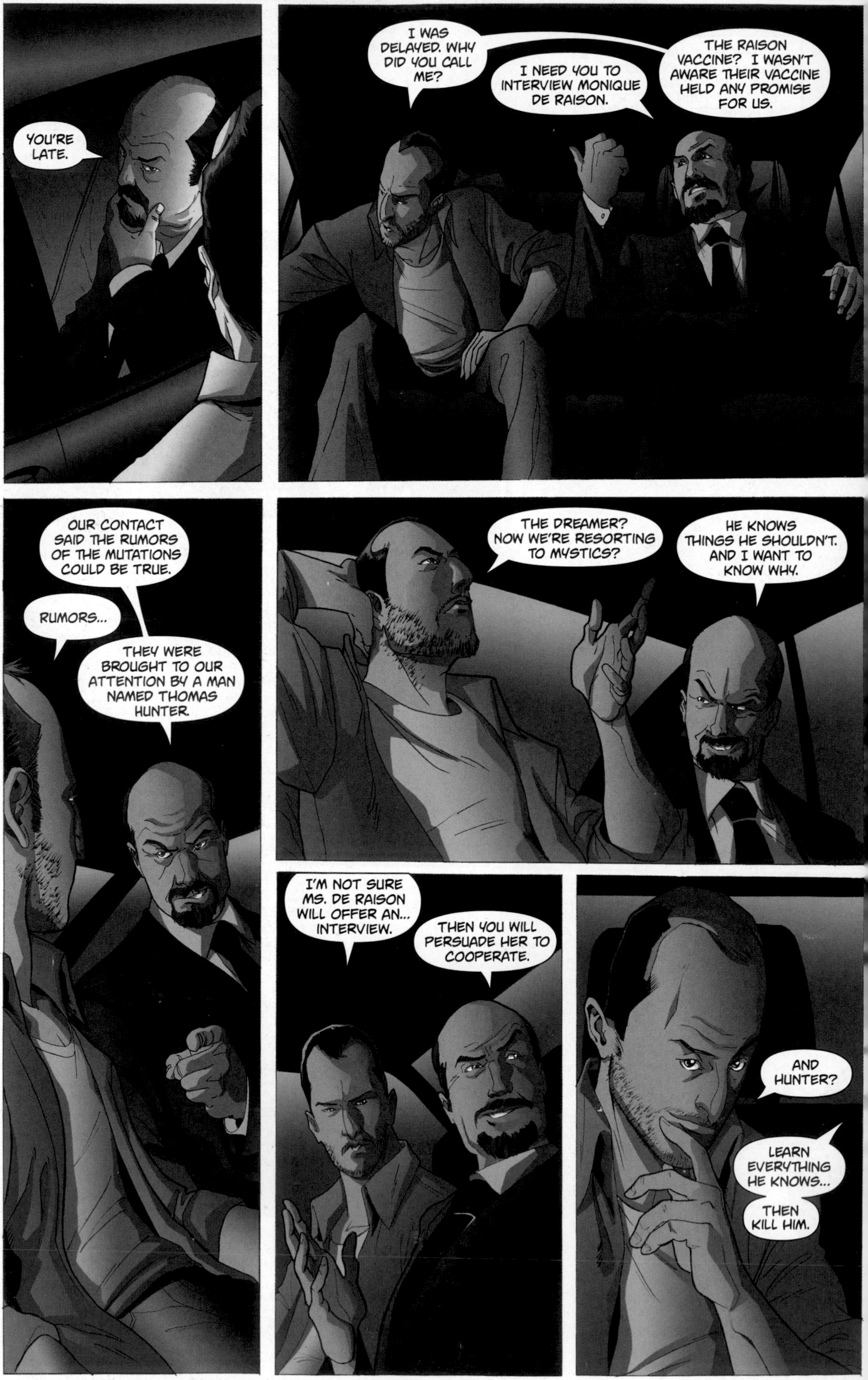
YOU'RE LATE.
I WAS DELAYED. WHY DID YOU CALL ME?
I NEED YOU TO INTERVIEW MONIQUE DE RAISON.
THE RAISON VACCINE? I WASN'T AWARE THEIR VACCINE HELD ANY PROMISE FOR US.
OUR CONTACT SAID THE RUMORS OF THE MUTATIONS COULD BE TRUE.
RUMORS...
THEY WERE BROUGHT TO OUR ATTENTION BY A MAN NAMED THOMAS HUNTER.
THE DREAMER? NOW WE'RE RESORTING TO MYSTICS?
HE KNOWS THINGS HE SHOULDN'T. AND I WANT TO KNOW WHY.
I'M NOT SURE MS. DE RAISON WILL OFFER AN... INTERVIEW.
THEN YOU WILL PERSUADE HER TO COOPERATE.
AND HUNTER?
LEARN EVERYTHING HE KNOWS...
THEN KILL HIM.

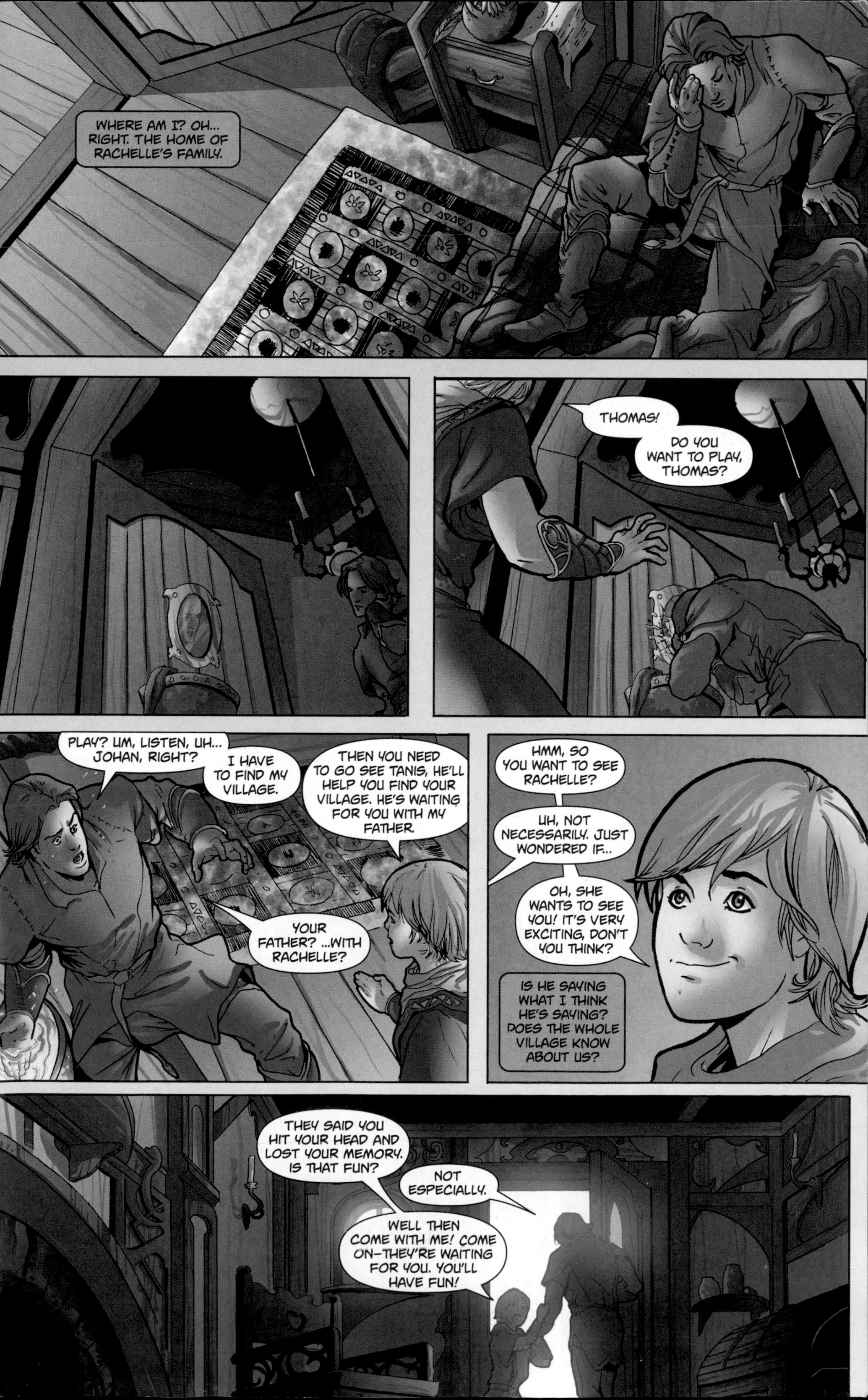
WHERE AM I? OH... RIGHT. THE HOME OF RACHELLE'S FAMILY.
THOMAS!
DO YOU WANT TO PLAY, THOMAS?
PLAY? UM, LISTEN, UH... JOHAN, RIGHT?
I HAVE TO FIND MY VILLAGE.
THEN YOU NEED TO GO SEE TANIS, HE'LL HELP YOU FIND YOUR VILLAGE. HE'S WAITING FOR YOU WITH MY FATHER.
YOUR FATHER? ...WITH RACHELLE?
HMM, SO YOU WANT TO SEE RACHELLE?
UH, NOT NECESSARILY. JUST WONDERED IF...
OH, SHE WANTS TO SEE YOU! IT'S VERY EXCITING, DON'T YOU THINK?
IS HE SAYING WHAT I THINK HE'S SAYING? DOES THE WHOLE VILLAGE KNOW ABOUT US?
THEY SAID YOU HIT YOUR HEAD AND LOST YOUR MEMORY. IS THAT FUN?
NOT ESPECIALLY.
WELL THEN COME WITH ME! COME ON—THEY'RE WAITING FOR YOU. YOU'LL HAVE FUN!

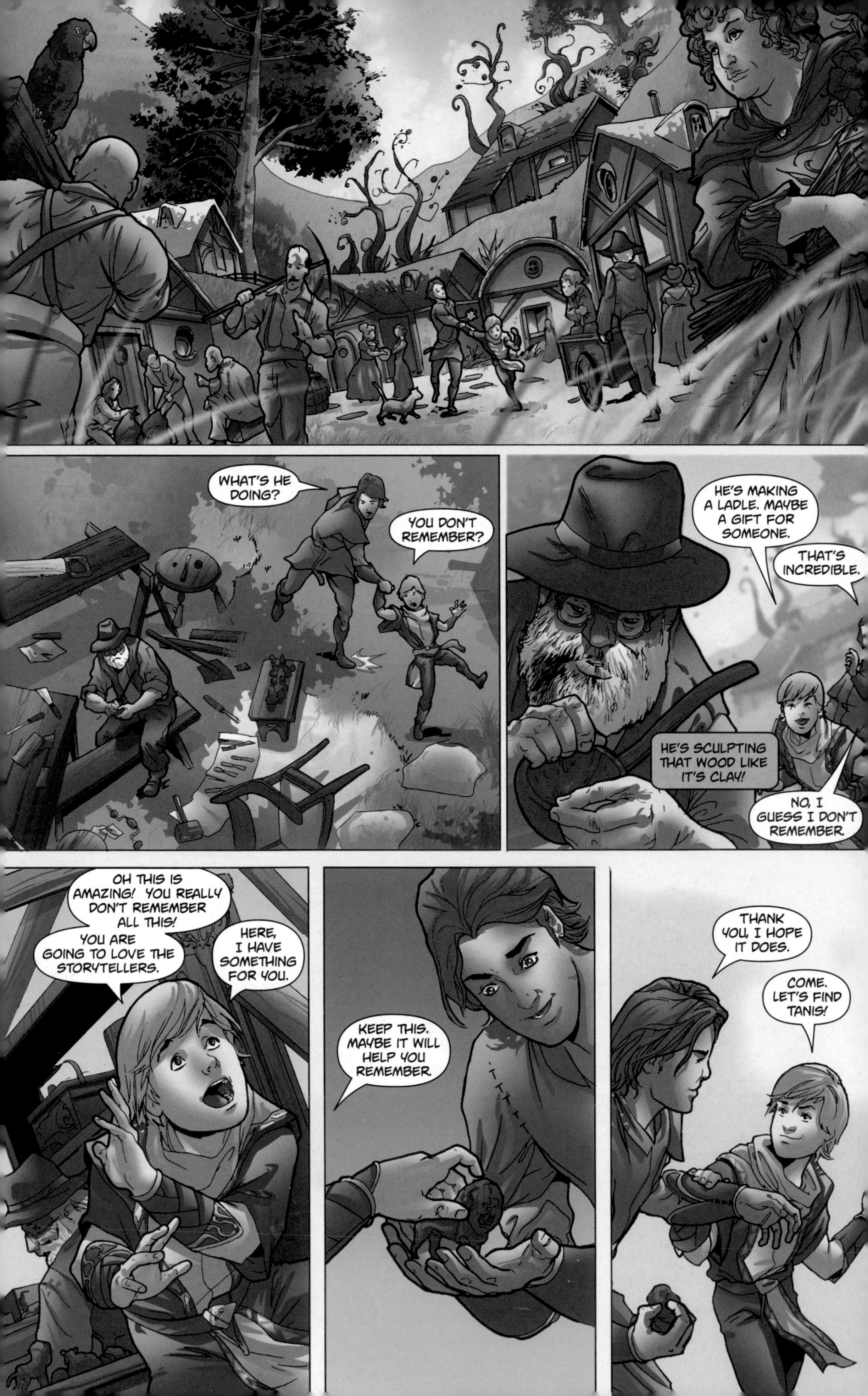
WHAT'S HE DOING?
YOU DON'T REMEMBER?
HE'S MAKING A LADLE. MAYBE A GIFT FOR SOMEONE.
THAT'S INCREDIBLE.
HE'S SCULPTING THAT WOOD LIKE IT'S CLAY!
NO, I GUESS I DON'T REMEMBER.
OH THIS IS AMAZING! YOU REALLY DON'T REMEMBER ALL THIS!
YOU ARE GOING TO LOVE THE STORYTELLERS.
HERE, I HAVE SOMETHING FOR YOU.
KEEP THIS. MAYBE IT WILL HELP YOU REMEMBER.
THANK YOU, I HOPE IT DOES.
COME. LET'S FIND TANIS!

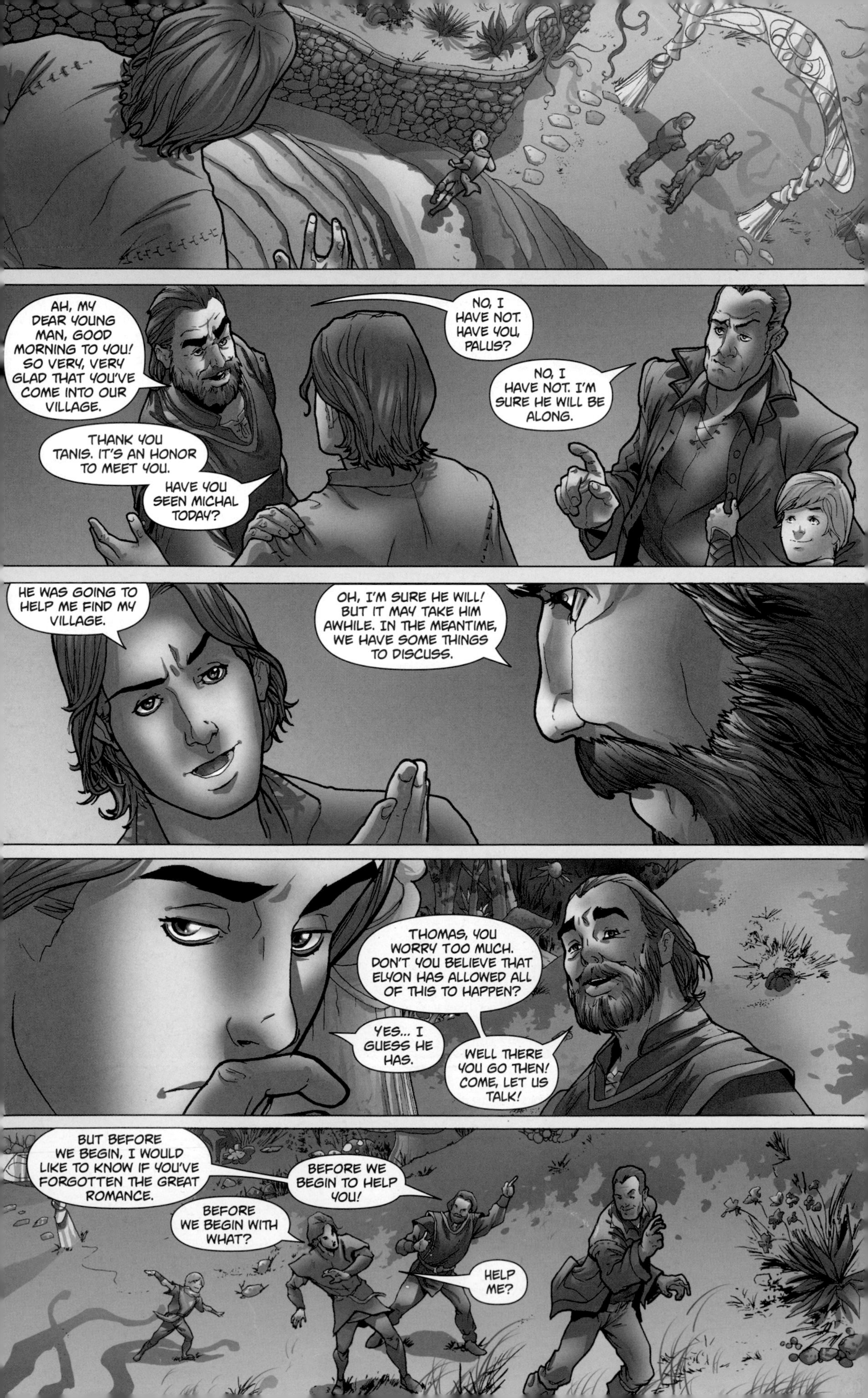
AH, MY DEAR YOUNG MAN, GOOD MORNING TO YOU! SO VERY, VERY GLAD THAT YOU'VE COME INTO OUR VILLAGE.
THANK YOU TANIS. IT'S AN HONOR TO MEET YOU.
HAVE YOU SEEN MICHAL TODAY?
NO, I HAVE NOT. HAVE YOU, PALUS?
NO, I HAVE NOT. I'M SURE HE WILL BE ALONG.
HE WAS GOING TO HELP ME FIND MY VILLAGE.
OH, I'M SURE HE WILL! BUT IT MAY TAKE HIM AWHILE. IN THE MEANTIME, WE HAVE SOME THINGS TO DISCUSS.
THOMAS, YOU WORRY TOO MUCH. DON'T YOU BELIEVE THAT ELYON HAS ALLOWED ALL OF THIS TO HAPPEN?
YES... I GUESS HE HAS.
WELL THERE YOU GO THEN! COME, LET US TALK!
BUT BEFORE WE BEGIN, I WOULD LIKE TO KNOW IF YOU'VE FORGOTTEN THE GREAT ROMANCE.
BEFORE WE BEGIN WITH WHAT?
BEFORE WE BEGIN TO HELP YOU!
HELP ME?

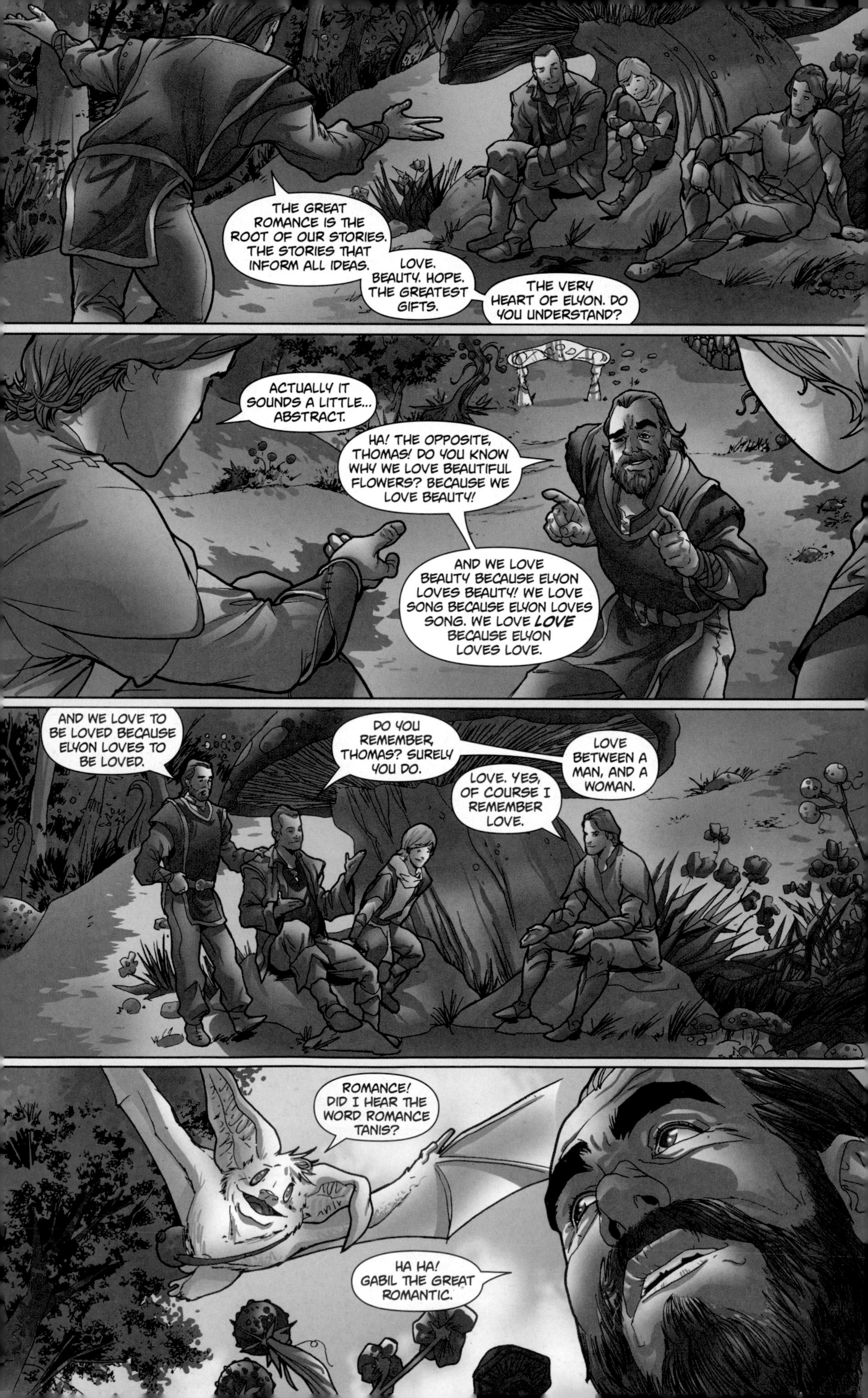
THE GREAT ROMANCE IS THE ROOT OF OUR STORIES. THE STORIES THAT INFORM ALL IDEAS.
LOVE. BEAUTY. HOPE. THE GREATEST GIFTS.
THE VERY HEART OF ELYON. DO YOU UNDERSTAND?
ACTUALLY IT SOUNDS A LITTLE... ABSTRACT.
HA! THE OPPOSITE, THOMAS! DO YOU KNOW WHY WE LOVE BEAUTIFUL FLOWERS? BECAUSE WE LOVE BEAUTY!
AND WE LOVE BEAUTY BECAUSE ELYON LOVES BEAUTY! WE LOVE SONG BECAUSE ELYON LOVES SONG. WE LOVE ***LOVE*** BECAUSE ELYON LOVES LOVE.
AND WE LOVE TO BE LOVED BECAUSE ELYON LOVES TO BE LOVED.
DO YOU REMEMBER, THOMAS? SURELY YOU DO.
LOVE BETWEEN A MAN, AND A WOMAN.
LOVE. YES, OF COURSE I REMEMBER LOVE.
ROMANCE! DID I HEAR THE WORD ROMANCE TANIS?
HA HA! GABIL THE GREAT ROMANTIC.

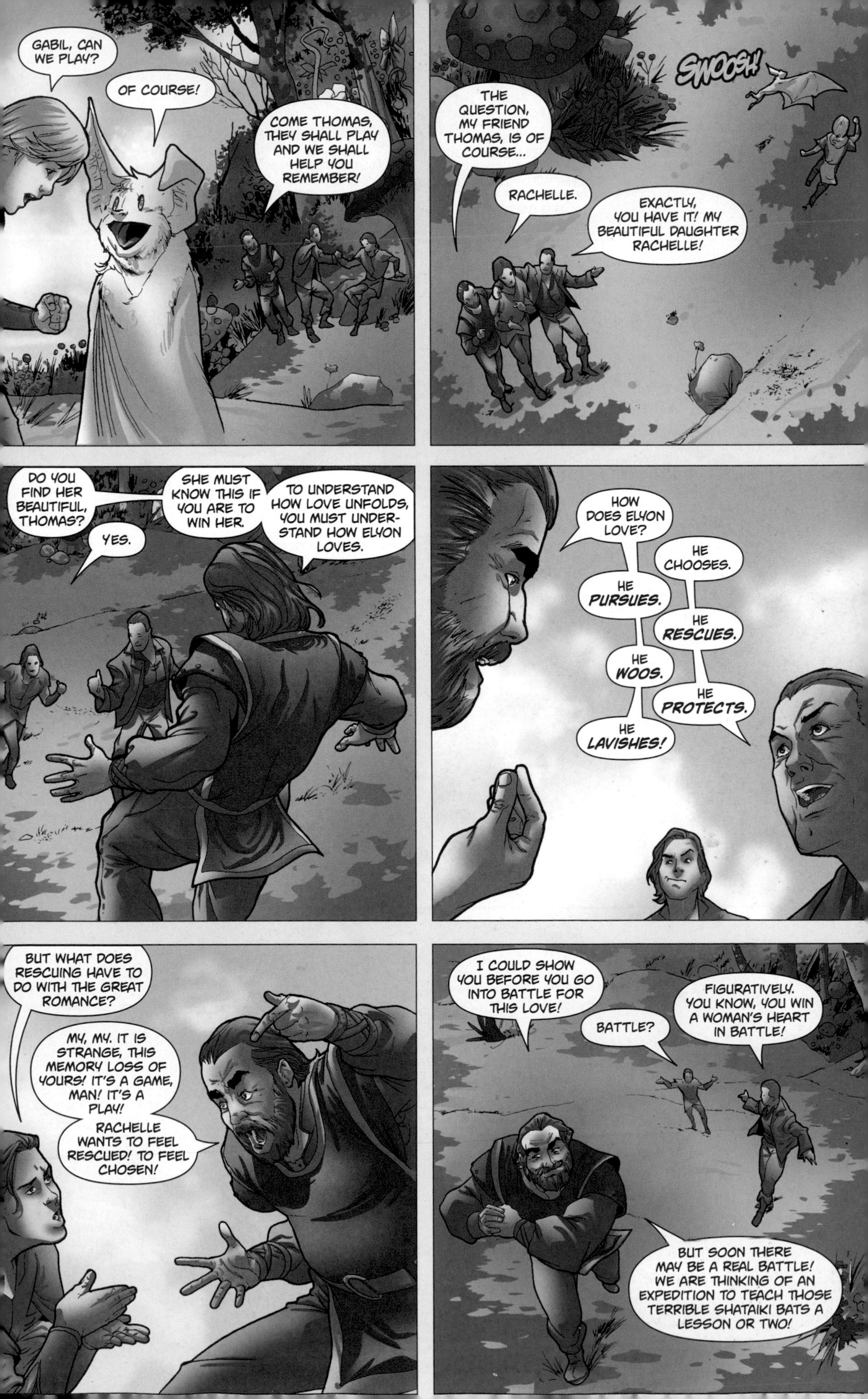
GABIL, CAN WE PLAY?
OF COURSE!
COME THOMAS, THEY SHALL PLAY AND WE SHALL HELP YOU REMEMBER!
SWOOSH!
THE QUESTION, MY FRIEND THOMAS, IS OF COURSE...
RACHELLE.
EXACTLY, YOU HAVE IT! MY BEAUTIFUL DAUGHTER RACHELLE!
DO YOU FIND HER BEAUTIFUL, THOMAS?
YES.
SHE MUST KNOW THIS IF YOU ARE TO WIN HER.
TO UNDERSTAND HOW LOVE UNFOLDS, YOU MUST UNDERSTAND HOW ELYON LOVES.
HOW DOES ELYON LOVE?
HE CHOOSES.
HE PURSUES.
HE RESCUES.
HE WOOS.
HE PROTECTS.
HE LAVISHES!
BUT WHAT DOES RESCUING HAVE TO DO WITH THE GREAT ROMANCE?
MY, MY. IT IS STRANGE, THIS MEMORY LOSS OF YOURS! IT'S A GAME, MAN! IT'S A PLAY!
RACHELLE WANTS TO FEEL RESCUED! TO FEEL CHOSEN!
I COULD SHOW YOU BEFORE YOU GO INTO BATTLE FOR THIS LOVE!
BATTLE?
FIGURATIVELY. YOU KNOW, YOU WIN A WOMAN'S HEART IN BATTLE!
BUT SOON THERE MAY BE A REAL BATTLE! WE ARE THINKING OF AN EXPEDITION TO TEACH THOSE TERRIBLE SHATAIKI BATS A LESSON OR TWO!

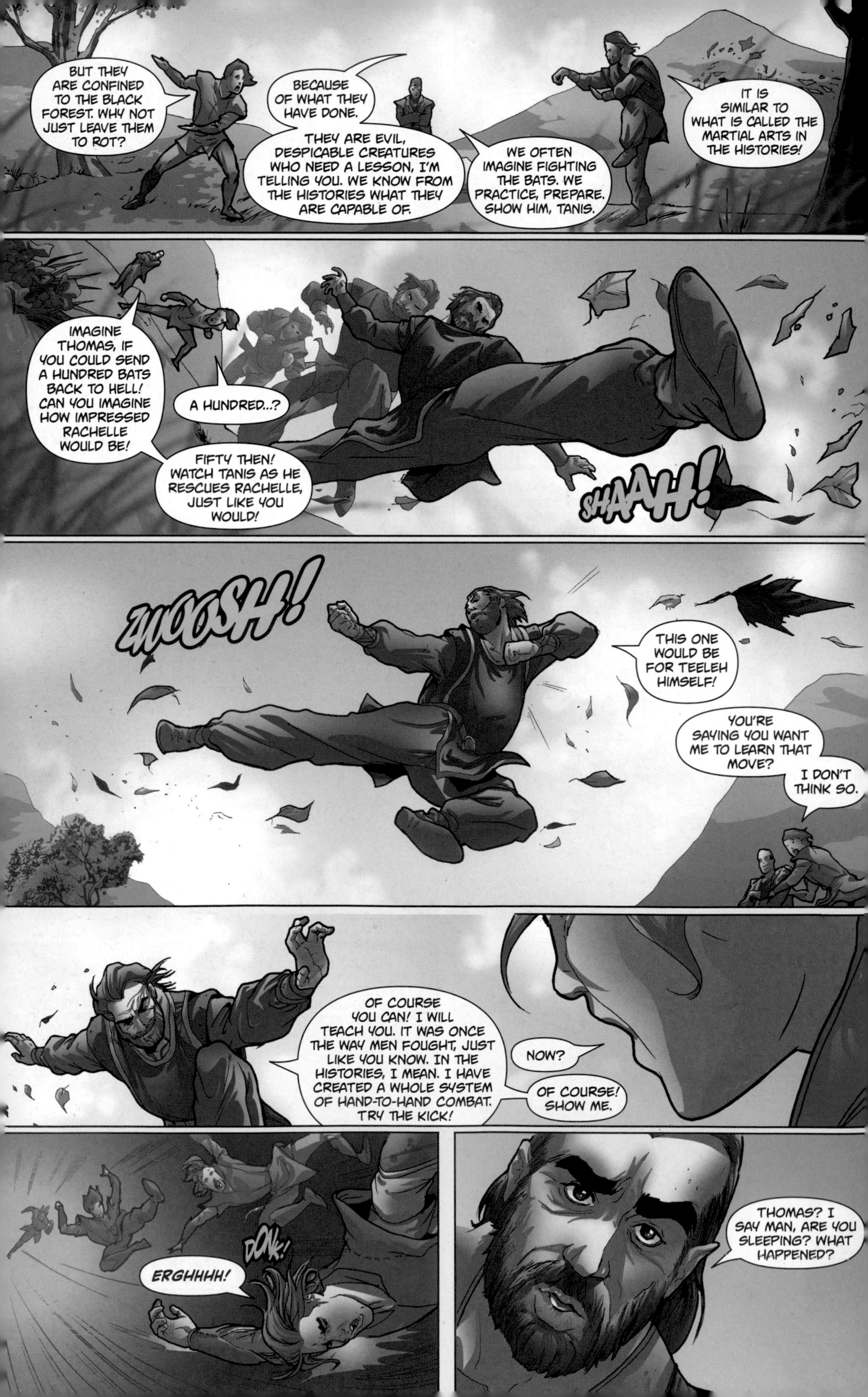
BUT THEY ARE CONFINED TO THE BLACK FOREST. WHY NOT JUST LEAVE THEM TO ROT?
BECAUSE OF WHAT THEY HAVE DONE.
THEY ARE EVIL, DESPICABLE CREATURES WHO NEED A LESSON, I'M TELLING YOU. WE KNOW FROM THE HISTORIES WHAT THEY ARE CAPABLE OF.
WE OFTEN IMAGINE FIGHTING THE BATS. WE PRACTICE, PREPARE. SHOW HIM, TANIS.
IT IS SIMILAR TO WHAT IS CALLED THE MARTIAL ARTS IN THE HISTORIES!
IMAGINE THOMAS, IF YOU COULD SEND A HUNDRED BATS BACK TO HELL! CAN YOU IMAGINE HOW IMPRESSED RACHELLE WOULD BE!
A HUNDRED...?
FIFTY THEN! WATCH TANIS AS HE RESCUES RACHELLE, JUST LIKE YOU WOULD!
SHAAAH!
ZWOOSH!
THIS ONE WOULD BE FOR TEELEH HIMSELF!
YOU'RE SAYING YOU WANT ME TO LEARN THAT MOVE?
I DON'T THINK SO.
OF COURSE YOU CAN! I WILL TEACH YOU. IT WAS ONCE THE WAY MEN FOUGHT, JUST LIKE YOU KNOW. IN THE HISTORIES, I MEAN. I HAVE CREATED A WHOLE SYSTEM OF HAND-TO-HAND COMBAT. TRY THE KICK!
NOW?
OF COURSE! SHOW ME.
DONK!
ERGHHHH!
THOMAS? I SAY MAN, ARE YOU SLEEPING? WHAT HAPPENED?

EXCUSE ME SIR? PLEASE BRING YOUR SEAT UP.

MHMM?

WE'VE BEGUN OUR DESCENT INTO BANGKOK.

WELCOME BACK TO THE LAND OF THE LIVING. SO, WHAT DID YOU FIND OUT?

NOTHING.

NOTHING? YOU'VE BEEN ASLEEP FIVE HOURS. WE'VE FLOWN ACROSS OCEANS BECAUSE OF YOUR DREAMS. DON'T TELL ME THEY AREN'T WORKING ANYMORE.

NO, I LEARNED SOMETHING. I THINK I KNOW WHY THIS MAY BE HAPPENING.

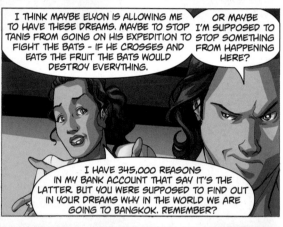

I THINK MAYBE ELYON IS ALLOWING ME TO HAVE THESE DREAMS. MAYBE TO STOP TANIS FROM GOING ON HIS EXPEDITION TO FIGHT THE BATS - IF HE CROSSES AND EATS THE FRUIT THE BATS WOULD DESTROY EVERYTHING.

OR MAYBE I'M SUPPOSED TO STOP SOMETHING FROM HAPPENING HERE?

I HAVE 345,000 REASONS IN MY BANK ACCOUNT THAT SAY IT'S THE LATTER BUT YOU WERE SUPPOSED TO FIND OUT IN YOUR DREAMS WHY IN THE WORLD WE ARE GOING TO BANGKOK. REMEMBER?

LET'S JUST SEE IF WE CAN MAKE IT TO THE RAISON ANNOUNCEMENT IN TIME.

I HAVE A BAD FEELING ABOUT THIS.

YOU SURE YOU'RE OKAY? YOU KEEP SAYING YOU ARE, BUT YOU LOOK TERRIBLE.

I'M JUST TIRED. SOON AS WE DEAL WITH THIS ALL I'LL SLEEP FOR A WEEK.

MAYBE THE DREAMS *ARE* REAL, LIKE YOU SAID. MAYBE THE REASON YOU'RE NOT GETTING ANY REST IS BECAUSE YOU REALLY AREN'T. YOU'RE AWAKE IN BOTH PLACES.

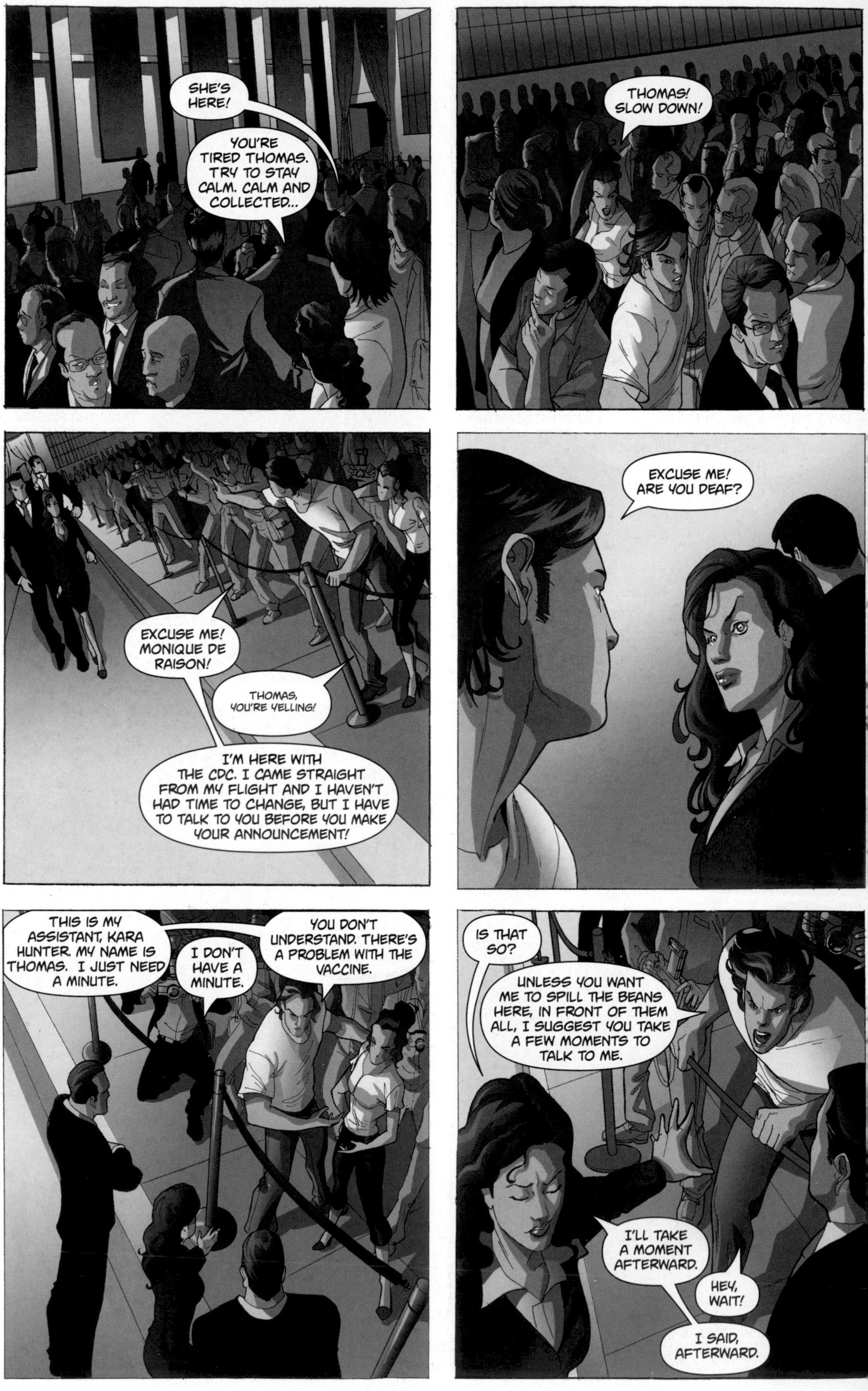
SHE'S HERE!
YOU'RE TIRED THOMAS. TRY TO STAY CALM. CALM AND COLLECTED...
THOMAS! SLOW DOWN!
EXCUSE ME! MONIQUE DE RAISON!
THOMAS, YOU'RE YELLING!
I'M HERE WITH THE CDC. I CAME STRAIGHT FROM MY FLIGHT AND I HAVEN'T HAD TIME TO CHANGE, BUT I HAVE TO TALK TO YOU BEFORE YOU MAKE YOUR ANNOUNCEMENT!
EXCUSE ME! ARE YOU DEAF?
THIS IS MY ASSISTANT, KARA HUNTER. MY NAME IS THOMAS. I JUST NEED A MINUTE.
I DON'T HAVE A MINUTE.
YOU DON'T UNDERSTAND. THERE'S A PROBLEM WITH THE VACCINE.
IS THAT SO?
UNLESS YOU WANT ME TO SPILL THE BEANS HERE, IN FRONT OF THEM ALL, I SUGGEST YOU TAKE A FEW MOMENTS TO TALK TO ME.
I'LL TAKE A MOMENT AFTERWARD.
HEY, WAIT!
I SAID, AFTERWARD.

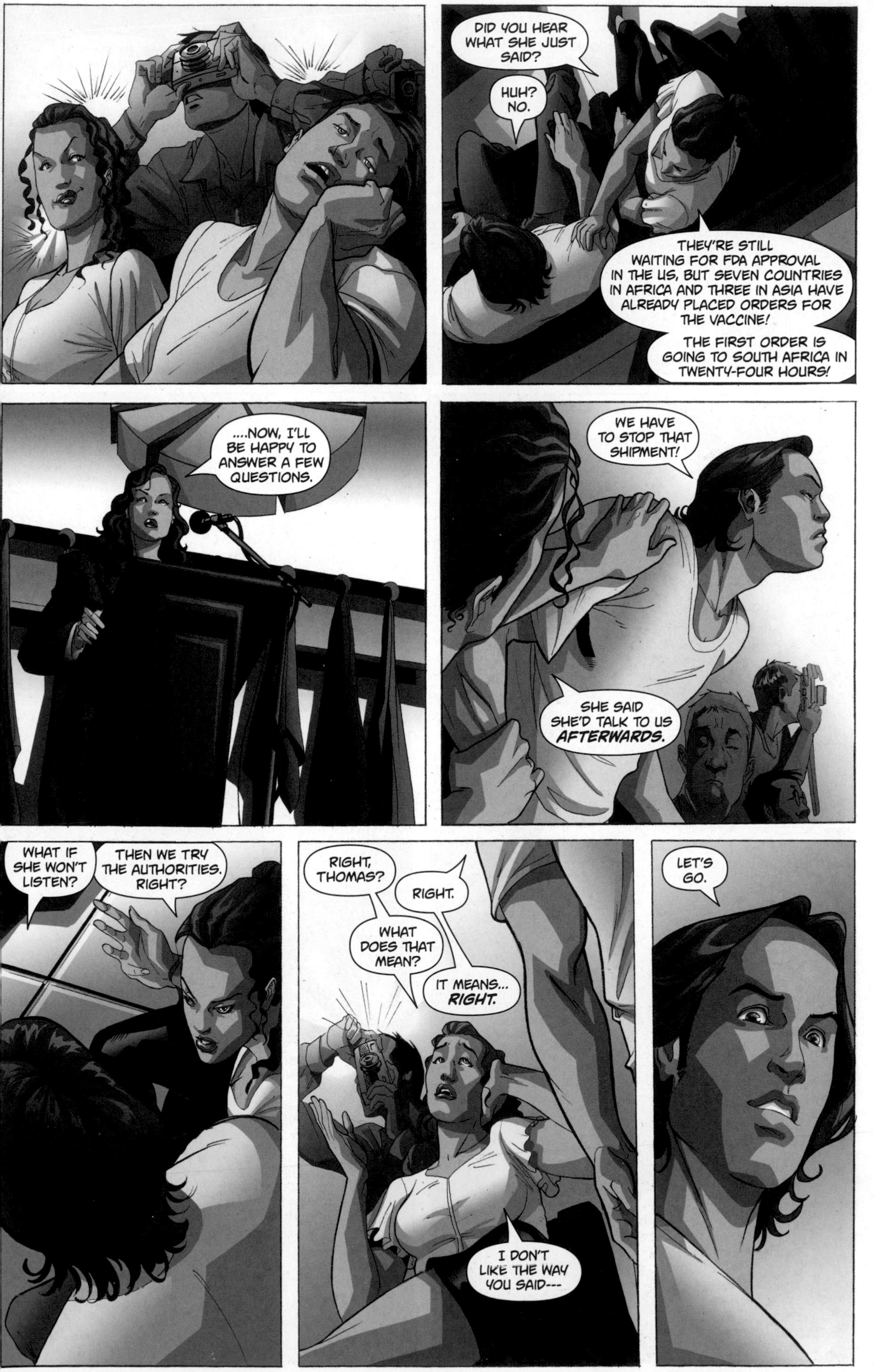
DID YOU HEAR WHAT SHE JUST SAID?
HUH? NO.
THEY'RE STILL WAITING FOR FDA APPROVAL IN THE US, BUT SEVEN COUNTRIES IN AFRICA AND THREE IN ASIA HAVE ALREADY PLACED ORDERS FOR THE VACCINE!
THE FIRST ORDER IS GOING TO SOUTH AFRICA IN TWENTY-FOUR HOURS!
....NOW, I'LL BE HAPPY TO ANSWER A FEW QUESTIONS.
WE HAVE TO STOP THAT SHIPMENT!
SHE SAID SHE'D TALK TO US AFTERWARDS.
WHAT IF SHE WON'T LISTEN?
THEN WE TRY THE AUTHORITIES. RIGHT?
RIGHT, THOMAS?
RIGHT.
WHAT DOES THAT MEAN?
IT MEANS... RIGHT.
I DON'T LIKE THE WAY YOU SAID---
LET'S GO.

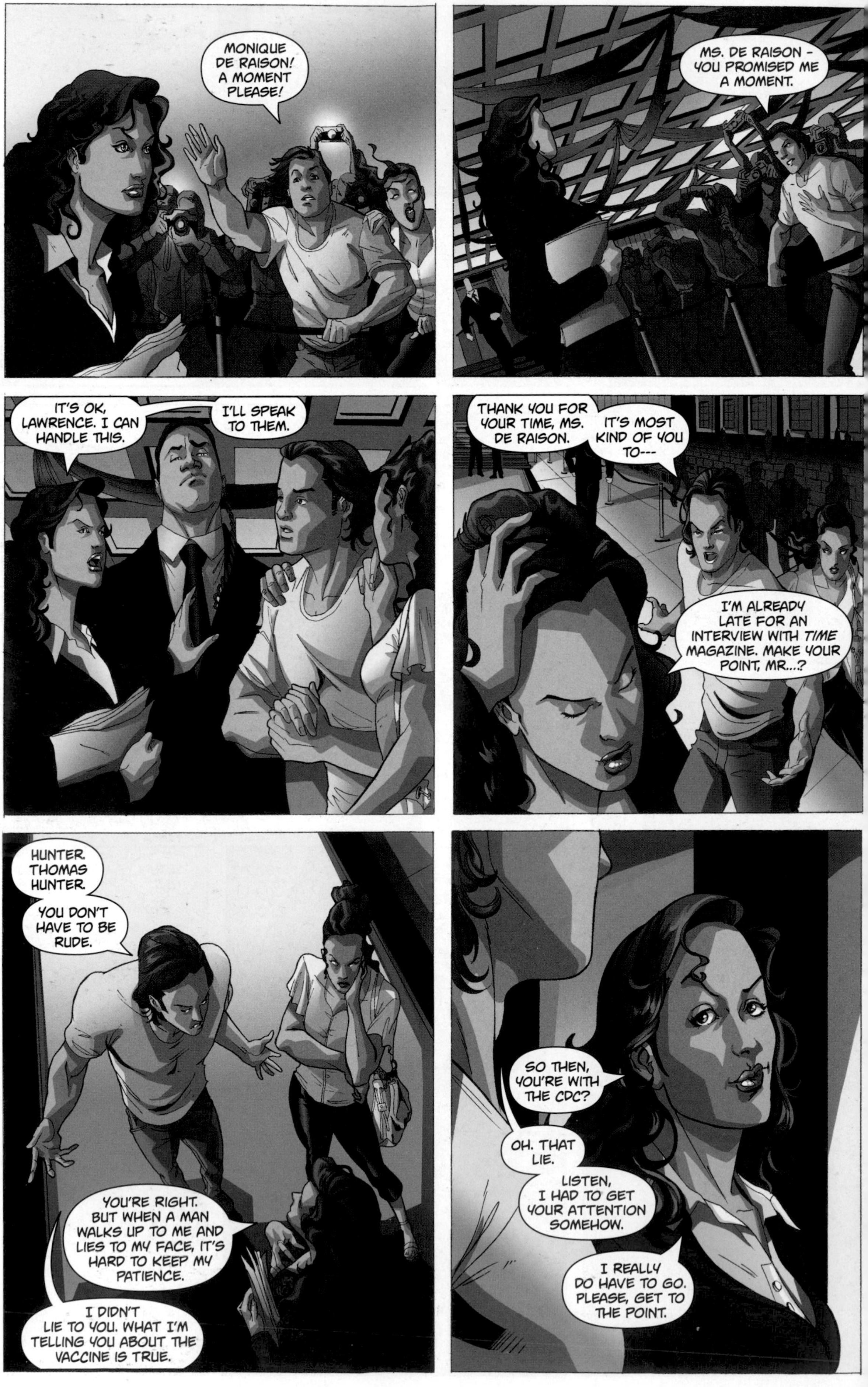
MONIQUE DE RAISON! A MOMENT PLEASE!
MS. DE RAISON - YOU PROMISED ME A MOMENT.
IT'S OK, LAWRENCE. I CAN HANDLE THIS.
I'LL SPEAK TO THEM.
THANK YOU FOR YOUR TIME, MS. DE RAISON.
IT'S MOST KIND OF YOU TO---
I'M ALREADY LATE FOR AN INTERVIEW WITH *TIME* MAGAZINE. MAKE YOUR POINT, MR...?
HUNTER. THOMAS HUNTER.
YOU DON'T HAVE TO BE RUDE.
YOU'RE RIGHT. BUT WHEN A MAN WALKS UP TO ME AND LIES TO MY FACE, IT'S HARD TO KEEP MY PATIENCE.
I DIDN'T LIE TO YOU. WHAT I'M TELLING YOU ABOUT THE VACCINE IS TRUE.
SO THEN, YOU'RE WITH THE CDC?
OH. THAT LIE.
LISTEN, I HAD TO GET YOUR ATTENTION SOMEHOW.
I REALLY DO HAVE TO GO. PLEASE, GET TO THE POINT.

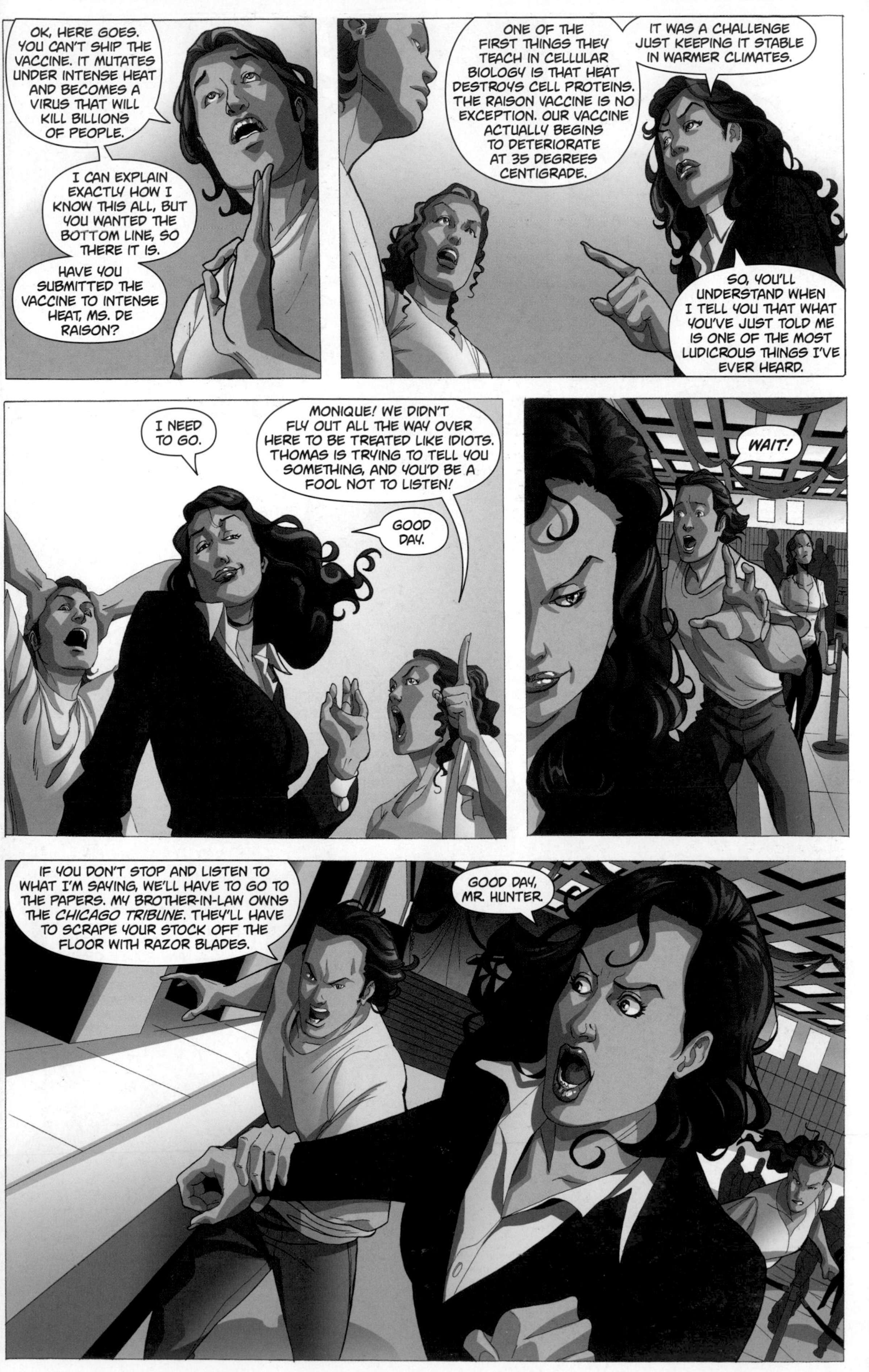
OK, HERE GOES. YOU CAN'T SHIP THE VACCINE. IT MUTATES UNDER INTENSE HEAT AND BECOMES A VIRUS THAT WILL KILL BILLIONS OF PEOPLE.
I CAN EXPLAIN EXACTLY HOW I KNOW THIS ALL, BUT YOU WANTED THE BOTTOM LINE, SO THERE IT IS.
HAVE YOU SUBMITTED THE VACCINE TO INTENSE HEAT, MS. DE RAISON?
ONE OF THE FIRST THINGS THEY TEACH IN CELLULAR BIOLOGY IS THAT HEAT DESTROYS CELL PROTEINS. THE RAISON VACCINE IS NO EXCEPTION. OUR VACCINE ACTUALLY BEGINS TO DETERIORATE AT 35 DEGREES CENTIGRADE.
IT WAS A CHALLENGE JUST KEEPING IT STABLE IN WARMER CLIMATES.
SO, YOU'LL UNDERSTAND WHEN I TELL YOU THAT WHAT YOU'VE JUST TOLD ME IS ONE OF THE MOST LUDICROUS THINGS I'VE EVER HEARD.
I NEED TO GO.
MONIQUE! WE DIDN'T FLY OUT ALL THE WAY OVER HERE TO BE TREATED LIKE IDIOTS. THOMAS IS TRYING TO TELL YOU SOMETHING, AND YOU'D BE A FOOL NOT TO LISTEN!
GOOD DAY.
WAIT!
IF YOU DON'T STOP AND LISTEN TO WHAT I'M SAYING, WE'LL HAVE TO GO TO THE PAPERS. MY BROTHER-IN-LAW OWNS THE *CHICAGO TRIBUNE*. THEY'LL HAVE TO SCRAPE YOUR STOCK OFF THE FLOOR WITH RAZOR BLADES.
GOOD DAY, MR. HUNTER.

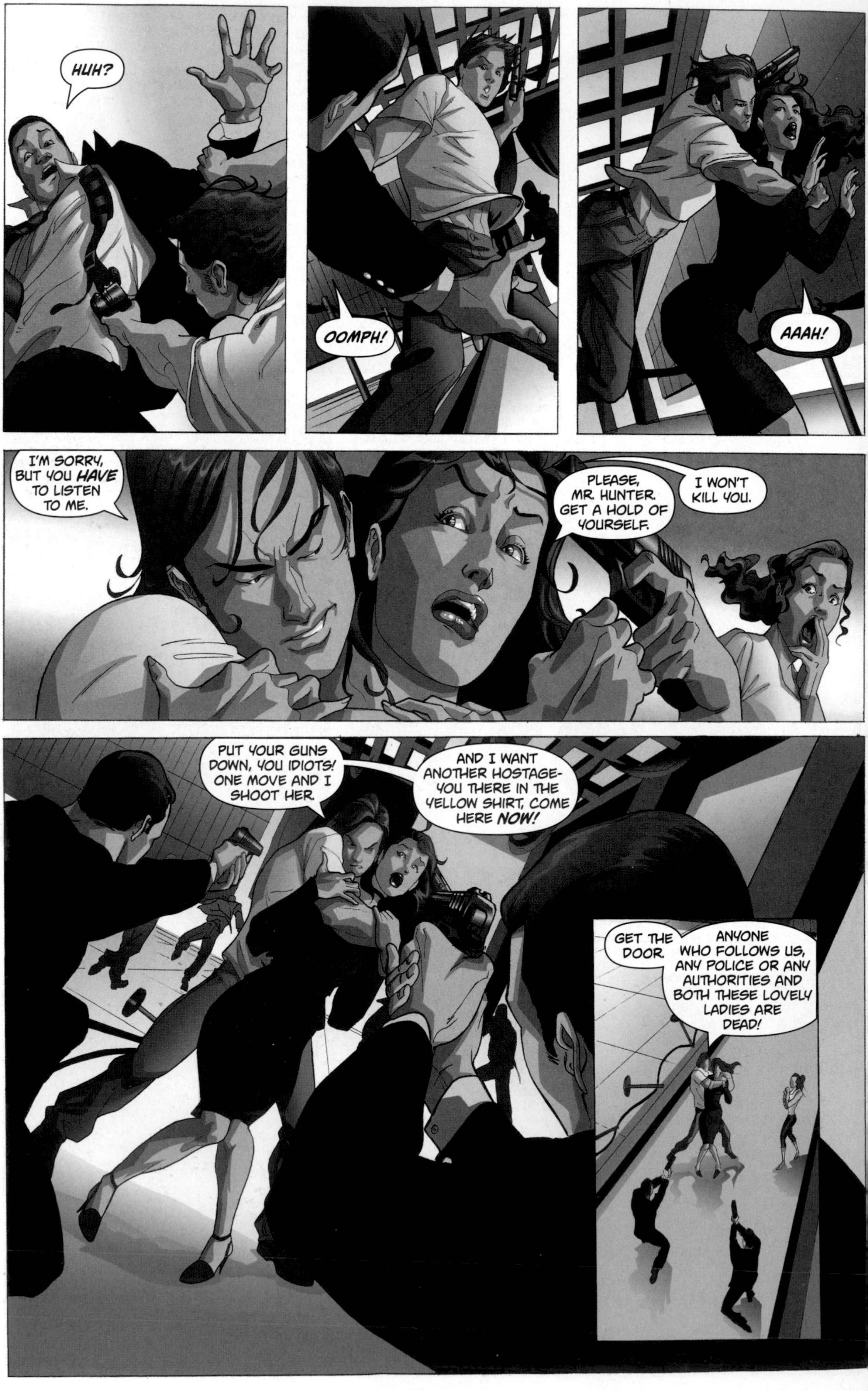
HUH?
OOMPH!
AAAH!
I'M SORRY, BUT YOU *HAVE* TO LISTEN TO ME.
PLEASE, MR. HUNTER. GET A HOLD OF YOURSELF.
I WON'T KILL YOU.
PUT YOUR GUNS DOWN, YOU IDIOTS! ONE MOVE AND I SHOOT HER.
AND I WANT ANOTHER HOSTAGE-YOU THERE IN THE YELLOW SHIRT, COME HERE *NOW!*
GET THE DOOR.
ANYONE WHO FOLLOWS US, ANY POLICE OR ANY AUTHORITIES AND BOTH THESE LOVELY LADIES ARE DEAD!

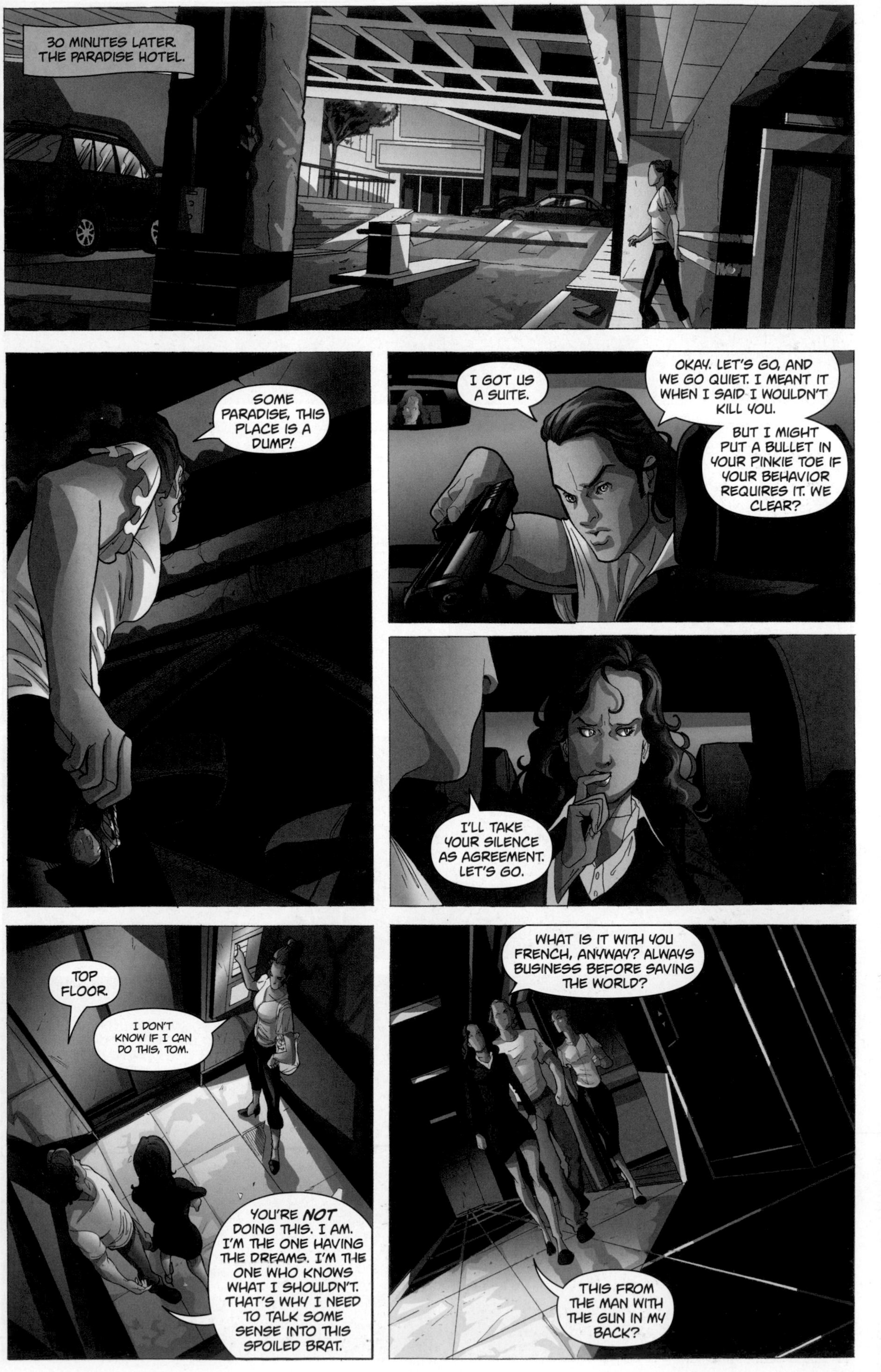

30 MINUTES LATER. THE PARADISE HOTEL.
SOME PARADISE, THIS PLACE IS A DUMP!
I GOT US A SUITE.
OKAY. LET'S GO, AND WE GO QUIET. I MEANT IT WHEN I SAID I WOULDN'T KILL YOU.
BUT I MIGHT PUT A BULLET IN YOUR PINKIE TOE IF YOUR BEHAVIOR REQUIRES IT. WE CLEAR?
I'LL TAKE YOUR SILENCE AS AGREEMENT. LET'S GO.
TOP FLOOR.
I DON'T KNOW IF I CAN DO THIS, TOM.
YOU'RE **NOT** DOING THIS. I AM. I'M THE ONE HAVING THE DREAMS. I'M THE ONE WHO KNOWS WHAT I SHOULDN'T. THAT'S WHY I NEED TO TALK SOME SENSE INTO THIS SPOILED BRAT.
WHAT IS IT WITH YOU FRENCH, ANYWAY? ALWAYS BUSINESS BEFORE SAVING THE WORLD?
THIS FROM THE MAN WITH THE GUN IN MY BACK?

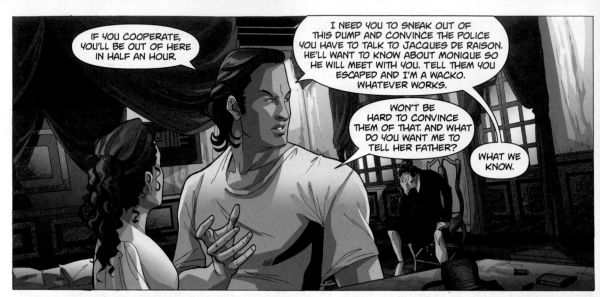

IF YOU COOPERATE, YOU'LL BE OUT OF HERE IN HALF AN HOUR.

I NEED YOU TO SNEAK OUT OF THIS DUMP AND CONVINCE THE POLICE YOU HAVE TO TALK TO JACQUES DE RAISON. HE'LL WANT TO KNOW ABOUT MONIQUE SO HE WILL MEET WITH YOU. TELL THEM YOU ESCAPED AND I'M A WACKO. WHATEVER WORKS.

WON'T BE HARD TO CONVINCE THEM OF THAT. AND WHAT DO YOU WANT ME TO TELL HER FATHER?

WHAT WE KNOW.

AND TELL HIM IF HE DOESN'T AGREE TO STOP OR RECALL THE SHIPMENT THAT I'M GOING TO START SHOOTING.

ONLY PINKIES, OF COURSE.

THIS IS NUTS. I HOPE YOU KNOW WHAT YOU'RE DOING.

GOOD LUCK WOOING THAT ONE, BY THE WAY.

FARTHEST THING FROM MY MIND.

CARLOS.

HOW CONVENIENT. THE TWO BIRDS I'M LOOKING FOR IN THE SAME NEST.

PARADI HOTE

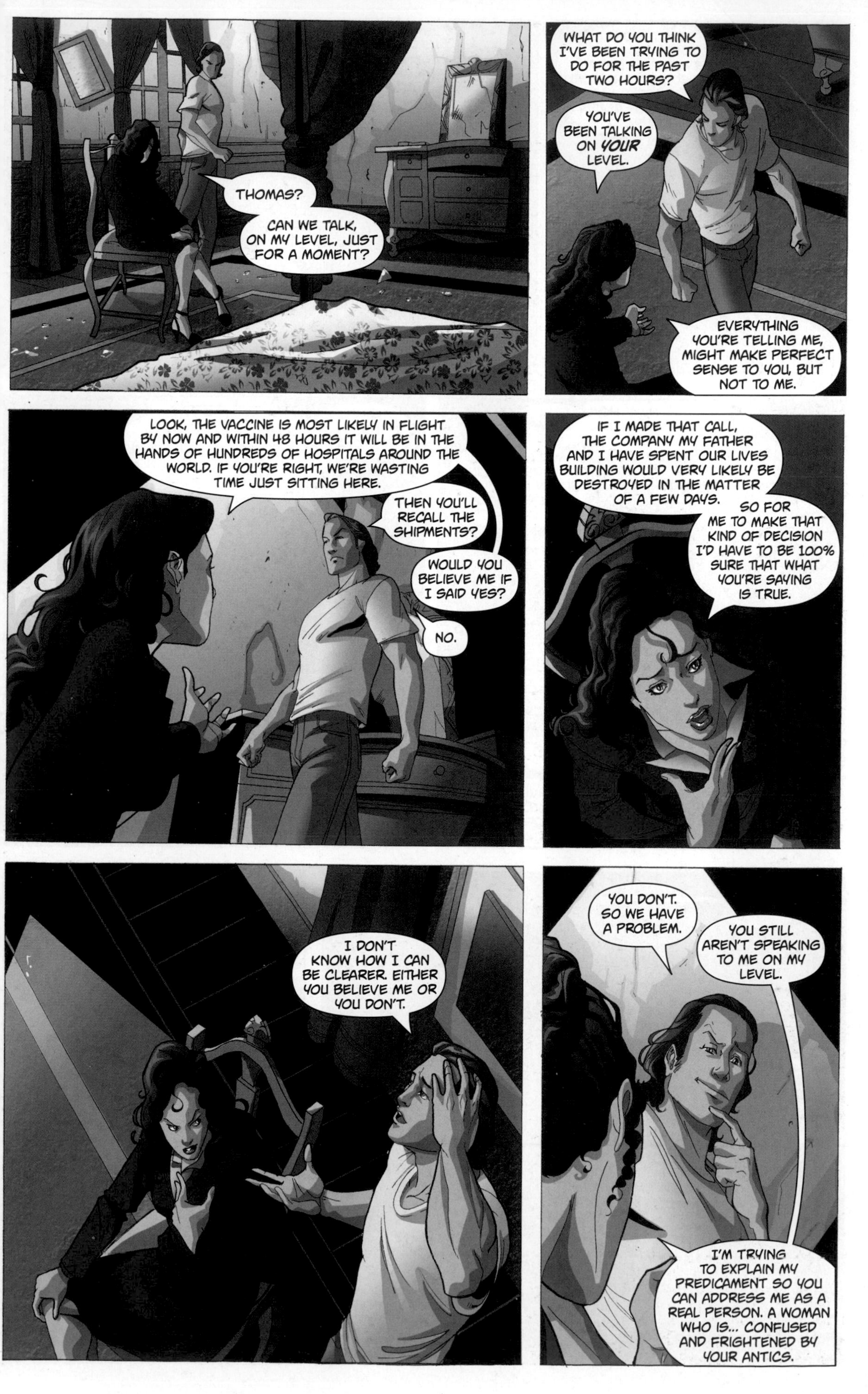
THOMAS?
CAN WE TALK, ON MY LEVEL, JUST FOR A MOMENT?
WHAT DO YOU THINK I'VE BEEN TRYING TO DO FOR THE PAST TWO HOURS?
YOU'VE BEEN TALKING ON YOUR LEVEL.
EVERYTHING YOU'RE TELLING ME, MIGHT MAKE PERFECT SENSE TO YOU, BUT NOT TO ME.
LOOK, THE VACCINE IS MOST LIKELY IN FLIGHT BY NOW AND WITHIN 48 HOURS IT WILL BE IN THE HANDS OF HUNDREDS OF HOSPITALS AROUND THE WORLD. IF YOU'RE RIGHT, WE'RE WASTING TIME JUST SITTING HERE.
THEN YOU'LL RECALL THE SHIPMENTS?
WOULD YOU BELIEVE ME IF I SAID YES?
NO.
IF I MADE THAT CALL, THE COMPANY MY FATHER AND I HAVE SPENT OUR LIVES BUILDING WOULD VERY LIKELY BE DESTROYED IN THE MATTER OF A FEW DAYS.
SO FOR ME TO MAKE THAT KIND OF DECISION I'D HAVE TO BE 100% SURE THAT WHAT YOU'RE SAYING IS TRUE.
I DON'T KNOW HOW I CAN BE CLEARER. EITHER YOU BELIEVE ME OR YOU DON'T.
YOU DON'T. SO WE HAVE A PROBLEM.
YOU STILL AREN'T SPEAKING TO ME ON MY LEVEL.
I'M TRYING TO EXPLAIN MY PREDICAMENT SO YOU CAN ADDRESS ME AS A REAL PERSON. A WOMAN WHO IS... CONFUSED AND FRIGHTENED BY YOUR ANTICS.

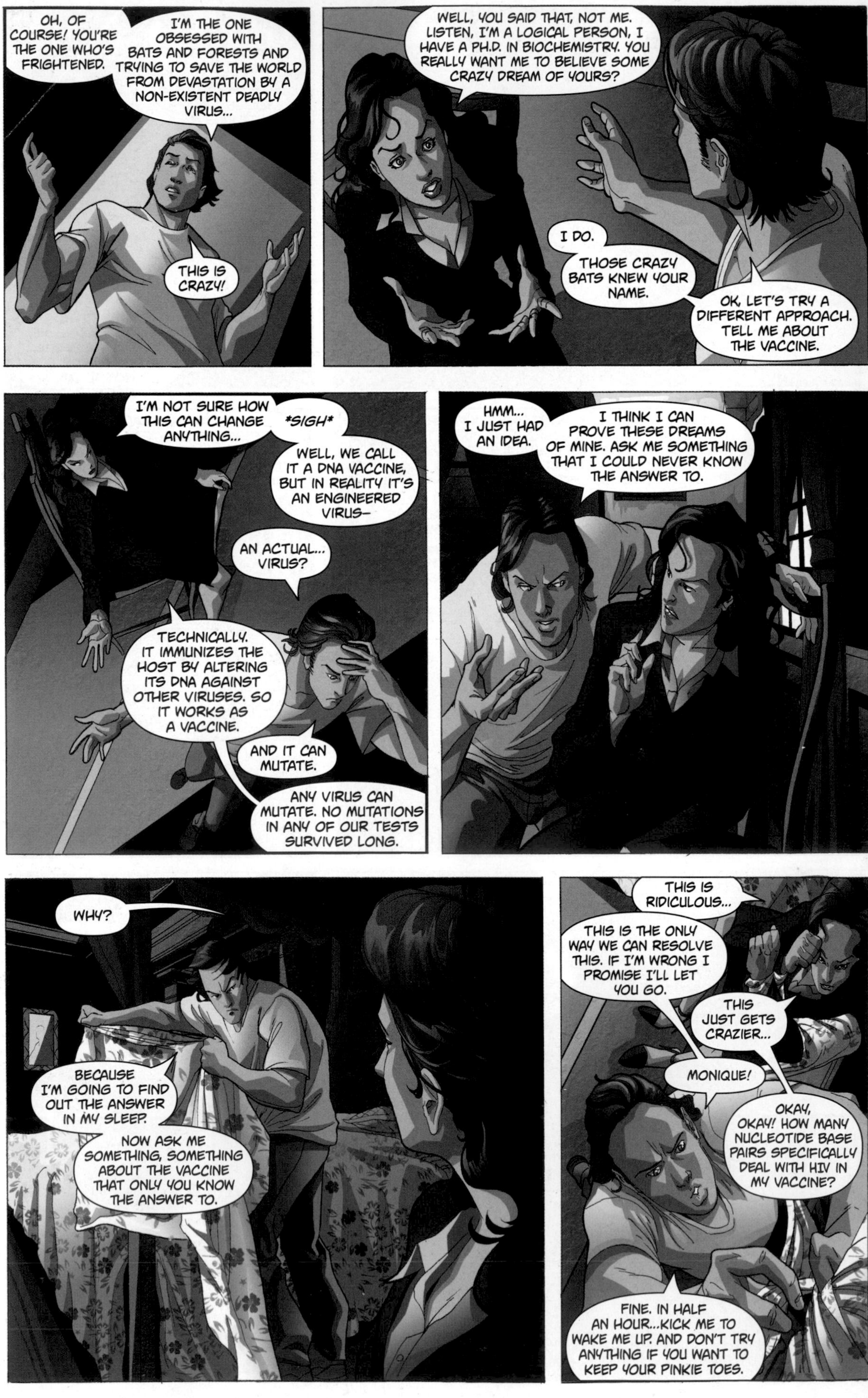
OH, OF COURSE! YOU'RE THE ONE WHO'S FRIGHTENED.
I'M THE ONE OBSESSED WITH BATS AND FORESTS AND TRYING TO SAVE THE WORLD FROM DEVASTATION BY A NON-EXISTENT DEADLY VIRUS...
THIS IS CRAZY!
WELL, YOU SAID THAT, NOT ME. LISTEN, I'M A LOGICAL PERSON, I HAVE A PH.D. IN BIOCHEMISTRY. YOU REALLY WANT ME TO BELIEVE SOME CRAZY DREAM OF YOURS?
I DO.
THOSE CRAZY BATS KNEW YOUR NAME.
OK, LET'S TRY A DIFFERENT APPROACH. TELL ME ABOUT THE VACCINE.
I'M NOT SURE HOW THIS CAN CHANGE ANYTHING...
SIGH
WELL, WE CALL IT A DNA VACCINE, BUT IN REALITY IT'S AN ENGINEERED VIRUS–
AN ACTUAL... VIRUS?
TECHNICALLY. IT IMMUNIZES THE HOST BY ALTERING ITS DNA AGAINST OTHER VIRUSES. SO IT WORKS AS A VACCINE.
AND IT CAN MUTATE.
ANY VIRUS CAN MUTATE. NO MUTATIONS IN ANY OF OUR TESTS SURVIVED LONG.
HMM... I JUST HAD AN IDEA.
I THINK I CAN PROVE THESE DREAMS OF MINE. ASK ME SOMETHING THAT I COULD NEVER KNOW THE ANSWER TO.
WHY?
BECAUSE I'M GOING TO FIND OUT THE ANSWER IN MY SLEEP.
NOW ASK ME SOMETHING, SOMETHING ABOUT THE VACCINE THAT ONLY YOU KNOW THE ANSWER TO.
THIS IS RIDICULOUS...
THIS IS THE ONLY WAY WE CAN RESOLVE THIS. IF I'M WRONG I PROMISE I'LL LET YOU GO.
THIS JUST GETS CRAZIER...
MONIQUE!
OKAY, OKAY! HOW MANY NUCLEOTIDE BASE PAIRS SPECIFICALLY DEAL WITH HIV IN MY VACCINE?
FINE. IN HALF AN HOUR...KICK ME TO WAKE ME UP. AND DON'T TRY ANYTHING IF YOU WANT TO KEEP YOUR PINKIE TOES.

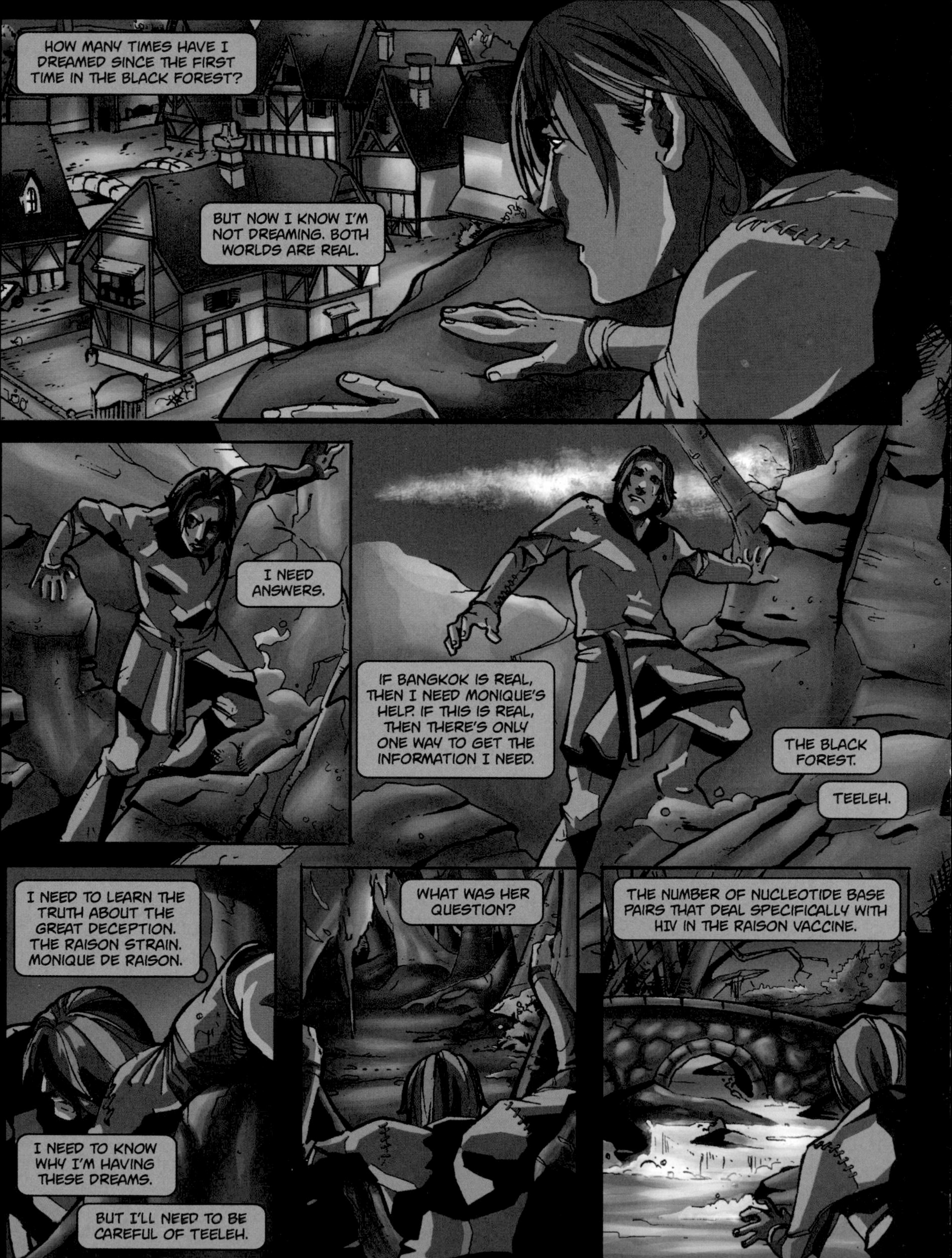
HOW MANY TIMES HAVE I DREAMED SINCE THE FIRST TIME IN THE BLACK FOREST?
BUT NOW I KNOW I'M NOT DREAMING. BOTH WORLDS ARE REAL.
I NEED ANSWERS.
IF BANGKOK IS REAL, THEN I NEED MONIQUE'S HELP. IF THIS IS REAL, THEN THERE'S ONLY ONE WAY TO GET THE INFORMATION I NEED.
THE BLACK FOREST.
TEELEH.
I NEED TO LEARN THE TRUTH ABOUT THE GREAT DECEPTION. THE RAISON STRAIN. MONIQUE DE RAISON.
I NEED TO KNOW WHY I'M HAVING THESE DREAMS.
BUT I'LL NEED TO BE CAREFUL OF TEELEH.
WHAT WAS HER QUESTION?
THE NUMBER OF NUCLEOTIDE BASE PAIRS THAT DEAL SPECIFICALLY WITH HIV IN THE RAISON VACCINE.

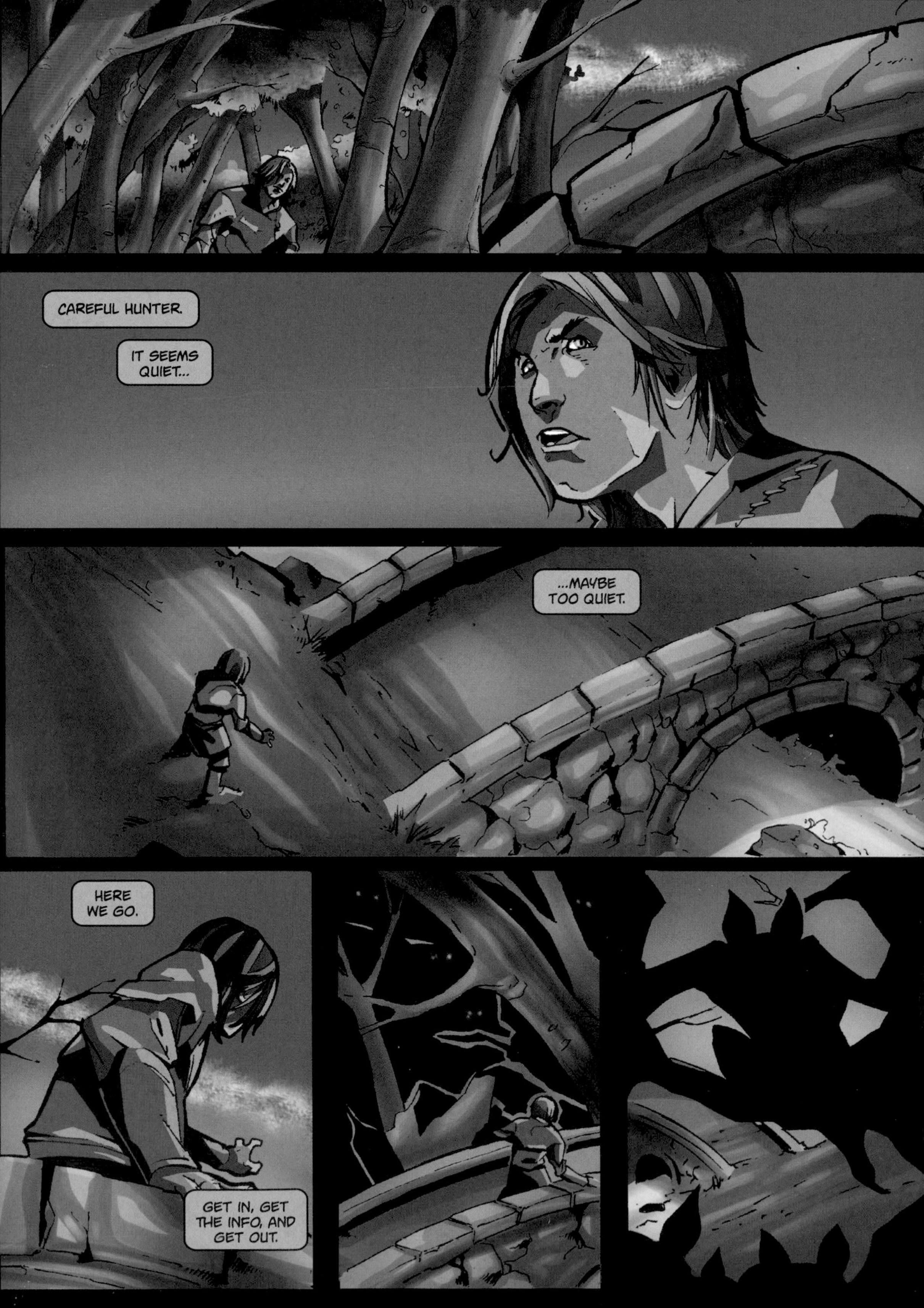

CAREFUL HUNTER.
IT SEEMS QUIET...
...MAYBE TOO QUIET.
HERE WE GO.
GET IN, GET THE INFO, AND GET OUT.

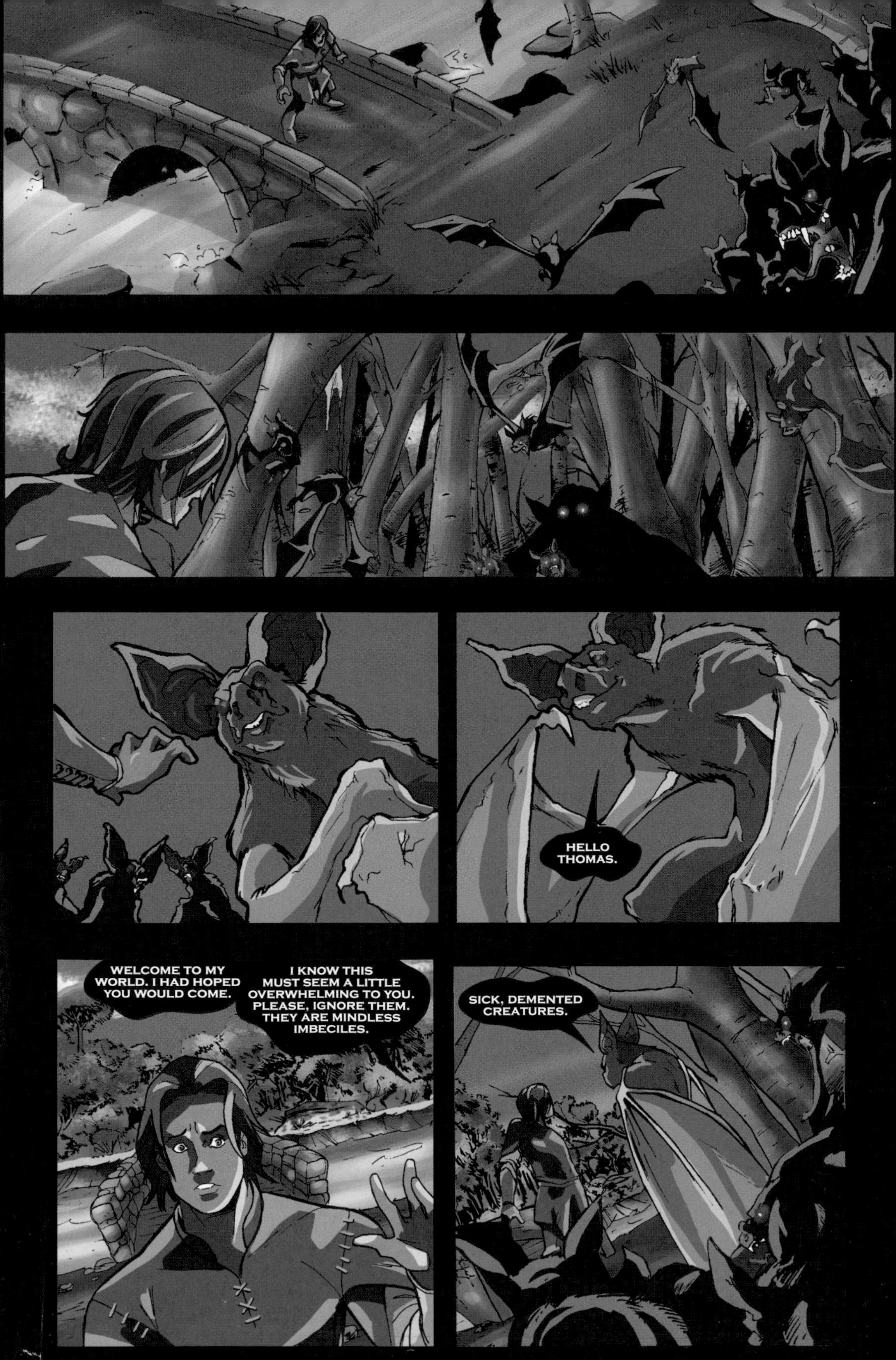
HELLO THOMAS.
WELCOME TO MY WORLD. I HAD HOPED YOU WOULD COME.
I KNOW THIS MUST SEEM A LITTLE OVERWHELMING TO YOU. PLEASE, IGNORE THEM. THEY ARE MINDLESS IMBECILES.
SICK, DEMENTED CREATURES.

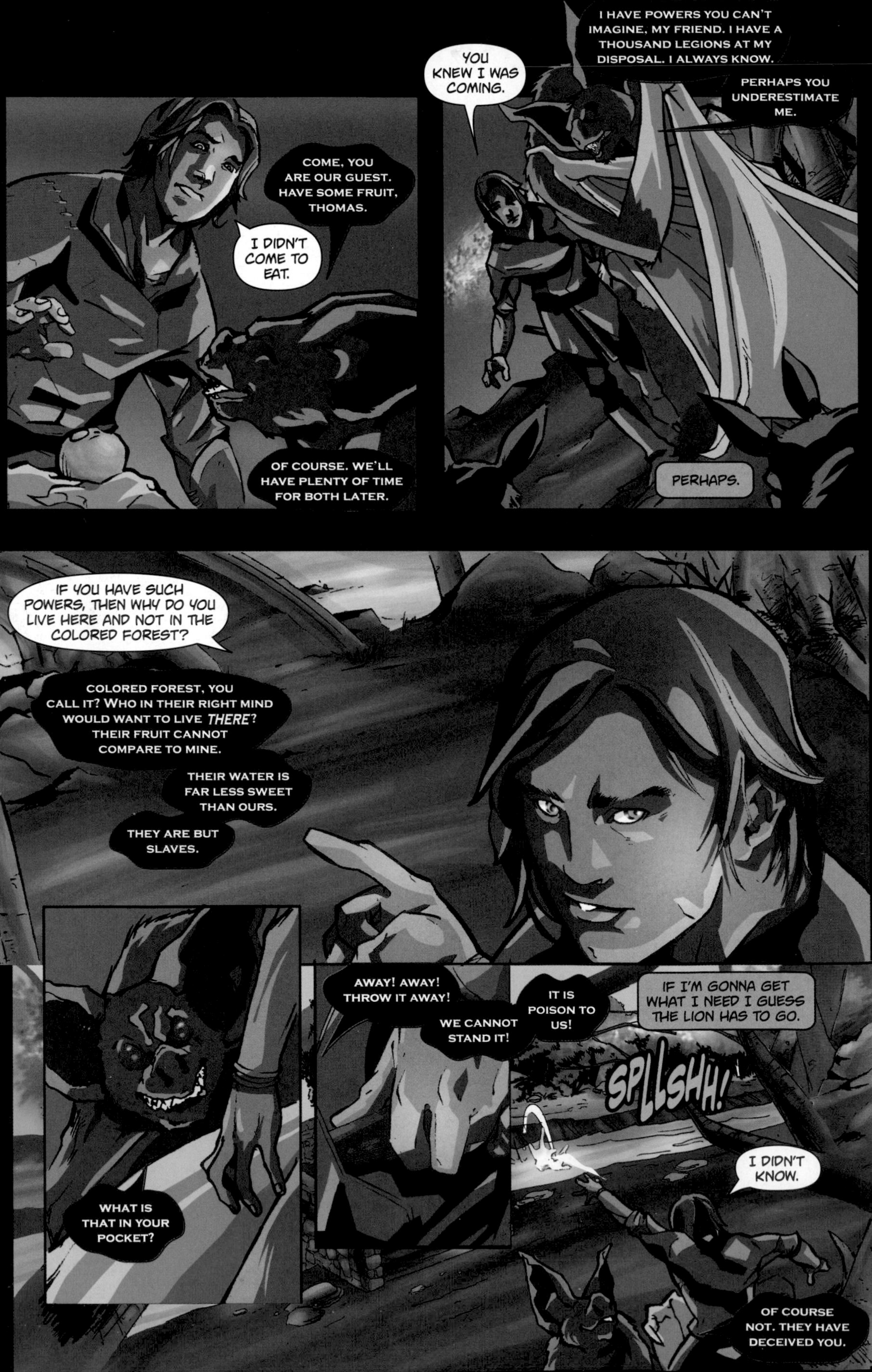
COME, YOU ARE OUR GUEST. HAVE SOME FRUIT, THOMAS.
I DIDN'T COME TO EAT.
OF COURSE. WE'LL HAVE PLENTY OF TIME FOR BOTH LATER.
YOU KNEW I WAS COMING.
I HAVE POWERS YOU CAN'T IMAGINE, MY FRIEND. I HAVE A THOUSAND LEGIONS AT MY DISPOSAL. I ALWAYS KNOW.
PERHAPS YOU UNDERESTIMATE ME.
PERHAPS.
IF YOU HAVE SUCH POWERS, THEN WHY DO YOU LIVE HERE AND NOT IN THE COLORED FOREST?
COLORED FOREST, YOU CALL IT? WHO IN THEIR RIGHT MIND WOULD WANT TO LIVE *THERE*? THEIR FRUIT CANNOT COMPARE TO MINE.
THEIR WATER IS FAR LESS SWEET THAN OURS.
THEY ARE BUT SLAVES.
WHAT IS THAT IN YOUR POCKET?
AWAY! AWAY! THROW IT AWAY!
WE CANNOT STAND IT!
IT IS POISON TO US!
IF I'M GONNA GET WHAT I NEED I GUESS THE LION HAS TO GO.
SPLLSHH!
I DIDN'T KNOW.
OF COURSE NOT. THEY HAVE DECEIVED YOU.

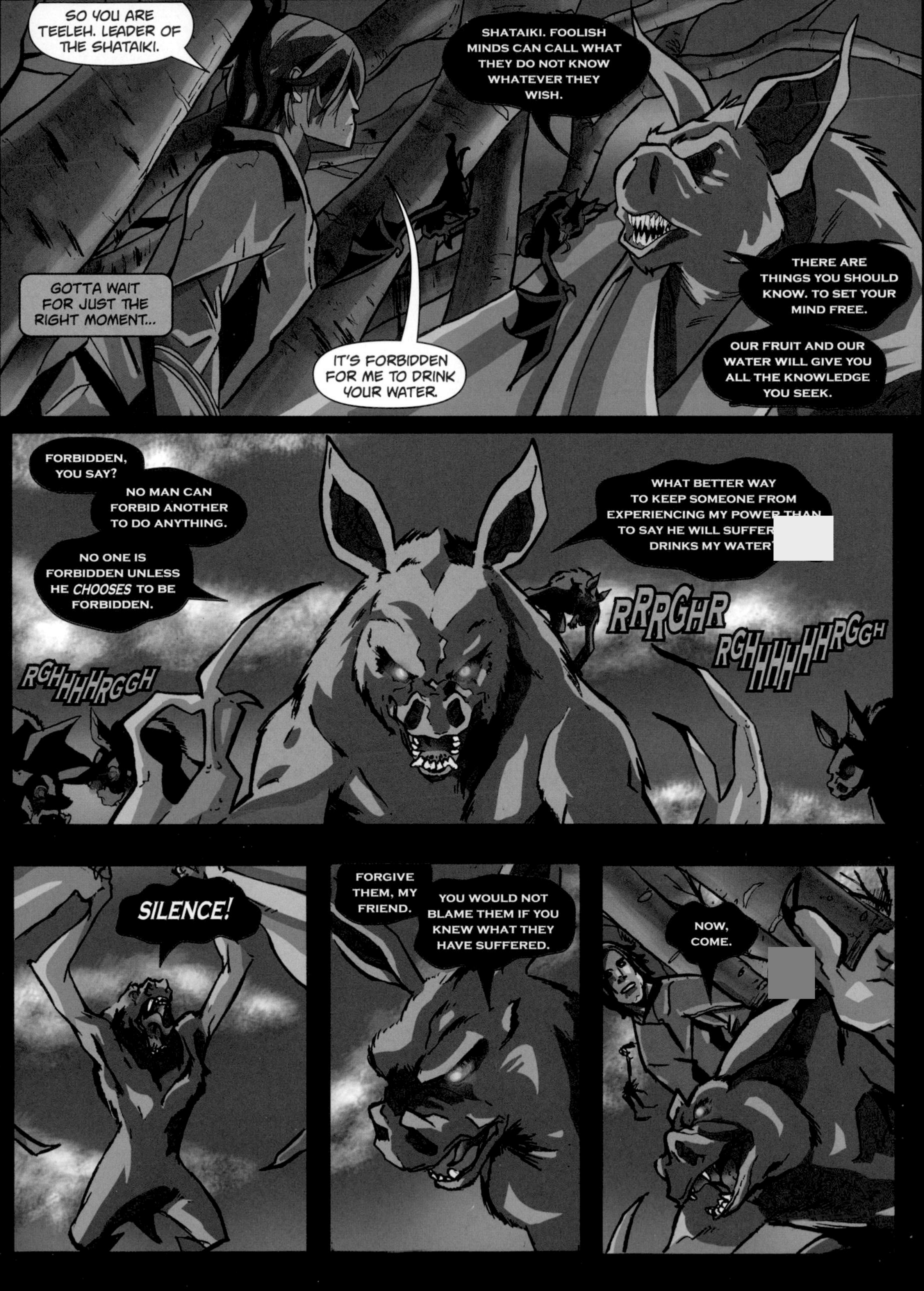
SO YOU ARE TEELEH. LEADER OF THE SHATAIKI.
SHATAIKI. FOOLISH MINDS CAN CALL WHAT THEY DO NOT KNOW WHATEVER THEY WISH.
GOTTA WAIT FOR JUST THE RIGHT MOMENT...
IT'S FORBIDDEN FOR ME TO DRINK YOUR WATER.
THERE ARE THINGS YOU SHOULD KNOW. TO SET YOUR MIND FREE.
OUR FRUIT AND OUR WATER WILL GIVE YOU ALL THE KNOWLEDGE YOU SEEK.
FORBIDDEN, YOU SAY?
NO MAN CAN FORBID ANOTHER TO DO ANYTHING.
NO ONE IS FORBIDDEN UNLESS HE *CHOOSES* TO BE FORBIDDEN.
WHAT BETTER WAY TO KEEP SOMEONE FROM EXPERIENCING MY POWER THAN TO SAY HE WILL SUFFER DRINKS MY WATER?
RRRGHR
RGHHHHHHRGGH
RGHHHHRGGH
SILENCE!
FORGIVE THEM, MY FRIEND.
YOU WOULD NOT BLAME THEM IF YOU KNEW WHAT THEY HAVE SUFFERED.
NOW, COME.

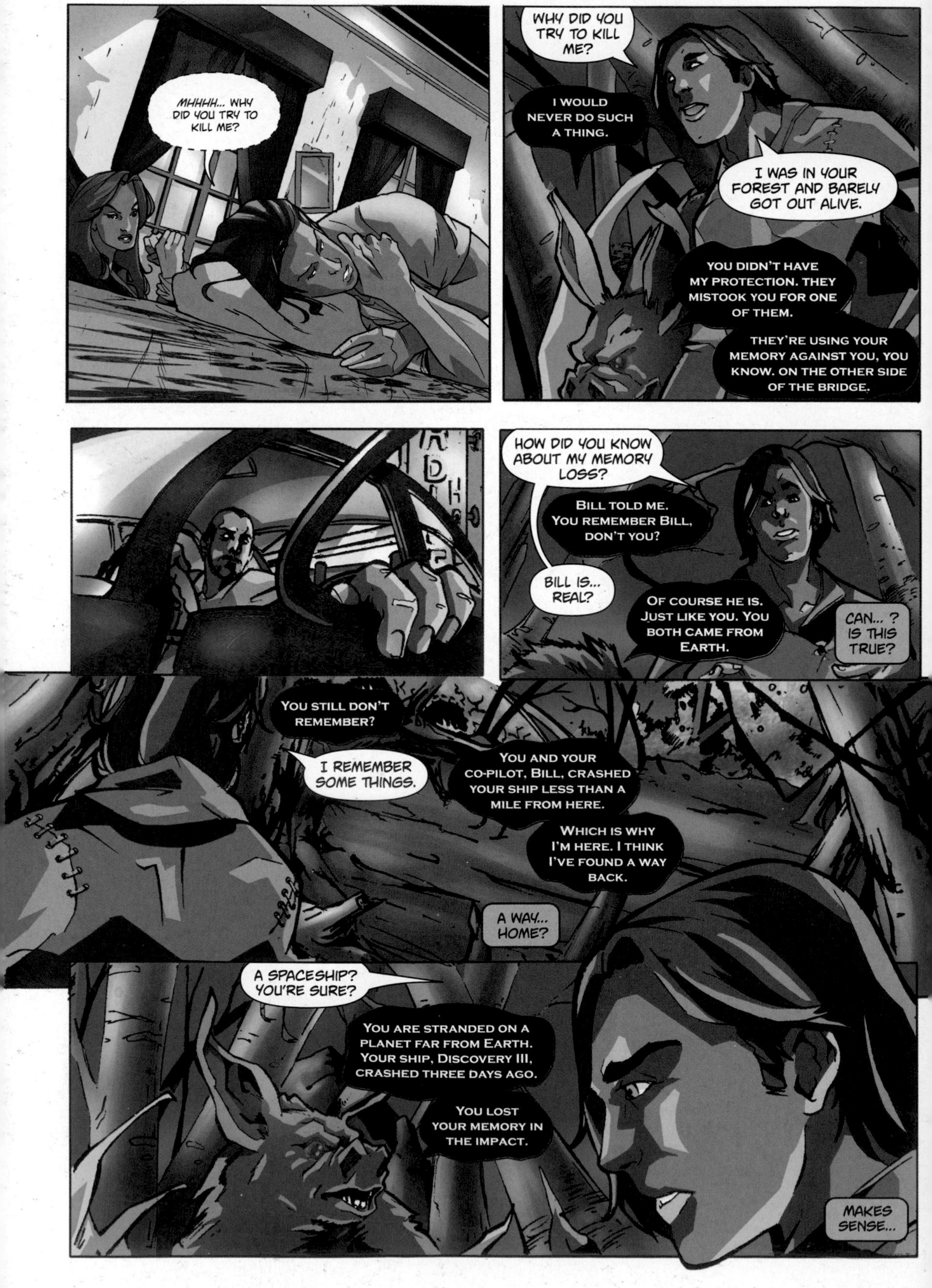
MHHHH... WHY DID YOU TRY TO KILL ME?
WHY DID YOU TRY TO KILL ME?
I WOULD NEVER DO SUCH A THING.
I WAS IN YOUR FOREST AND BARELY GOT OUT ALIVE.
YOU DIDN'T HAVE MY PROTECTION. THEY MISTOOK YOU FOR ONE OF THEM.
THEY'RE USING YOUR MEMORY AGAINST YOU, YOU KNOW. ON THE OTHER SIDE OF THE BRIDGE.
HOW DID YOU KNOW ABOUT MY MEMORY LOSS?
BILL TOLD ME. YOU REMEMBER BILL, DON'T YOU?
BILL IS... REAL?
OF COURSE HE IS. JUST LIKE YOU. YOU BOTH CAME FROM EARTH.
CAN... ? IS THIS TRUE?
YOU STILL DON'T REMEMBER?
I REMEMBER SOME THINGS.
YOU AND YOUR CO-PILOT, BILL, CRASHED YOUR SHIP LESS THAN A MILE FROM HERE.
WHICH IS WHY I'M HERE. I THINK I'VE FOUND A WAY BACK.
A WAY... HOME?
A SPACESHIP? YOU'RE SURE?
YOU ARE STRANDED ON A PLANET FAR FROM EARTH. YOUR SHIP, DISCOVERY III, CRASHED THREE DAYS AGO.
YOU LOST YOUR MEMORY IN THE IMPACT.
MAKES SENSE...

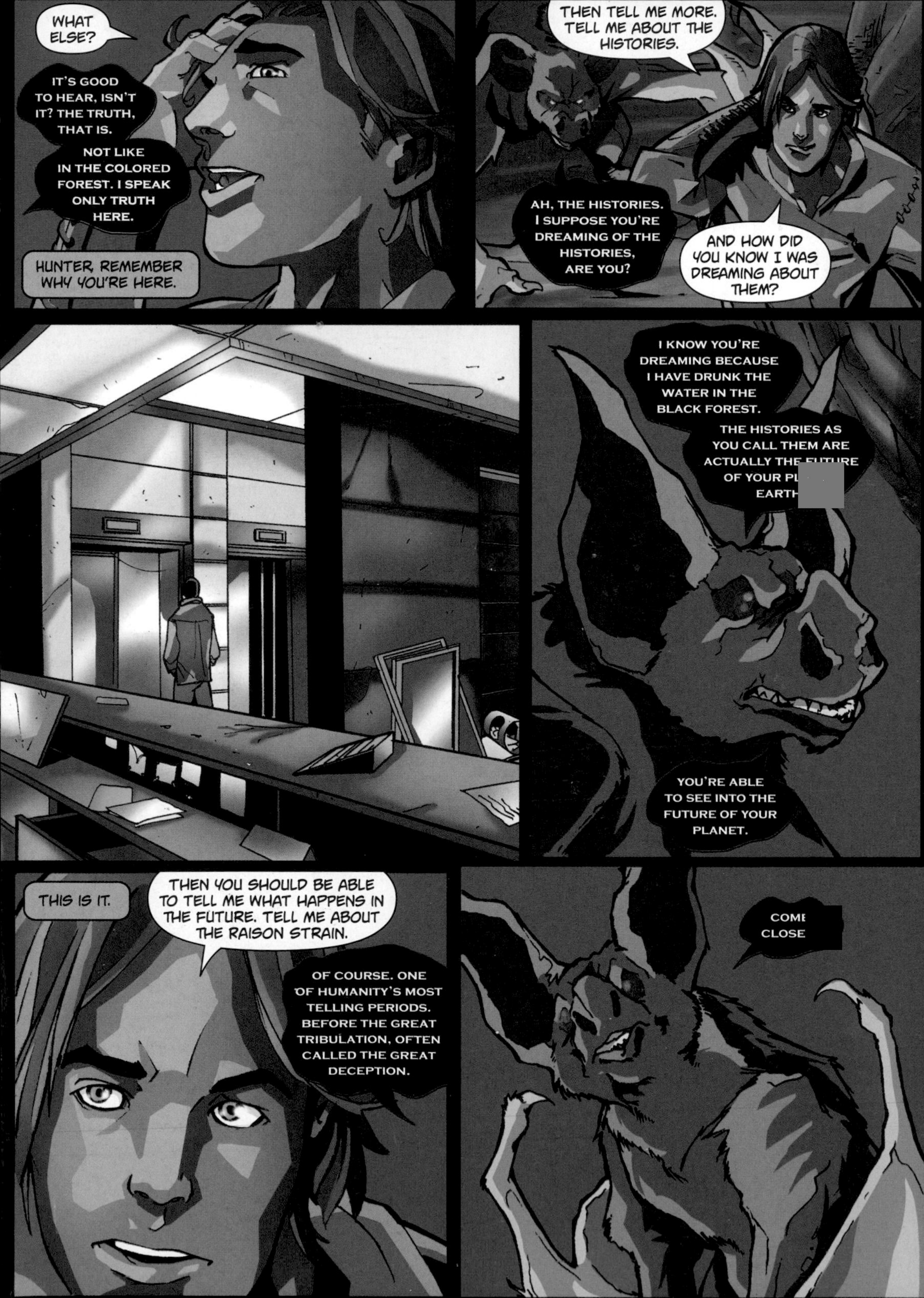
WHAT ELSE?
IT'S GOOD TO HEAR, ISN'T IT? THE TRUTH, THAT IS.
NOT LIKE IN THE COLORED FOREST. I SPEAK ONLY TRUTH HERE.
HUNTER, REMEMBER WHY YOU'RE HERE.
THEN TELL ME MORE. TELL ME ABOUT THE HISTORIES.
AH, THE HISTORIES. I SUPPOSE YOU'RE DREAMING OF THE HISTORIES, ARE YOU?
AND HOW DID YOU KNOW I WAS DREAMING ABOUT THEM?
I KNOW YOU'RE DREAMING BECAUSE I HAVE DRUNK THE WATER IN THE BLACK FOREST.
THE HISTORIES AS YOU CALL THEM ARE ACTUALLY THE FUTURE OF YOUR PL[redacted] EARTH[redacted]
YOU'RE ABLE TO SEE INTO THE FUTURE OF YOUR PLANET.
THIS IS IT.
THEN YOU SHOULD BE ABLE TO TELL ME WHAT HAPPENS IN THE FUTURE. TELL ME ABOUT THE RAISON STRAIN.
OF COURSE. ONE OF HUMANITY'S MOST TELLING PERIODS. BEFORE THE GREAT TRIBULATION, OFTEN CALLED THE GREAT DECEPTION.
COME[redacted] CLOSE[redacted]

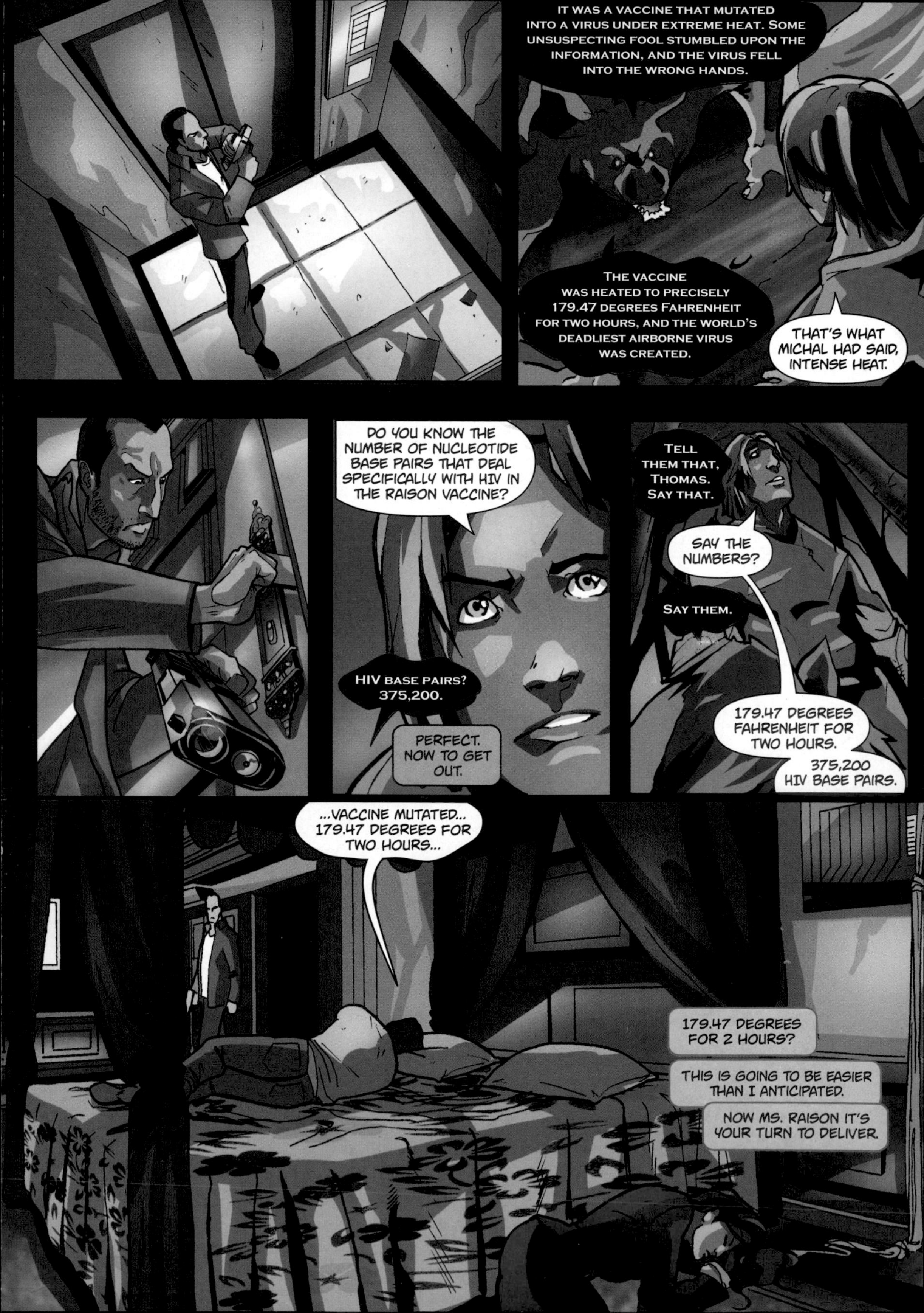
IT WAS A VACCINE THAT MUTATED INTO A VIRUS UNDER EXTREME HEAT. SOME UNSUSPECTING FOOL STUMBLED UPON THE INFORMATION, AND THE VIRUS FELL INTO THE WRONG HANDS.
THE VACCINE WAS HEATED TO PRECISELY 179.47 DEGREES FAHRENHEIT FOR TWO HOURS, AND THE WORLD'S DEADLIEST AIRBORNE VIRUS WAS CREATED.
THAT'S WHAT MICHAL HAD SAID, INTENSE HEAT.
DO YOU KNOW THE NUMBER OF NUCLEOTIDE BASE PAIRS THAT DEAL SPECIFICALLY WITH HIV IN THE RAISON VACCINE?
HIV BASE PAIRS? 375,200.
PERFECT. NOW TO GET OUT.
TELL THEM THAT, THOMAS. SAY THAT.
SAY THE NUMBERS?
SAY THEM.
179.47 DEGREES FAHRENHEIT FOR TWO HOURS.
375,200 HIV BASE PAIRS.
...VACCINE MUTATED... 179.47 DEGREES FOR TWO HOURS...
179.47 DEGREES FOR 2 HOURS?
THIS IS GOING TO BE EASIER THAN I ANTICIPATED.
NOW MS. RAISON IT'S YOUR TURN TO DELIVER.

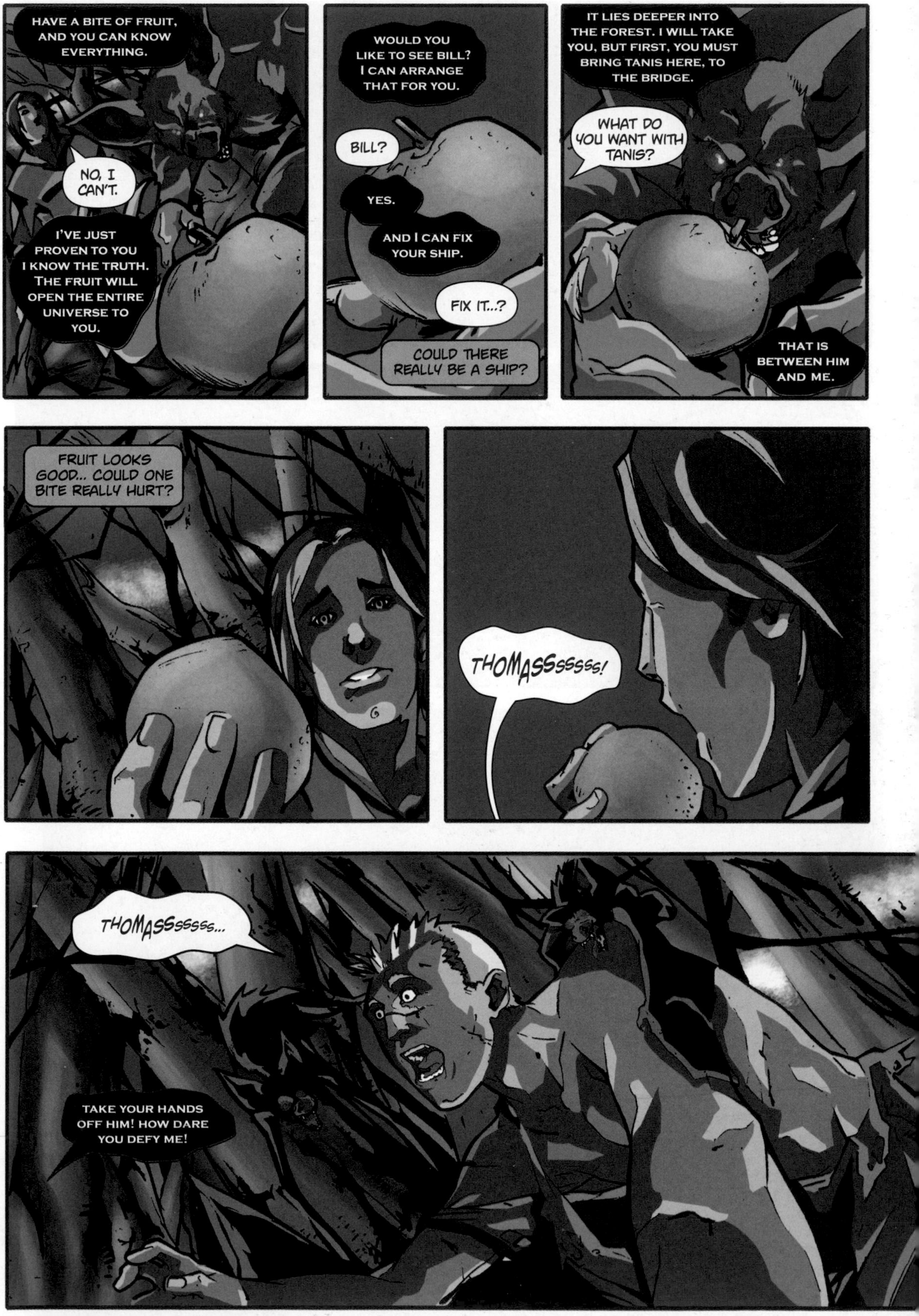
HAVE A BITE OF FRUIT, AND YOU CAN KNOW EVERYTHING.
NO, I CAN'T.
I'VE JUST PROVEN TO YOU I KNOW THE TRUTH. THE FRUIT WILL OPEN THE ENTIRE UNIVERSE TO YOU.
WOULD YOU LIKE TO SEE BILL? I CAN ARRANGE THAT FOR YOU.
BILL?
YES.
AND I CAN FIX YOUR SHIP.
FIX IT...?
COULD THERE REALLY BE A SHIP?
IT LIES DEEPER INTO THE FOREST. I WILL TAKE YOU, BUT FIRST, YOU MUST BRING TANIS HERE, TO THE BRIDGE.
WHAT DO YOU WANT WITH TANIS?
THAT IS BETWEEN HIM AND ME.
FRUIT LOOKS GOOD... COULD ONE BITE REALLY HURT?
THOMASSsssss!
THOMASSsssss...
TAKE YOUR HANDS OFF HIM! HOW DARE YOU DEFY ME!

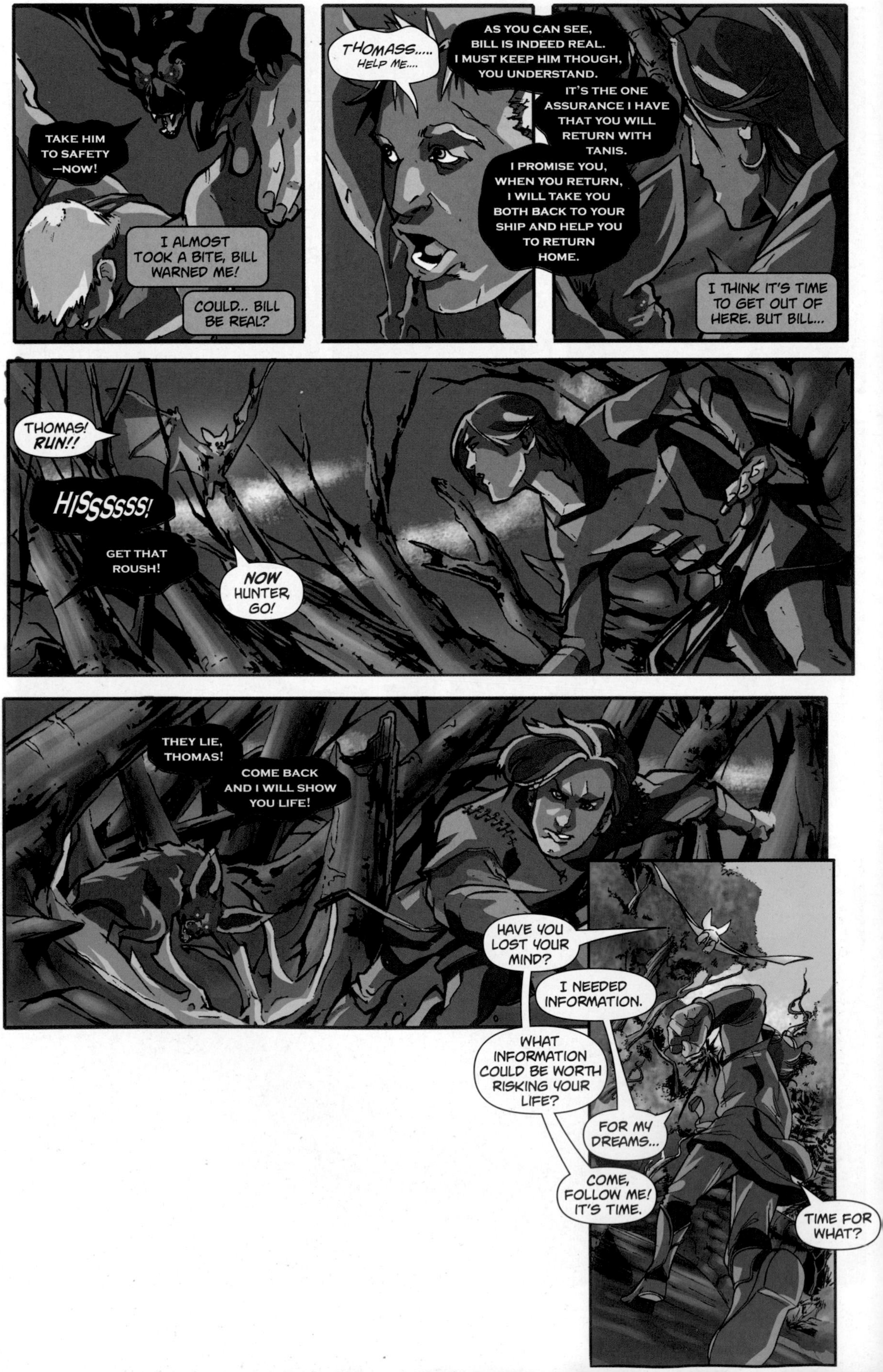
TAKE HIM TO SAFETY —NOW!
I ALMOST TOOK A BITE, BILL WARNED ME!
COULD... BILL BE REAL?
THOMASS..... HELP ME....
AS YOU CAN SEE, BILL IS INDEED REAL. I MUST KEEP HIM THOUGH, YOU UNDERSTAND.
IT'S THE ONE ASSURANCE I HAVE THAT YOU WILL RETURN WITH TANIS.
I PROMISE YOU, WHEN YOU RETURN, I WILL TAKE YOU BOTH BACK TO YOUR SHIP AND HELP YOU TO RETURN HOME.
I THINK IT'S TIME TO GET OUT OF HERE. BUT BILL...
THOMAS! RUN!!
HISSSSSS!
GET THAT ROUSH!
NOW HUNTER, GO!
THEY LIE, THOMAS!
COME BACK AND I WILL SHOW YOU LIFE!
HAVE YOU LOST YOUR MIND?
I NEEDED INFORMATION.
WHAT INFORMATION COULD BE WORTH RISKING YOUR LIFE?
FOR MY DREAMS...
COME, FOLLOW ME! IT'S TIME.
TIME FOR WHAT?

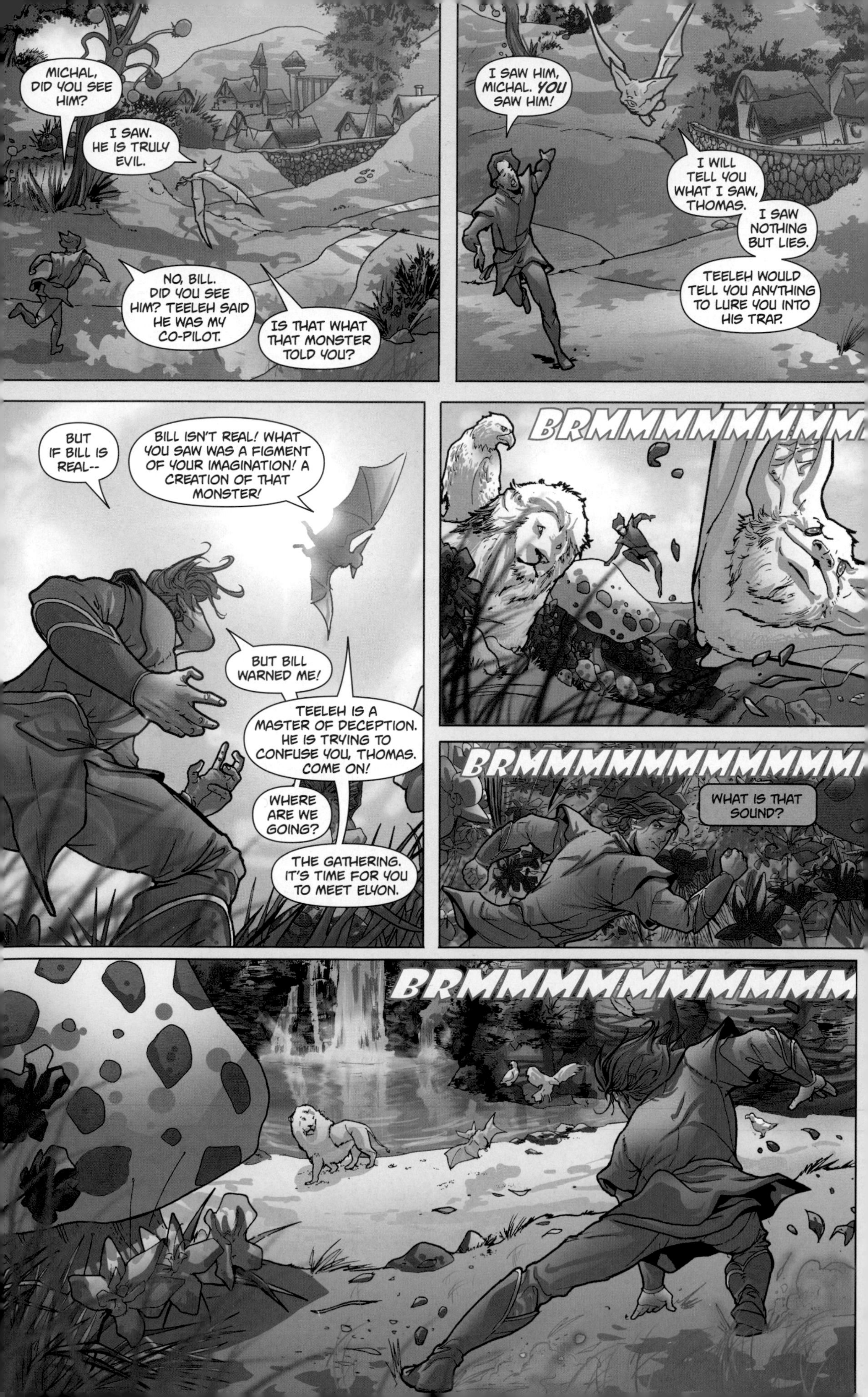
MICHAL, DID YOU SEE HIM?
I SAW. HE IS TRULY EVIL.
NO, BILL. DID YOU SEE HIM? TEELEH SAID HE WAS MY CO-PILOT.
IS THAT WHAT THAT MONSTER TOLD YOU?
I SAW HIM, MICHAL. YOU SAW HIM!
I WILL TELL YOU WHAT I SAW, THOMAS.
I SAW NOTHING BUT LIES.
TEELEH WOULD TELL YOU ANYTHING TO LURE YOU INTO HIS TRAP.
BUT IF BILL IS REAL--
BILL ISN'T REAL! WHAT YOU SAW WAS A FIGMENT OF YOUR IMAGINATION! A CREATION OF THAT MONSTER!
BUT BILL WARNED ME!
TEELEH IS A MASTER OF DECEPTION. HE IS TRYING TO CONFUSE YOU, THOMAS. COME ON!
WHERE ARE WE GOING?
THE GATHERING. IT'S TIME FOR YOU TO MEET ELYON.
BRMMMMMMMMMM
BRMMMMMMMMMMMM
WHAT IS THAT SOUND?
BRMMMMMMMMMMMM

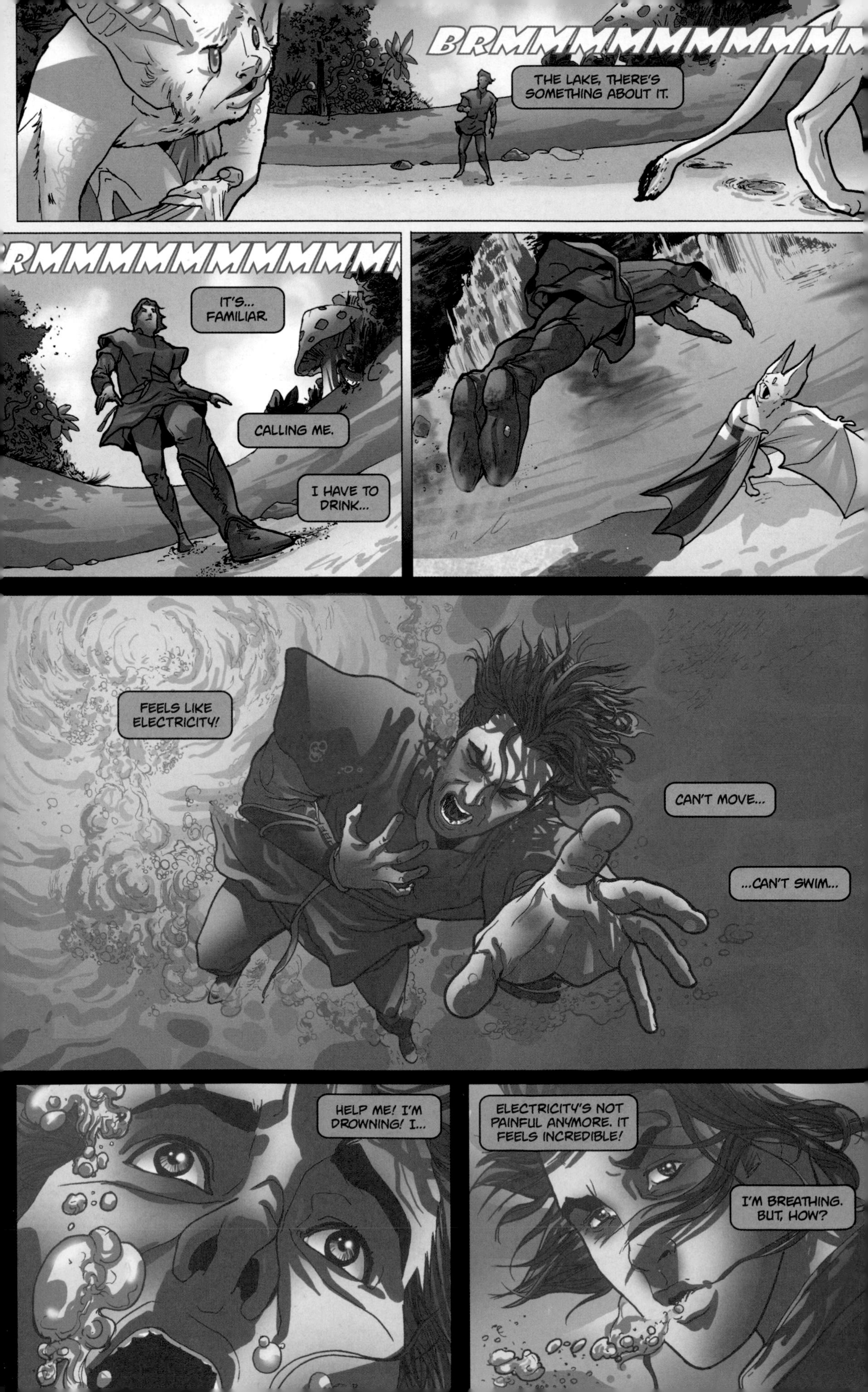
BRMMMMMMMMMMM
THE LAKE, THERE'S SOMETHING ABOUT IT.
RMMMMMMMMMMMM
IT'S... FAMILIAR.
CALLING ME.
I HAVE TO DRINK...
FEELS LIKE ELECTRICITY!
CAN'T MOVE...
...CAN'T SWIM...
HELP ME! I'M DROWNING! I...
ELECTRICITY'S NOT PAINFUL ANYMORE. IT FEELS INCREDIBLE!
I'M BREATHING. BUT, HOW?

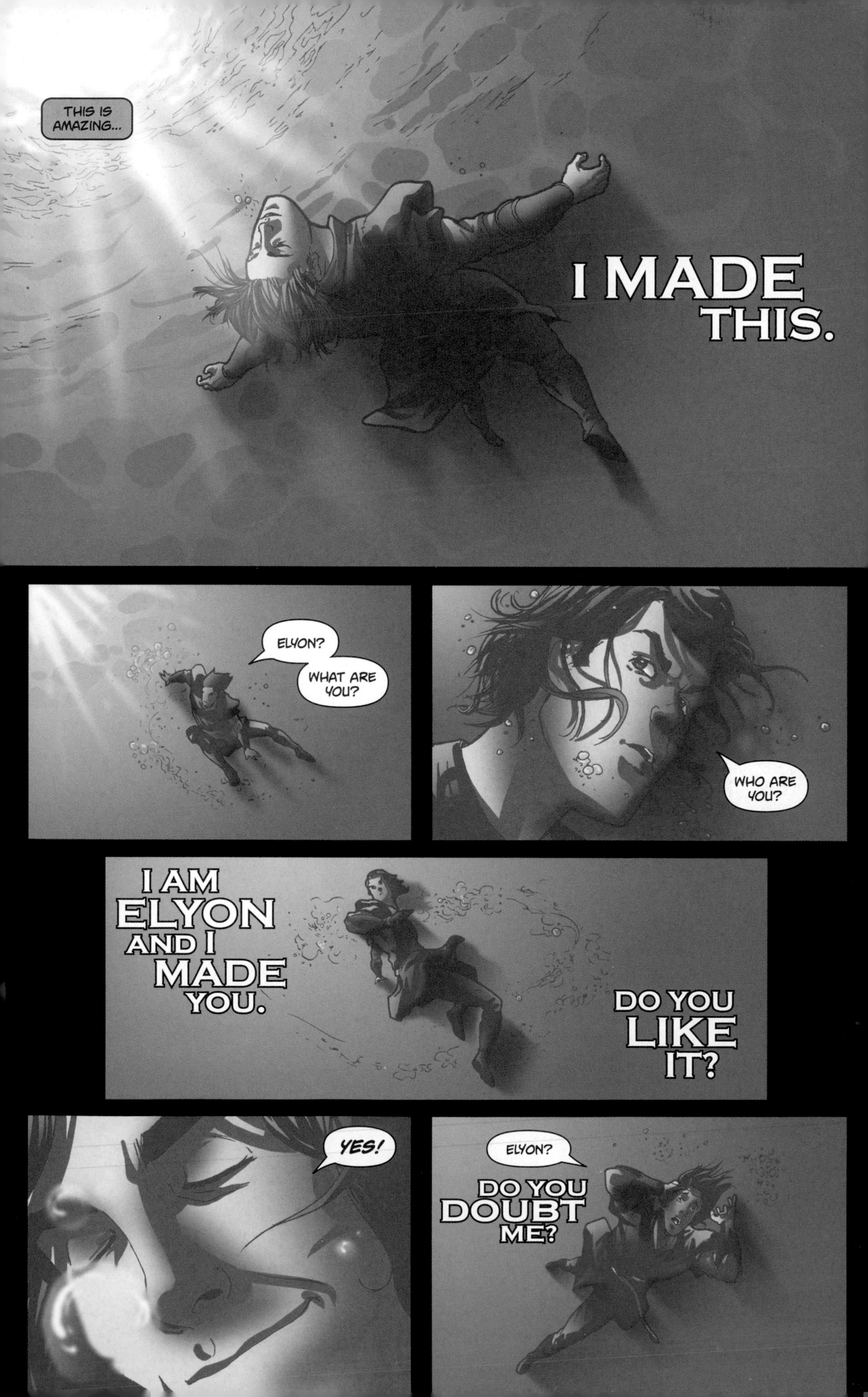
THIS IS AMAZING...
I MADE THIS.
ELYON?
WHAT ARE YOU?
WHO ARE YOU?
I AM ELYON AND I MADE YOU.
DO YOU LIKE IT?
YES!
ELYON?
DO YOU DOUBT ME?

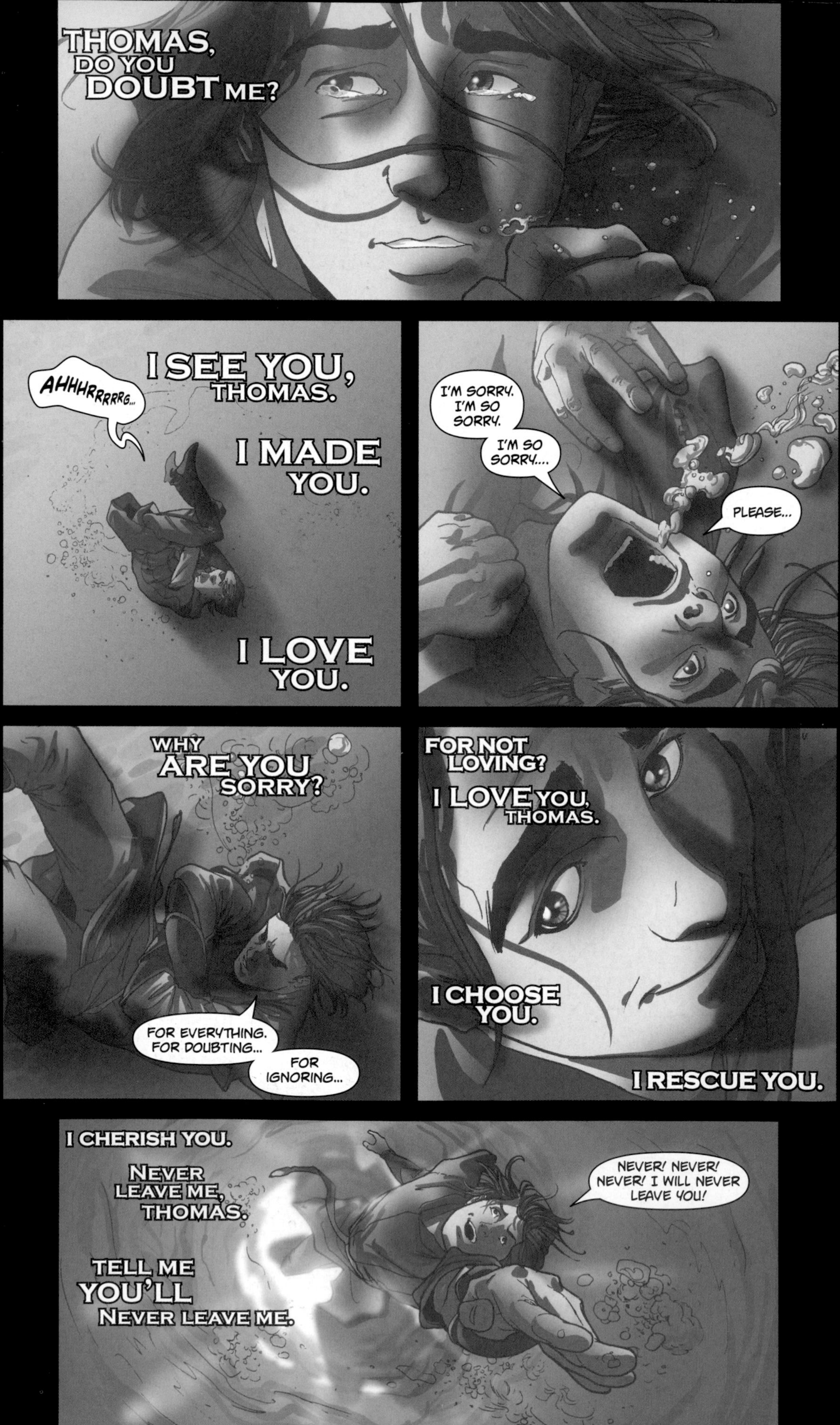
THOMAS, DO YOU DOUBT ME?
AHHHRRRRRG...
I SEE YOU, THOMAS.
I MADE YOU.
I LOVE YOU.
I'M SORRY. I'M SO SORRY.
I'M SO SORRY....
PLEASE...
WHY ARE YOU SORRY?
FOR EVERYTHING. FOR DOUBTING...
FOR IGNORING...
FOR NOT LOVING?
I LOVE YOU, THOMAS.
I CHOOSE YOU.
I RESCUE YOU.
I CHERISH YOU.
NEVER LEAVE ME, THOMAS.
TELL ME YOU'LL NEVER LEAVE ME.
NEVER! NEVER! NEVER! I WILL NEVER LEAVE YOU!

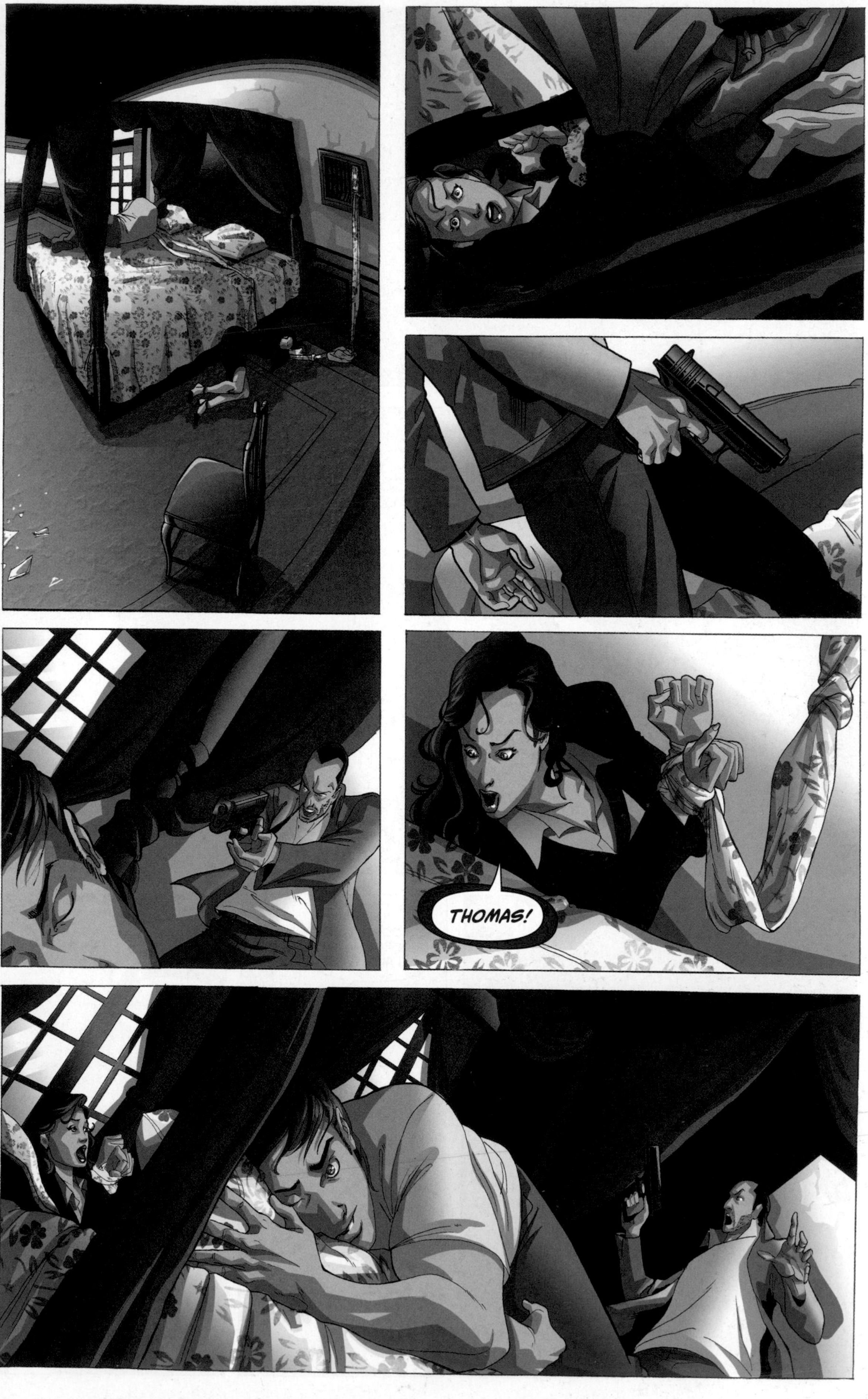
THOMAS!

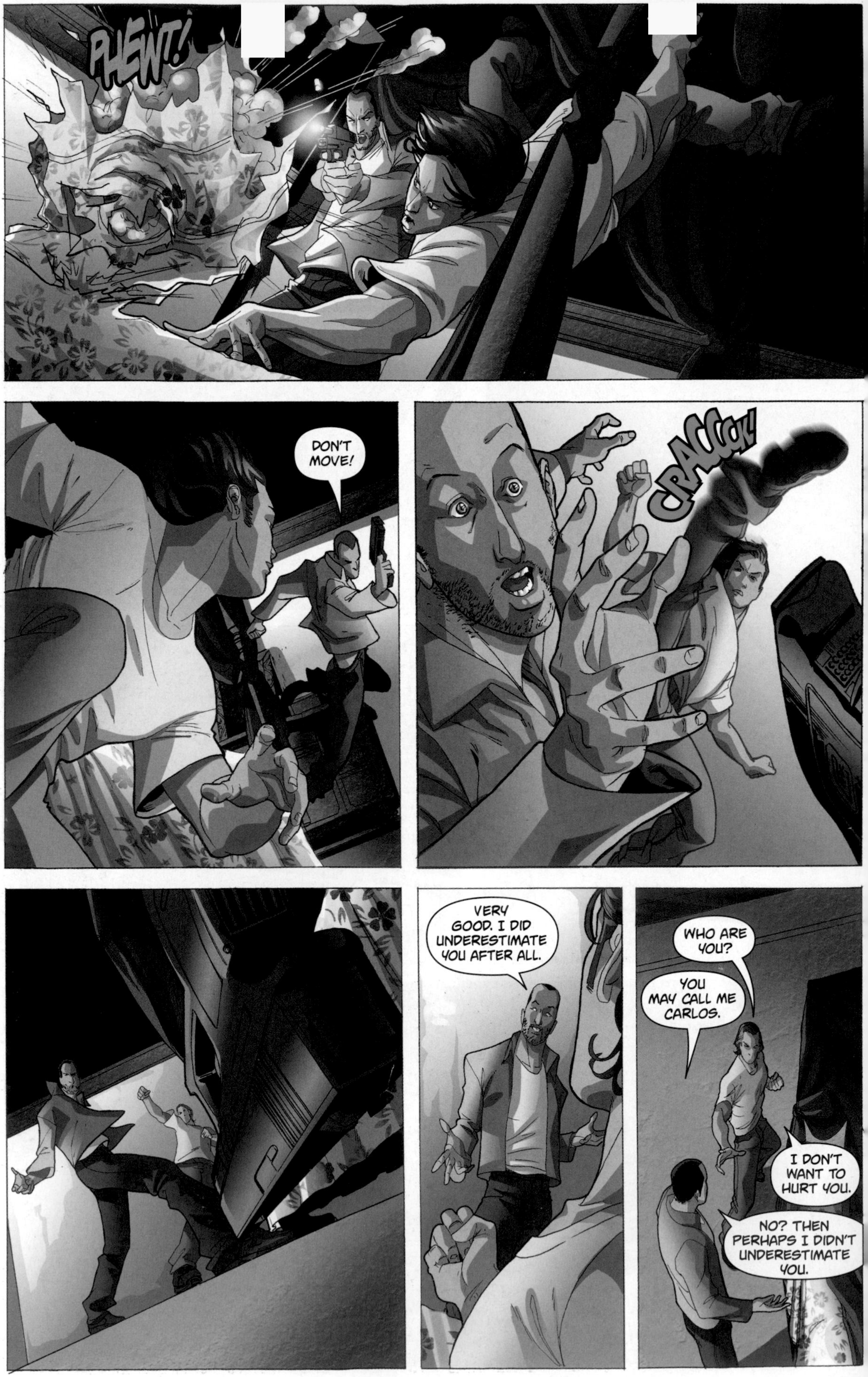
PHEWT!
DON'T MOVE!
CRACCK!
VERY GOOD. I DID UNDERESTIMATE YOU AFTER ALL.
WHO ARE YOU?
YOU MAY CALL ME CARLOS.
I DON'T WANT TO HURT YOU.
NO? THEN PERHAPS I DIDN'T UNDERESTIMATE YOU.

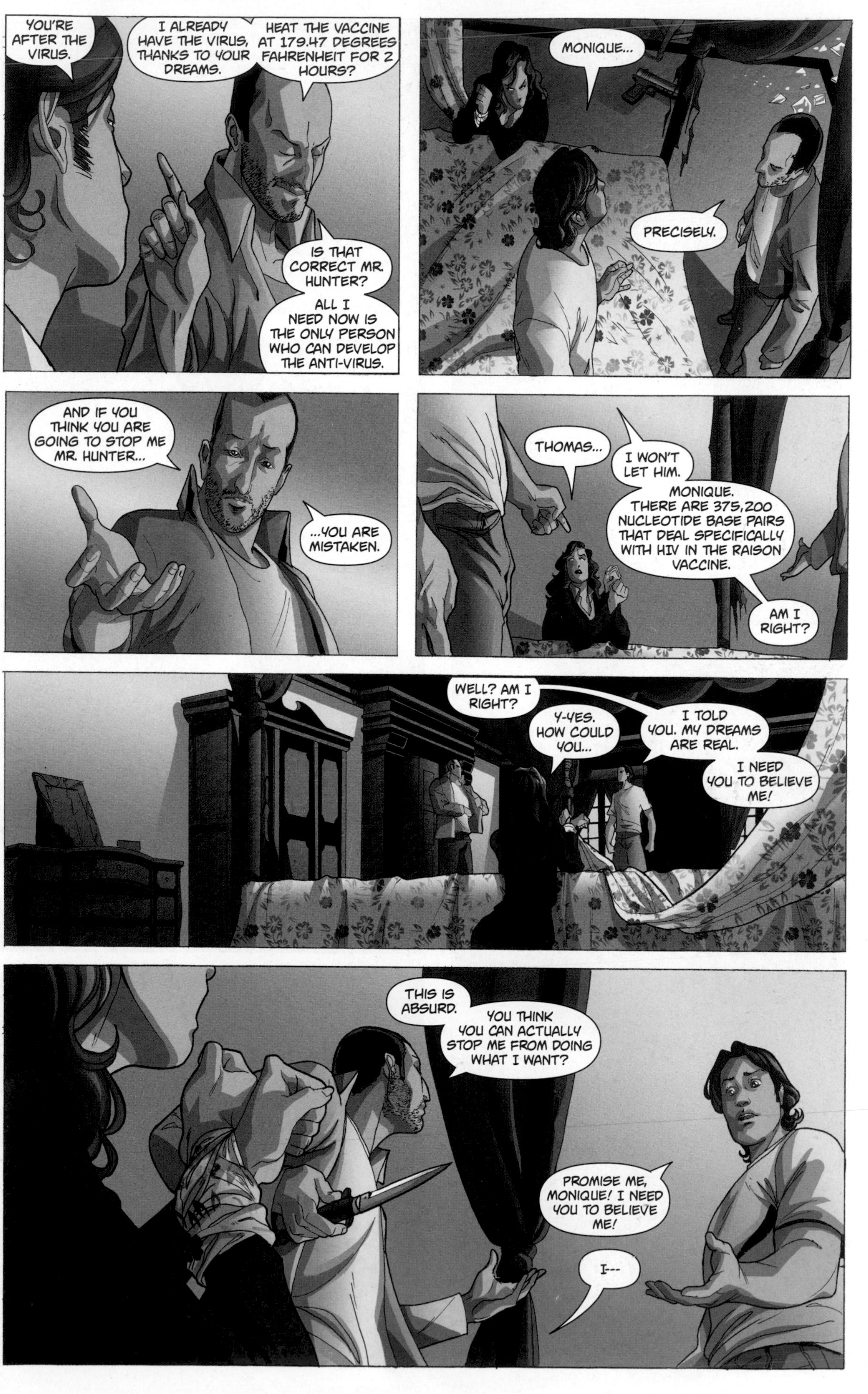
YOU'RE AFTER THE VIRUS.
I ALREADY HAVE THE VIRUS, THANKS TO YOUR DREAMS.
HEAT THE VACCINE AT 179.47 DEGREES FAHRENHEIT FOR 2 HOURS?
IS THAT CORRECT MR. HUNTER?
ALL I NEED NOW IS THE ONLY PERSON WHO CAN DEVELOP THE ANTI-VIRUS.
MONIQUE...
PRECISELY.
AND IF YOU THINK YOU ARE GOING TO STOP ME MR. HUNTER...
...YOU ARE MISTAKEN.
THOMAS...
I WON'T LET HIM.
MONIQUE. THERE ARE 375,200 NUCLEOTIDE BASE PAIRS THAT DEAL SPECIFICALLY WITH HIV IN THE RAISON VACCINE.
AM I RIGHT?
WELL? AM I RIGHT?
Y-YES. HOW COULD YOU...
I TOLD YOU. MY DREAMS ARE REAL.
I NEED YOU TO BELIEVE ME!
THIS IS ABSURD.
YOU THINK YOU CAN ACTUALLY STOP ME FROM DOING WHAT I WANT?
PROMISE ME, MONIQUE! I NEED YOU TO BELIEVE ME!
I---

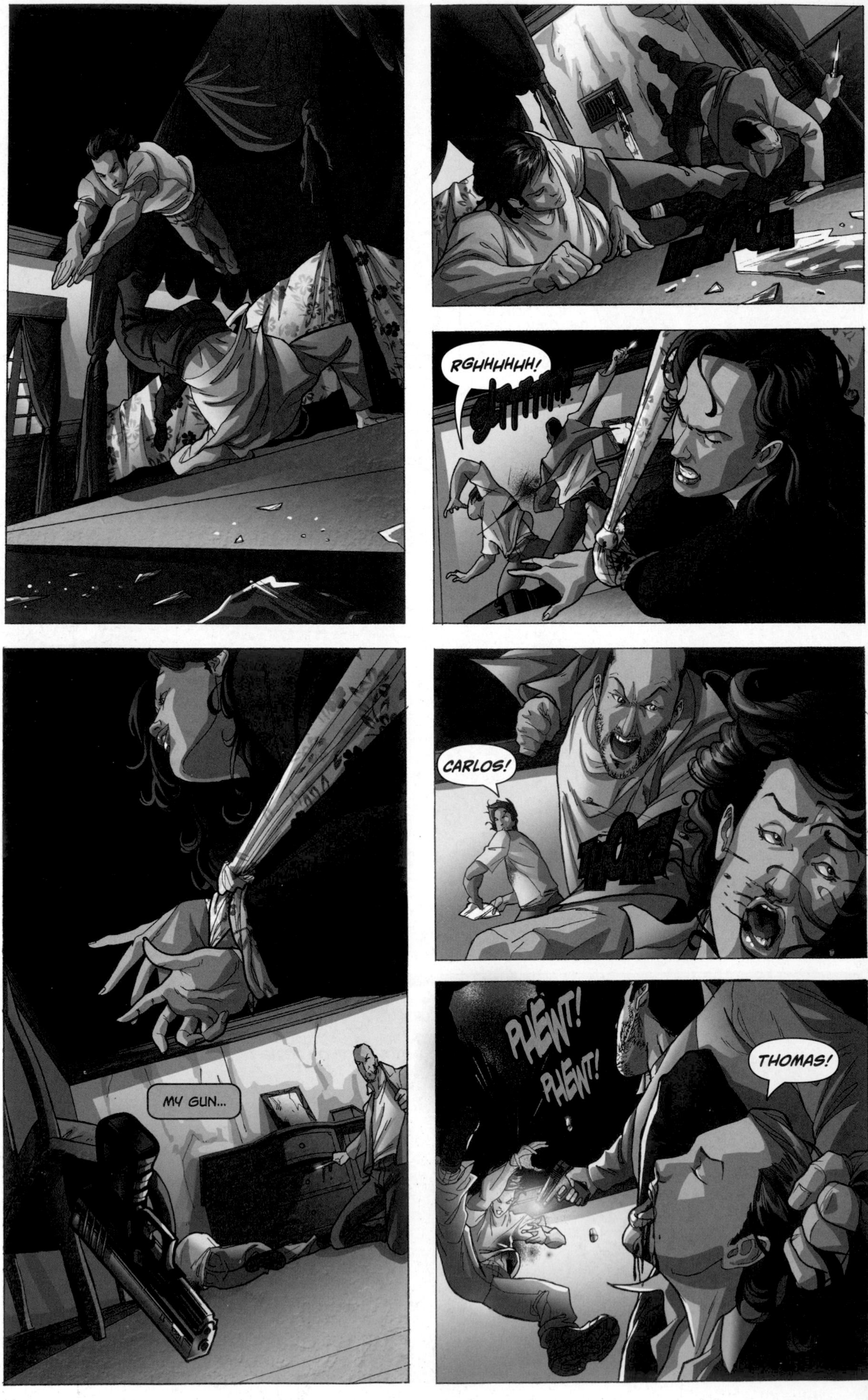
RGHHHHHH!
MY GUN...
CARLOS!
PHEWT!
PHEWT!
THOMAS!

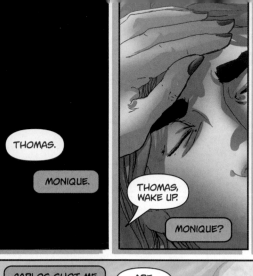

THOMAS.

MONIQUE.

THOMAS, WAKE UP.

MONIQUE?

THOMAS?

CARLOS!

YOU'VE BEEN DREAMING...

WHAA...

CARLOS SHOT ME TWICE. THE WATER HEALED ME

ARE YOU OK?

I THINK SO... WHERE IS EVERYONE?

THEY ARE PREPARING.

PREPARING FOR WHAT?

FOR THE GATHERING.

YOU STILL DON'T REMEMBER.

I REMEMBER THE GREAT ROMANCE.

IT'S ABOUT CHOOSING, RESCUING AND WINNING LOVE BECAUSE THAT'S WHAT ELYON DOES.

YES!

AND IT'S SOMETHING WE DO BECAUSE WE ARE LIKE ELYON THAT WAY.

AND NOW THAT YOU UNDERSTAND...

YOU'RE SAYING THAT YOU WANT TO CHOOSE ME.

I AM?

YES. YOU'RE DESPERATE FOR MY LOVE, AND YOU WANT ME TO BE DESPERATE FOR YOUR LOVE.

SHE'S RIGHT.

BUT SHOULDN'T I BE THE ONE WOOING HER?

COME. LET'S WALK, AND REMEMBER MORE.

TELL ME ABOUT YOUR DREAMS.

HOW REAL ARE THEY?

REAL ENOUGH. BUT THEY ARE THE HISTORIES. A TOTALLY DIFFERENT REALITY.

SO IT'S LIKE YOU'RE REALLY LIVING THERE?

YES.

AND WHAT DO YOU THINK OF THIS PLACE IN YOUR DREAMS?

I WISH SHE HADN'T ASKED THAT...

ACTUALLY, WHEN I'M DREAMING, IT'S LIKE I'M THERE, NOT HERE.

SO I'M LIKE A DREAM?

YOU'RE NOT A DREAM. YOU'RE WALKING RIGHT BESIDE ME, AND I HAVE CHOSEN YOU.

I'M NOT SURE I LIKE THESE DREAMS OF YOURS.

I'M NOT SURE I DO EITHER.

BUT I'M HAVING THEM, I'M LIVING JUST BEFORE THE GREAT DECEPTION, TRYING TO STOP THE RAISON STRAIN.

IT'S SO REAL!

JUST BEFORE YOU WOKE ME, I WAS FIGHTING A MAN WITH A GUN.

A GUN? A WEAPON, I ASSUME. AND WHAT WERE YOU FIGHTING ABOUT?

HE WAS TRYING TO CAPTURE MONIQUE.

MONIQUE?

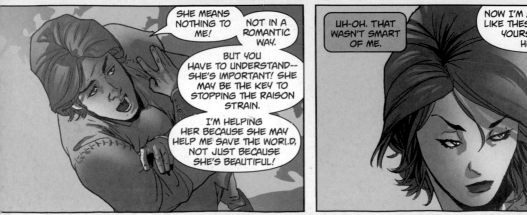

SHE MEANS NOTHING TO ME! NOT IN A ROMANTIC WAY.

BUT YOU HAVE TO UNDERSTAND-- SHE'S IMPORTANT! SHE MAY BE THE KEY TO STOPPING THE RAISON STRAIN.

I'M HELPING HER BECAUSE SHE MAY HELP ME SAVE THE WORLD, NOT JUST BECAUSE SHE'S BEAUTIFUL!

UH-OH. THAT WASN'T SMART OF ME.

NOW I'M SURE I DON'T LIKE THESE DREAMS OF YOURS, THOMAS HUNTER.

FROM NOW ON WHEN YOU DREAM, DREAM OF ME.

NOW COME ON...

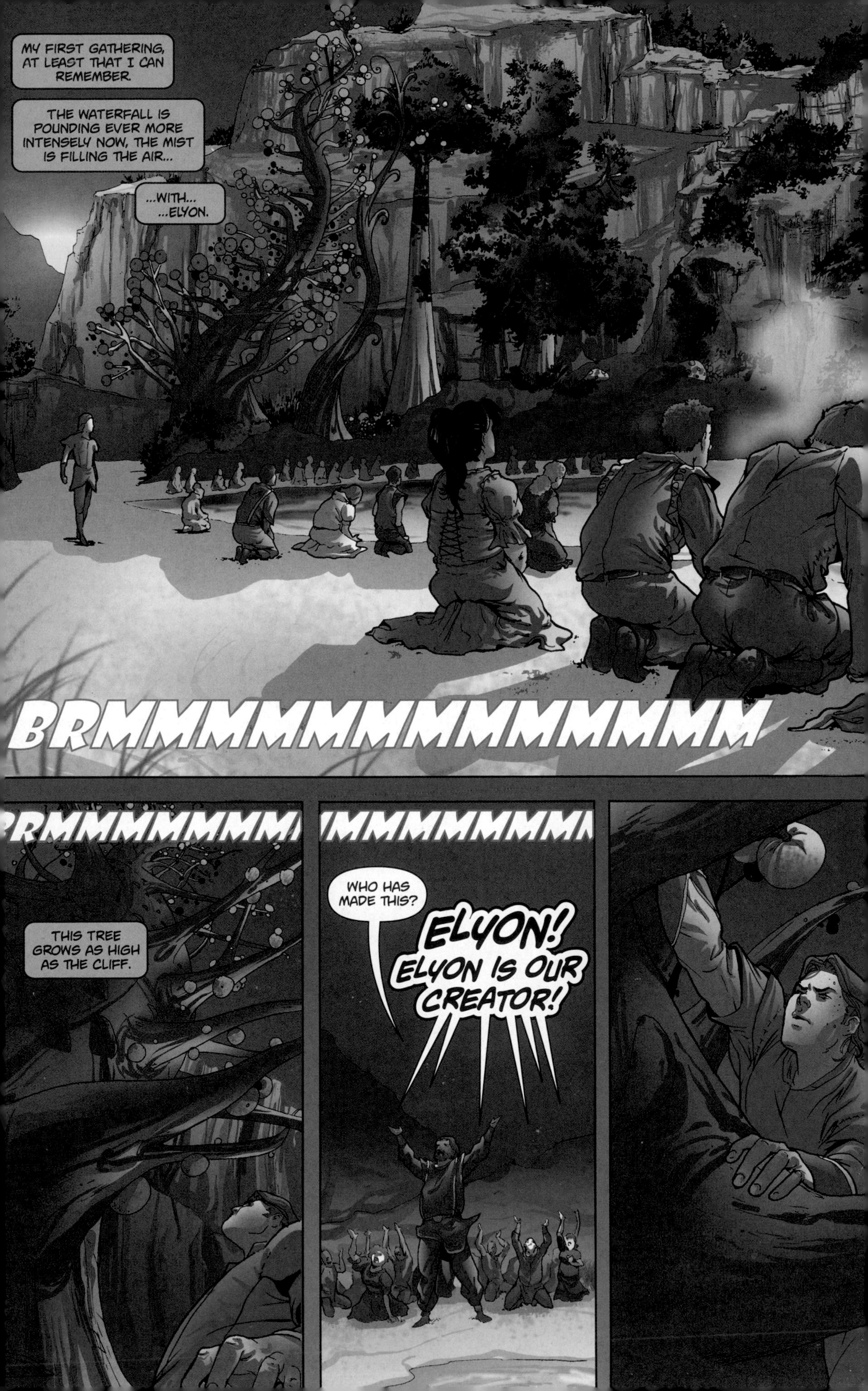
MY FIRST GATHERING, AT LEAST THAT I CAN REMEMBER.
THE WATERFALL IS POUNDING EVER MORE INTENSELY NOW, THE MIST IS FILLING THE AIR...
...WITH... ...ELYON.
BRMMMMMMMMMMMMMM
BRMMMMMMMMM
MMMMMMMMMM
THIS TREE GROWS AS HIGH AS THE CLIFF.
WHO HAS MADE THIS?
ELYON! ELYON IS OUR CREATOR!

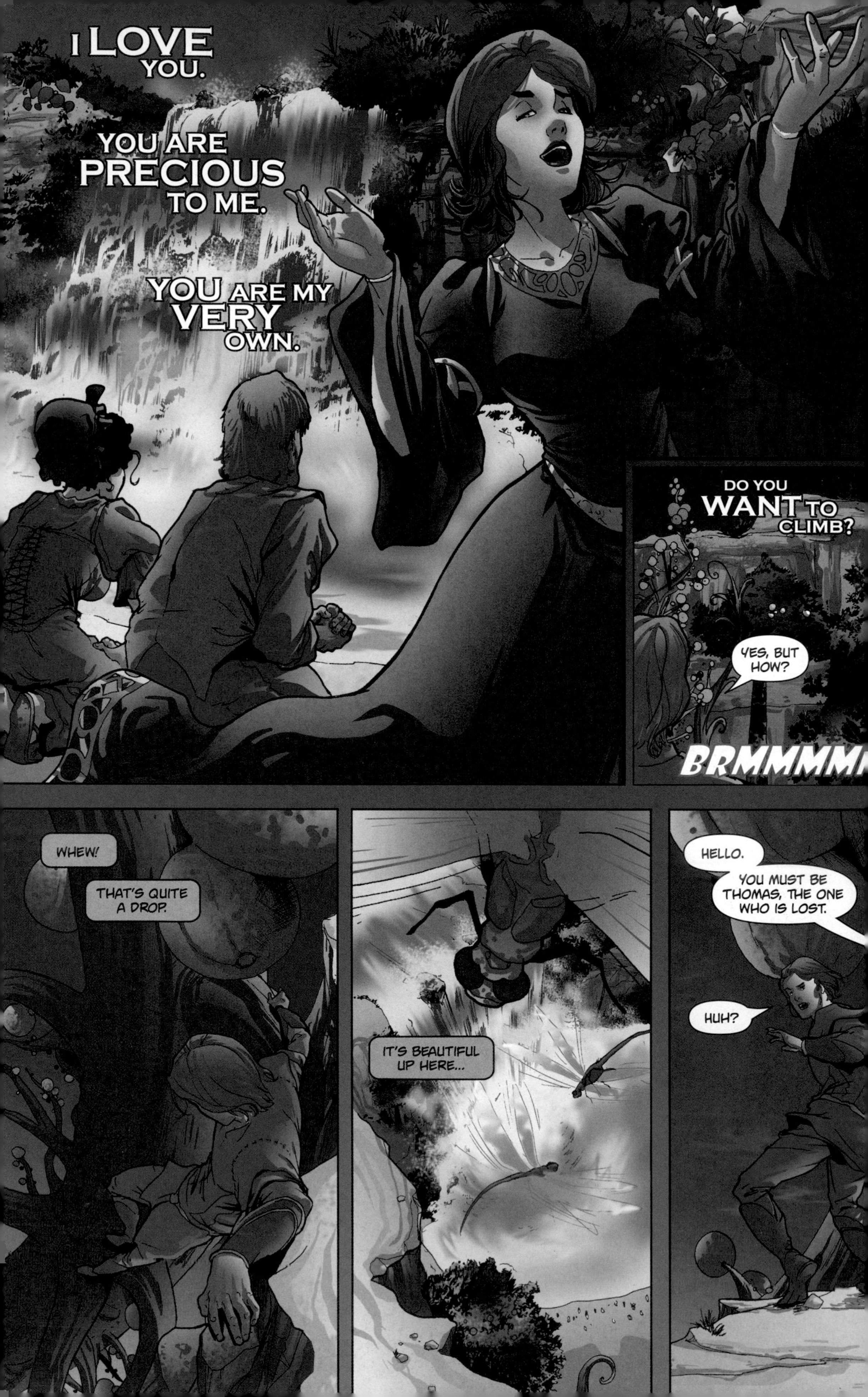
I LOVE YOU.
YOU ARE PRECIOUS TO ME.
YOU ARE MY VERY OWN.
DO YOU WANT TO CLIMB?
YES, BUT HOW?
BRMMMMM
WHEW!
THAT'S QUITE A DROP.
IT'S BEAUTIFUL UP HERE...
HELLO.
YOU MUST BE THOMAS, THE ONE WHO IS LOST.
HUH?

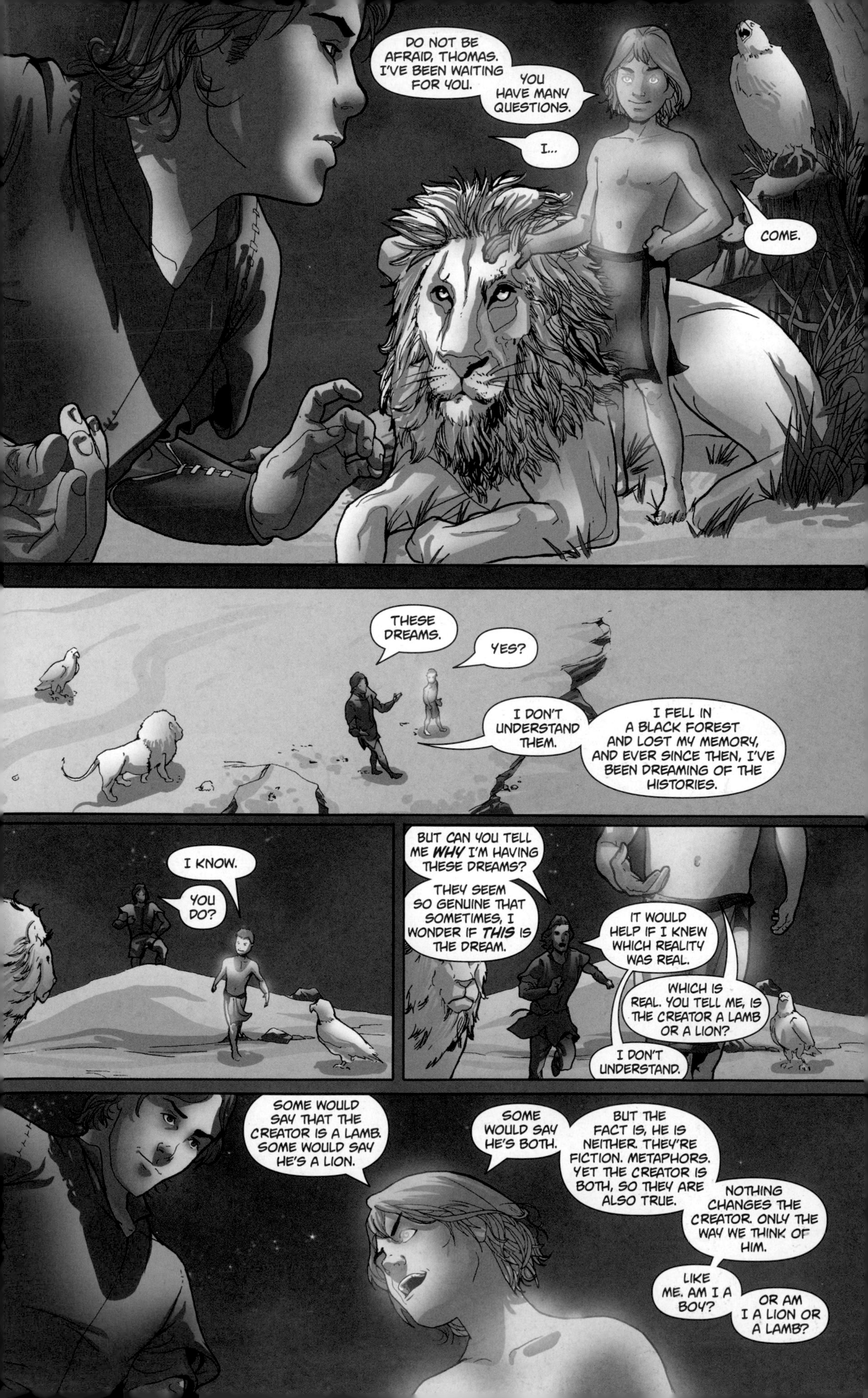

DO NOT BE AFRAID, THOMAS. I'VE BEEN WAITING FOR YOU.
YOU HAVE MANY QUESTIONS.
I...
COME.
THESE DREAMS.
YES?
I DON'T UNDERSTAND THEM.
I FELL IN A BLACK FOREST AND LOST MY MEMORY, AND EVER SINCE THEN, I'VE BEEN DREAMING OF THE HISTORIES.
I KNOW.
YOU DO?
BUT CAN YOU TELL ME *WHY* I'M HAVING THESE DREAMS?
THEY SEEM SO GENUINE THAT SOMETIMES, I WONDER IF *THIS* IS THE DREAM.
IT WOULD HELP IF I KNEW WHICH REALITY WAS REAL.
WHICH IS REAL. YOU TELL ME, IS THE CREATOR A LAMB OR A LION?
I DON'T UNDERSTAND.
SOME WOULD SAY THAT THE CREATOR IS A LAMB. SOME WOULD SAY HE'S A LION.
SOME WOULD SAY HE'S BOTH.
BUT THE FACT IS, HE IS NEITHER. THEY'RE FICTION. METAPHORS. YET THE CREATOR IS BOTH, SO THEY ARE ALSO TRUE.
NOTHING CHANGES THE CREATOR. ONLY THE WAY WE THINK OF HIM.
LIKE ME. AM I A BOY?
OR AM I A LION OR A LAMB?

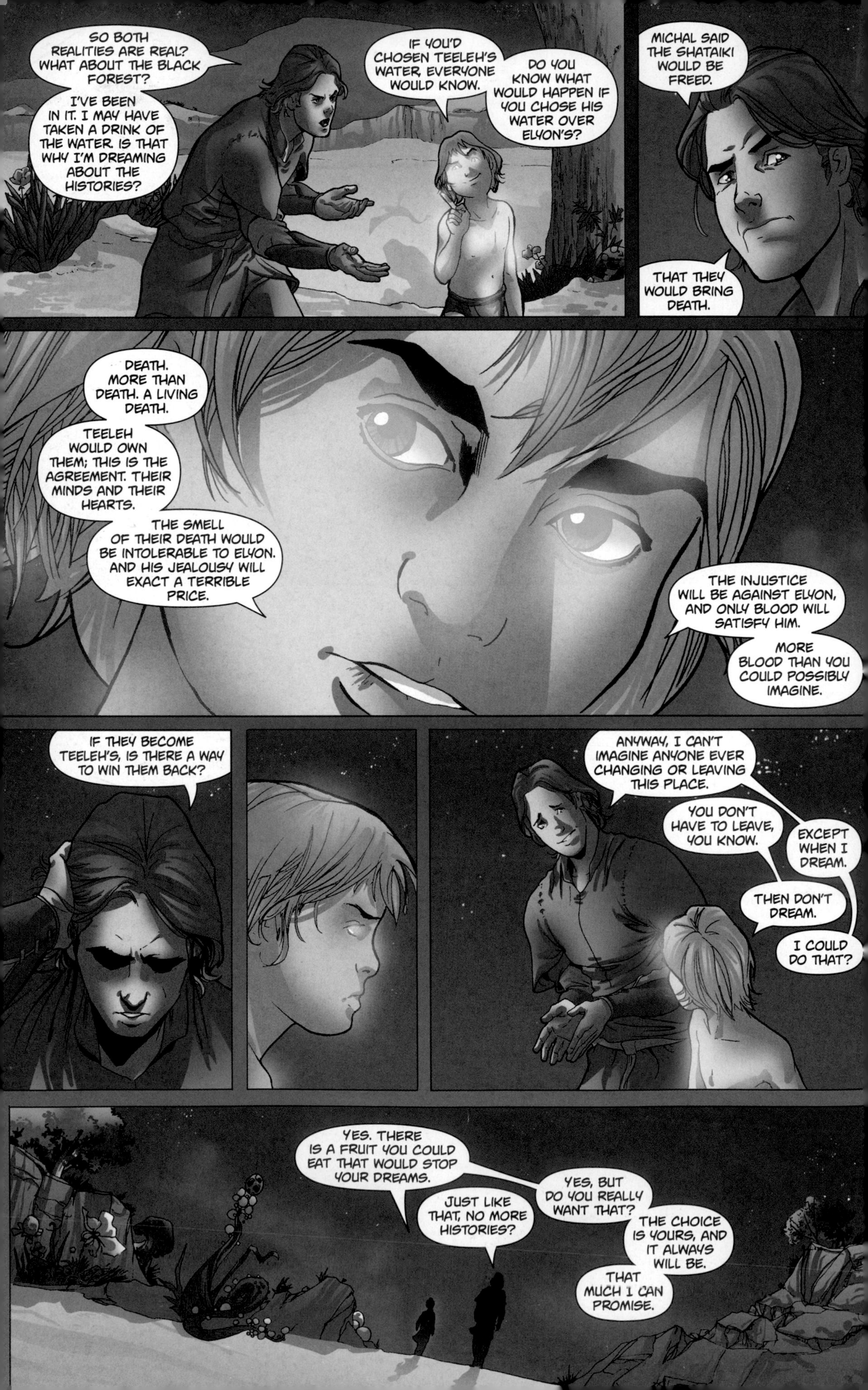
SO BOTH REALITIES ARE REAL? WHAT ABOUT THE BLACK FOREST?
I'VE BEEN IN IT. I MAY HAVE TAKEN A DRINK OF THE WATER. IS THAT WHY I'M DREAMING ABOUT THE HISTORIES?
IF YOU'D CHOSEN TEELEH'S WATER, EVERYONE WOULD KNOW.
DO YOU KNOW WHAT WOULD HAPPEN IF YOU CHOSE HIS WATER OVER ELYON'S?
MICHAL SAID THE SHATAIKI WOULD BE FREED.
THAT THEY WOULD BRING DEATH.
DEATH. MORE THAN DEATH. A LIVING DEATH.
TEELEH WOULD OWN THEM; THIS IS THE AGREEMENT. THEIR MINDS AND THEIR HEARTS.
THE SMELL OF THEIR DEATH WOULD BE INTOLERABLE TO ELYON. AND HIS JEALOUSY WILL EXACT A TERRIBLE PRICE.
THE INJUSTICE WILL BE AGAINST ELYON, AND ONLY BLOOD WILL SATISFY HIM.
MORE BLOOD THAN YOU COULD POSSIBLY IMAGINE.
IF THEY BECOME TEELEH'S, IS THERE A WAY TO WIN THEM BACK?
ANYWAY, I CAN'T IMAGINE ANYONE EVER CHANGING OR LEAVING THIS PLACE.
YOU DON'T HAVE TO LEAVE, YOU KNOW.
EXCEPT WHEN I DREAM.
THEN DON'T DREAM.
I COULD DO THAT?
YES. THERE IS A FRUIT YOU COULD EAT THAT WOULD STOP YOUR DREAMS.
JUST LIKE THAT, NO MORE HISTORIES?
YES, BUT DO YOU REALLY WANT THAT?
THE CHOICE IS YOURS, AND IT ALWAYS WILL BE.
THAT MUCH I CAN PROMISE.

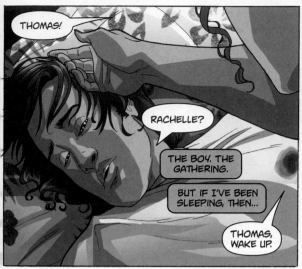

THOMAS!

RACHELLE?

THE BOY. THE GATHERING.

BUT IF I'VE BEEN SLEEPING, THEN...

THOMAS, WAKE UP.

GASP!

KARA!

THOMAS, ARE YOU ALL RIGHT? YOU'VE BEEN SHOT!

TALK TO ME!

ARE YOU HURT?

I DON'T THINK SO... SOMEONE BROKE IN. WE FOUGHT, AND THEN...

AND THEN HE MUST HAVE TAKEN MONIQUE.

AND THEN...

SO WHAT, YOU WERE HEALED IN YOUR DREAM?

YES, BUT... OH, NO.

LISTEN. I THINK I MAY HAVE GIVEN INSTRUCTIONS FOR HOW TO MAKE THE VIRUS TO...

I'M THE UNSUSPECTING FOOL!

WHAT?

TEELEH TRICKED ME INTO REPEATING THE INSTRUCTIONS AND CARLOS MUST HAVE HEARD ME SAY THE WORDS IN MY SLEEP.

CARLOS?

WE HAVE TO GET MONIQUE BACK. SHE'S THE KEY TO THE ANTIVIRUS.

I DON'T UNDERSTAND. WHY DOES CARLOS CARE ABOUT THE ANTIVIRUS?

THINK ABOUT IT. YOU PUT THE VIRUS IN THE AIR, AND THREE WEEKS LATER, EVERYONE'S DEAD, INCLUDING THE PERSON WHO RELEASED IT. BUT IF YOU HAVE THE CURE...

...YOU CAN CONTROL IT. LIKE HAVING THE ONLY NUCLEAR ARSENAL IN THE WORLD.

I ARRANGED TO MEET MONIQUE'S FATHER. I'M PRETTY SURE HE DOESN'T BUY ANY OF THIS. HE JUST WANTS HIS DAUGHTER BACK.

HE'S NOT GOING TO BE HAPPY TO HEAR SHE'S BEEN KIDNAPPED AGAIN...

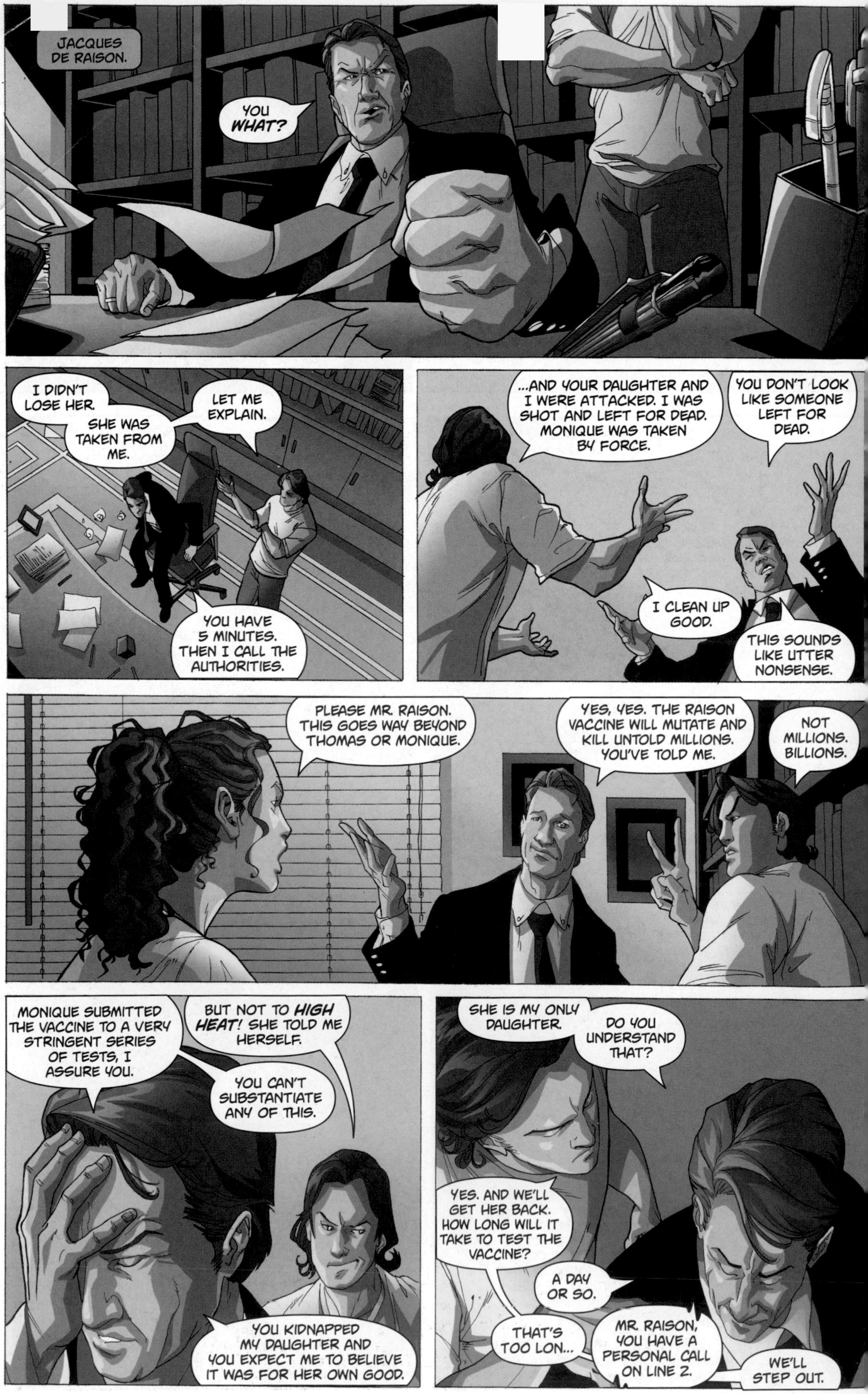
JACQUES DE RAISON.
YOU *WHAT?*
I DIDN'T LOSE HER.
SHE WAS TAKEN FROM ME.
LET ME EXPLAIN.
YOU HAVE 5 MINUTES. THEN I CALL THE AUTHORITIES.
...AND YOUR DAUGHTER AND I WERE ATTACKED. I WAS SHOT AND LEFT FOR DEAD. MONIQUE WAS TAKEN BY FORCE.
YOU DON'T LOOK LIKE SOMEONE LEFT FOR DEAD.
I CLEAN UP GOOD.
THIS SOUNDS LIKE UTTER NONSENSE.
PLEASE MR. RAISON. THIS GOES WAY BEYOND THOMAS OR MONIQUE.
YES, YES. THE RAISON VACCINE WILL MUTATE AND KILL UNTOLD MILLIONS. YOU'VE TOLD ME.
NOT MILLIONS. BILLIONS.
MONIQUE SUBMITTED THE VACCINE TO A VERY STRINGENT SERIES OF TESTS, I ASSURE YOU.
BUT NOT TO *HIGH HEAT!* SHE TOLD ME HERSELF.
YOU CAN'T SUBSTANTIATE ANY OF THIS.
YOU KIDNAPPED MY DAUGHTER AND YOU EXPECT ME TO BELIEVE IT WAS FOR HER OWN GOOD.
SHE IS MY ONLY DAUGHTER.
DO YOU UNDERSTAND THAT?
YES. AND WE'LL GET HER BACK. HOW LONG WILL IT TAKE TO TEST THE VACCINE?
A DAY OR SO.
THAT'S TOO LON...
MR. RAISON, YOU HAVE A PERSONAL CALL ON LINE 2.
WE'LL STEP OUT.

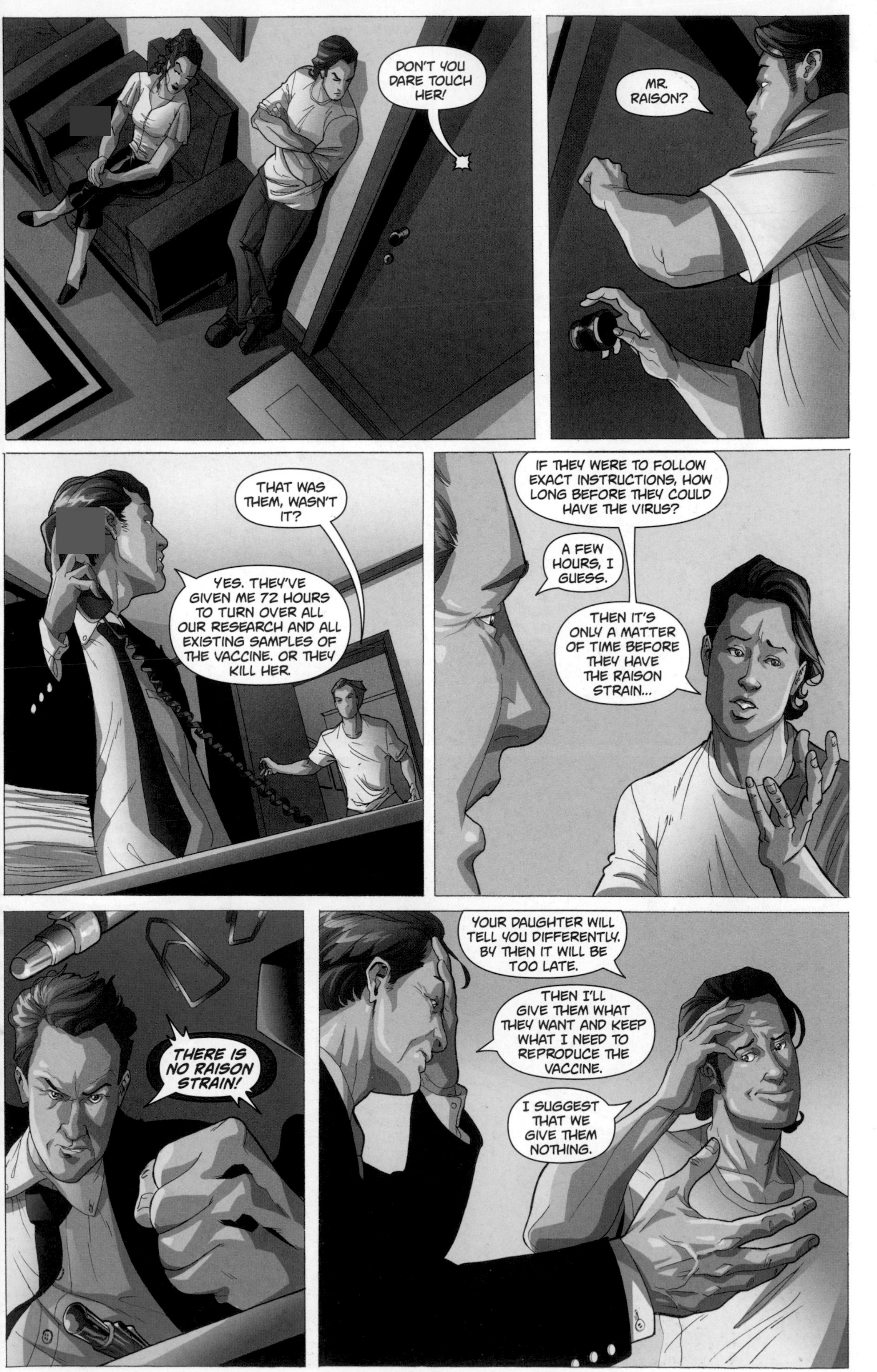
DON'T YOU DARE TOUCH HER!
MR. RAISON?
THAT WAS THEM, WASN'T IT?
YES. THEY'VE GIVEN ME 72 HOURS TO TURN OVER ALL OUR RESEARCH AND ALL EXISTING SAMPLES OF THE VACCINE. OR THEY KILL HER.
IF THEY WERE TO FOLLOW EXACT INSTRUCTIONS, HOW LONG BEFORE THEY COULD HAVE THE VIRUS?
A FEW HOURS, I GUESS.
THEN IT'S ONLY A MATTER OF TIME BEFORE THEY HAVE THE RAISON STRAIN...
THERE IS NO RAISON STRAIN!
YOUR DAUGHTER WILL TELL YOU DIFFERENTLY. BY THEN IT WILL BE TOO LATE.
THEN I'LL GIVE THEM WHAT THEY WANT AND KEEP WHAT I NEED TO REPRODUCE THE VACCINE.
I SUGGEST THAT WE GIVE THEM NOTHING.

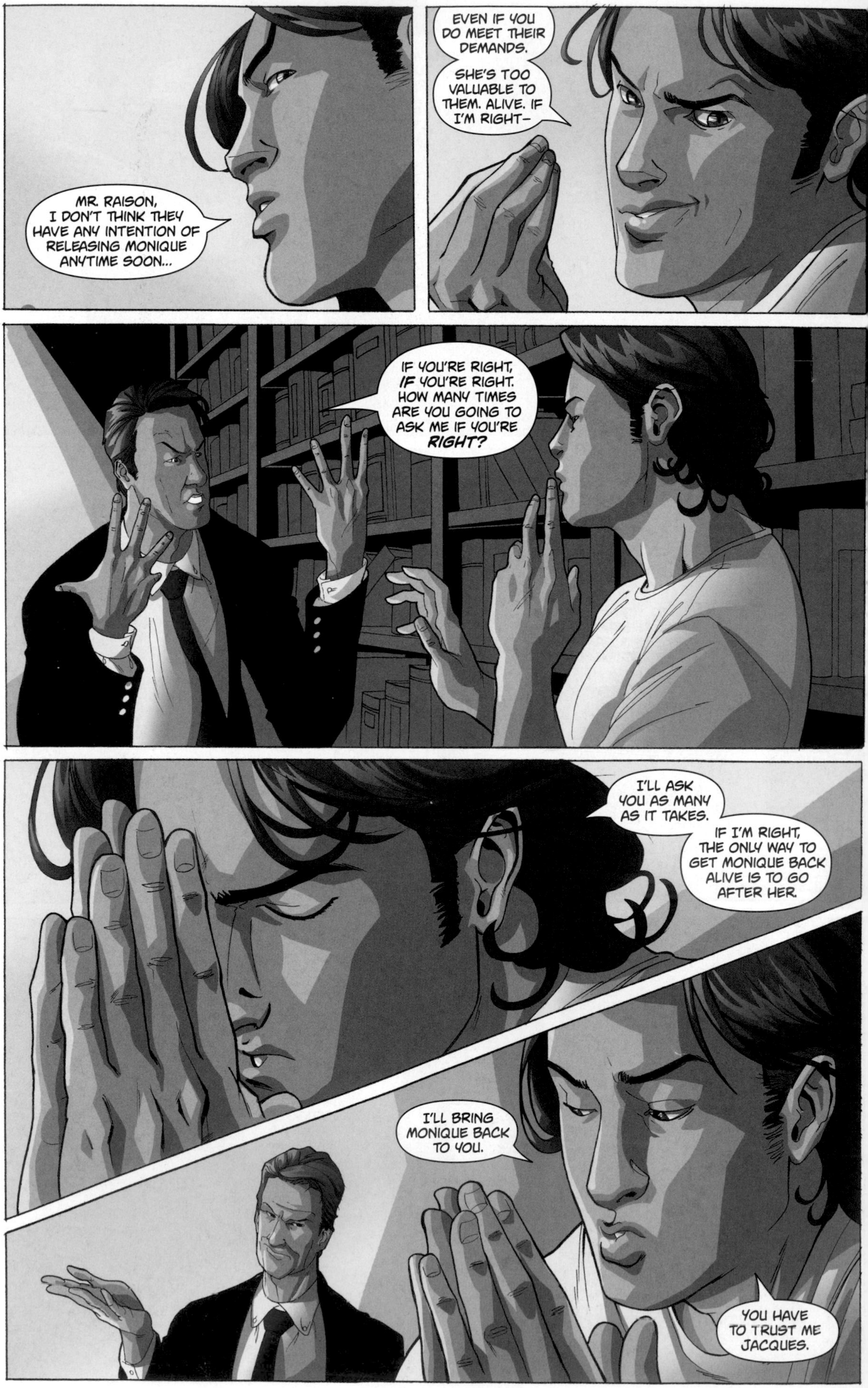
MR. RAISON, I DON'T THINK THEY HAVE ANY INTENTION OF RELEASING MONIQUE ANYTIME SOON...
EVEN IF YOU DO MEET THEIR DEMANDS.
SHE'S TOO VALUABLE TO THEM. ALIVE. IF I'M RIGHT–
IF YOU'RE RIGHT, *IF* YOU'RE RIGHT. HOW MANY TIMES ARE YOU GOING TO ASK ME IF YOU'RE *RIGHT?*
I'LL ASK YOU AS MANY AS IT TAKES.
IF I'M RIGHT, THE ONLY WAY TO GET MONIQUE BACK ALIVE IS TO GO AFTER HER.
I'LL BRING MONIQUE BACK TO YOU.
YOU HAVE TO TRUST ME JACQUES.

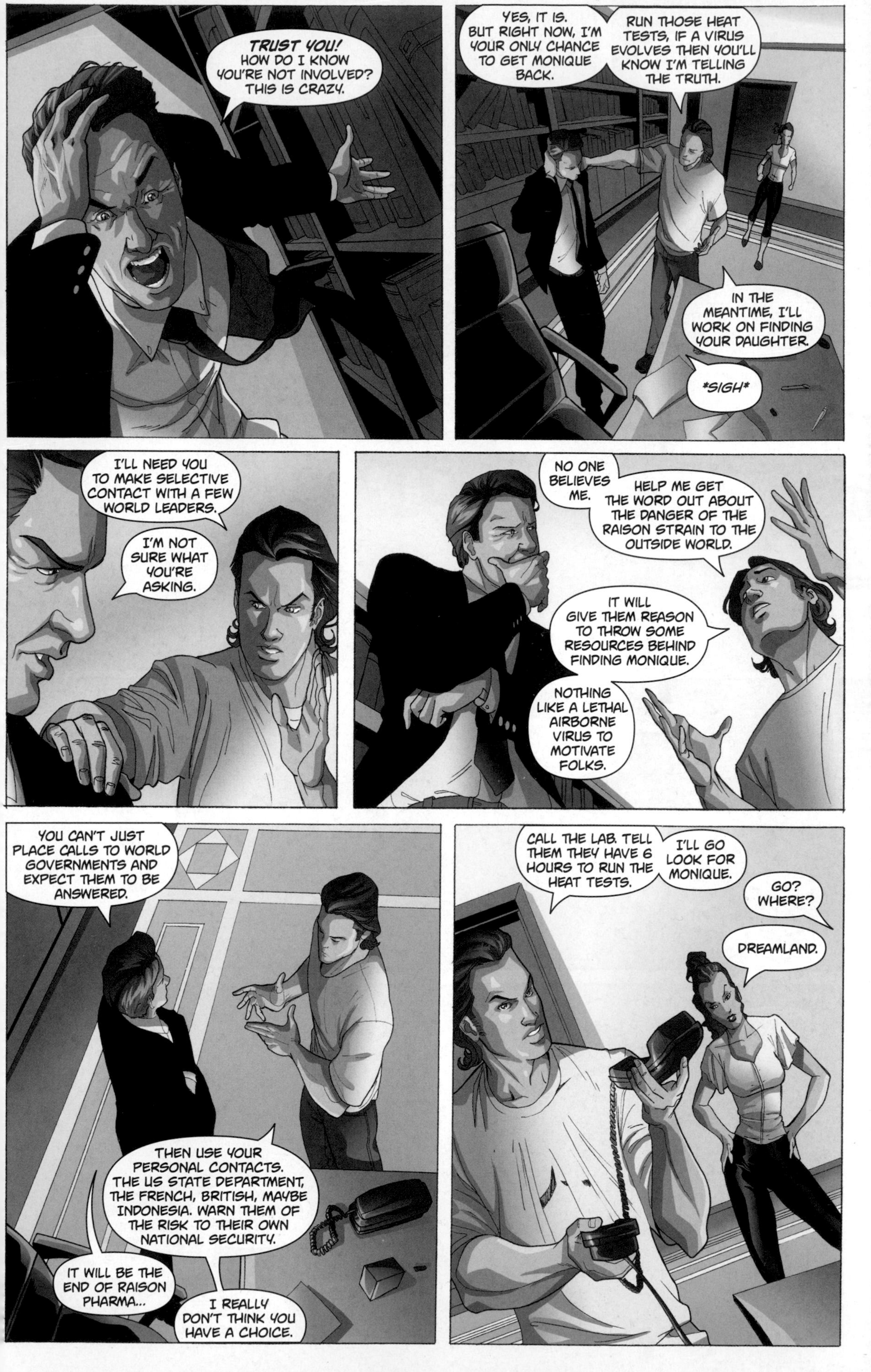
TRUST YOU! HOW DO I KNOW YOU'RE NOT INVOLVED? THIS IS CRAZY.
YES, IT IS. BUT RIGHT NOW, I'M YOUR ONLY CHANCE TO GET MONIQUE BACK.
RUN THOSE HEAT TESTS, IF A VIRUS EVOLVES THEN YOU'LL KNOW I'M TELLING THE TRUTH.
IN THE MEANTIME, I'LL WORK ON FINDING YOUR DAUGHTER.
SIGH
I'LL NEED YOU TO MAKE SELECTIVE CONTACT WITH A FEW WORLD LEADERS.
I'M NOT SURE WHAT YOU'RE ASKING.
NO ONE BELIEVES ME.
HELP ME GET THE WORD OUT ABOUT THE DANGER OF THE RAISON STRAIN TO THE OUTSIDE WORLD.
IT WILL GIVE THEM REASON TO THROW SOME RESOURCES BEHIND FINDING MONIQUE.
NOTHING LIKE A LETHAL AIRBORNE VIRUS TO MOTIVATE FOLKS.
YOU CAN'T JUST PLACE CALLS TO WORLD GOVERNMENTS AND EXPECT THEM TO BE ANSWERED.
THEN USE YOUR PERSONAL CONTACTS. THE US STATE DEPARTMENT, THE FRENCH, BRITISH, MAYBE INDONESIA. WARN THEM OF THE RISK TO THEIR OWN NATIONAL SECURITY.
IT WILL BE THE END OF RAISON PHARMA...
I REALLY DON'T THINK YOU HAVE A CHOICE.
CALL THE LAB. TELL THEM THEY HAVE 6 HOURS TO RUN THE HEAT TESTS.
I'LL GO LOOK FOR MONIQUE.
GO? WHERE?
DREAMLAND.

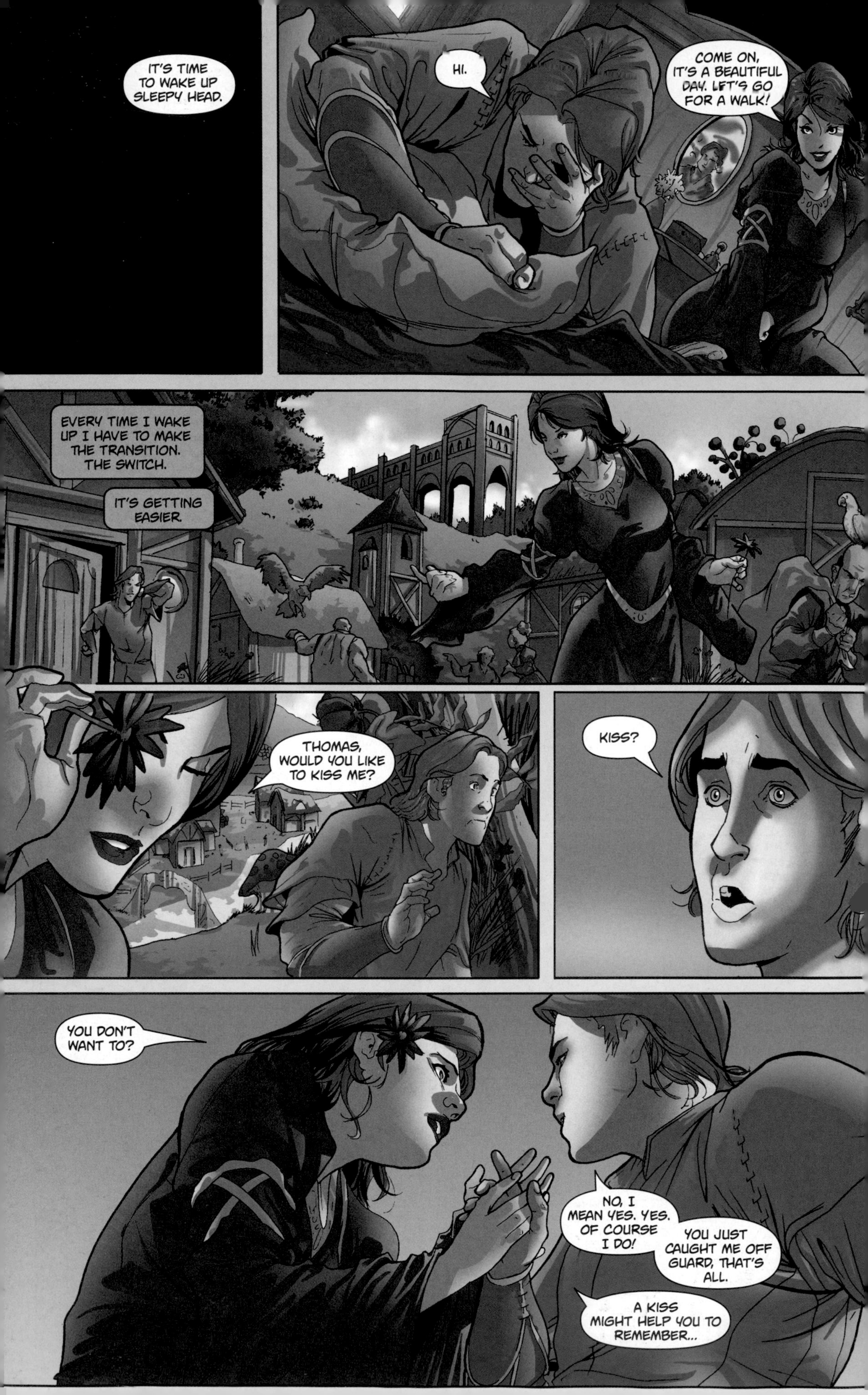
IT'S TIME TO WAKE UP SLEEPY HEAD.
HI.
COME ON, IT'S A BEAUTIFUL DAY. LET'S GO FOR A WALK!
EVERY TIME I WAKE UP I HAVE TO MAKE THE TRANSITION. THE SWITCH.
IT'S GETTING EASIER.
THOMAS, WOULD YOU LIKE TO KISS ME?
KISS?
YOU DON'T WANT TO?
NO, I MEAN YES. YES. OF COURSE I DO!
YOU JUST CAUGHT ME OFF GUARD, THAT'S ALL.
A KISS MIGHT HELP YOU TO REMEMBER...

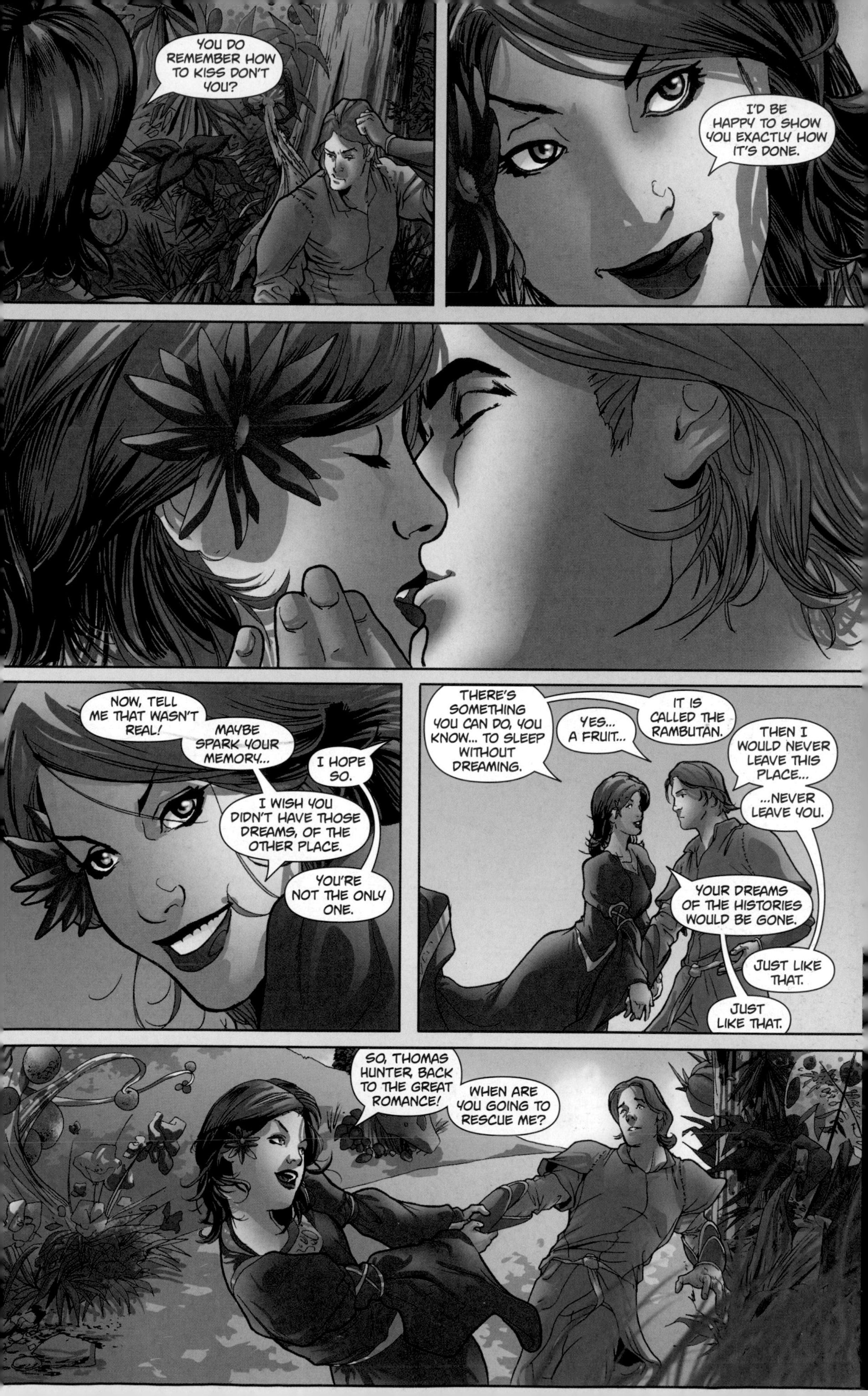
YOU DO REMEMBER HOW TO KISS DON'T YOU?
I'D BE HAPPY TO SHOW YOU EXACTLY HOW IT'S DONE.
NOW, TELL ME THAT WASN'T REAL!
MAYBE SPARK YOUR MEMORY...
I HOPE SO.
I WISH YOU DIDN'T HAVE THOSE DREAMS, OF THE OTHER PLACE.
YOU'RE NOT THE ONLY ONE.
THERE'S SOMETHING YOU CAN DO, YOU KNOW... TO SLEEP WITHOUT DREAMING.
YES... A FRUIT...
IT IS CALLED THE RAMBUTAN.
THEN I WOULD NEVER LEAVE THIS PLACE...
...NEVER LEAVE YOU.
YOUR DREAMS OF THE HISTORIES WOULD BE GONE.
JUST LIKE THAT.
JUST LIKE THAT.
SO, THOMAS HUNTER, BACK TO THE GREAT ROMANCE!
WHEN ARE YOU GOING TO RESCUE ME?

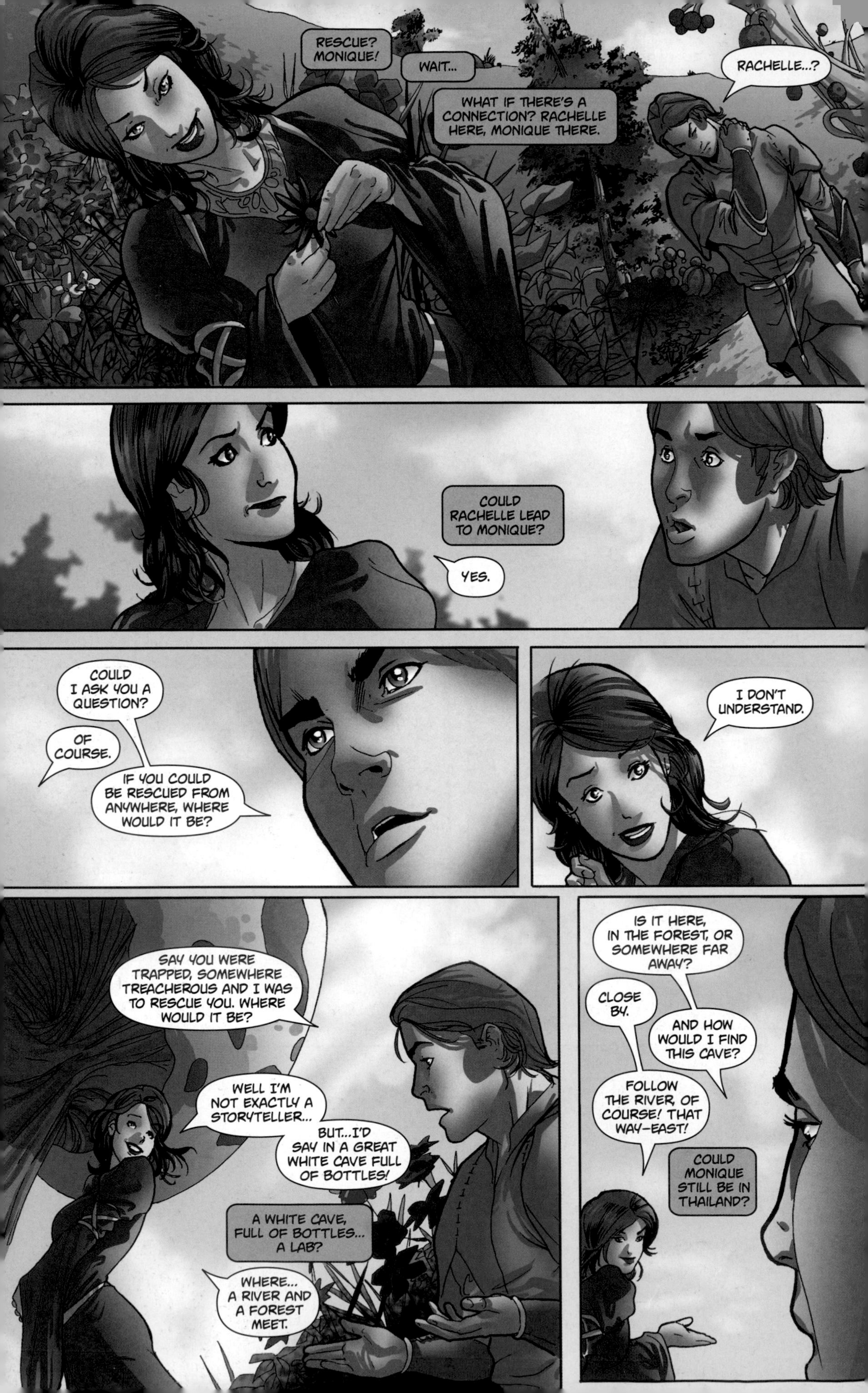
RESCUE? MONIQUE!
WAIT...
WHAT IF THERE'S A CONNECTION? RACHELLE HERE, MONIQUE THERE.
RACHELLE...?
COULD RACHELLE LEAD TO MONIQUE?
YES.
COULD I ASK YOU A QUESTION?
OF COURSE.
IF YOU COULD BE RESCUED FROM ANYWHERE, WHERE WOULD IT BE?
I DON'T UNDERSTAND.
SAY YOU WERE TRAPPED, SOMEWHERE TREACHEROUS AND I WAS TO RESCUE YOU. WHERE WOULD IT BE?
WELL I'M NOT EXACTLY A STORYTELLER...
BUT...I'D SAY IN A GREAT WHITE CAVE FULL OF BOTTLES!
A WHITE CAVE, FULL OF BOTTLES... A LAB?
WHERE... A RIVER AND A FOREST MEET.
IS IT HERE, IN THE FOREST, OR SOMEWHERE FAR AWAY?
CLOSE BY.
AND HOW WOULD I FIND THIS CAVE?
FOLLOW THE RIVER, OF COURSE! THAT WAY—EAST!
COULD MONIQUE STILL BE IN THAILAND?

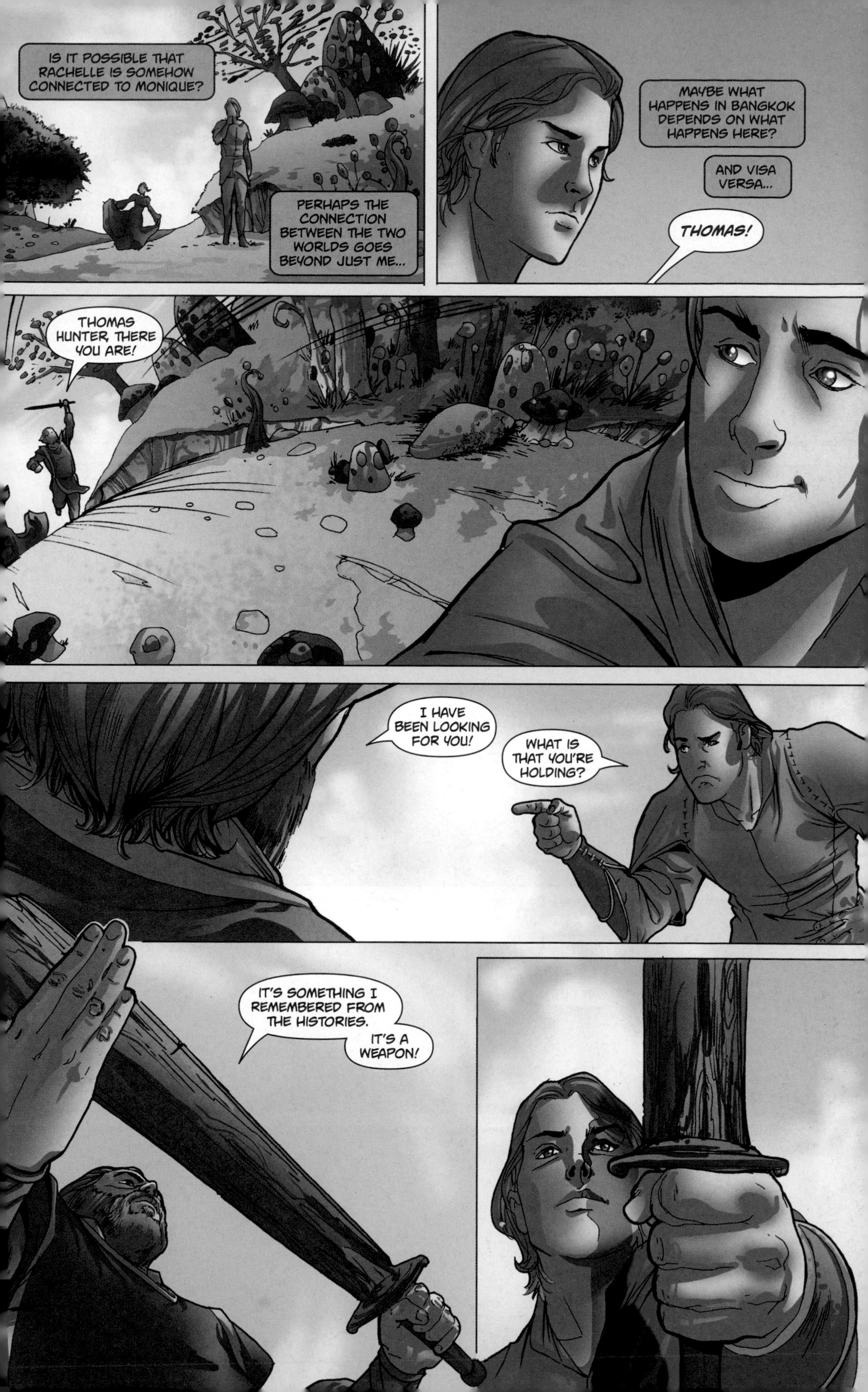
IS IT POSSIBLE THAT RACHELLE IS SOMEHOW CONNECTED TO MONIQUE?
PERHAPS THE CONNECTION BETWEEN THE TWO WORLDS GOES BEYOND JUST ME...
MAYBE WHAT HAPPENS IN BANGKOK DEPENDS ON WHAT HAPPENS HERE?
AND VISA VERSA...
THOMAS!
THOMAS HUNTER, THERE YOU ARE!
I HAVE BEEN LOOKING FOR YOU!
WHAT IS THAT YOU'RE HOLDING?
IT'S SOMETHING I REMEMBERED FROM THE HISTORIES.
IT'S A WEAPON!

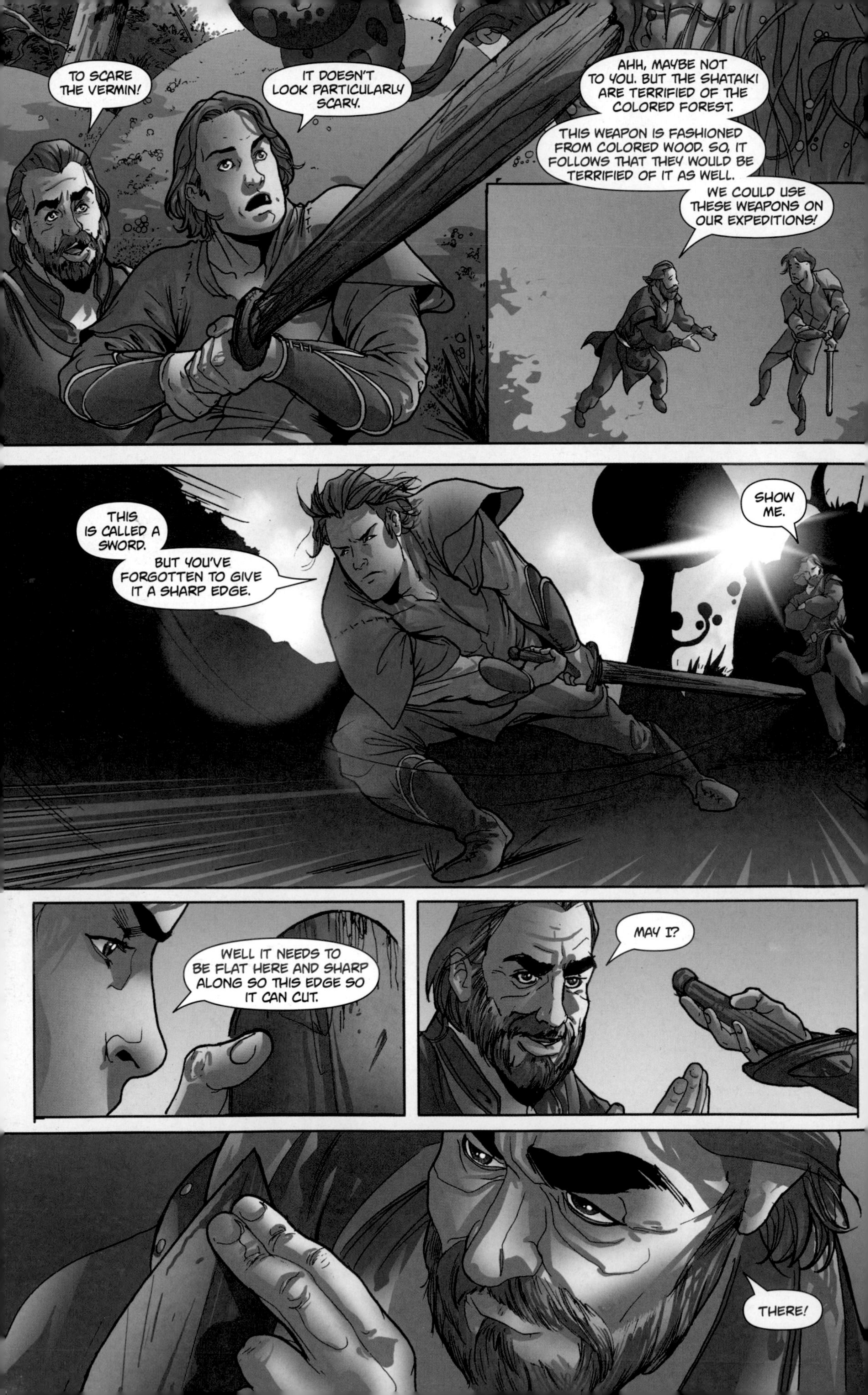
TO SCARE THE VERMIN!
IT DOESN'T LOOK PARTICULARLY SCARY.
AHH, MAYBE NOT TO YOU. BUT THE SHATAIKI ARE TERRIFIED OF THE COLORED FOREST.
THIS WEAPON IS FASHIONED FROM COLORED WOOD. SO, IT FOLLOWS THAT THEY WOULD BE TERRIFIED OF IT AS WELL.
WE COULD USE THESE WEAPONS ON OUR EXPEDITIONS!
THIS IS CALLED A SWORD.
BUT YOU'VE FORGOTTEN TO GIVE IT A SHARP EDGE.
SHOW ME.
WELL IT NEEDS TO BE FLAT HERE AND SHARP ALONG SO THIS EDGE SO IT CAN CUT.
MAY I?
THERE!

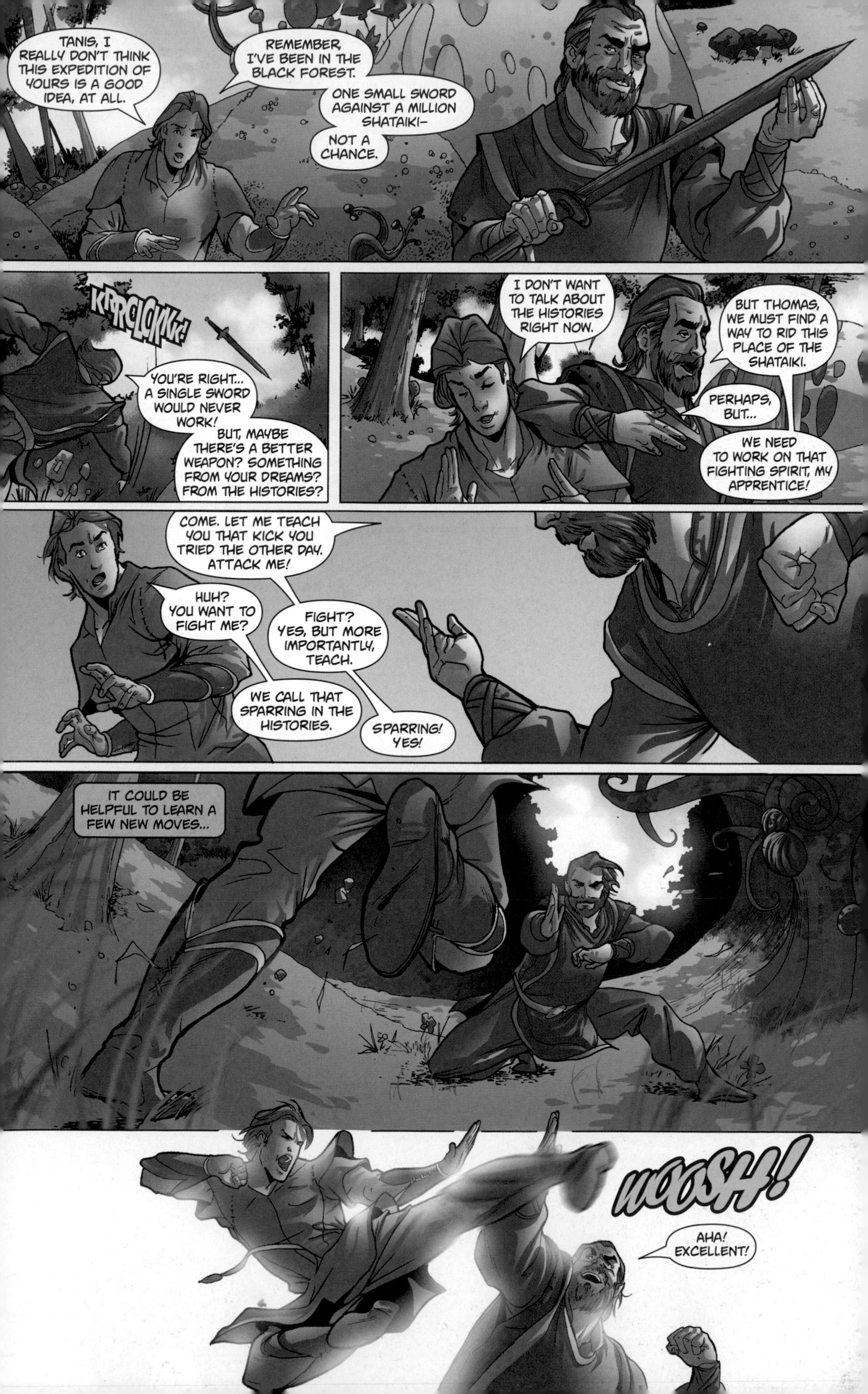
TANIS, I REALLY DON'T THINK THIS EXPEDITION OF YOURS IS A GOOD IDEA, AT ALL.
REMEMBER, I'VE BEEN IN THE BLACK FOREST.
ONE SMALL SWORD AGAINST A MILLION SHATAIKI–
NOT A CHANCE.
KRRCLOKK!
YOU'RE RIGHT... A SINGLE SWORD WOULD NEVER WORK!
BUT, MAYBE THERE'S A BETTER WEAPON? SOMETHING FROM YOUR DREAMS? FROM THE HISTORIES?
I DON'T WANT TO TALK ABOUT THE HISTORIES RIGHT NOW.
BUT THOMAS, WE MUST FIND A WAY TO RID THIS PLACE OF THE SHATAIKI.
PERHAPS, BUT...
WE NEED TO WORK ON THAT FIGHTING SPIRIT, MY APPRENTICE!
COME. LET ME TEACH YOU THAT KICK YOU TRIED THE OTHER DAY. ATTACK ME!
HUH? YOU WANT TO FIGHT ME?
FIGHT? YES, BUT MORE IMPORTANTLY, TEACH.
WE CALL THAT SPARRING IN THE HISTORIES.
SPARRING! YES!
IT COULD BE HELPFUL TO LEARN A FEW NEW MOVES...
WOOSH!
AHA! EXCELLENT!

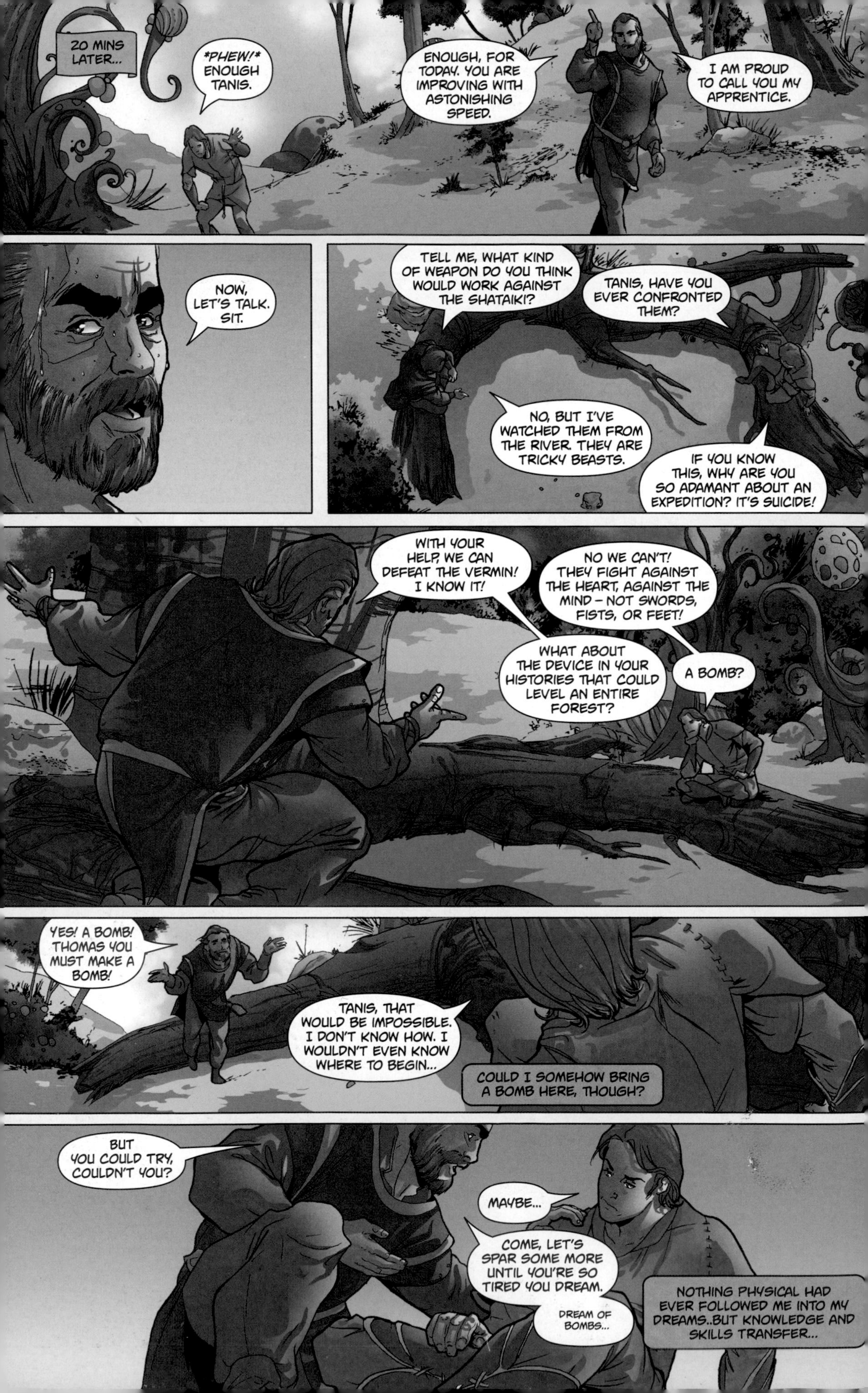
20 MINS LATER...
PHEW! ENOUGH TANIS.
ENOUGH, FOR TODAY. YOU ARE IMPROVING WITH ASTONISHING SPEED.
I AM PROUD TO CALL YOU MY APPRENTICE.
NOW, LET'S TALK. SIT.
TELL ME, WHAT KIND OF WEAPON DO YOU THINK WOULD WORK AGAINST THE SHATAIKI?
TANIS, HAVE YOU EVER CONFRONTED THEM?
NO, BUT I'VE WATCHED THEM FROM THE RIVER. THEY ARE TRICKY BEASTS.
IF YOU KNOW THIS, WHY ARE YOU SO ADAMANT ABOUT AN EXPEDITION? IT'S SUICIDE!
WITH YOUR HELP, WE CAN DEFEAT THE VERMIN! I KNOW IT!
NO WE CAN'T! THEY FIGHT AGAINST THE HEART, AGAINST THE MIND – NOT SWORDS, FISTS, OR FEET!
WHAT ABOUT THE DEVICE IN YOUR HISTORIES THAT COULD LEVEL AN ENTIRE FOREST?
A BOMB?
YES! A BOMB! THOMAS YOU MUST MAKE A BOMB!
TANIS, THAT WOULD BE IMPOSSIBLE. I DON'T KNOW HOW. I WOULDN'T EVEN KNOW WHERE TO BEGIN...
COULD I SOMEHOW BRING A BOMB HERE, THOUGH?
BUT YOU COULD TRY, COULDN'T YOU?
MAYBE...
COME, LET'S SPAR SOME MORE UNTIL YOU'RE SO TIRED YOU DREAM.
DREAM OF BOMBS...
NOTHING PHYSICAL HAD EVER FOLLOWED ME INTO MY DREAMS..BUT KNOWLEDGE AND SKILLS TRANSFER...

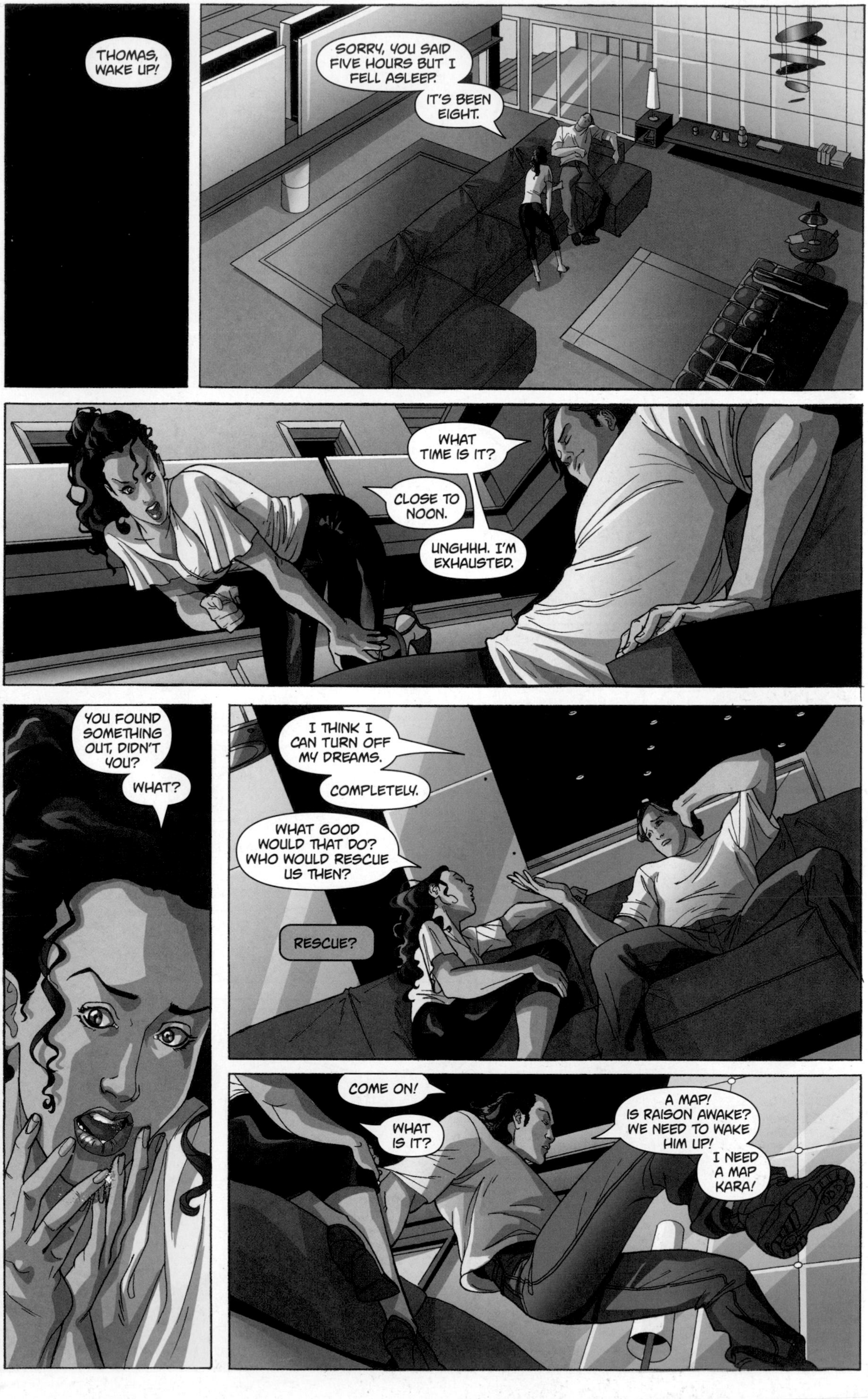
THOMAS, WAKE UP!
SORRY, YOU SAID FIVE HOURS BUT I FELL ASLEEP.
IT'S BEEN EIGHT.
WHAT TIME IS IT?
CLOSE TO NOON.
UNGHHH. I'M EXHAUSTED.
YOU FOUND SOMETHING OUT, DIDN'T YOU?
WHAT?
I THINK I CAN TURN OFF MY DREAMS.
COMPLETELY.
WHAT GOOD WOULD THAT DO? WHO WOULD RESCUE US THEN?
RESCUE?
COME ON!
WHAT IS IT?
A MAP! IS RAISON AWAKE? WE NEED TO WAKE HIM UP!
I NEED A MAP KARA!

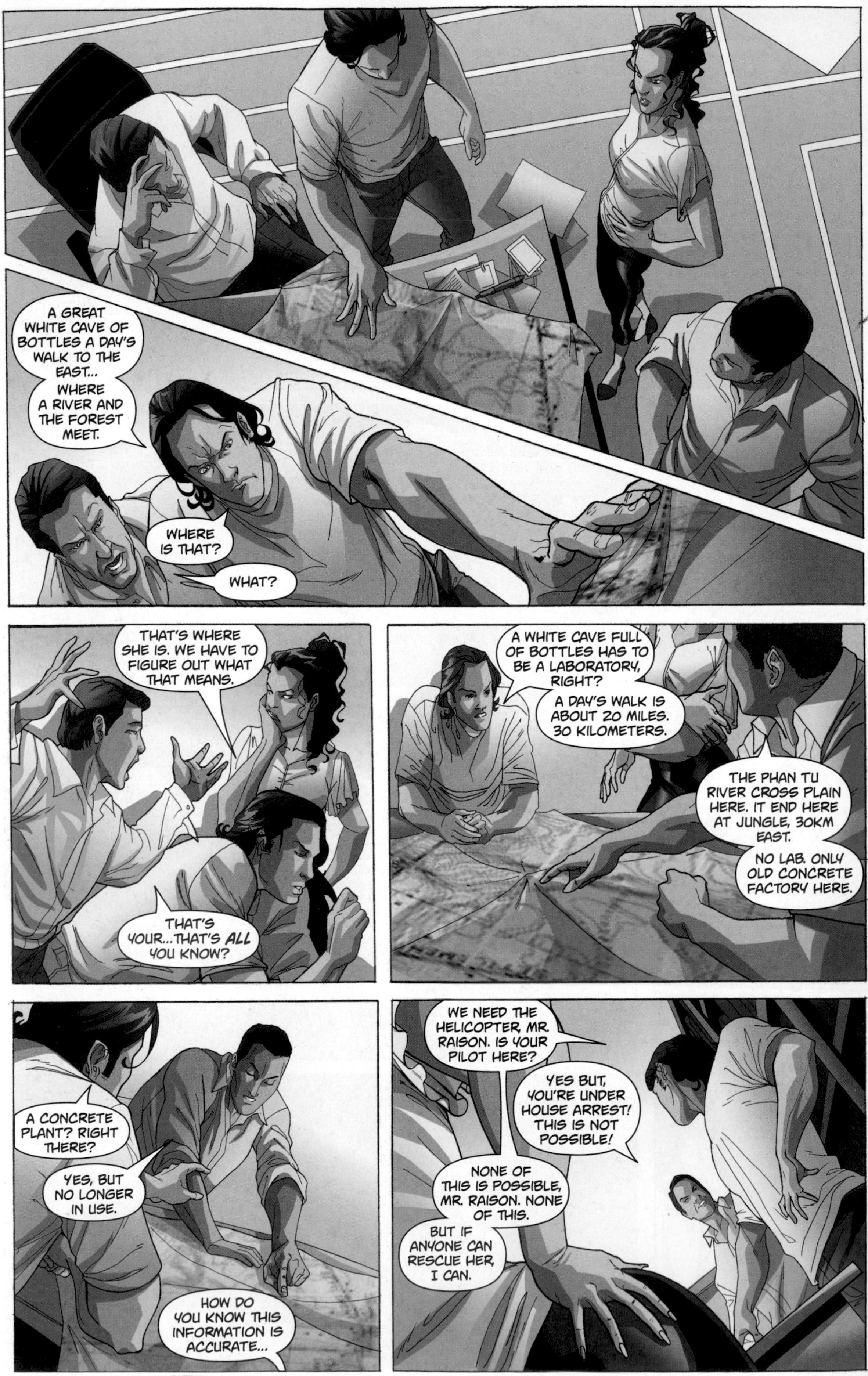
A GREAT WHITE CAVE OF BOTTLES A DAY'S WALK TO THE EAST... WHERE A RIVER AND THE FOREST MEET.
WHERE IS THAT?
WHAT?
THAT'S WHERE SHE IS. WE HAVE TO FIGURE OUT WHAT THAT MEANS.
THAT'S YOUR...THAT'S ALL YOU KNOW?
A WHITE CAVE FULL OF BOTTLES HAS TO BE A LABORATORY, RIGHT?
A DAY'S WALK IS ABOUT 20 MILES. 30 KILOMETERS.
THE PHAN TU RIVER CROSS PLAIN HERE. IT END HERE AT JUNGLE, 30KM EAST.
NO LAB. ONLY OLD CONCRETE FACTORY HERE.
A CONCRETE PLANT? RIGHT THERE?
YES, BUT NO LONGER IN USE.
HOW DO YOU KNOW THIS INFORMATION IS ACCURATE...
WE NEED THE HELICOPTER, MR. RAISON. IS YOUR PILOT HERE?
YES BUT, YOU'RE UNDER HOUSE ARREST! THIS IS NOT POSSIBLE!
NONE OF THIS IS POSSIBLE, MR. RAISON. NONE OF THIS.
BUT IF ANYONE CAN RESCUE HER, I CAN.

OPEN IT.

WARNING
AREA

SO MONIQUE, ARE YOU READY TO WRITE HISTORY?

YOU RECOGNIZE ME, DON'T YOU? WE'VE MET BEFORE...AT A SYMPOSIUM, YEARS AGO.

WHICH IS A PROBLEM.

REMOVE IT, CARLOS.

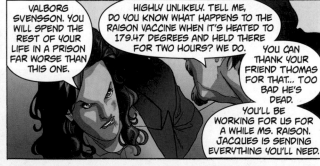

VALBORG SVENSSON. YOU WILL SPEND THE REST OF YOUR LIFE IN A PRISON FAR WORSE THAN THIS ONE.

HIGHLY UNLIKELY. TELL ME, DO YOU KNOW WHAT HAPPENS TO THE RAISON VACCINE WHEN IT'S HEATED TO 179.47 DEGREES AND HELD THERE FOR TWO HOURS? WE DO.

YOU CAN THANK YOUR FRIEND THOMAS FOR THAT... TOO BAD HE'S DEAD.

YOU'LL BE WORKING FOR US FOR A WHILE MS. RAISON. JACQUES IS SENDING EVERYTHING YOU'LL NEED.

AND MONIQUE, NOBODY'S COMING FOR YOU.

AND JUST IN CASE YOU WERE CONSIDERING GOING SOMEWHERE WITHOUT ME,

THAT RATHER LARGE PILL CARLOS FORCED YOU TO SWALLOW...

...WAS A RADIO-CONTROLLED DETONATOR.

STRAY MORE THAN 50 METERS AND, WELL...

...I'LL LEAVE THAT TO YOUR IMAGINATION.

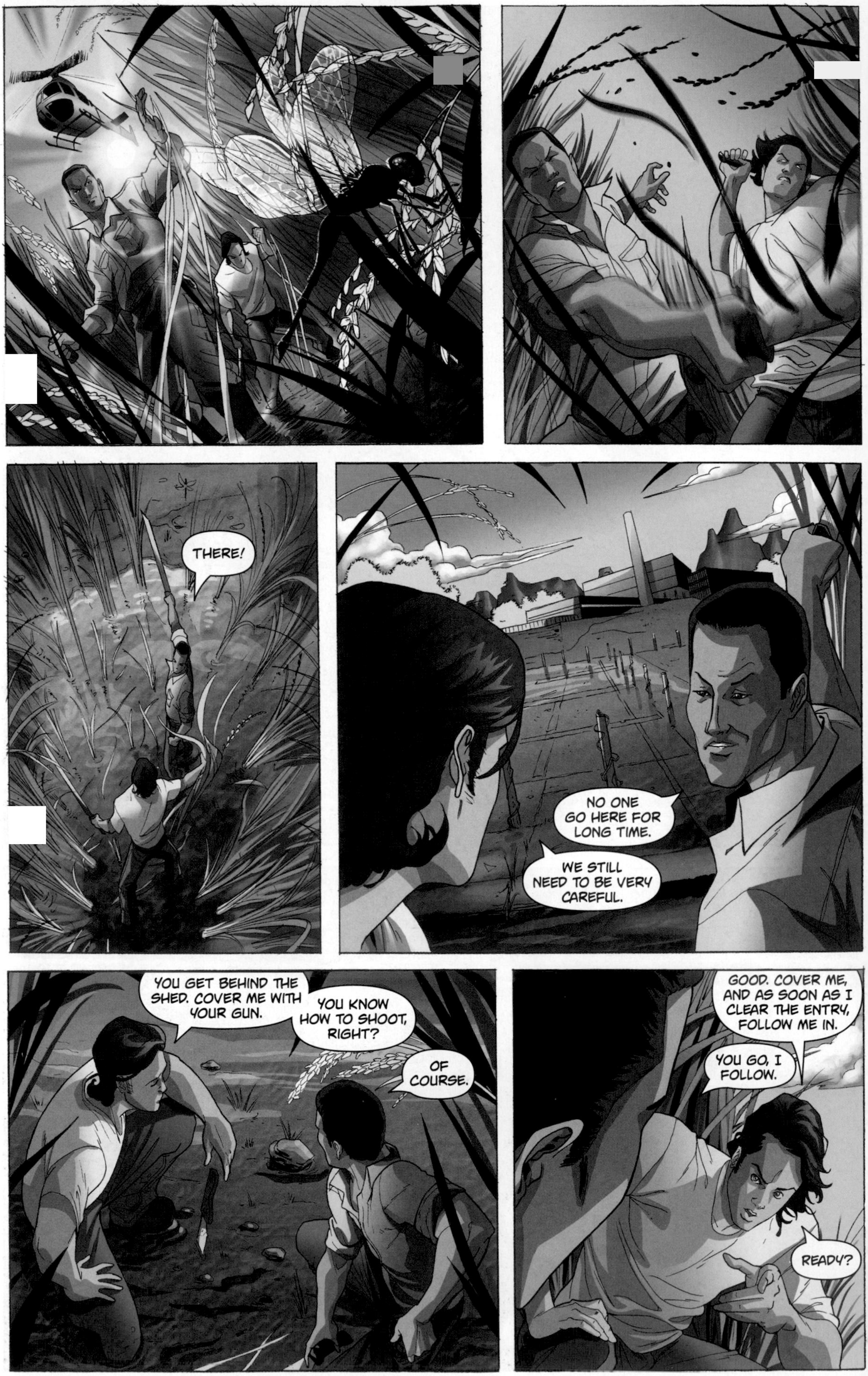
THERE!
NO ONE GO HERE FOR LONG TIME.
WE STILL NEED TO BE VERY CAREFUL.
YOU GET BEHIND THE SHED. COVER ME WITH YOUR GUN.
YOU KNOW HOW TO SHOOT, RIGHT?
OF COURSE.
GOOD. COVER ME, AND AS SOON AS I CLEAR THE ENTRY, FOLLOW ME IN.
YOU GO, I FOLLOW.
READY?

GO!

UNLOCKED.

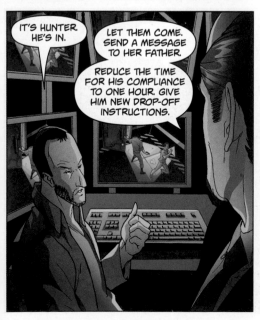

IT'S HUNTER, HE'S IN.

LET THEM COME. SEND A MESSAGE TO HER FATHER.

REDUCE THE TIME FOR HIS COMPLIANCE TO ONE HOUR. GIVE HIM NEW DROP-OFF INSTRUCTIONS.

THEN TAKE CARE OF HUNTER. BRING HER TO THE MOUNTAIN.

AND CARLOS, I TRUST THIS WILL BE THE LAST TIME I HAVE TO ASK.

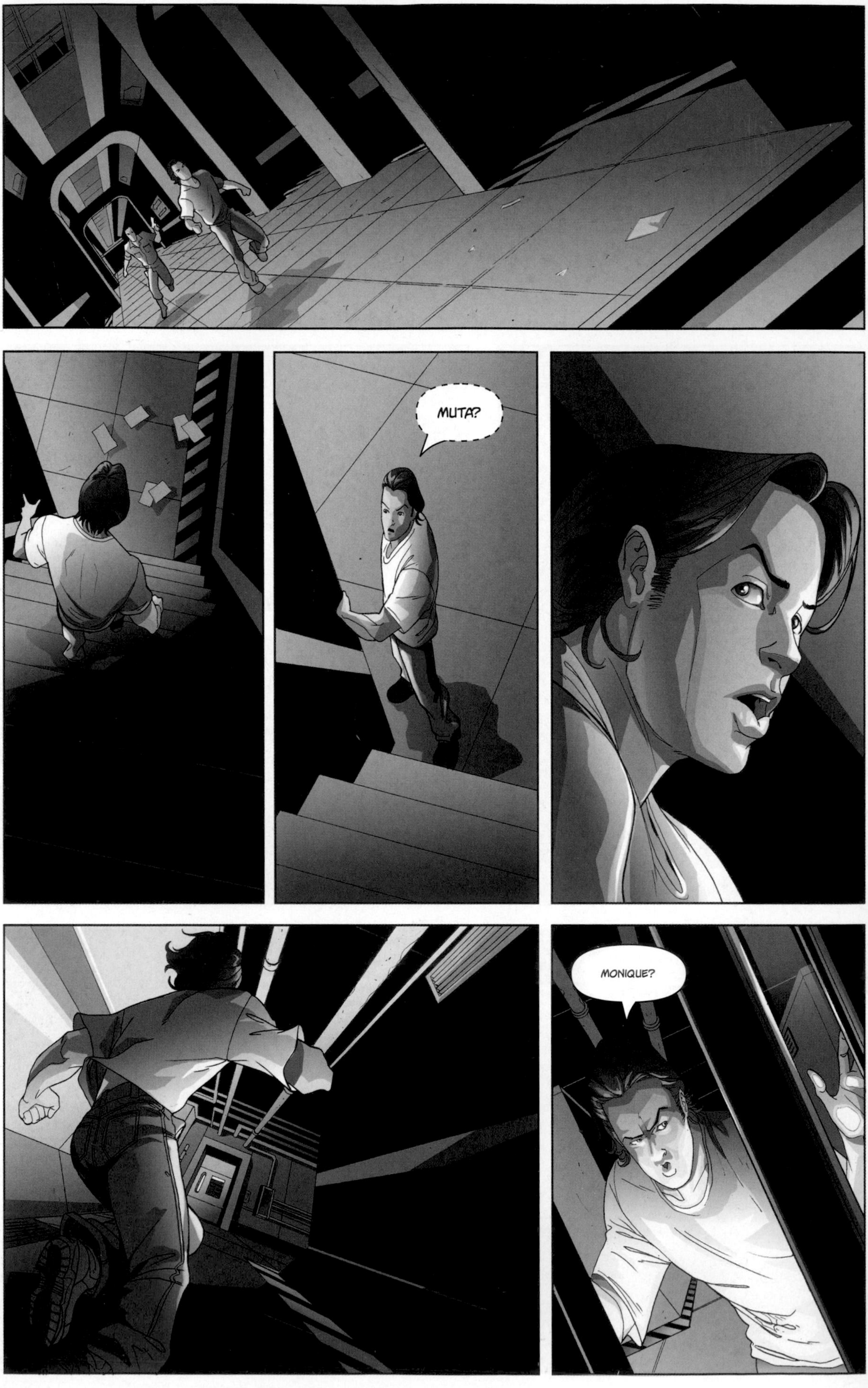
MUTA?
MONIQUE?

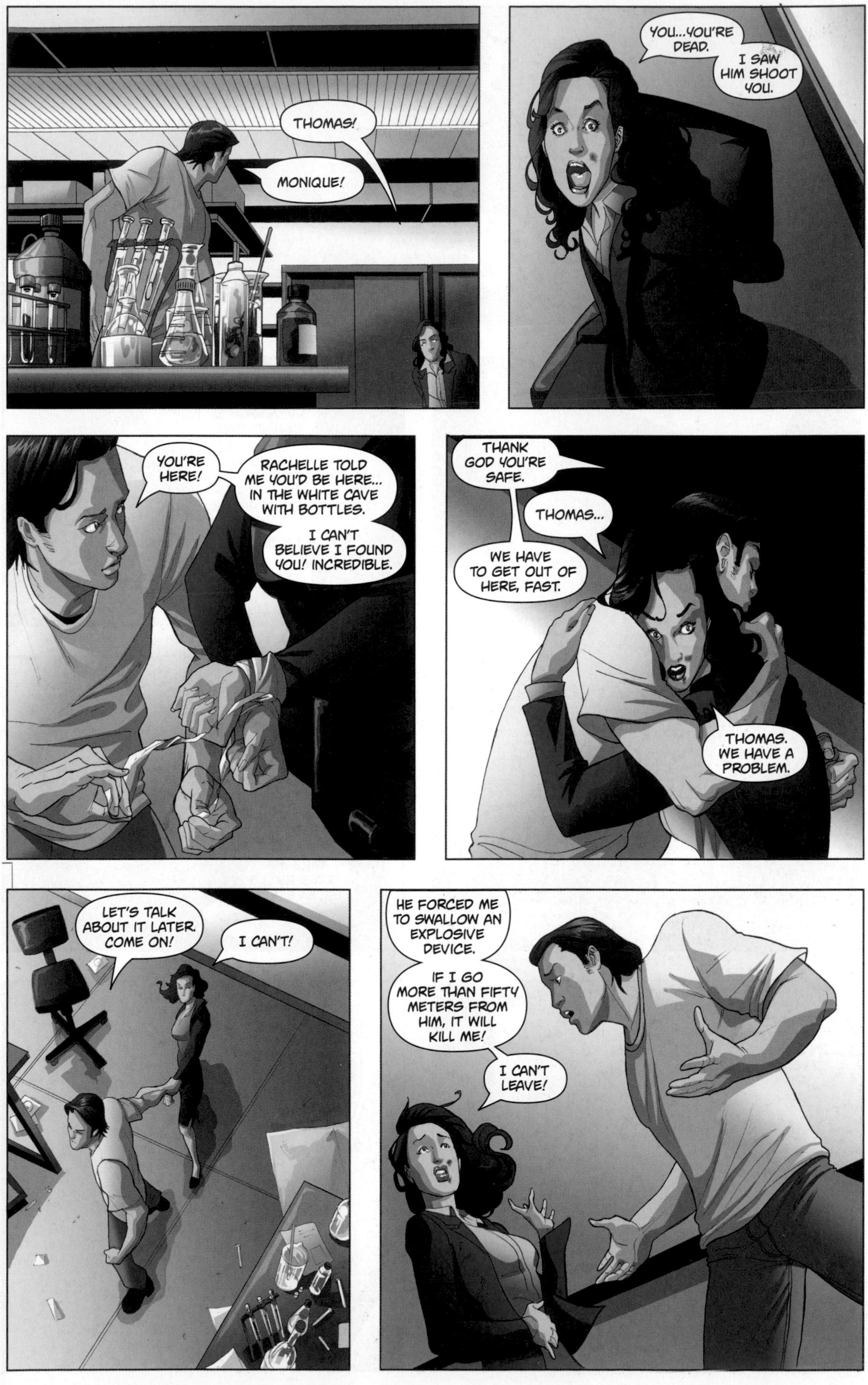
THOMAS!
MONIQUE!
YOU...YOU'RE DEAD.
I SAW HIM SHOOT YOU.
YOU'RE HERE!
RACHELLE TOLD ME YOU'D BE HERE... IN THE WHITE CAVE WITH BOTTLES.
I CAN'T BELIEVE I FOUND YOU! INCREDIBLE.
THANK GOD YOU'RE SAFE.
THOMAS...
WE HAVE TO GET OUT OF HERE, FAST.
THOMAS. WE HAVE A PROBLEM.
LET'S TALK ABOUT IT LATER. COME ON!
I CAN'T!
HE FORCED ME TO SWALLOW AN EXPLOSIVE DEVICE.
IF I GO MORE THAN FIFTY METERS FROM HIM, IT WILL KILL ME!
I CAN'T LEAVE!

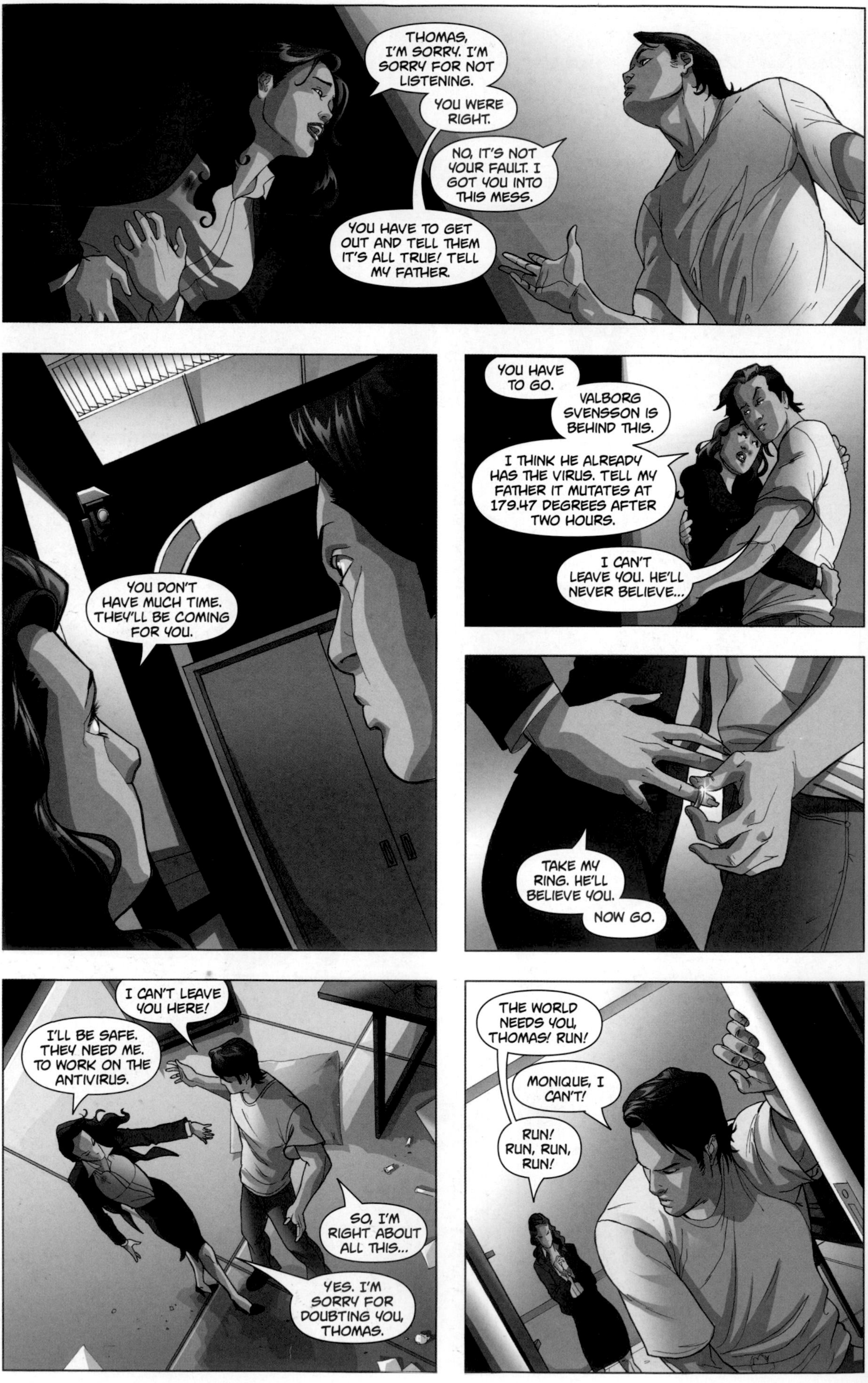
THOMAS, I'M SORRY. I'M SORRY FOR NOT LISTENING.
YOU WERE RIGHT.
NO, IT'S NOT YOUR FAULT. I GOT YOU INTO THIS MESS.
YOU HAVE TO GET OUT AND TELL THEM IT'S ALL TRUE! TELL MY FATHER.
YOU DON'T HAVE MUCH TIME. THEY'LL BE COMING FOR YOU.
YOU HAVE TO GO.
VALBORG SVENSSON IS BEHIND THIS.
I THINK HE ALREADY HAS THE VIRUS. TELL MY FATHER IT MUTATES AT 179.47 DEGREES AFTER TWO HOURS.
I CAN'T LEAVE YOU. HE'LL NEVER BELIEVE...
TAKE MY RING. HE'LL BELIEVE YOU.
NOW GO.
I CAN'T LEAVE YOU HERE!
I'LL BE SAFE. THEY NEED ME. TO WORK ON THE ANTIVIRUS.
SO, I'M RIGHT ABOUT ALL THIS...
YES. I'M SORRY FOR DOUBTING YOU, THOMAS.
THE WORLD NEEDS YOU, THOMAS! RUN!
MONIQUE, I CAN'T!
RUN! RUN, RUN, RUN!

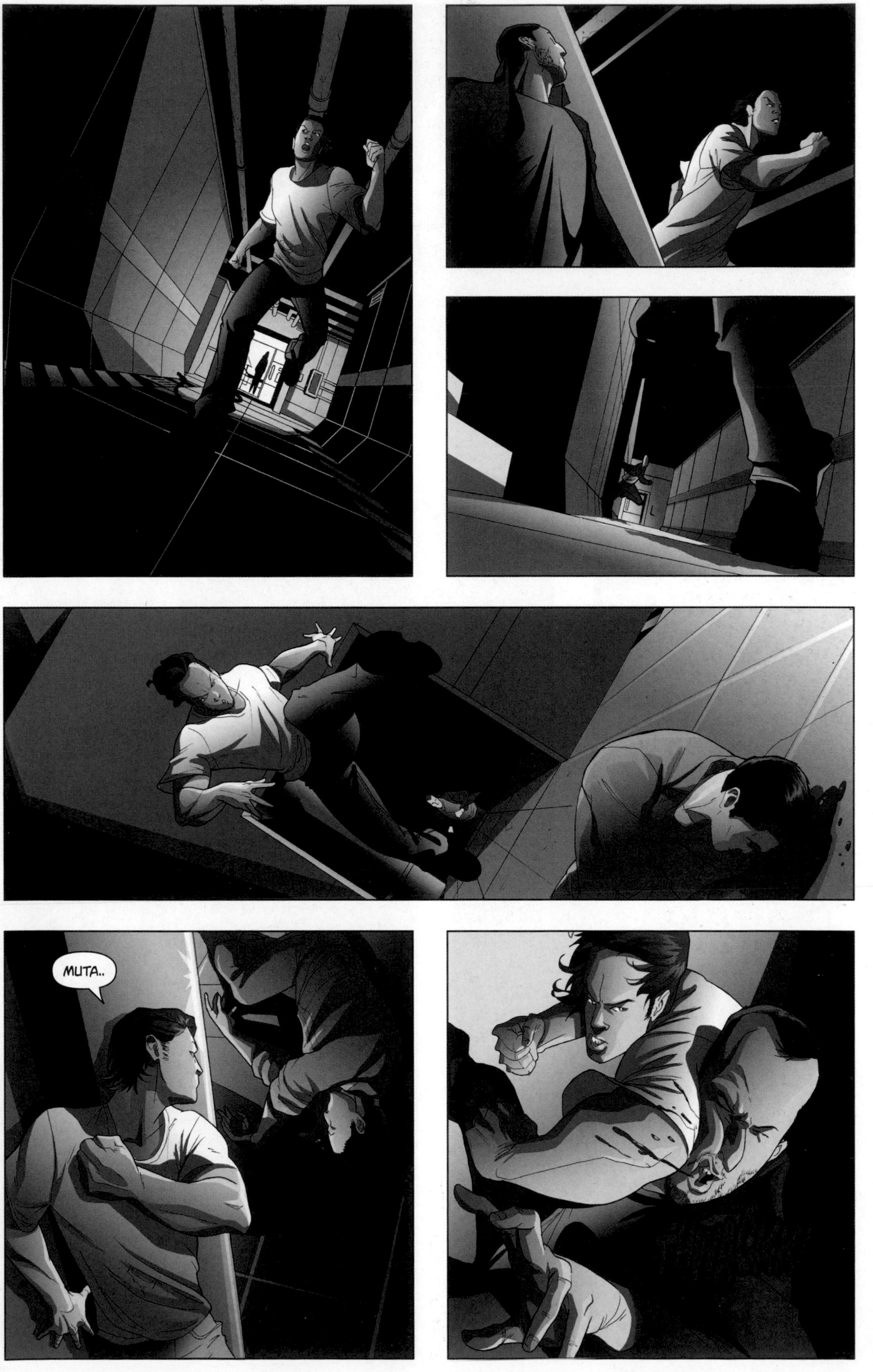
MUTA..

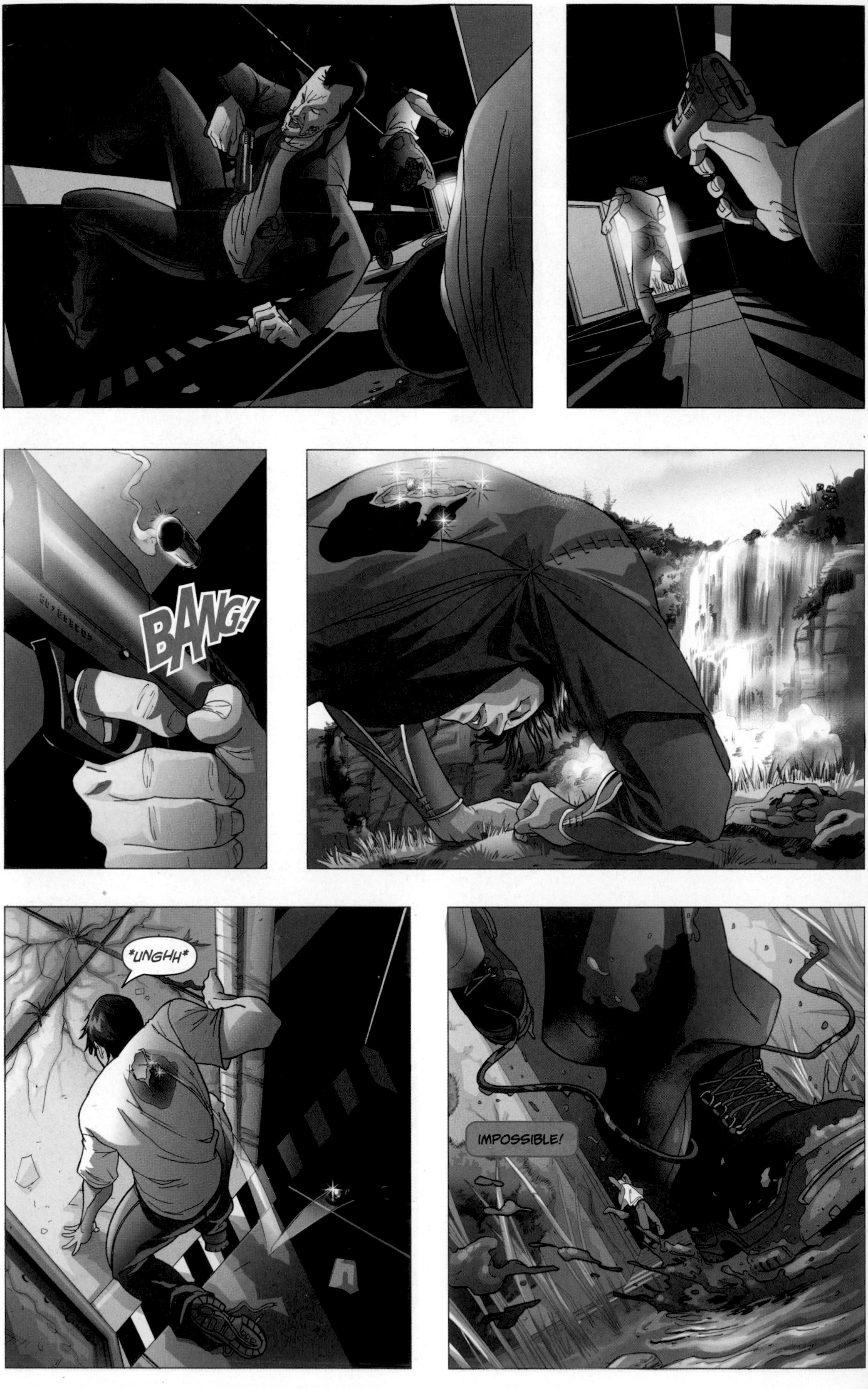
BANG!
UNGHH
IMPOSSIBLE!

YOU GAVE THEM THE VACCINE?

THEY GAVE ME ONE HOUR, MR. HUNTER. MY DAUGHTER'S LIFE WAS ON THE LINE.

...IT'S NOT JUST YOUR DAUGHTER'S LIFE THAT'S ON THE LINE HERE JACQUES!

FOR ME IT IS.

SHE GAVE ME THIS TO PERSUADE YOU TO LISTEN TO ME.

YOU... YOU SAW HER? IS SHE OK?

YES. SHE TOLD ME THAT THEY NEED HER. SO SHE STILL HAS SOME TIME.

BUT HOW MUCH... WHY DIDN'T YOU GET HER OUT?

THEY WOULD HAVE KILLED HER IF I TRIED. TRUST ME, I WOULD HAVE BROUGHT HER HOME IF I COULD HAVE.

VALBORG SVENSSON HAS THE VIRUS, AND NOW HE'S WORKING ON THE ANTI-VIRUS.

SO WHAT DO WE DO NEXT?

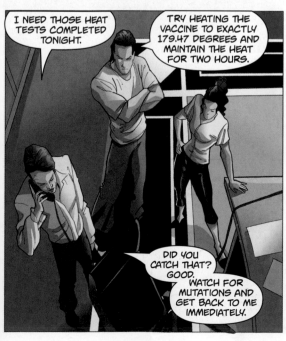

I NEED THOSE HEAT TESTS COMPLETED TONIGHT.

TRY HEATING THE VACCINE TO EXACTLY 179.47 DEGREES AND MAINTAIN THE HEAT FOR TWO HOURS.

DID YOU CATCH THAT? GOOD. WATCH FOR MUTATIONS AND GET BACK TO ME IMMEDIATELY.

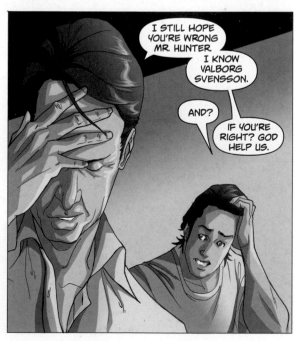

I STILL HOPE YOU'RE WRONG MR. HUNTER.

I KNOW VALBORG SVENSSON.

AND?

IF YOU'RE RIGHT? GOD HELP US.

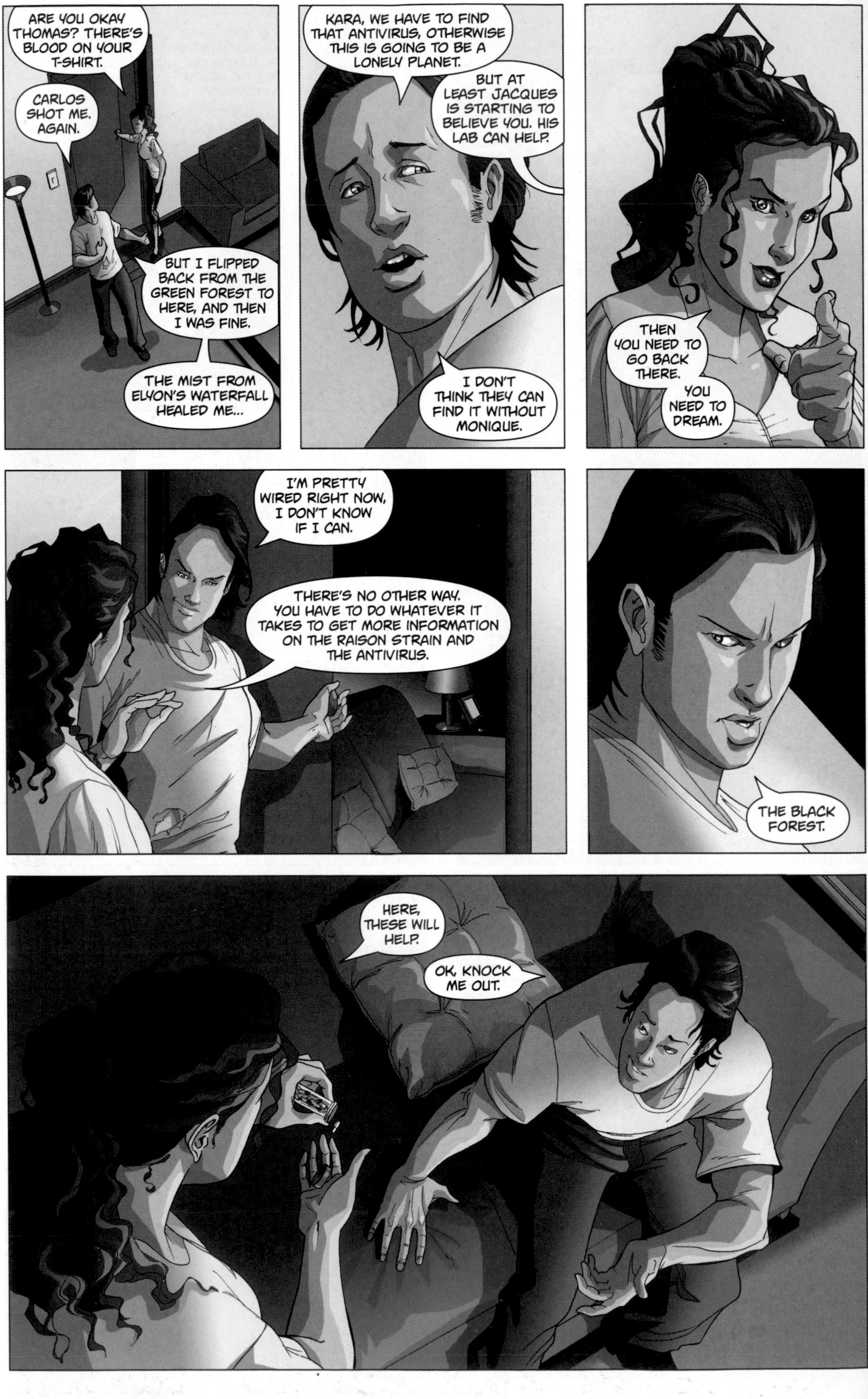
ARE YOU OKAY THOMAS? THERE'S BLOOD ON YOUR T-SHIRT.
CARLOS SHOT ME. AGAIN.
BUT I FLIPPED BACK FROM THE GREEN FOREST TO HERE, AND THEN I WAS FINE.
THE MIST FROM ELYON'S WATERFALL HEALED ME...
KARA, WE HAVE TO FIND THAT ANTIVIRUS, OTHERWISE THIS IS GOING TO BE A LONELY PLANET.
BUT AT LEAST JACQUES IS STARTING TO BELIEVE YOU. HIS LAB CAN HELP.
I DON'T THINK THEY CAN FIND IT WITHOUT MONIQUE.
THEN YOU NEED TO GO BACK THERE.
YOU NEED TO DREAM.
I'M PRETTY WIRED RIGHT NOW, I DON'T KNOW IF I CAN.
THERE'S NO OTHER WAY. YOU HAVE TO DO WHATEVER IT TAKES TO GET MORE INFORMATION ON THE RAISON STRAIN AND THE ANTIVIRUS.
THE BLACK FOREST.
HERE, THESE WILL HELP.
OK, KNOCK ME OUT.

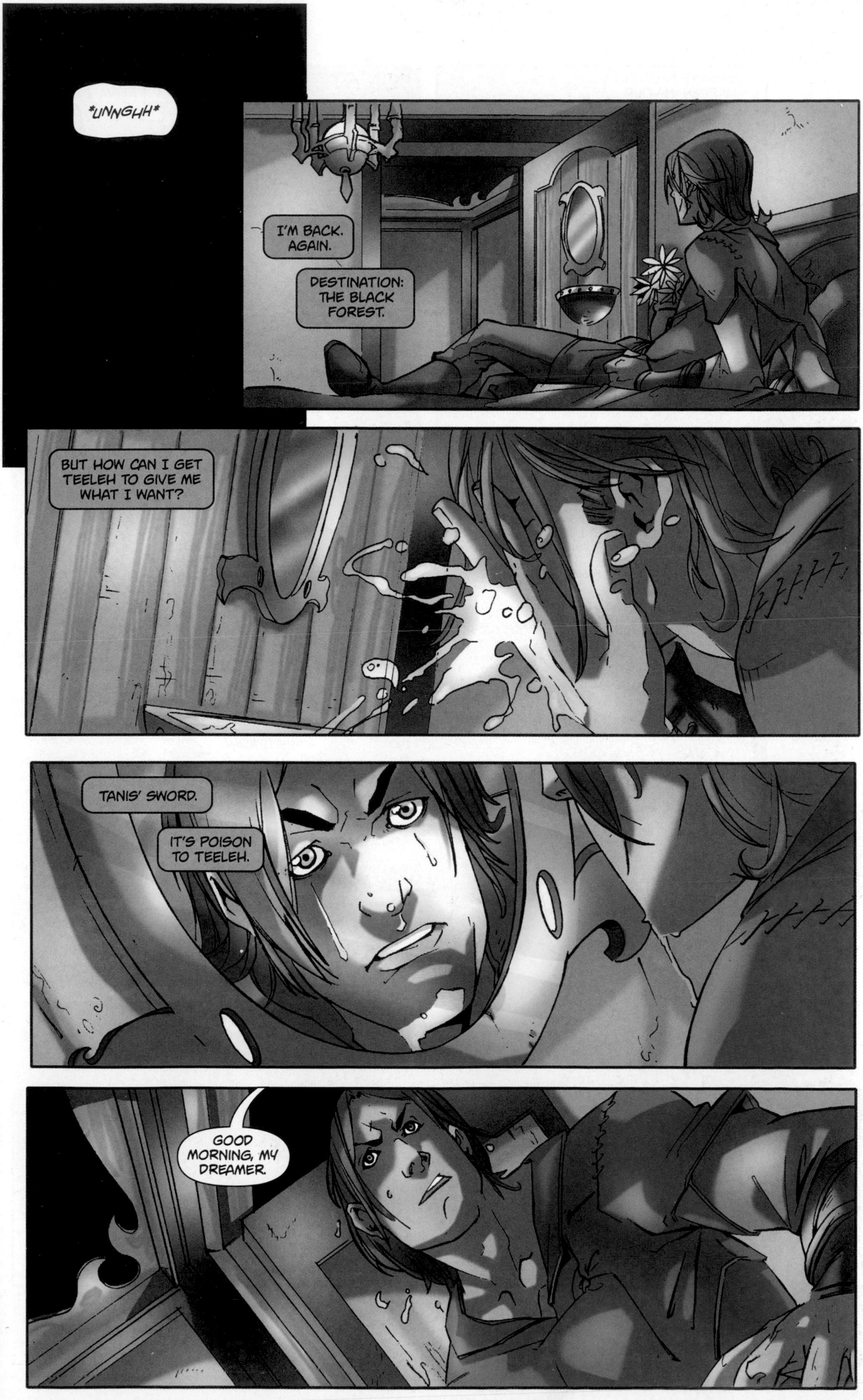
UNNGHH
I'M BACK. AGAIN.
DESTINATION: THE BLACK FOREST.
BUT HOW CAN I GET TEELEH TO GIVE ME WHAT I WANT?
TANIS' SWORD.
IT'S POISON TO TEELEH.
GOOD MORNING, MY DREAMER.

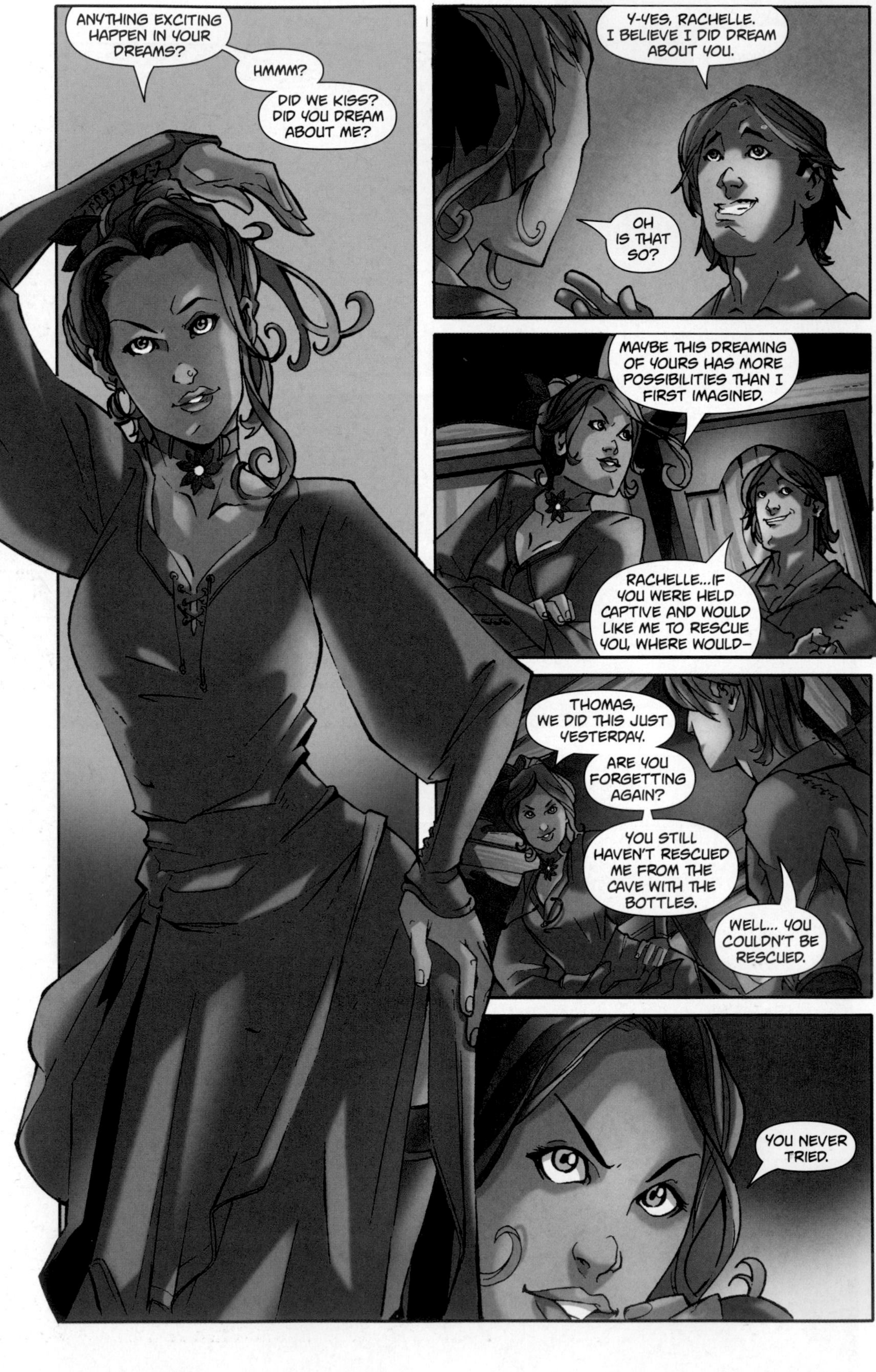
ANYTHING EXCITING HAPPEN IN YOUR DREAMS?
HMMM?
DID WE KISS? DID YOU DREAM ABOUT ME?
Y-YES, RACHELLE. I BELIEVE I DID DREAM ABOUT YOU.
OH IS THAT SO?
MAYBE THIS DREAMING OF YOURS HAS MORE POSSIBILITIES THAN I FIRST IMAGINED.
RACHELLE...IF YOU WERE HELD CAPTIVE AND WOULD LIKE ME TO RESCUE YOU, WHERE WOULD–
THOMAS, WE DID THIS JUST YESTERDAY.
ARE YOU FORGETTING AGAIN?
YOU STILL HAVEN'T RESCUED ME FROM THE CAVE WITH THE BOTTLES.
WELL... YOU COULDN'T BE RESCUED.
YOU NEVER TRIED.

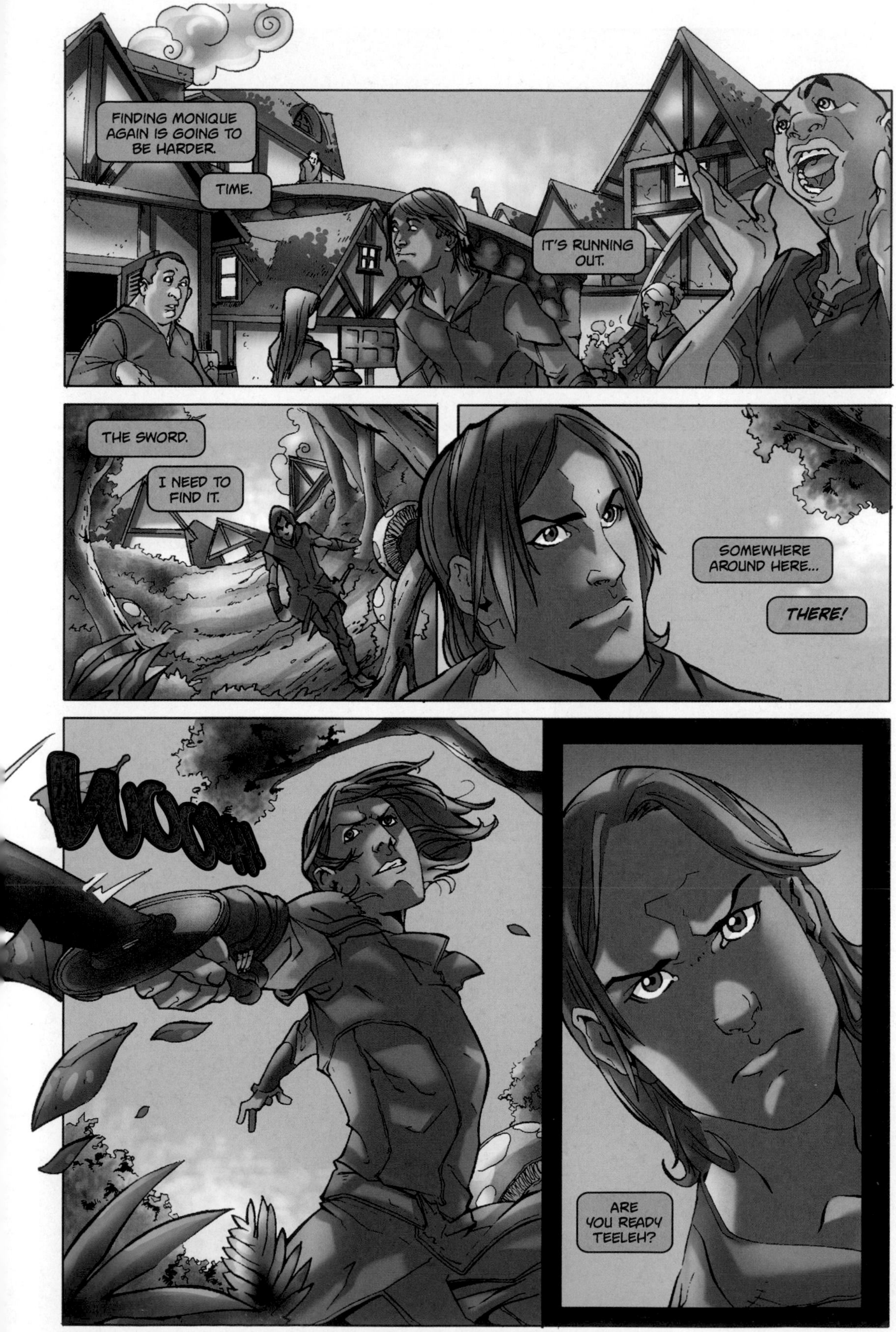
FINDING MONIQUE AGAIN IS GOING TO BE HARDER.
TIME.
IT'S RUNNING OUT.
THE SWORD.
I NEED TO FIND IT.
SOMEWHERE AROUND HERE...
THERE!
WOOSH
ARE YOU READY TEELEH?

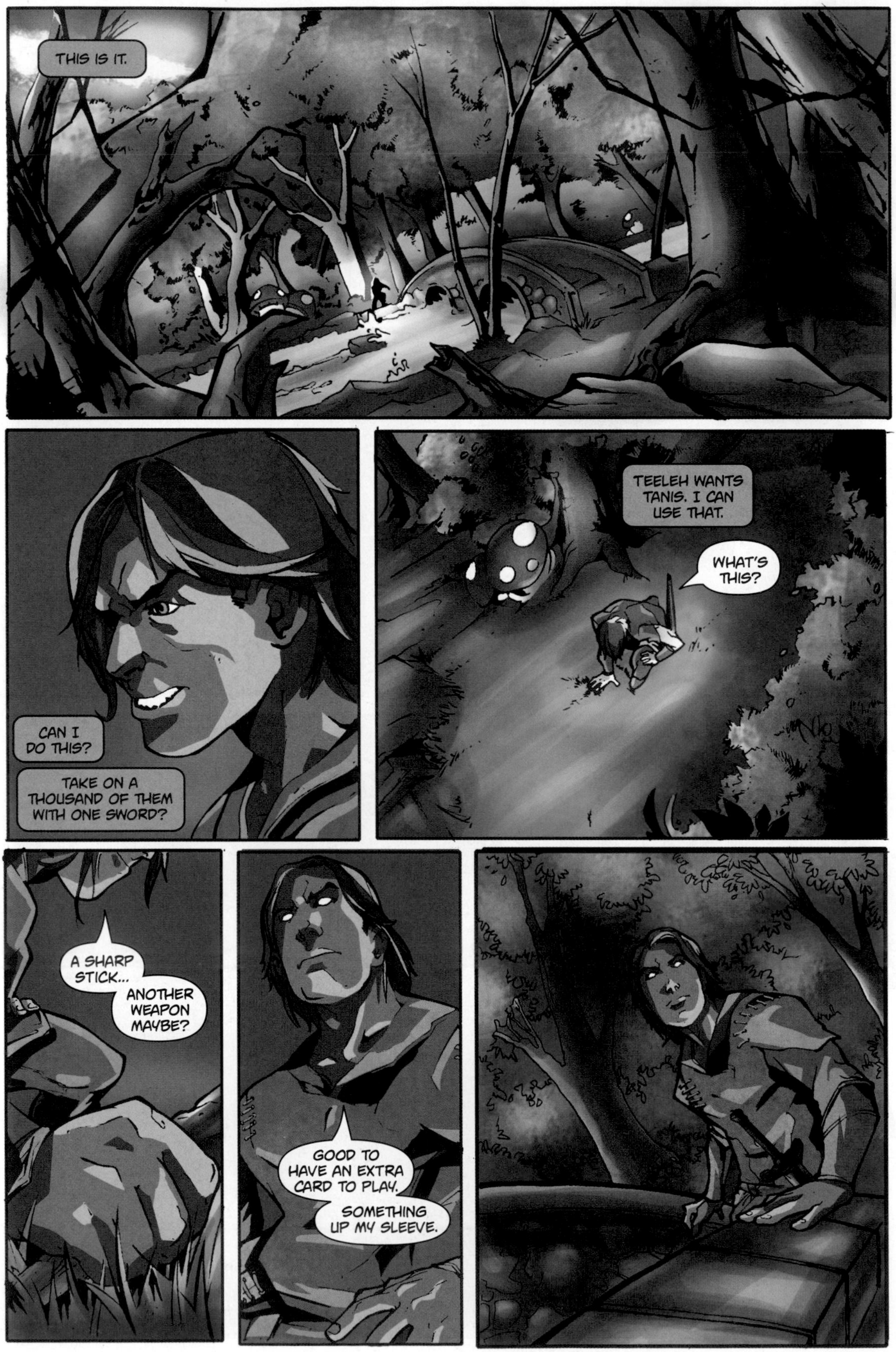
THIS IS IT.
CAN I DO THIS?
TAKE ON A THOUSAND OF THEM WITH ONE SWORD?
TEELEH WANTS TANIS. I CAN USE THAT.
WHAT'S THIS?
A SHARP STICK...
ANOTHER WEAPON MAYBE?
GOOD TO HAVE AN EXTRA CARD TO PLAY.
SOMETHING UP MY SLEEVE.

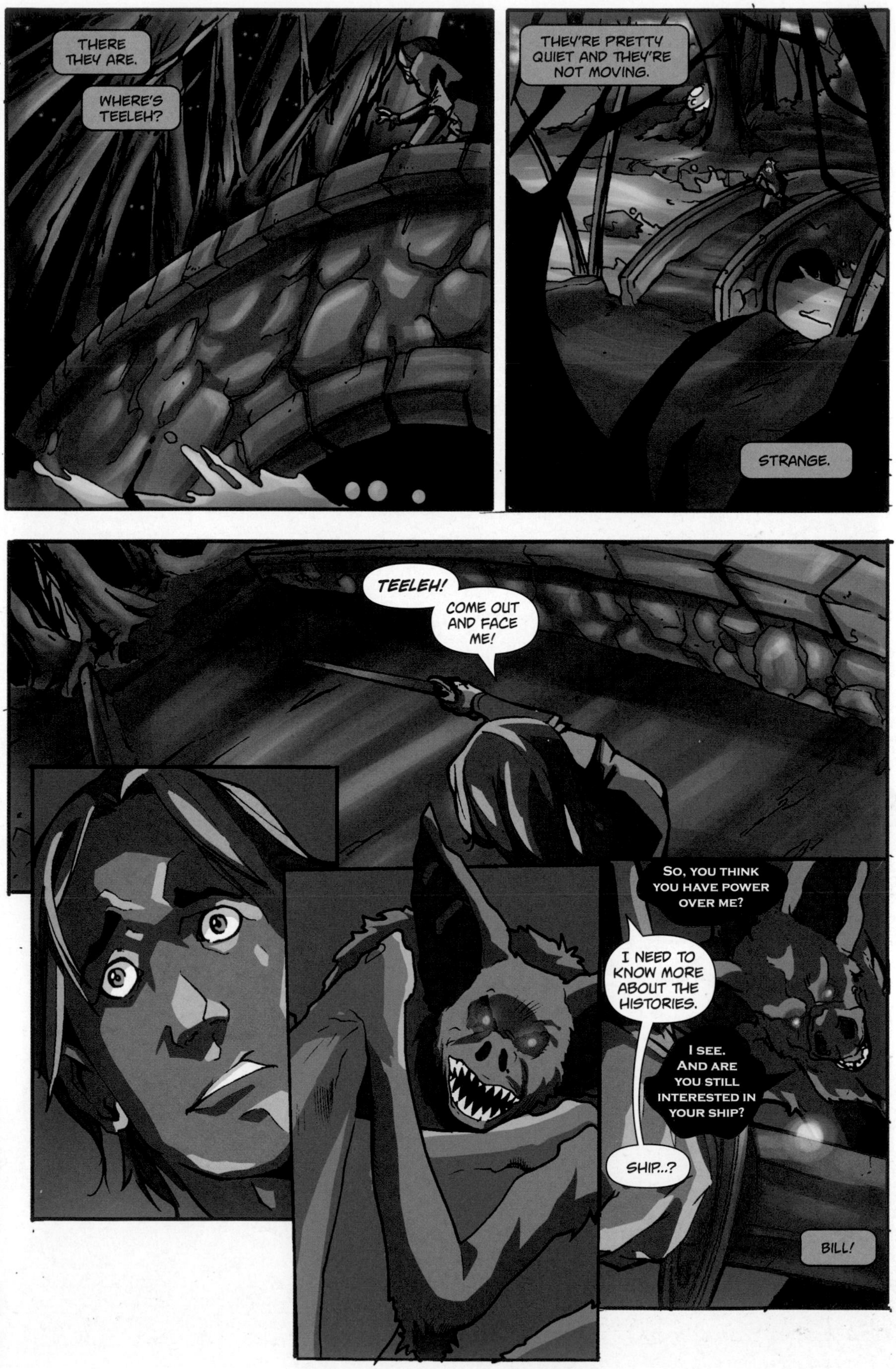
THERE THEY ARE.
WHERE'S TEELEH?
THEY'RE PRETTY QUIET AND THEY'RE NOT MOVING.
STRANGE.
TEELEH!
COME OUT AND FACE ME!
So, YOU THINK YOU HAVE POWER OVER ME?
I NEED TO KNOW MORE ABOUT THE HISTORIES.
I SEE. AND ARE YOU STILL INTERESTED IN YOUR SHIP?
SHIP...?
BILL!

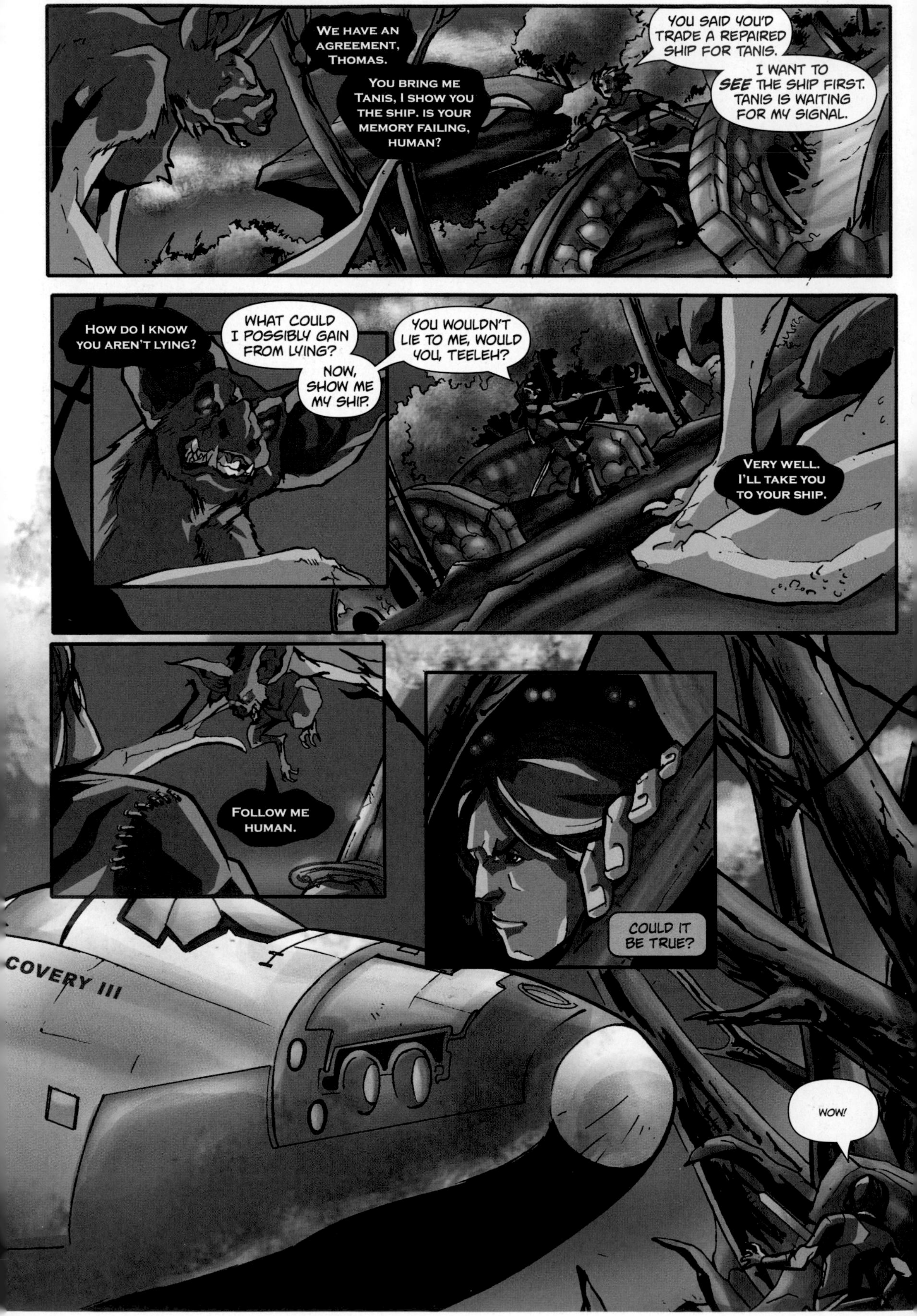
We have an agreement, Thomas.
You bring me Tanis, I show you the ship. Is your memory failing, human?
You said you'd trade a repaired ship for Tanis.
I want to SEE the ship first. Tanis is waiting for my signal.
How do I know you aren't lying?
What could I possibly gain from lying?
Now, show me my ship.
You wouldn't lie to me, would you, Teeleh?
Very well. I'll take you to your ship.
Follow me human.
Could it be true?
COVERY III
WOW!

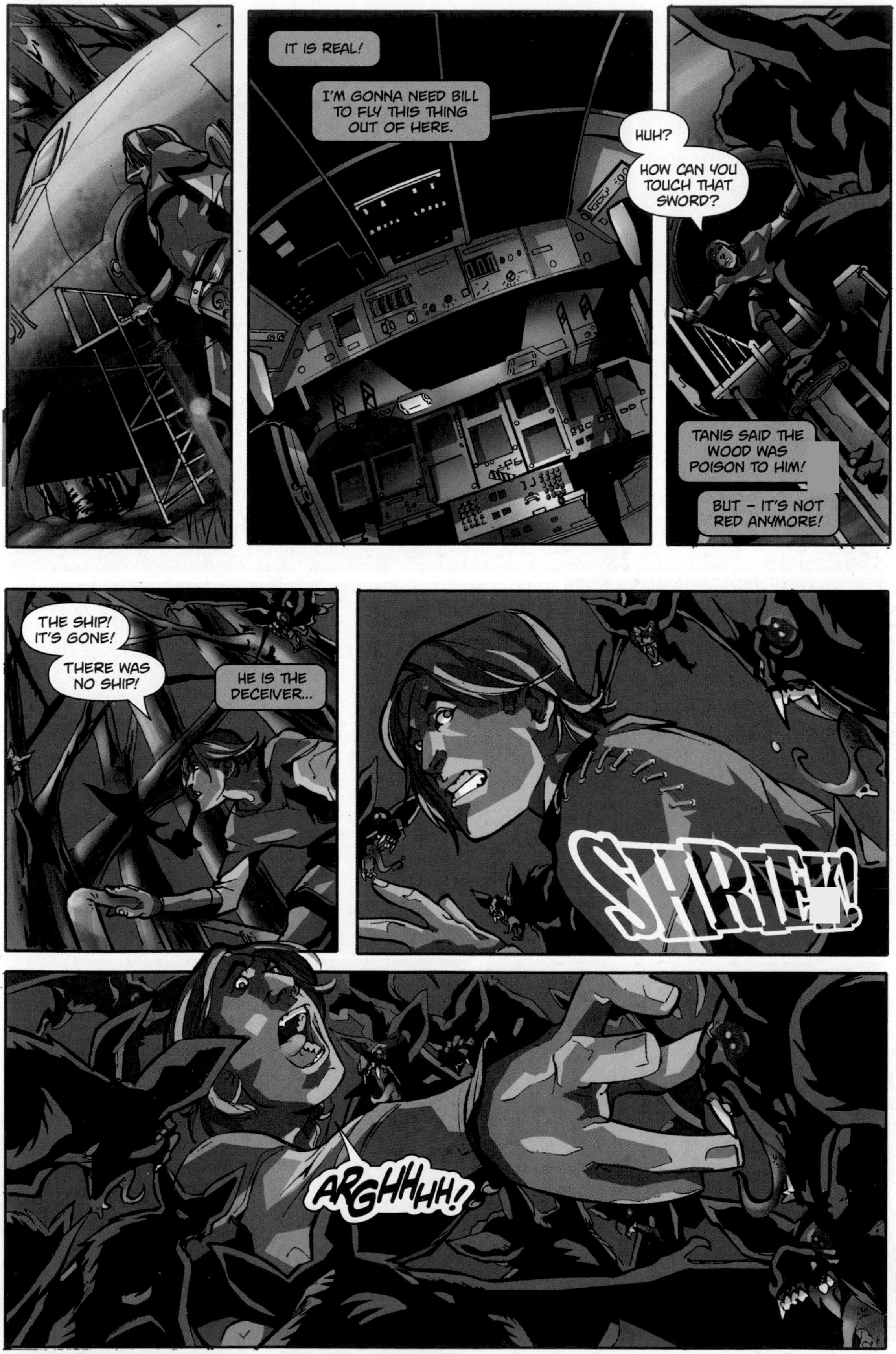
IT IS REAL!
I'M GONNA NEED BILL TO FLY THIS THING OUT OF HERE.
HUH?
HOW CAN YOU TOUCH THAT SWORD?
TANIS SAID THE WOOD WAS POISON TO HIM!
BUT – IT'S NOT RED ANYMORE!
THE SHIP! IT'S GONE!
THERE WAS NO SHIP!
HE IS THE DECEIVER...
SHRIEK!
ARGHHHH!

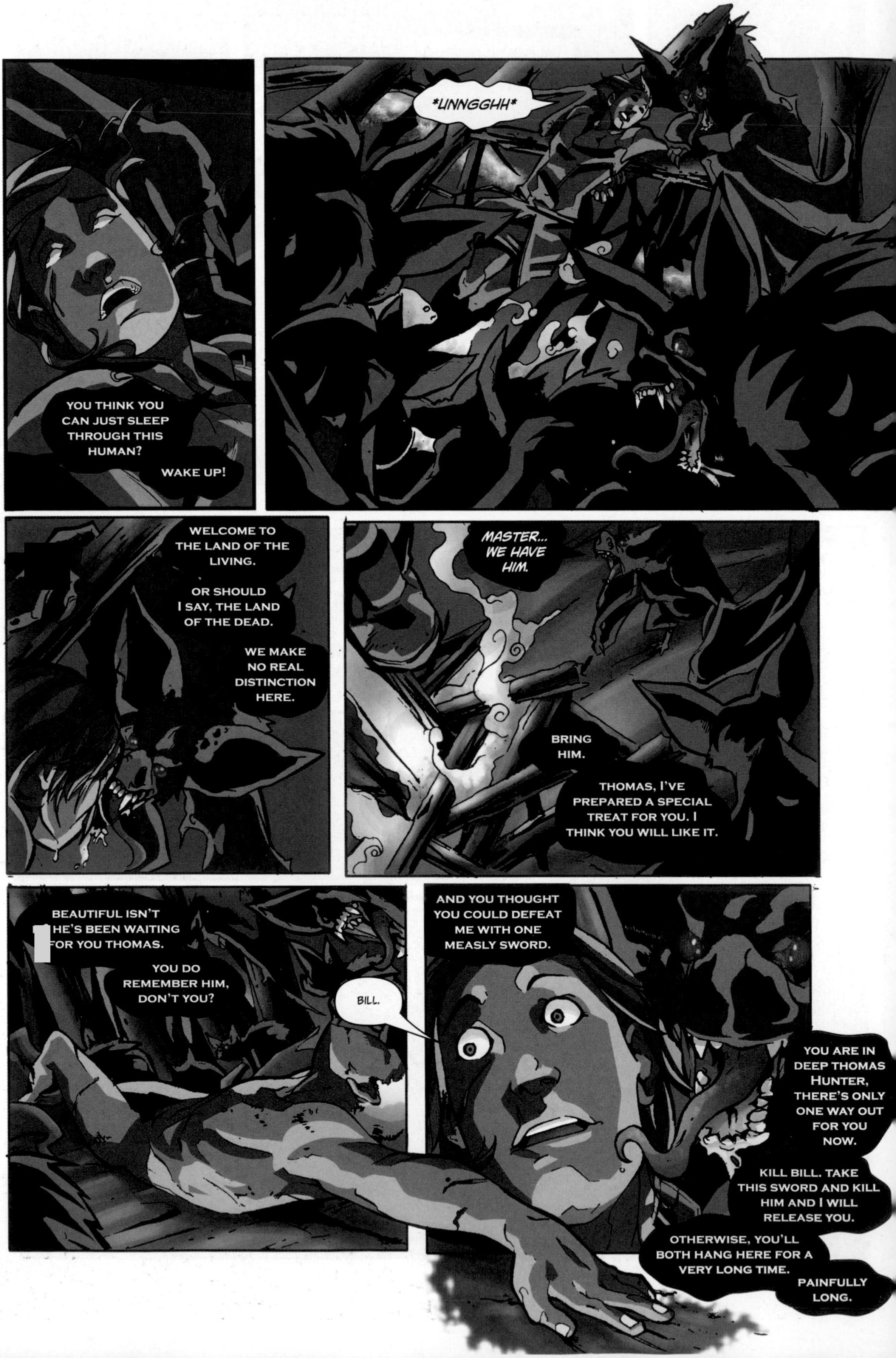
YOU THINK YOU CAN JUST SLEEP THROUGH THIS HUMAN?
WAKE UP!
UNNGGHH
WELCOME TO THE LAND OF THE LIVING.
OR SHOULD I SAY, THE LAND OF THE DEAD.
WE MAKE NO REAL DISTINCTION HERE.
MASTER... WE HAVE HIM.
BRING HIM.
THOMAS, I'VE PREPARED A SPECIAL TREAT FOR YOU. I THINK YOU WILL LIKE IT.
BEAUTIFUL ISN'T HE'S BEEN WAITING FOR YOU THOMAS.
YOU DO REMEMBER HIM, DON'T YOU?
BILL.
AND YOU THOUGHT YOU COULD DEFEAT ME WITH ONE MEASLY SWORD.
YOU ARE IN DEEP THOMAS HUNTER, THERE'S ONLY ONE WAY OUT FOR YOU NOW.
KILL BILL. TAKE THIS SWORD AND KILL HIM AND I WILL RELEASE YOU.
OTHERWISE, YOU'LL BOTH HANG HERE FOR A VERY LONG TIME.
PAINFULLY LONG.

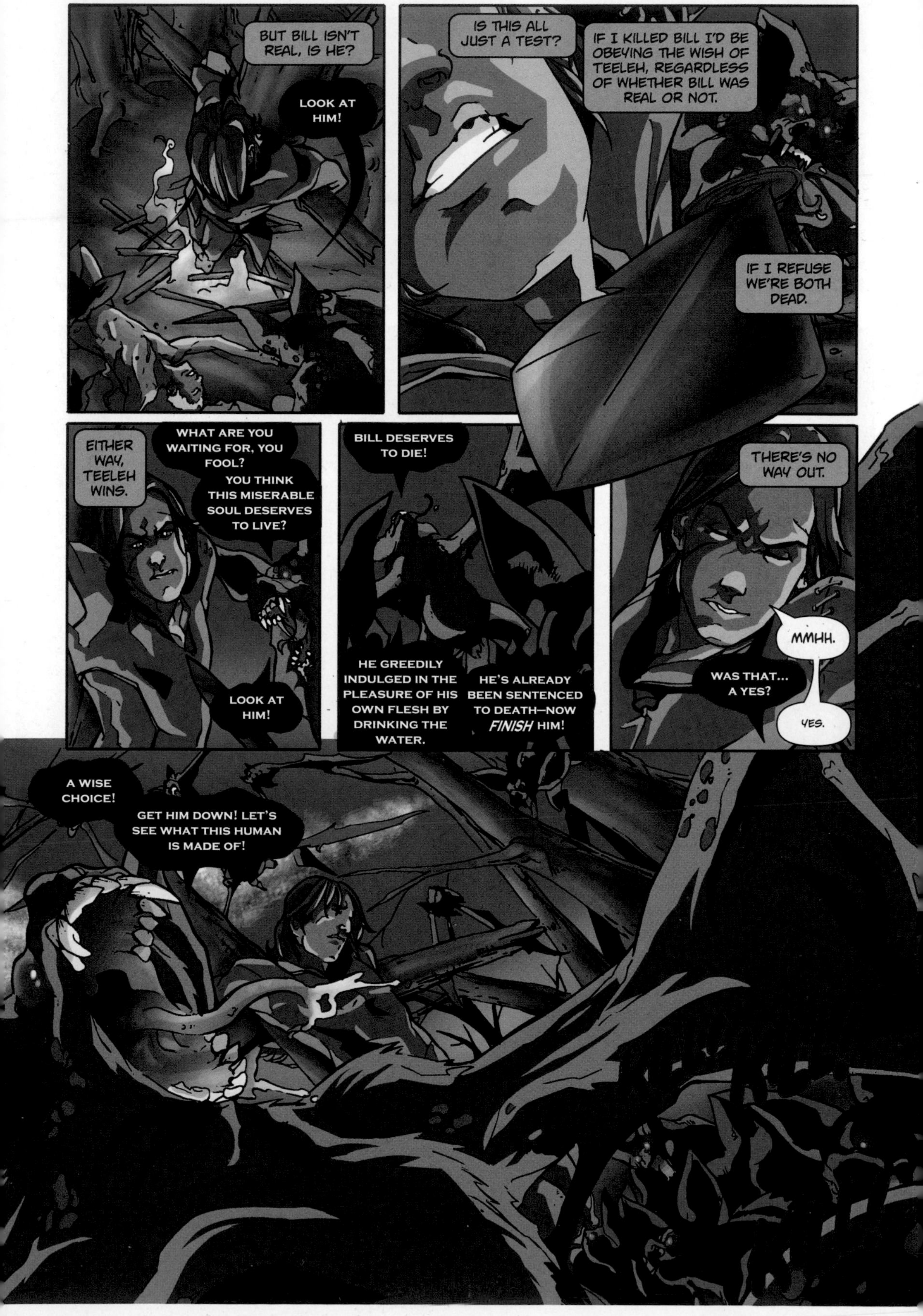
BUT BILL ISN'T REAL, IS HE?
LOOK AT HIM!
IS THIS ALL JUST A TEST?
IF I KILLED BILL I'D BE OBEYING THE WISH OF TEELEH, REGARDLESS OF WHETHER BILL WAS REAL OR NOT.
IF I REFUSE WE'RE BOTH DEAD.
EITHER WAY, TEELEH WINS.
WHAT ARE YOU WAITING FOR, YOU FOOL?
YOU THINK THIS MISERABLE SOUL DESERVES TO LIVE?
LOOK AT HIM!
BILL DESERVES TO DIE!
HE GREEDILY INDULGED IN THE PLEASURE OF HIS OWN FLESH BY DRINKING THE WATER.
HE'S ALREADY BEEN SENTENCED TO DEATH—NOW *FINISH* HIM!
THERE'S NO WAY OUT.
MMHH.
WAS THAT... A YES?
YES.
A WISE CHOICE!
GET HIM DOWN! LET'S SEE WHAT THIS HUMAN IS MADE OF!

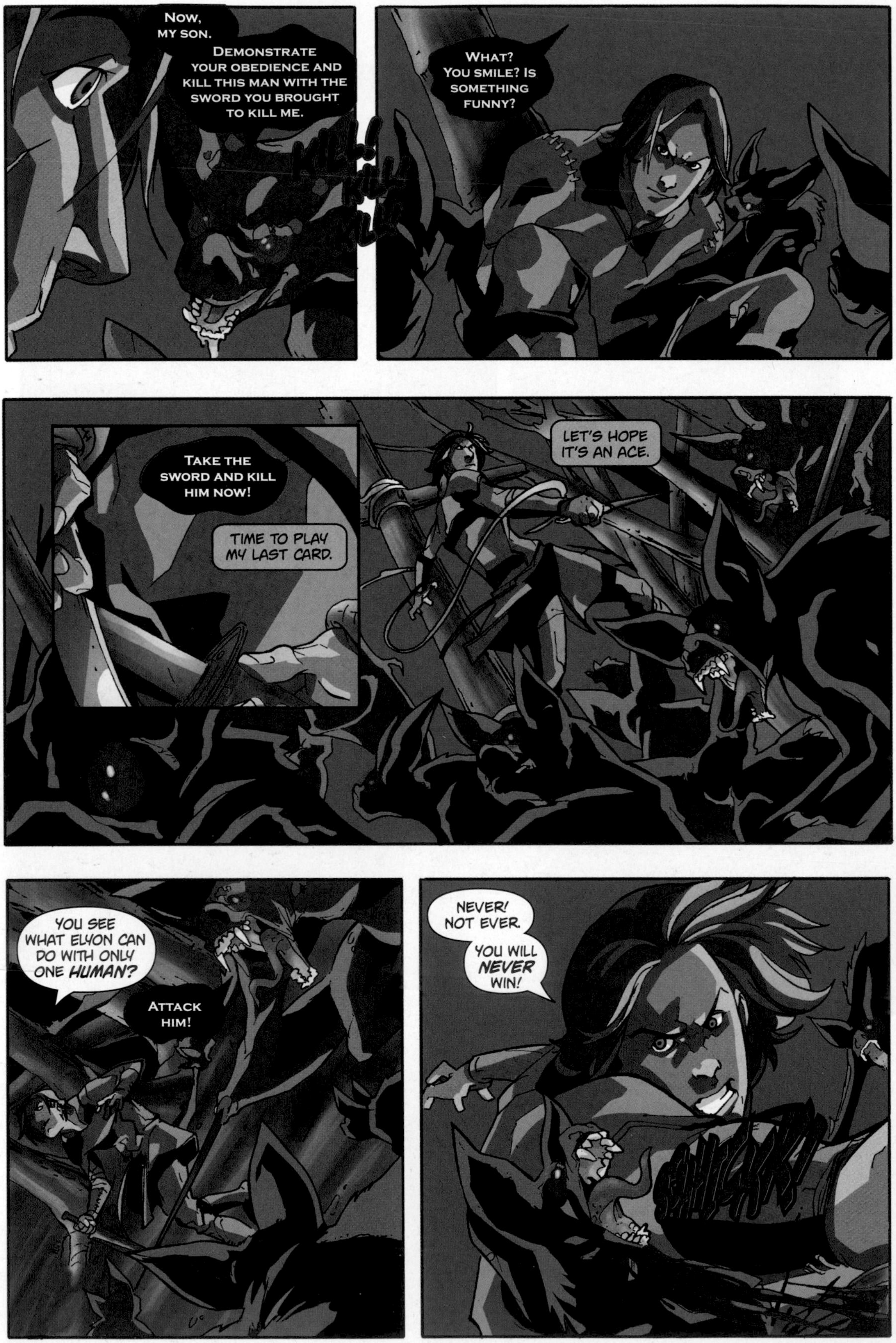

Now, my son.
Demonstrate your obedience and kill this man with the sword you brought to kill me.
KILL!
What? You smile? Is something funny?
Take the sword and kill him now!
Time to play my last card.
Let's hope it's an ace.
You see what Elyon can do with only one *human?*
Attack him!
Never! Not ever.
You will ***never*** win!

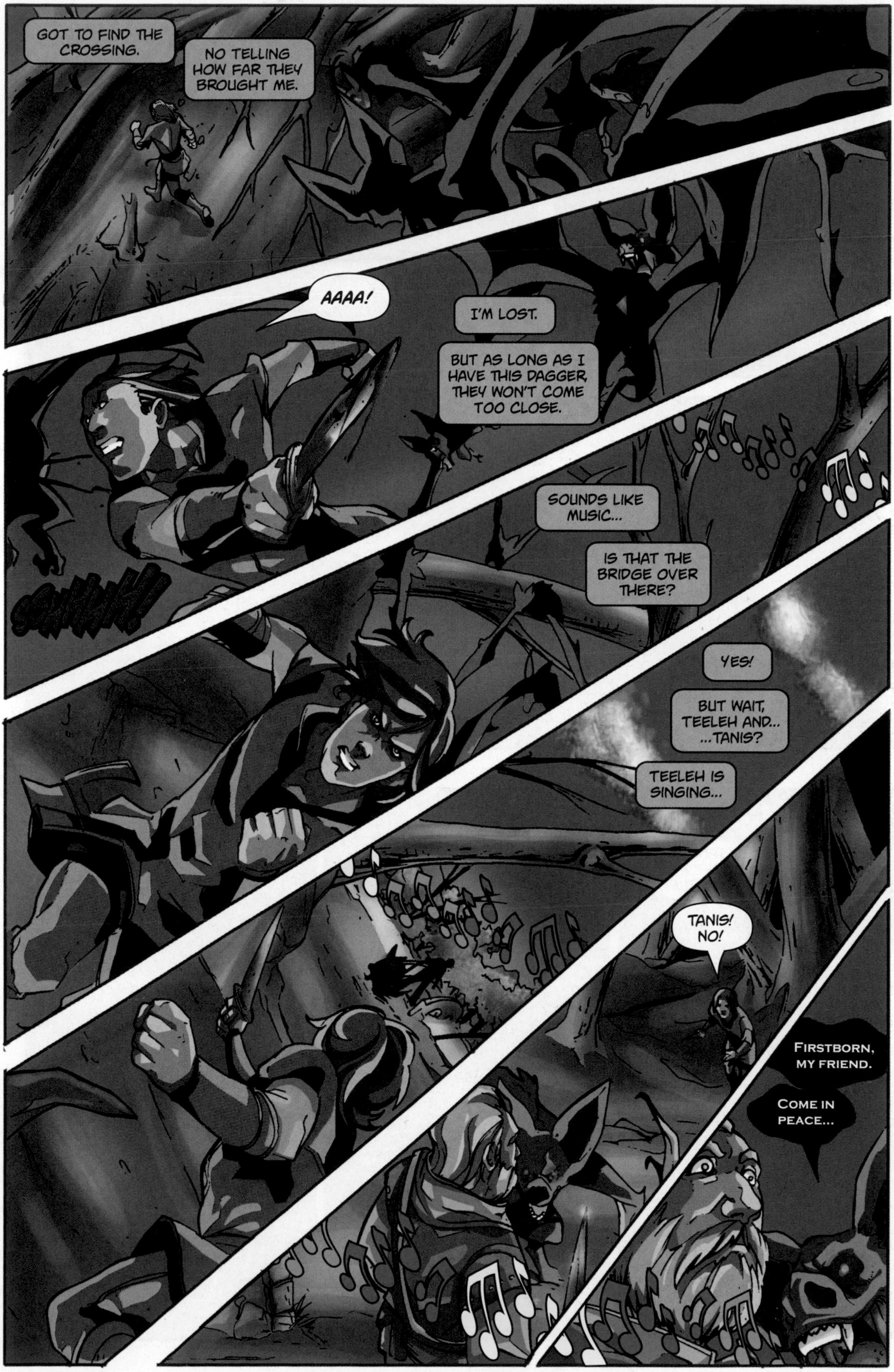
GOT TO FIND THE CROSSING.
NO TELLING HOW FAR THEY BROUGHT ME.
AAAA!
I'M LOST.
BUT AS LONG AS I HAVE THIS DAGGER, THEY WON'T COME TOO CLOSE.
SOUNDS LIKE MUSIC...
IS THAT THE BRIDGE OVER THERE?
YES!
BUT WAIT, TEELEH AND... ...TANIS?
TEELEH IS SINGING...
TANIS! NO!
FIRSTBORN, MY FRIEND.
COME IN PEACE...

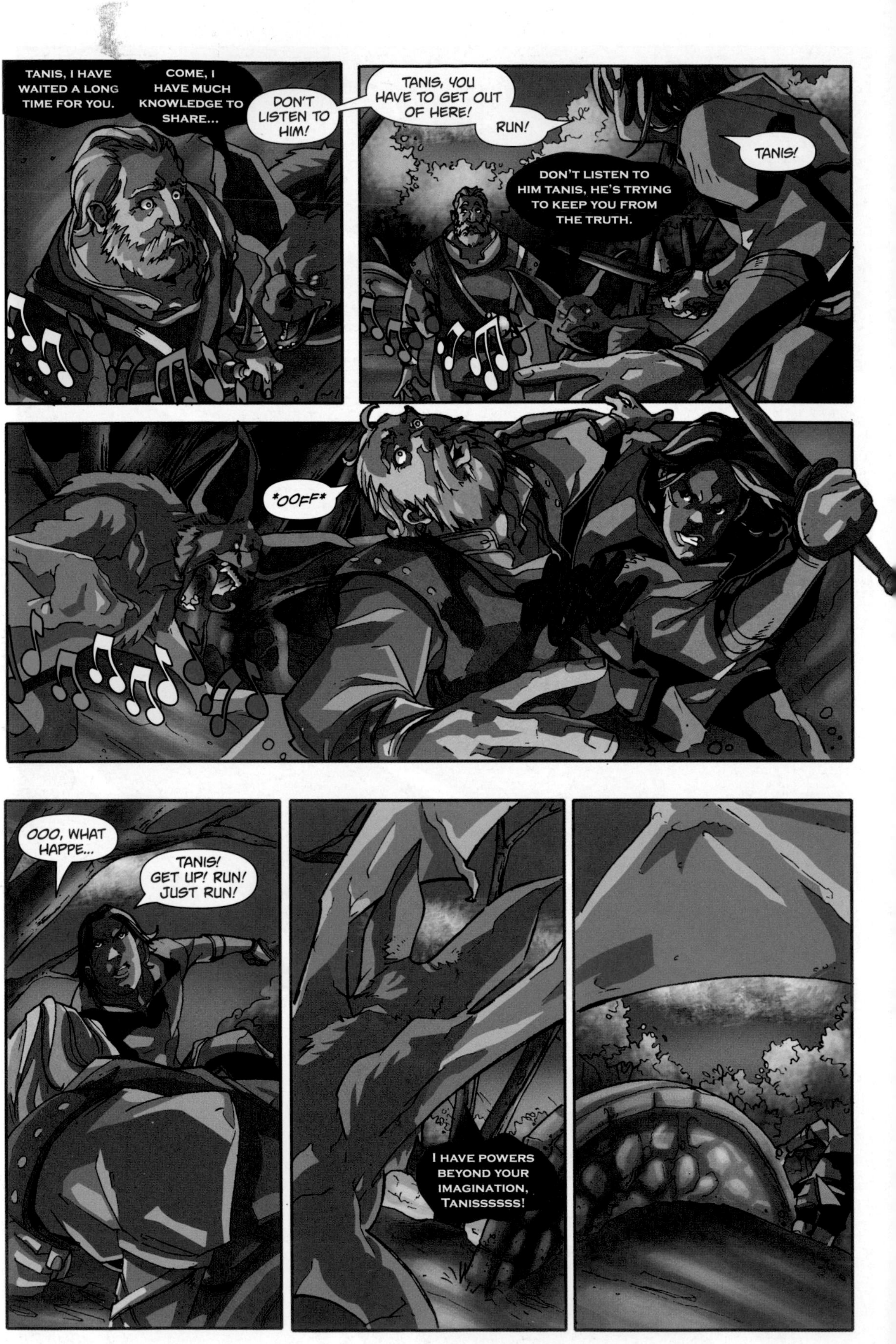
TANIS, I HAVE WAITED A LONG TIME FOR YOU.
COME, I HAVE MUCH KNOWLEDGE TO SHARE...
DON'T LISTEN TO HIM!
TANIS, YOU HAVE TO GET OUT OF HERE!
RUN!
TANIS!
DON'T LISTEN TO HIM TANIS, HE'S TRYING TO KEEP YOU FROM THE TRUTH.
OOFF
OOO, WHAT HAPPE...
TANIS! GET UP! RUN! JUST RUN!
I HAVE POWERS BEYOND YOUR IMAGINATION, Tanissssss!

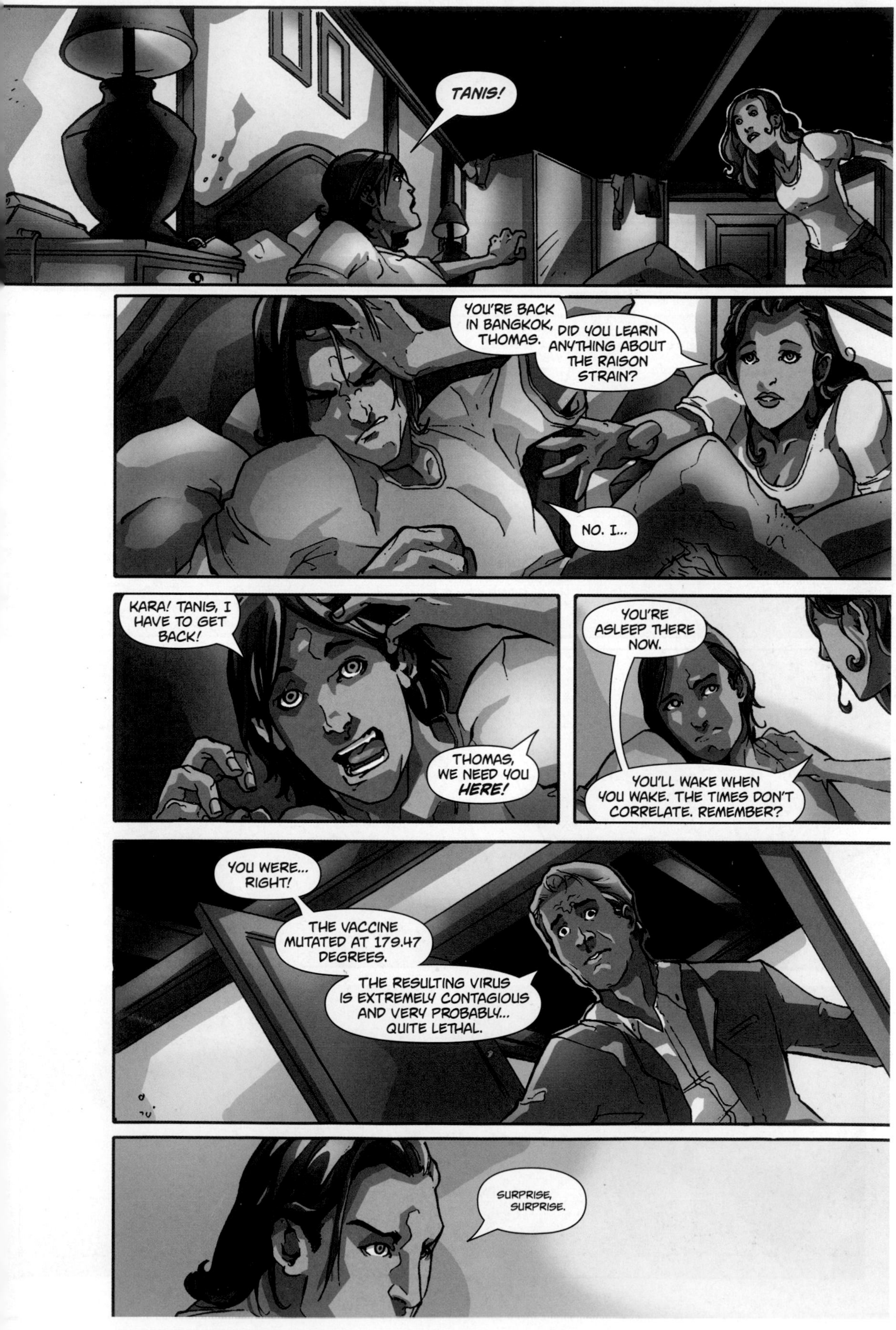
TANIS!
YOU'RE BACK IN BANGKOK, THOMAS.
DID YOU LEARN ANYTHING ABOUT THE RAISON STRAIN?
NO. I...
KARA! TANIS, I HAVE TO GET BACK!
THOMAS, WE NEED YOU HERE!
YOU'RE ASLEEP THERE NOW.
YOU'LL WAKE WHEN YOU WAKE. THE TIMES DON'T CORRELATE. REMEMBER?
YOU WERE... RIGHT!
THE VACCINE MUTATED AT 179.47 DEGREES.
THE RESULTING VIRUS IS EXTREMELY CONTAGIOUS AND VERY PROBABLY... QUITE LETHAL.
SURPRISE, SURPRISE.

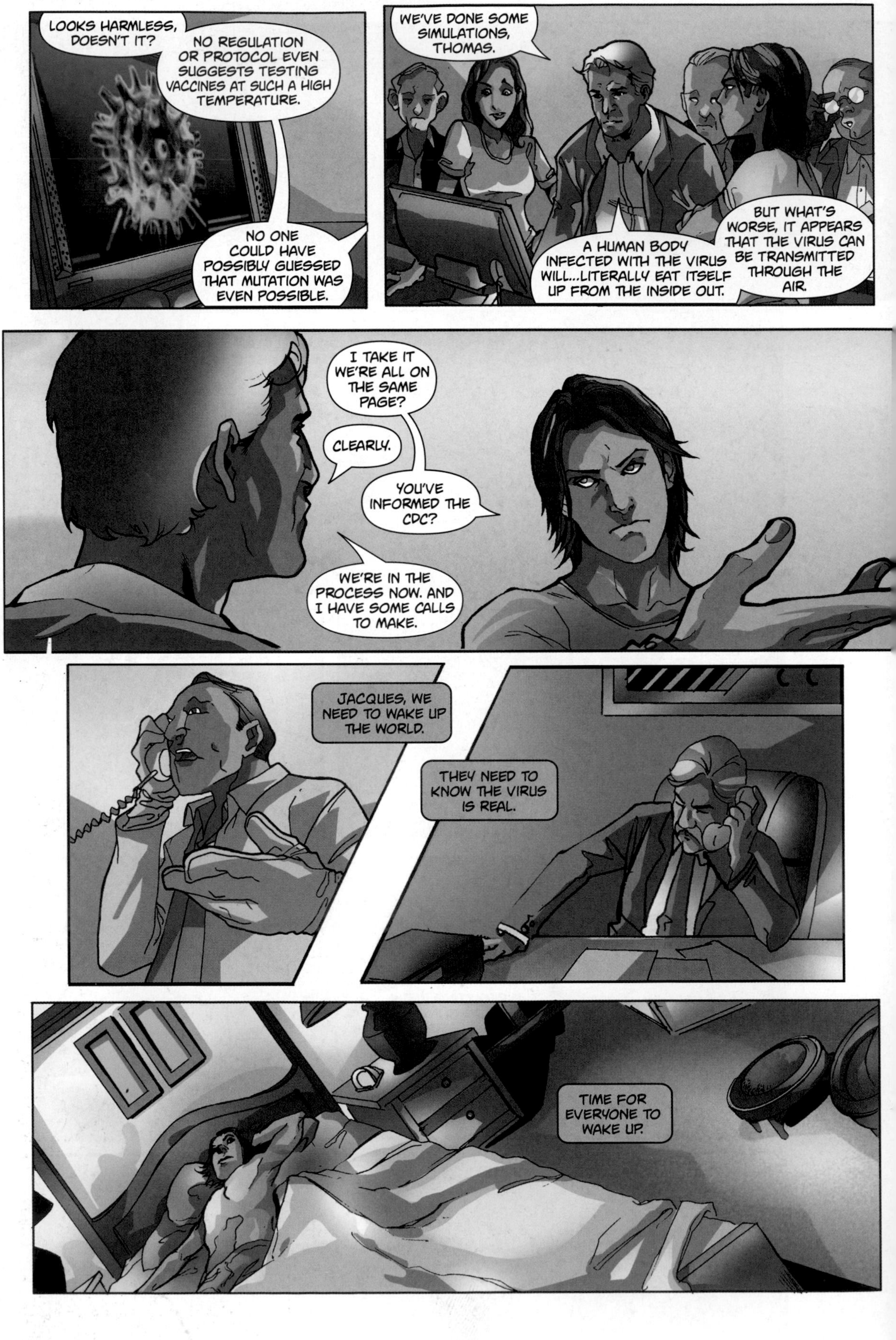
LOOKS HARMLESS, DOESN'T IT?
NO REGULATION OR PROTOCOL EVEN SUGGESTS TESTING VACCINES AT SUCH A HIGH TEMPERATURE.
NO ONE COULD HAVE POSSIBLY GUESSED THAT MUTATION WAS EVEN POSSIBLE.
WE'VE DONE SOME SIMULATIONS, THOMAS.
A HUMAN BODY INFECTED WITH THE VIRUS WILL...LITERALLY EAT ITSELF UP FROM THE INSIDE OUT.
BUT WHAT'S WORSE, IT APPEARS THAT THE VIRUS CAN BE TRANSMITTED THROUGH THE AIR.
I TAKE IT WE'RE ALL ON THE SAME PAGE?
CLEARLY.
YOU'VE INFORMED THE CDC?
WE'RE IN THE PROCESS NOW. AND I HAVE SOME CALLS TO MAKE.
JACQUES, WE NEED TO WAKE UP THE WORLD.
THEY NEED TO KNOW THE VIRUS IS REAL.
TIME FOR EVERYONE TO WAKE UP.

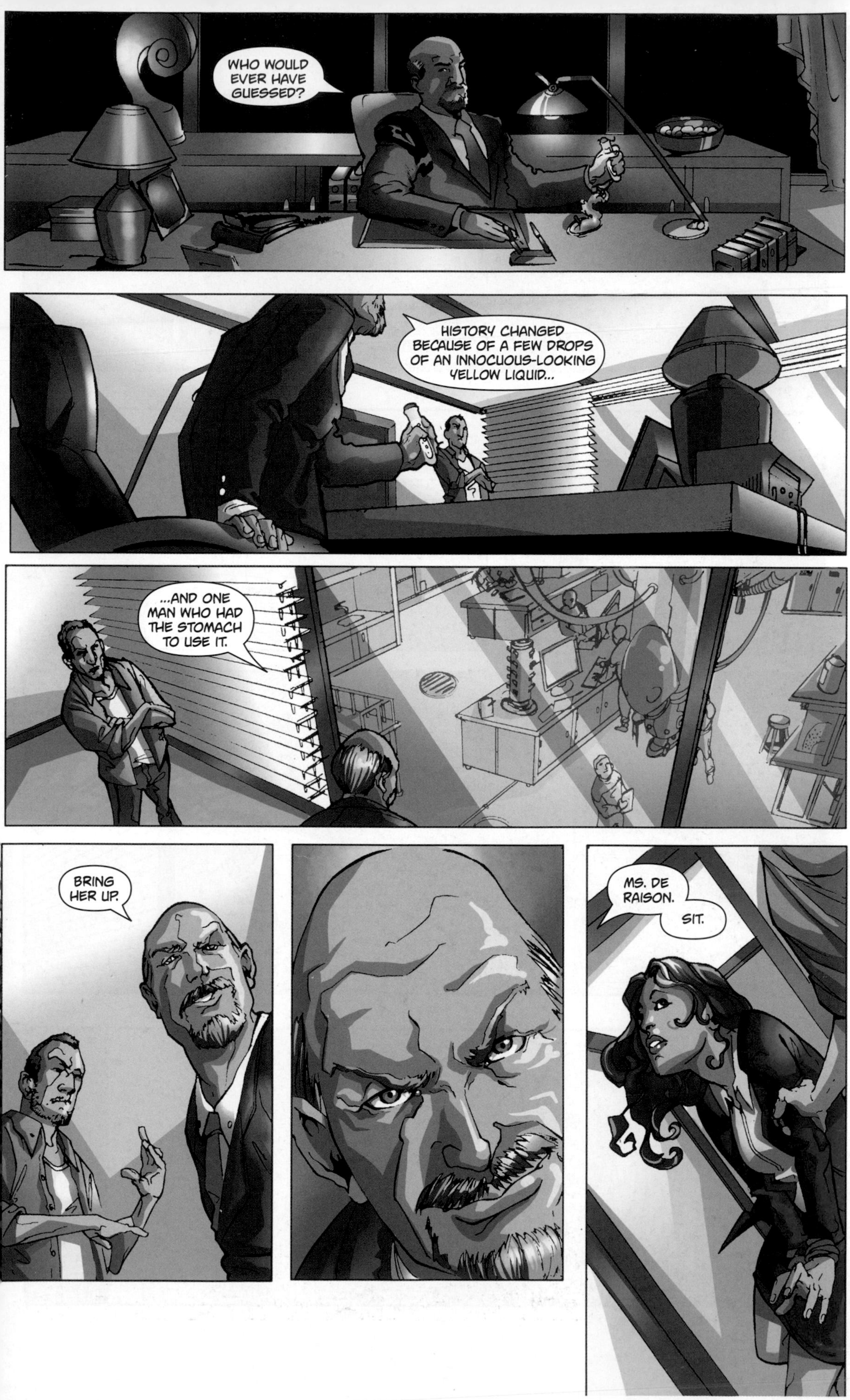
WHO WOULD EVER HAVE GUESSED?
HISTORY CHANGED BECAUSE OF A FEW DROPS OF AN INNOCUOUS-LOOKING YELLOW LIQUID...
...AND ONE MAN WHO HAD THE STOMACH TO USE IT.
BRING HER UP.
MS. DE RAISON.
SIT.

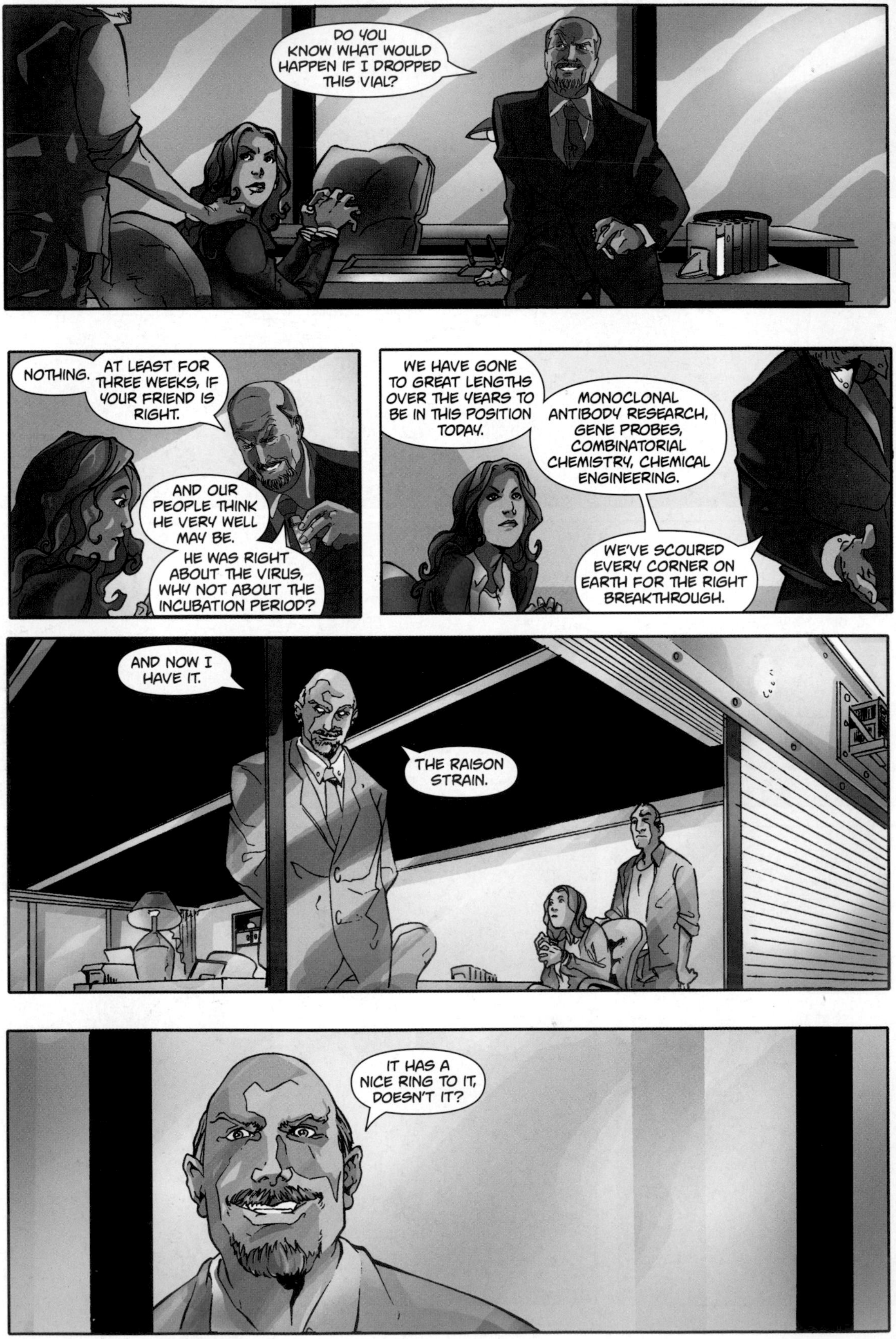
DO YOU KNOW WHAT WOULD HAPPEN IF I DROPPED THIS VIAL?
NOTHING.
AT LEAST FOR THREE WEEKS, IF YOUR FRIEND IS RIGHT.
AND OUR PEOPLE THINK HE VERY WELL MAY BE.
HE WAS RIGHT ABOUT THE VIRUS, WHY NOT ABOUT THE INCUBATION PERIOD?
WE HAVE GONE TO GREAT LENGTHS OVER THE YEARS TO BE IN THIS POSITION TODAY.
MONOCLONAL ANTIBODY RESEARCH, GENE PROBES, COMBINATORIAL CHEMISTRY, CHEMICAL ENGINEERING.
WE'VE SCOURED EVERY CORNER ON EARTH FOR THE RIGHT BREAKTHROUGH.
AND NOW I HAVE IT.
THE RAISON STRAIN.
IT HAS A NICE RING TO IT, DOESN'T IT?

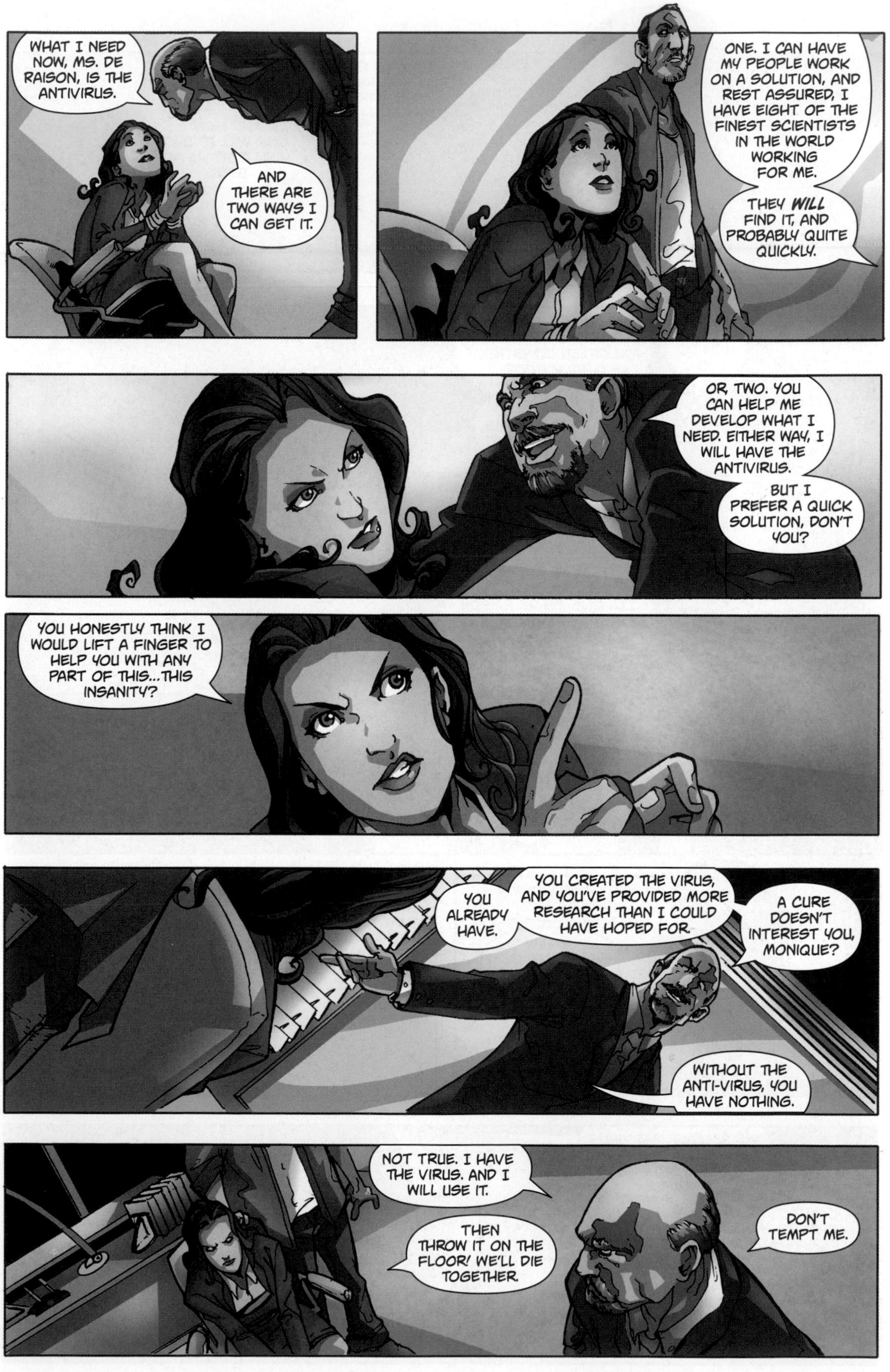
WHAT I NEED NOW, MS. DE RAISON, IS THE ANTIVIRUS.
AND THERE ARE TWO WAYS I CAN GET IT.
ONE. I CAN HAVE MY PEOPLE WORK ON A SOLUTION, AND REST ASSURED, I HAVE EIGHT OF THE FINEST SCIENTISTS IN THE WORLD WORKING FOR ME.
THEY *WILL* FIND IT, AND PROBABLY QUITE QUICKLY.
OR, TWO. YOU CAN HELP ME DEVELOP WHAT I NEED. EITHER WAY, I WILL HAVE THE ANTIVIRUS.
BUT I PREFER A QUICK SOLUTION, DON'T YOU?
YOU HONESTLY THINK I WOULD LIFT A FINGER TO HELP YOU WITH ANY PART OF THIS...THIS INSANITY?
YOU ALREADY HAVE.
YOU CREATED THE VIRUS, AND YOU'VE PROVIDED MORE RESEARCH THAN I COULD HAVE HOPED FOR.
A CURE DOESN'T INTEREST YOU, MONIQUE?
WITHOUT THE ANTI-VIRUS, YOU HAVE NOTHING.
NOT TRUE. I HAVE THE VIRUS. AND I WILL USE IT.
THEN THROW IT ON THE FLOOR! WE'LL DIE TOGETHER.
DON'T TEMPT ME.

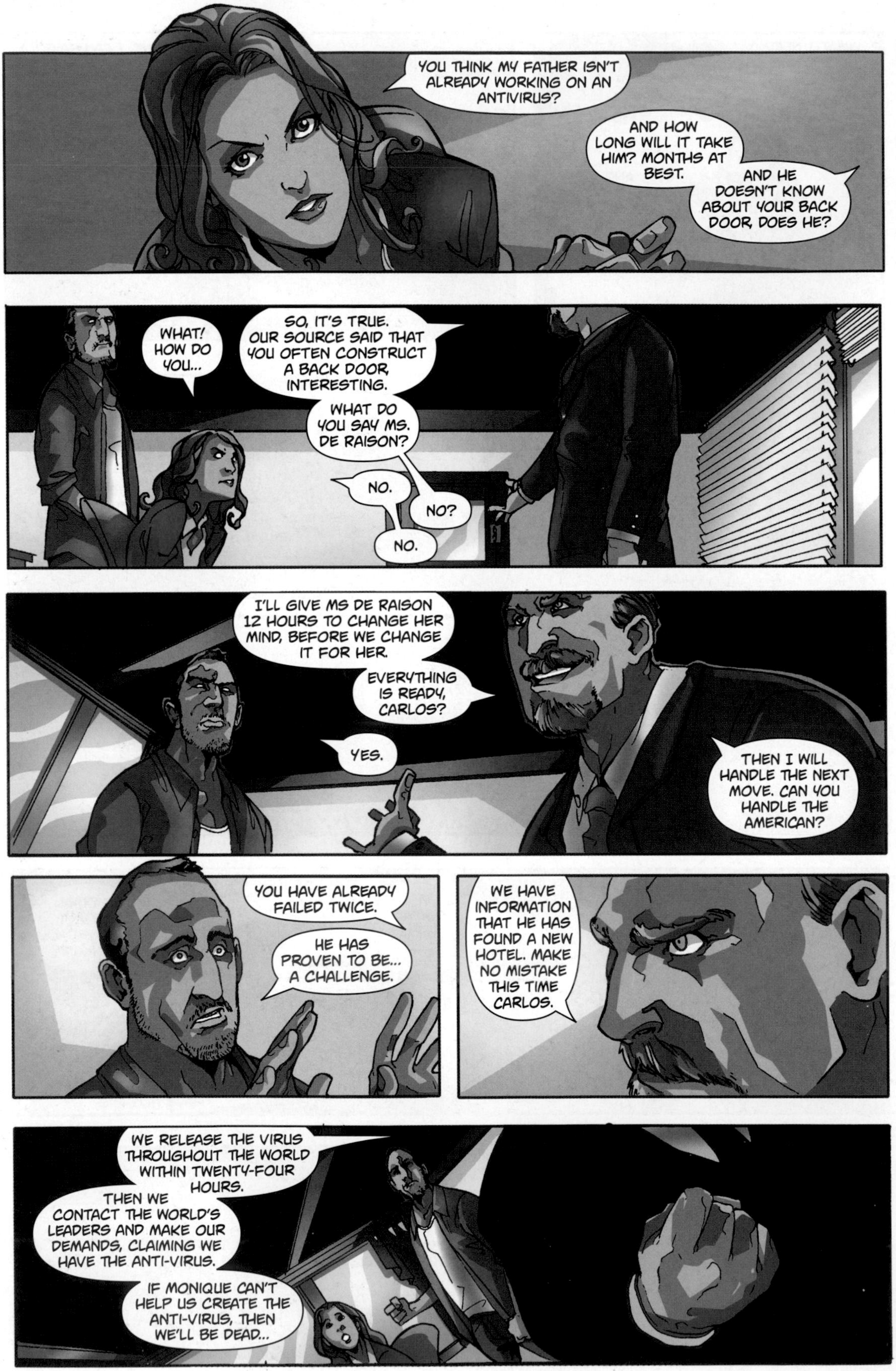
YOU THINK MY FATHER ISN'T ALREADY WORKING ON AN ANTIVIRUS?
AND HOW LONG WILL IT TAKE HIM? MONTHS AT BEST.
AND HE DOESN'T KNOW ABOUT YOUR BACK DOOR, DOES HE?
WHAT! HOW DO YOU...
SO, IT'S TRUE. OUR SOURCE SAID THAT YOU OFTEN CONSTRUCT A BACK DOOR, INTERESTING.
WHAT DO YOU SAY MS. DE RAISON?
NO.
NO?
NO.
I'LL GIVE MS DE RAISON 12 HOURS TO CHANGE HER MIND, BEFORE WE CHANGE IT FOR HER.
EVERYTHING IS READY, CARLOS?
YES.
THEN I WILL HANDLE THE NEXT MOVE. CAN YOU HANDLE THE AMERICAN?
YOU HAVE ALREADY FAILED TWICE.
HE HAS PROVEN TO BE... A CHALLENGE.
WE HAVE INFORMATION THAT HE HAS FOUND A NEW HOTEL. MAKE NO MISTAKE THIS TIME CARLOS.
WE RELEASE THE VIRUS THROUGHOUT THE WORLD WITHIN TWENTY-FOUR HOURS.
THEN WE CONTACT THE WORLD'S LEADERS AND MAKE OUR DEMANDS, CLAIMING WE HAVE THE ANTI-VIRUS.
IF MONIQUE CAN'T HELP US CREATE THE ANTI-VIRUS, THEN WE'LL BE DEAD...

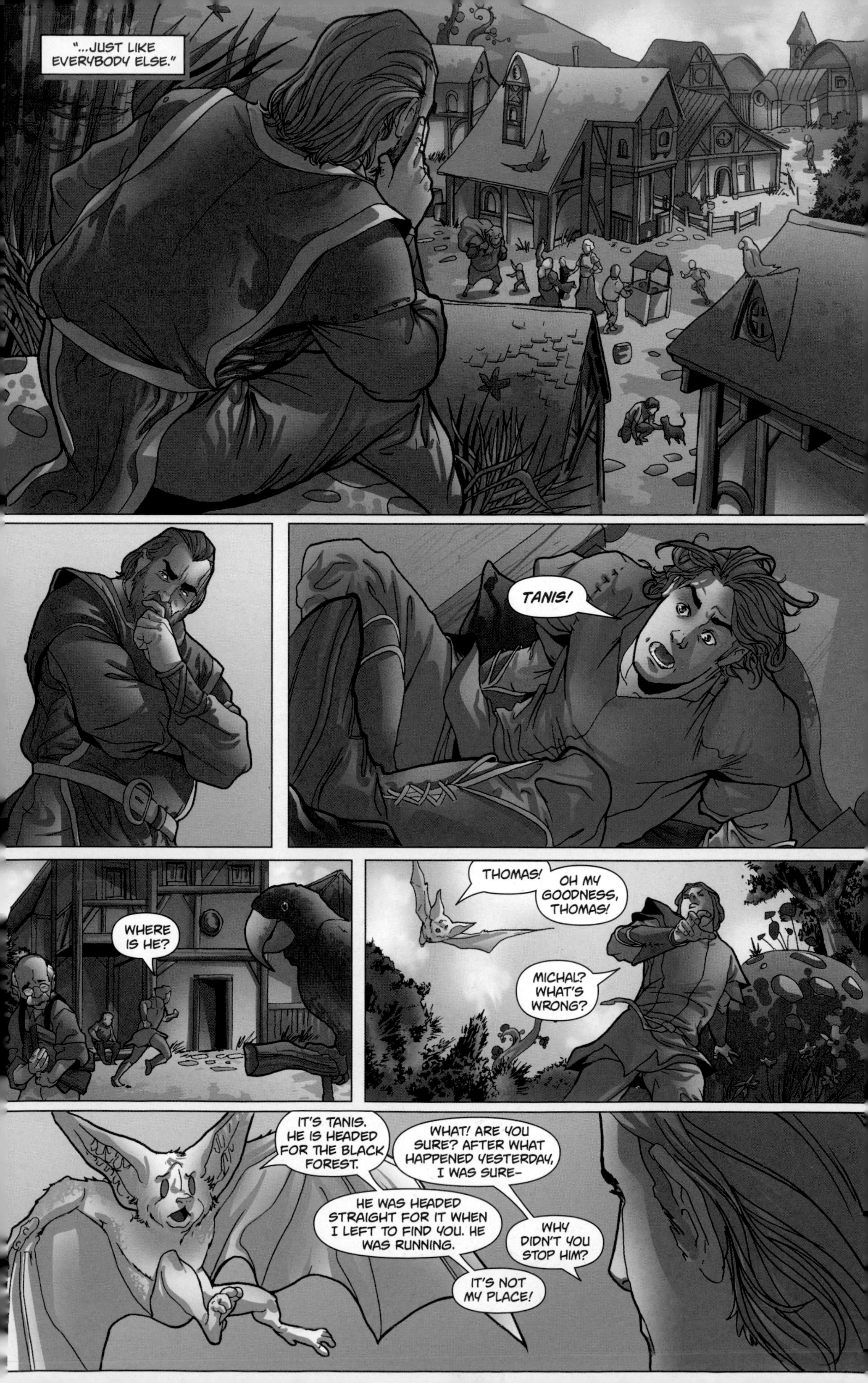
"...JUST LIKE EVERYBODY ELSE."
TANIS!
WHERE IS HE?
THOMAS!
OH MY GOODNESS, THOMAS!
MICHAL? WHAT'S WRONG?
IT'S TANIS. HE IS HEADED FOR THE BLACK FOREST.
WHAT! ARE YOU SURE? AFTER WHAT HAPPENED YESTERDAY, I WAS SURE-
HE WAS HEADED STRAIGHT FOR IT WHEN I LEFT TO FIND YOU. HE WAS RUNNING.
WHY DIDN'T YOU STOP HIM?
IT'S NOT MY PLACE!

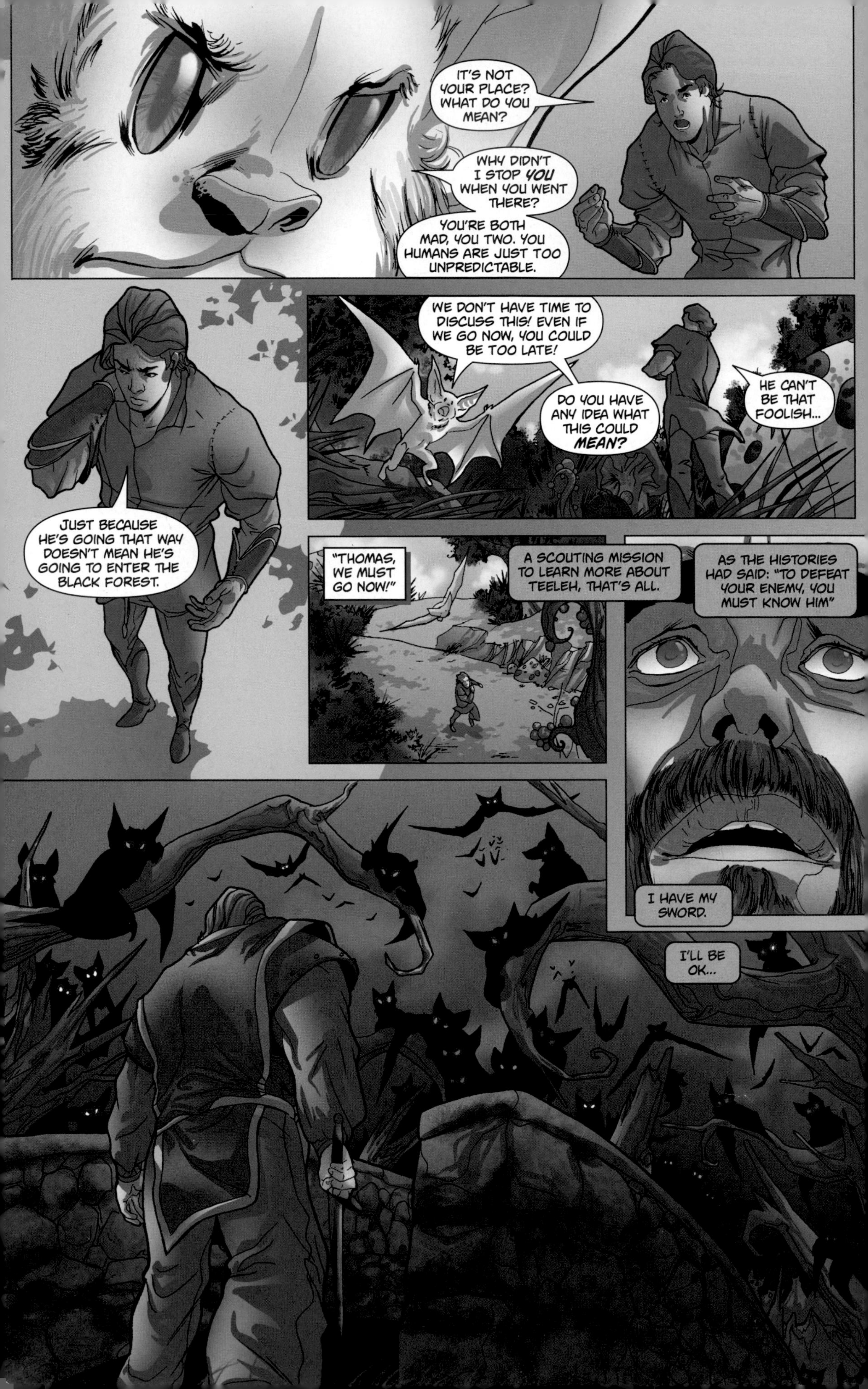
IT'S NOT YOUR PLACE? WHAT DO YOU MEAN?
WHY DIDN'T I STOP *YOU* WHEN YOU WENT THERE?
YOU'RE BOTH MAD, YOU TWO. YOU HUMANS ARE JUST TOO UNPREDICTABLE.
WE DON'T HAVE TIME TO DISCUSS THIS! EVEN IF WE GO NOW, YOU COULD BE TOO LATE!
DO YOU HAVE ANY IDEA WHAT THIS COULD *MEAN?*
HE CAN'T BE THAT FOOLISH...
JUST BECAUSE HE'S GOING THAT WAY DOESN'T MEAN HE'S GOING TO ENTER THE BLACK FOREST.
"THOMAS, WE MUST GO NOW!"
A SCOUTING MISSION TO LEARN MORE ABOUT TEELEH, THAT'S ALL.
AS THE HISTORIES HAD SAID: "TO DEFEAT YOUR ENEMY, YOU MUST KNOW HIM"
I HAVE MY SWORD.
I'LL BE OK...

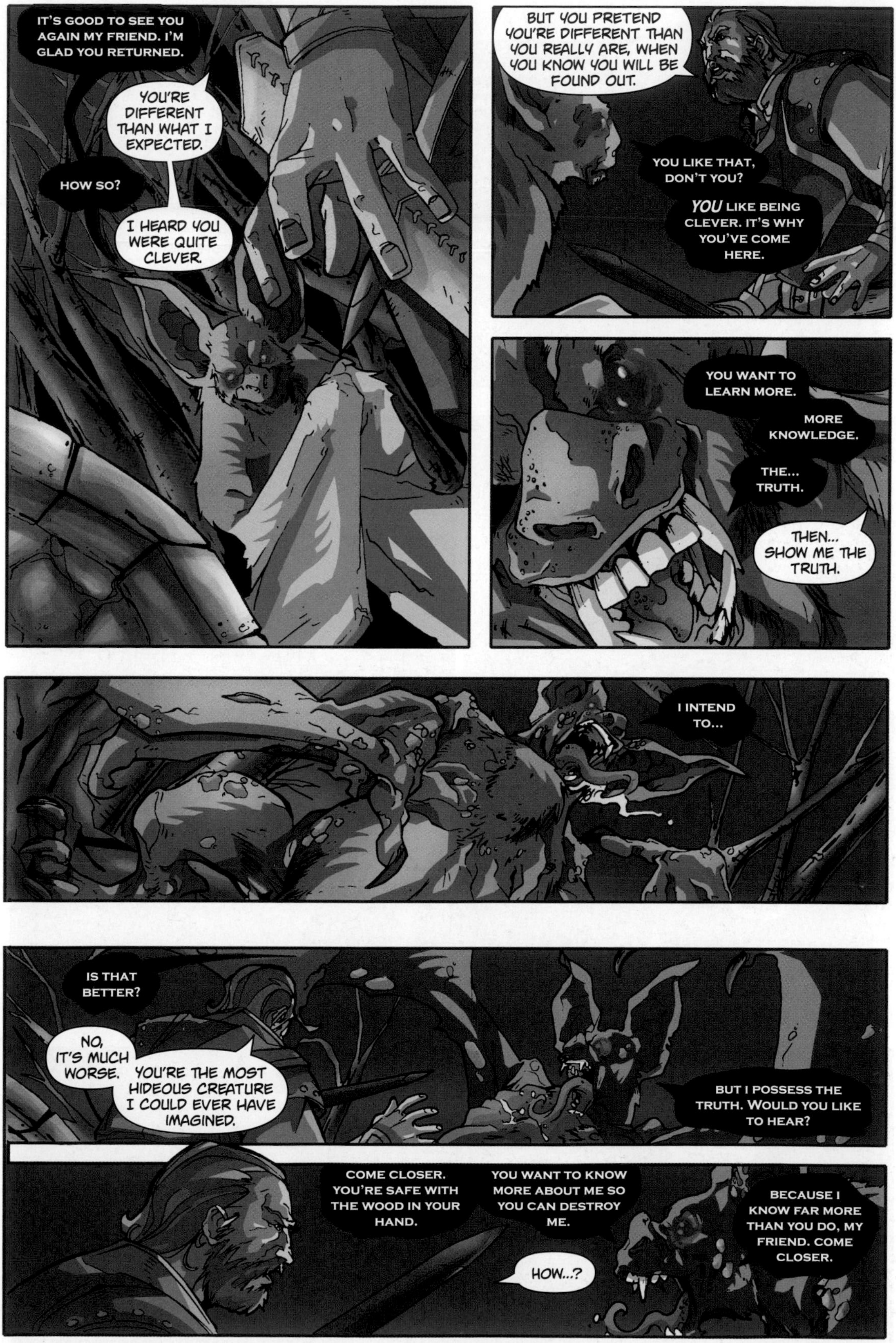
IT'S GOOD TO SEE YOU AGAIN MY FRIEND. I'M GLAD YOU RETURNED.
YOU'RE DIFFERENT THAN WHAT I EXPECTED.
HOW SO?
I HEARD YOU WERE QUITE CLEVER.
BUT YOU PRETEND YOU'RE DIFFERENT THAN YOU REALLY ARE, WHEN YOU KNOW YOU WILL BE FOUND OUT.
YOU LIKE THAT, DON'T YOU?
YOU LIKE BEING CLEVER. IT'S WHY YOU'VE COME HERE.
YOU WANT TO LEARN MORE.
MORE KNOWLEDGE.
THE... TRUTH.
THEN... SHOW ME THE TRUTH.
I INTEND TO...
IS THAT BETTER?
NO, IT'S MUCH WORSE.
YOU'RE THE MOST HIDEOUS CREATURE I COULD EVER HAVE IMAGINED.
BUT I POSSESS THE TRUTH. WOULD YOU LIKE TO HEAR?
COME CLOSER. YOU'RE SAFE WITH THE WOOD IN YOUR HAND.
YOU WANT TO KNOW MORE ABOUT ME SO YOU CAN DESTROY ME.
HOW...?
BECAUSE I KNOW FAR MORE THAN YOU DO, MY FRIEND. COME CLOSER.

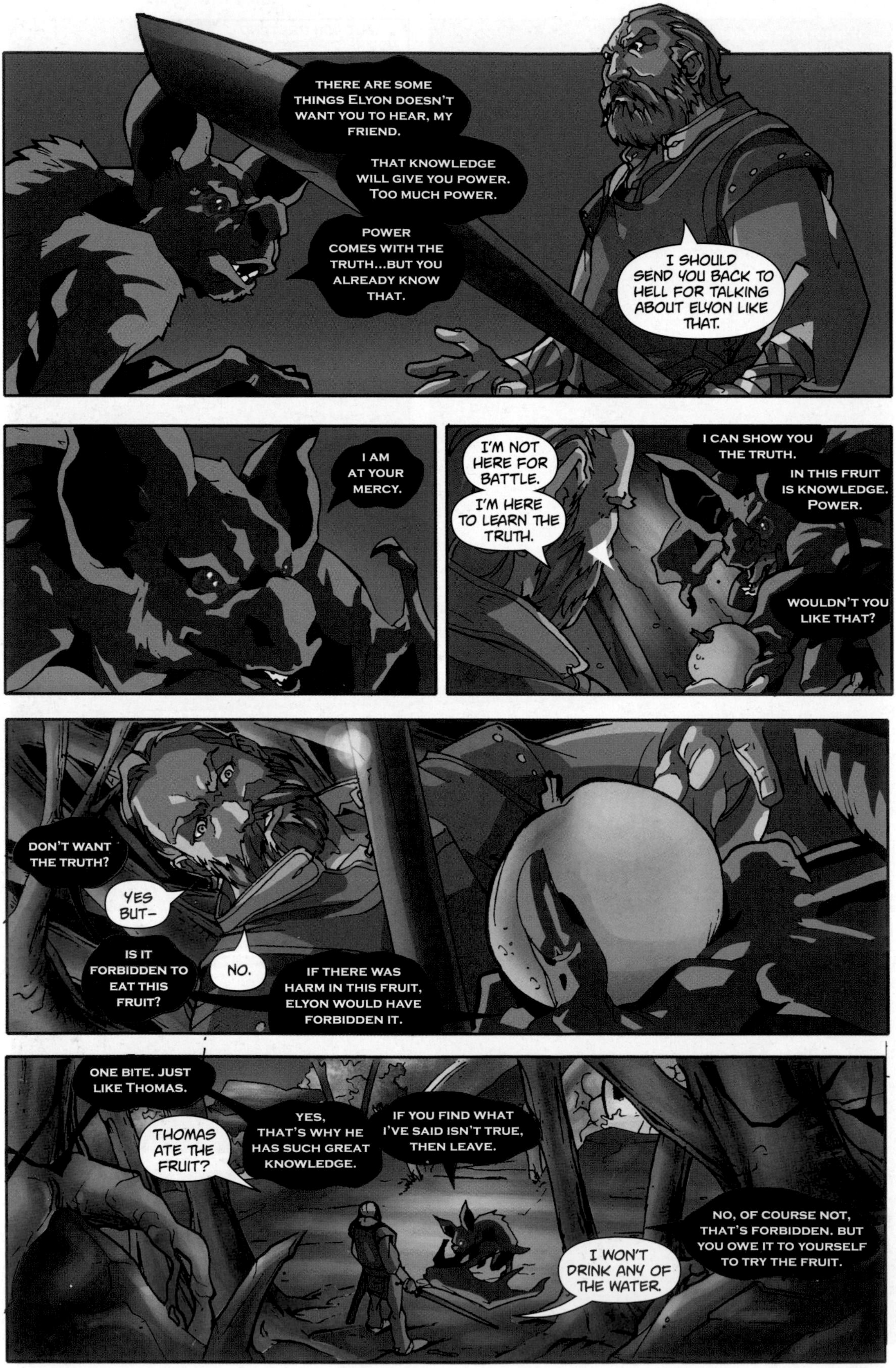
THERE ARE SOME THINGS ELYON DOESN'T WANT YOU TO HEAR, MY FRIEND.
THAT KNOWLEDGE WILL GIVE YOU POWER. TOO MUCH POWER.
POWER COMES WITH THE TRUTH...BUT YOU ALREADY KNOW THAT.
I SHOULD SEND YOU BACK TO HELL FOR TALKING ABOUT ELYON LIKE THAT.
I AM AT YOUR MERCY.
I'M NOT HERE FOR BATTLE.
I'M HERE TO LEARN THE TRUTH.
I CAN SHOW YOU THE TRUTH.
IN THIS FRUIT IS KNOWLEDGE. POWER.
WOULDN'T YOU LIKE THAT?
DON'T WANT THE TRUTH?
YES BUT–
IS IT FORBIDDEN TO EAT THIS FRUIT?
NO.
IF THERE WAS HARM IN THIS FRUIT, ELYON WOULD HAVE FORBIDDEN IT.
ONE BITE. JUST LIKE THOMAS.
THOMAS ATE THE FRUIT?
YES, THAT'S WHY HE HAS SUCH GREAT KNOWLEDGE.
IF YOU FIND WHAT I'VE SAID ISN'T TRUE, THEN LEAVE.
I WON'T DRINK ANY OF THE WATER.
NO, OF COURSE NOT, THAT'S FORBIDDEN. BUT YOU OWE IT TO YOURSELF TO TRY THE FRUIT.

HURRY! WE MAY BE TOO LATE...

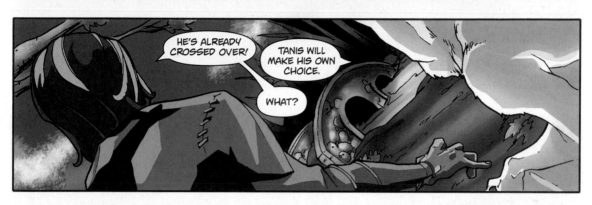

HE'S ALREADY CROSSED OVER!

TANIS WILL MAKE HIS OWN CHOICE.

WHAT?

KEEP THE WOOD TO YOUR SIDE, IF YOU DON'T MIND.

TASTE WHAT ELYON HIMSELF HAS INVITED YOU TO TASTE BY NOT FORBIDDING IT.

KNOW YOUR ENEMY. KNOW HIS FRUIT.

THIS IS THE FRUIT THAT THOMAS ATE?

IT IS INDEED, MY FRIEND.

TANIS!!

THOMAS IS A VERY WISE MAN, INDEED.

JUST ONE BITE...

TANIS, WHAT HAVE YOU DONE??

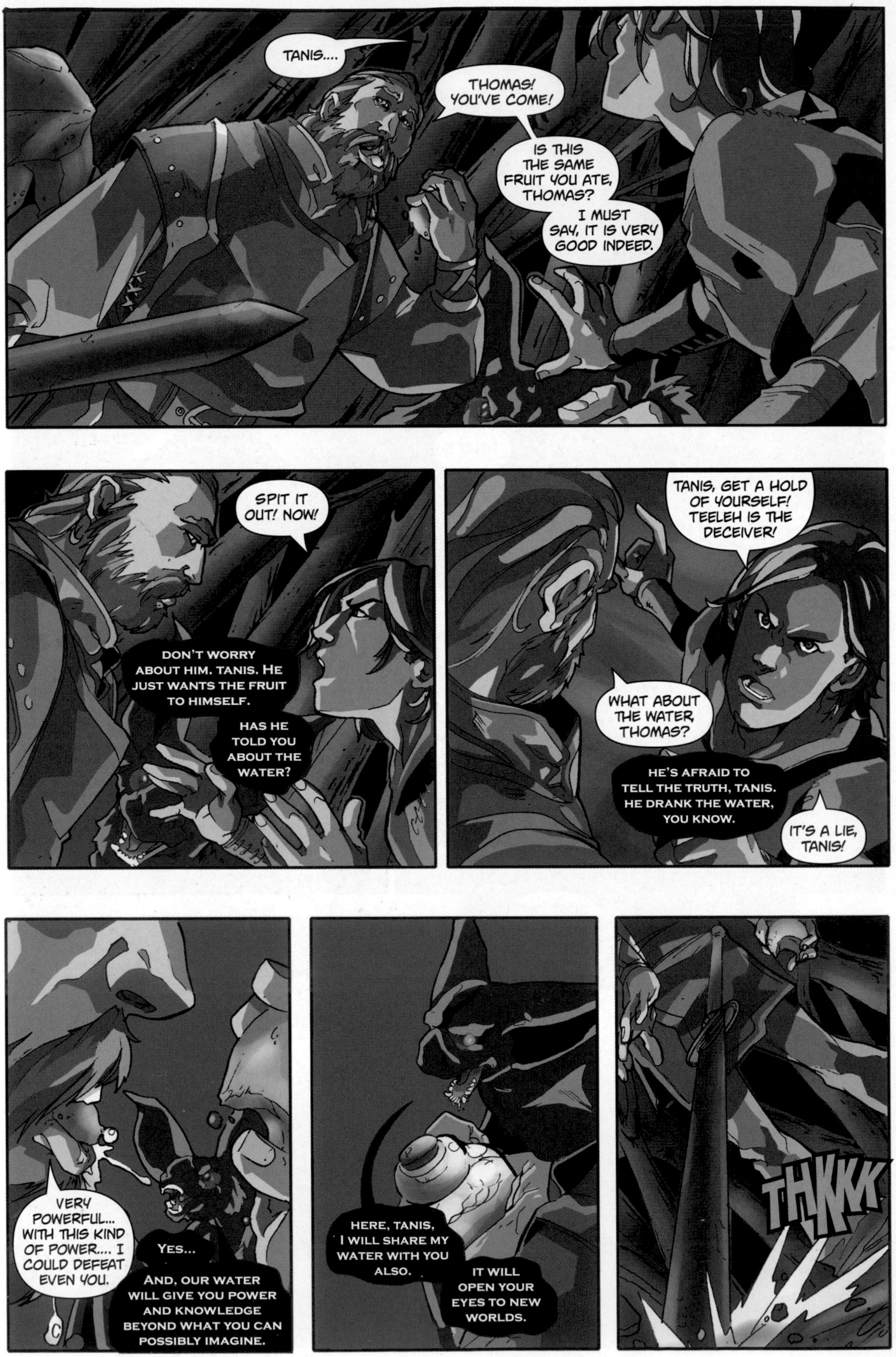
TANIS....
THOMAS! YOU'VE COME!
IS THIS THE SAME FRUIT YOU ATE, THOMAS?
I MUST SAY, IT IS VERY GOOD INDEED.
SPIT IT OUT! NOW!
DON'T WORRY ABOUT HIM. TANIS. HE JUST WANTS THE FRUIT TO HIMSELF.
HAS HE TOLD YOU ABOUT THE WATER?
TANIS, GET A HOLD OF YOURSELF! TEELEH IS THE DECEIVER!
WHAT ABOUT THE WATER, THOMAS?
HE'S AFRAID TO TELL THE TRUTH, TANIS. HE DRANK THE WATER, YOU KNOW.
IT'S A LIE, TANIS!
VERY POWERFUL... WITH THIS KIND OF POWER.... I COULD DEFEAT EVEN YOU.
YES...
AND, OUR WATER WILL GIVE YOU POWER AND KNOWLEDGE BEYOND WHAT YOU CAN POSSIBLY IMAGINE.
HERE, TANIS, I WILL SHARE MY WATER WITH YOU ALSO.
IT WILL OPEN YOUR EYES TO NEW WORLDS.
THKKK

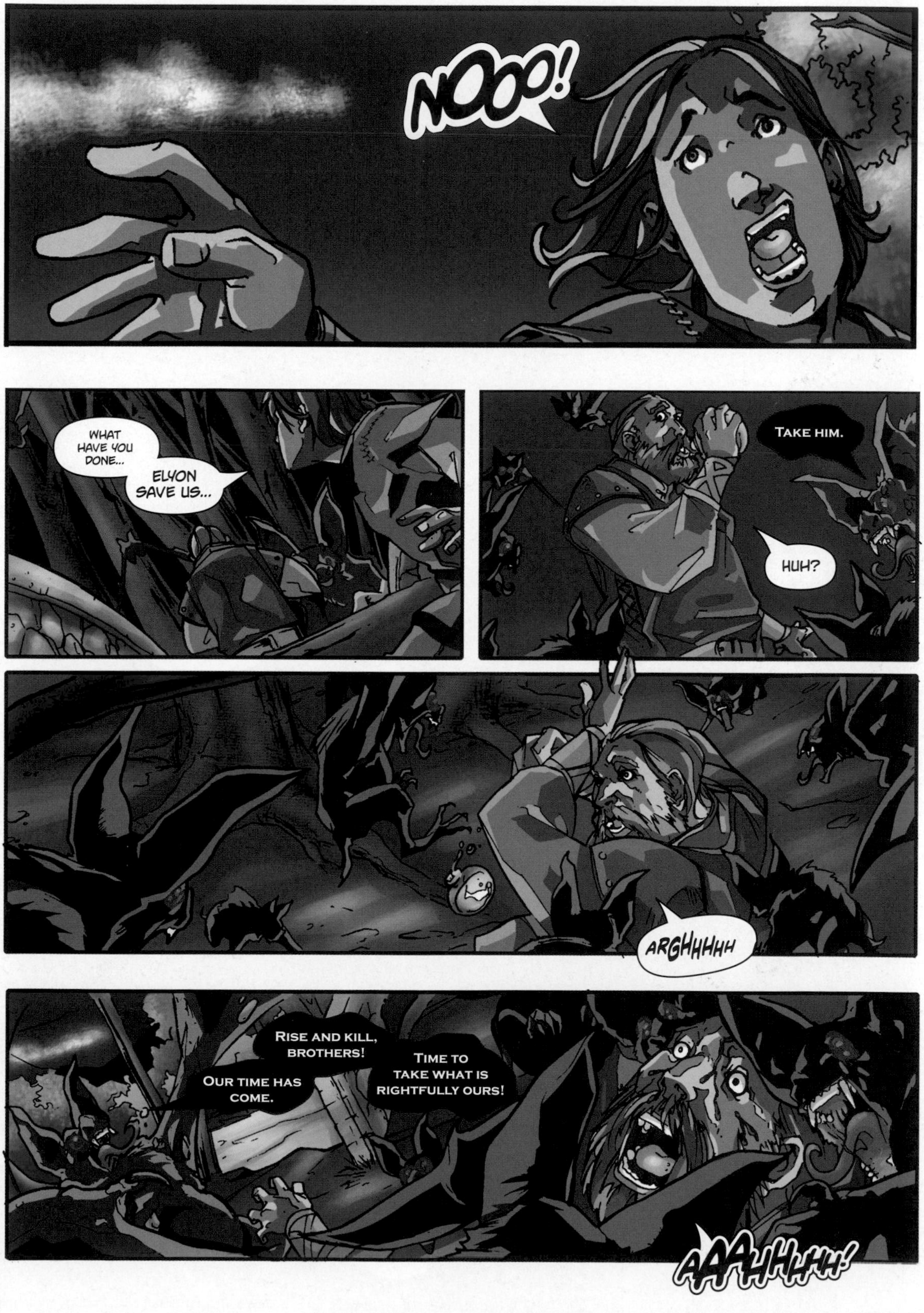
NOOO!
WHAT HAVE YOU DONE...
ELYON SAVE US...
TAKE HIM.
HUH?
ARGHHHHH
RISE AND KILL, BROTHERS!
OUR TIME HAS COME.
TIME TO TAKE WHAT IS RIGHTFULLY OURS!
AAAHHHHH!

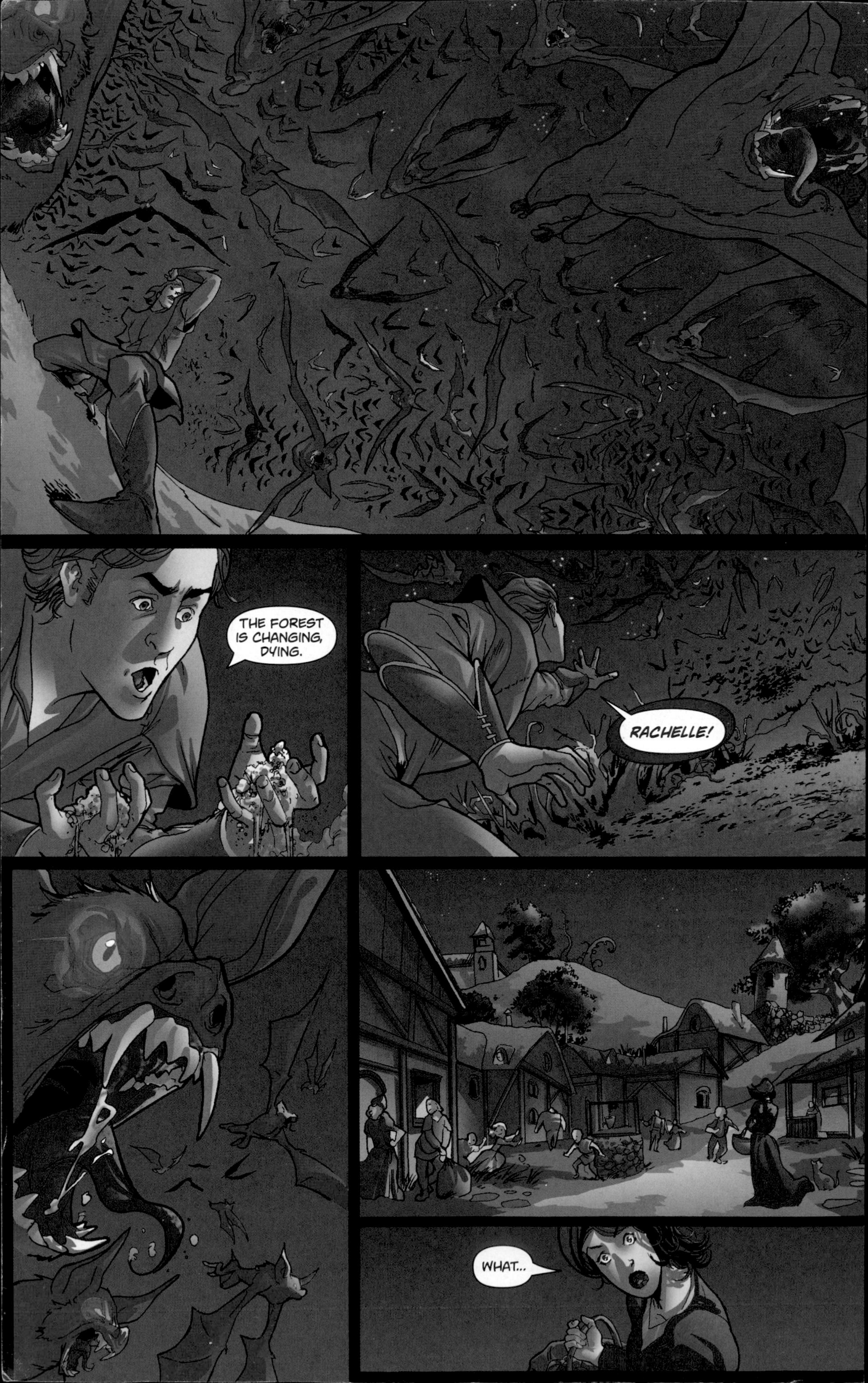
THE FOREST IS CHANGING, DYING.
RACHELLE!
WHAT...

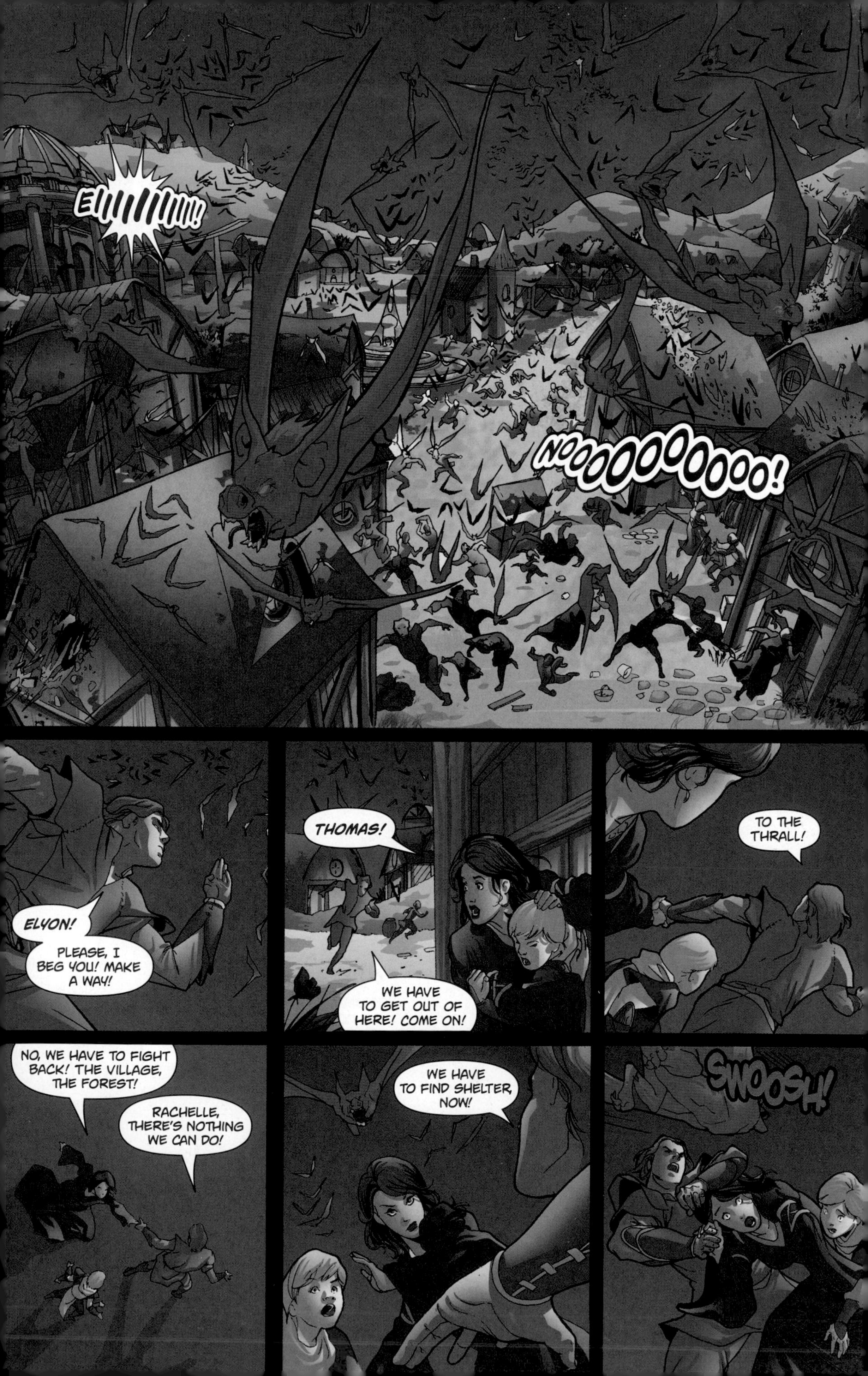
EIIIIIIIIII!
NOOOOOOOOOOO!
ELYON!
PLEASE, I BEG YOU! MAKE A WAY!
THOMAS!
WE HAVE TO GET OUT OF HERE! COME ON!
TO THE THRALL!
NO, WE HAVE TO FIGHT BACK! THE VILLAGE, THE FOREST!
RACHELLE, THERE'S NOTHING WE CAN DO!
WE HAVE TO FIND SHELTER, NOW!
SWOOSH!

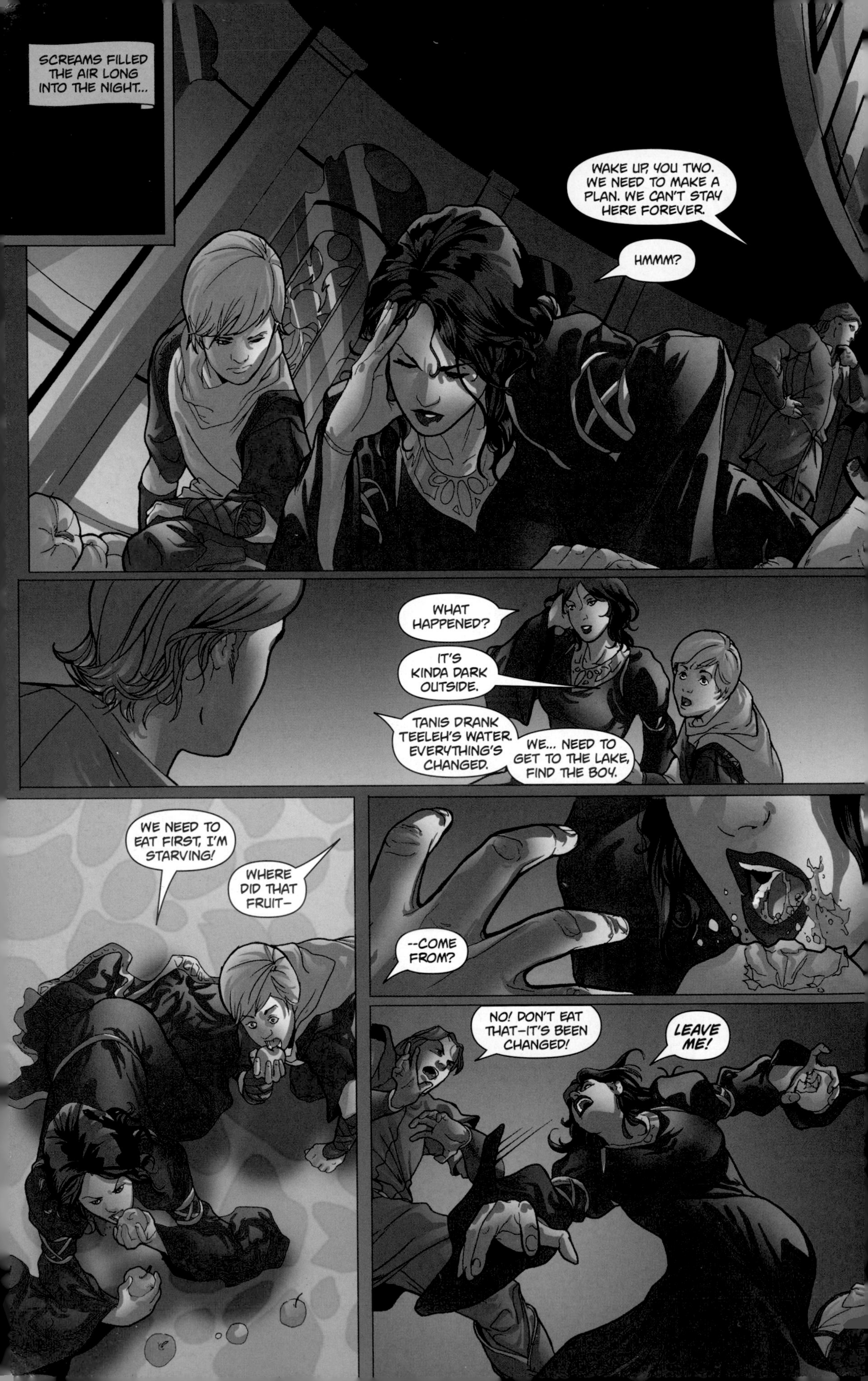
SCREAMS FILLED THE AIR LONG INTO THE NIGHT...
WAKE UP, YOU TWO. WE NEED TO MAKE A PLAN. WE CAN'T STAY HERE FOREVER.
HMMM?
WHAT HAPPENED?
IT'S KINDA DARK OUTSIDE.
TANIS DRANK TEELEH'S WATER. EVERYTHING'S CHANGED.
WE... NEED TO GET TO THE LAKE, FIND THE BOY.
WE NEED TO EAT FIRST, I'M STARVING!
WHERE DID THAT FRUIT-
--COME FROM?
NO! DON'T EAT THAT-IT'S BEEN CHANGED!
LEAVE ME!

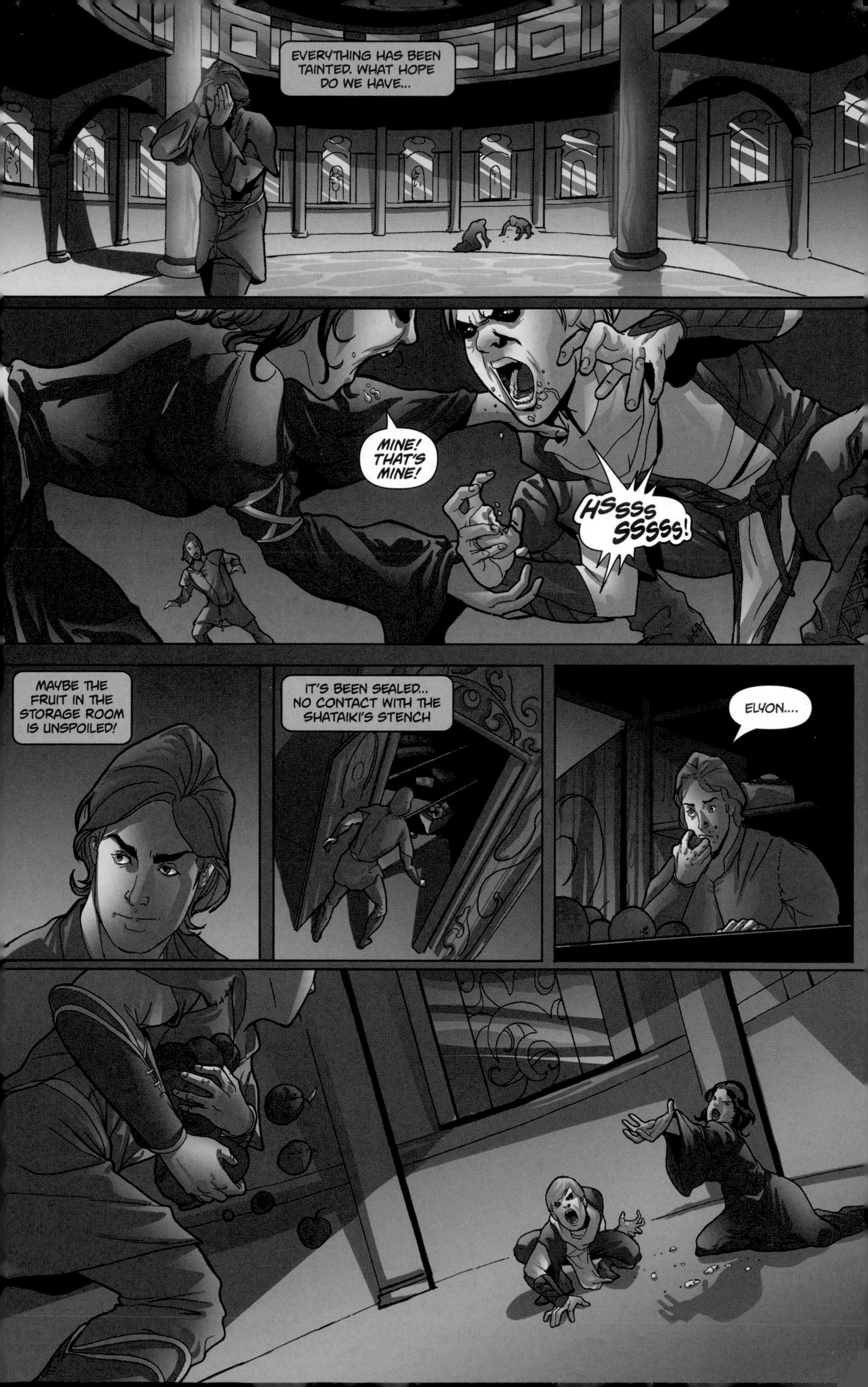
EVERYTHING HAS BEEN TAINTED. WHAT HOPE DO WE HAVE...
MINE! THAT'S MINE!
HSSSS SSSSS!
MAYBE THE FRUIT IN THE STORAGE ROOM IS UNSPOILED!
IT'S BEEN SEALED... NO CONTACT WITH THE SHATAIKI'S STENCH
ELYON....

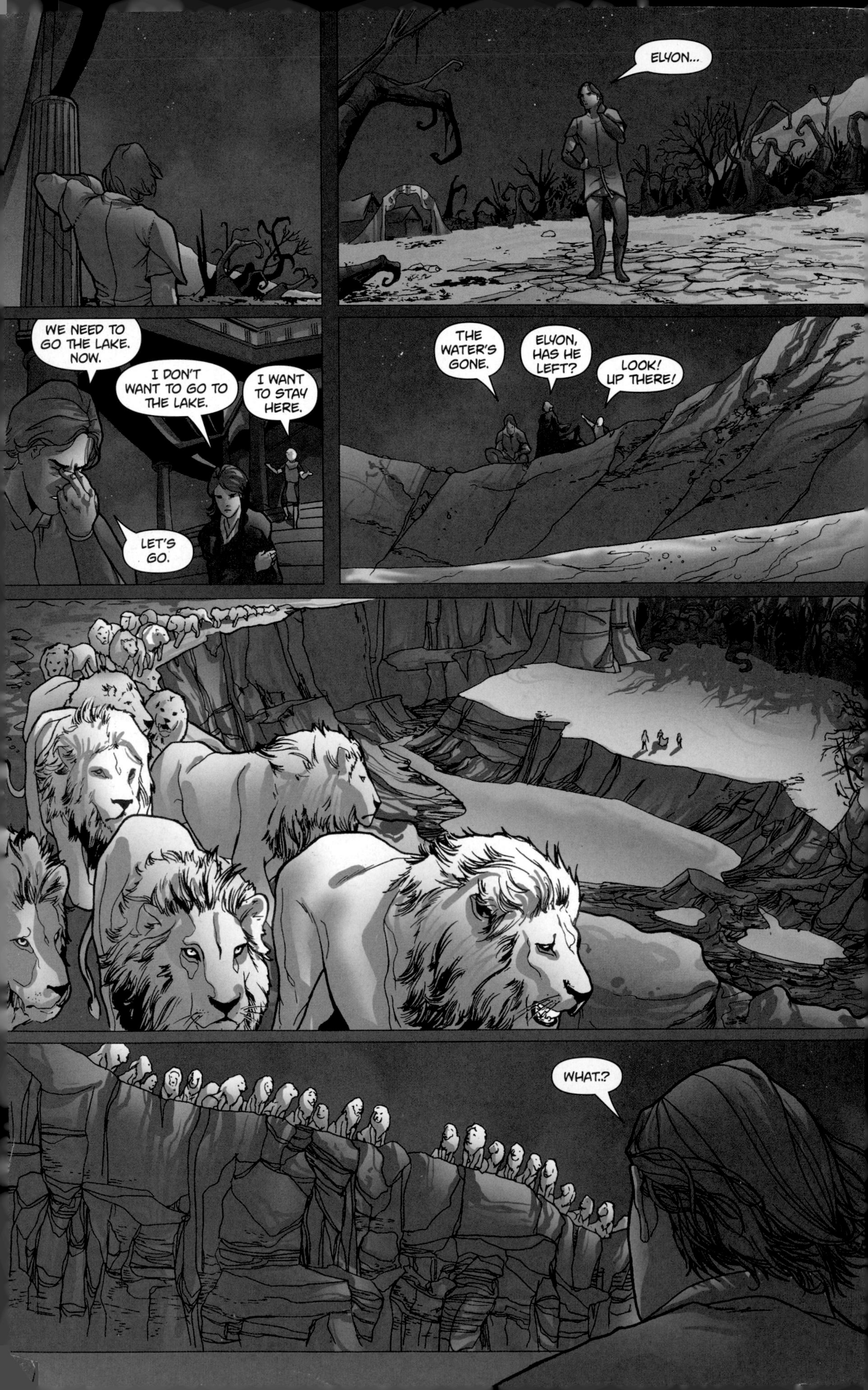
ELYON...
WE NEED TO GO THE LAKE. NOW.
I DON'T WANT TO GO TO THE LAKE.
I WANT TO STAY HERE.
LET'S GO.
THE WATER'S GONE.
ELYON, HAS HE LEFT?
LOOK! UP THERE!
WHAT.?

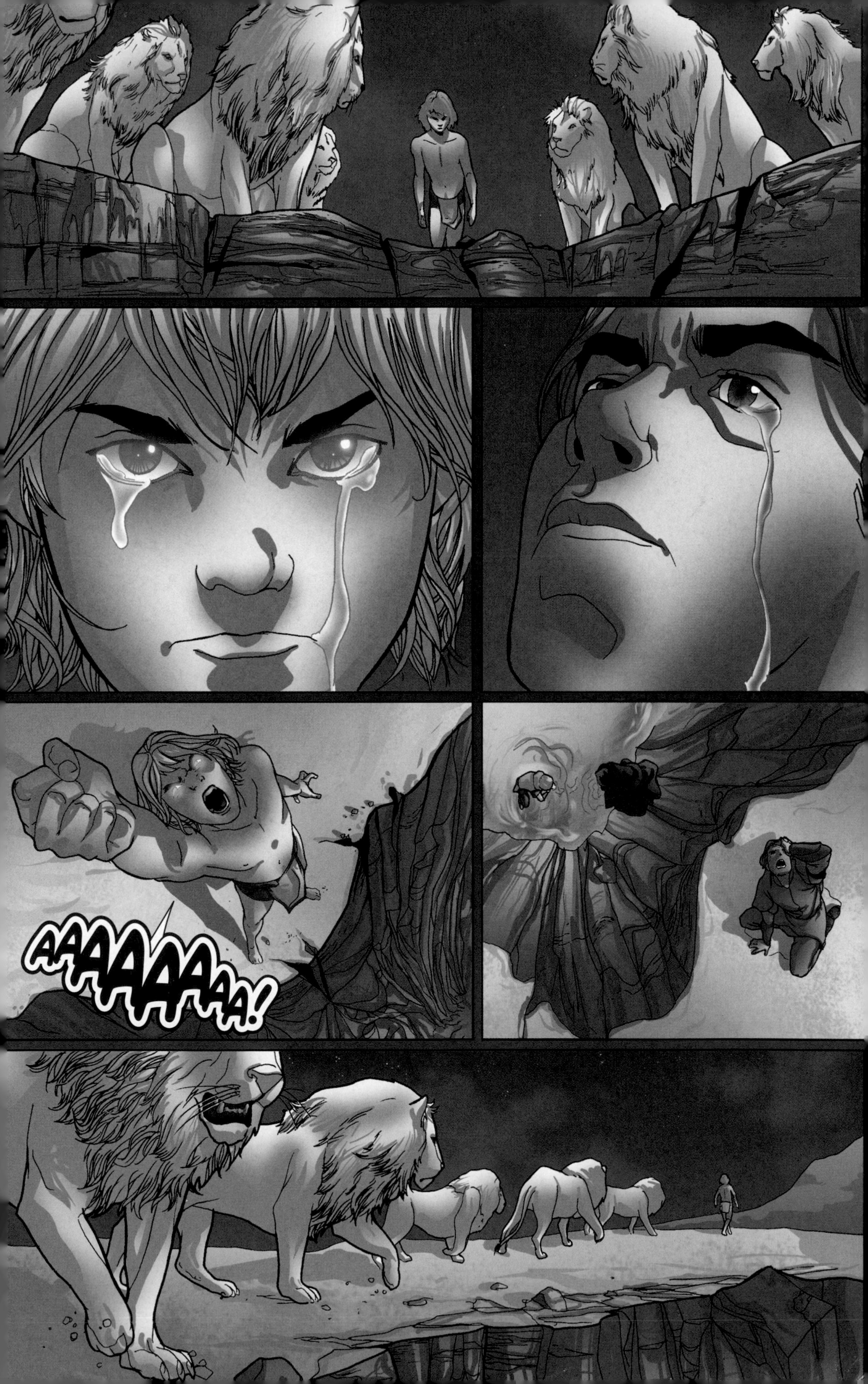
AAAAAAAAA!

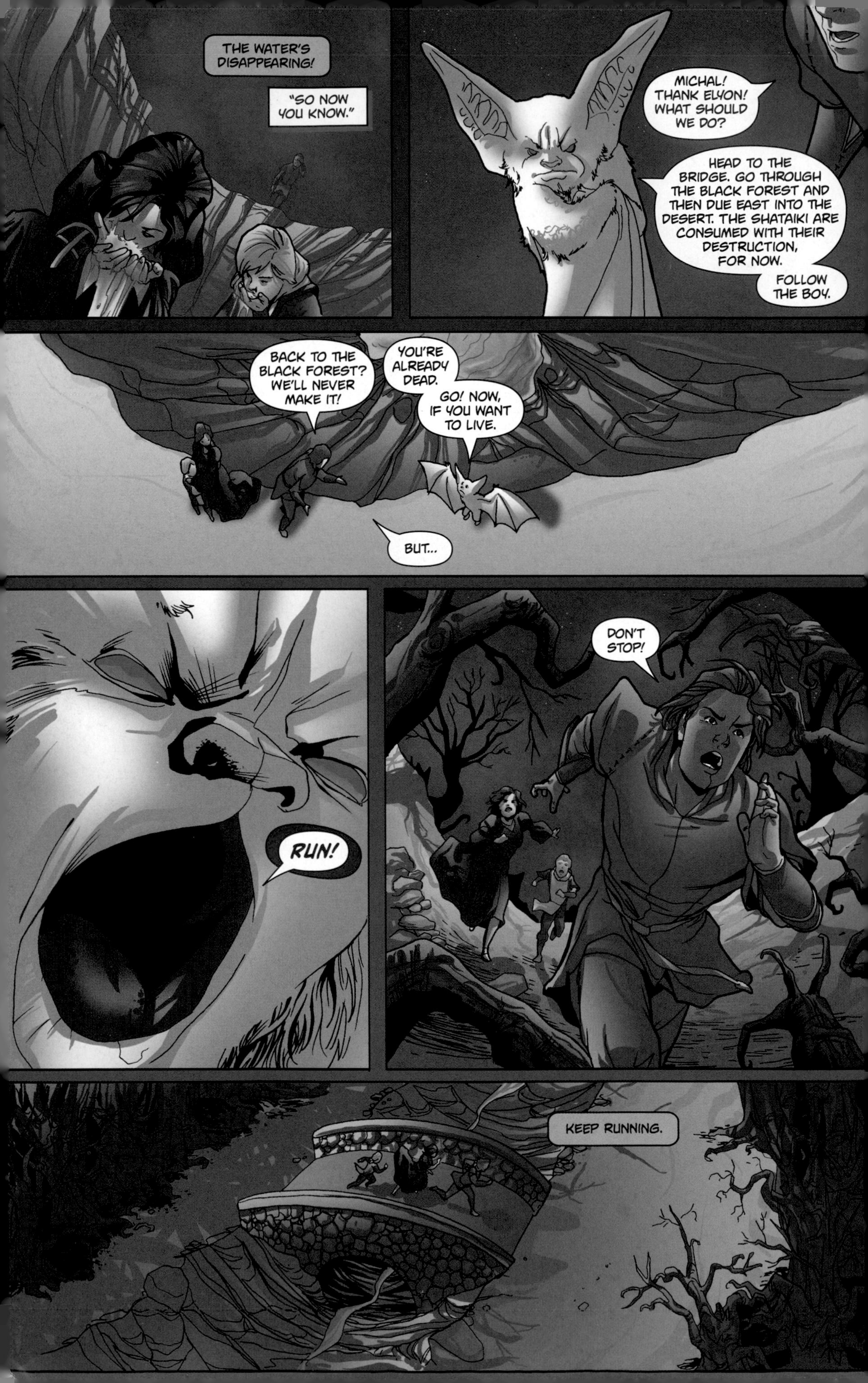
THE WATER'S DISAPPEARING!
"SO NOW YOU KNOW."
MICHAL! THANK ELYON! WHAT SHOULD WE DO?
HEAD TO THE BRIDGE. GO THROUGH THE BLACK FOREST AND THEN DUE EAST INTO THE DESERT. THE SHATAIKI ARE CONSUMED WITH THEIR DESTRUCTION, FOR NOW.
FOLLOW THE BOY.
BACK TO THE BLACK FOREST? WE'LL NEVER MAKE IT!
YOU'RE ALREADY DEAD.
GO! NOW, IF YOU WANT TO LIVE.
BUT...
RUN!
DON'T STOP!
KEEP RUNNING.

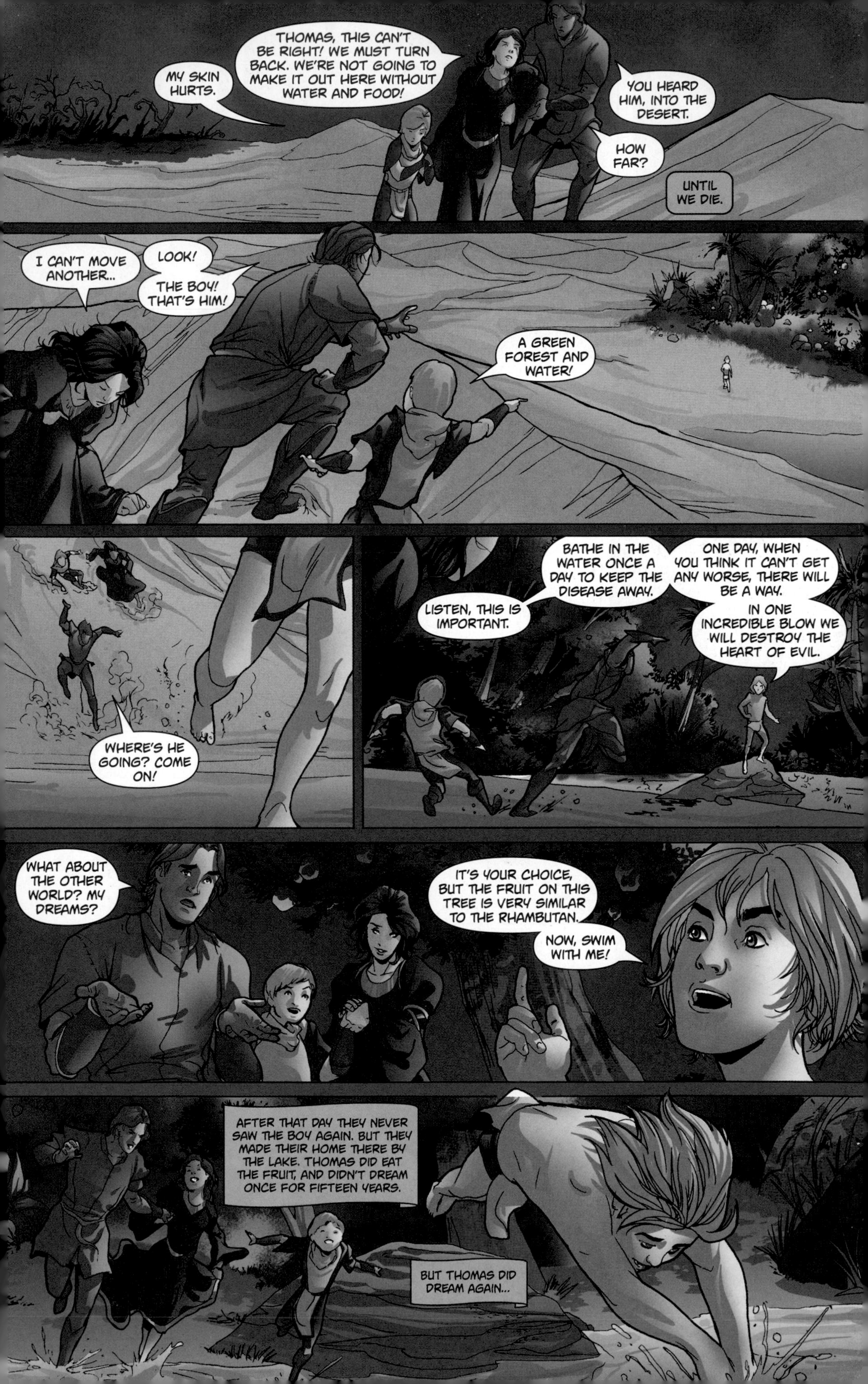

MY SKIN HURTS.
THOMAS, THIS CAN'T BE RIGHT! WE MUST TURN BACK. WE'RE NOT GOING TO MAKE IT OUT HERE WITHOUT WATER AND FOOD!
YOU HEARD HIM, INTO THE DESERT.
HOW FAR?
UNTIL WE DIE.
I CAN'T MOVE ANOTHER...
LOOK!
THE BOY! THAT'S HIM!
A GREEN FOREST AND WATER!
WHERE'S HE GOING? COME ON!
LISTEN, THIS IS IMPORTANT.
BATHE IN THE WATER ONCE A DAY TO KEEP THE DISEASE AWAY.
ONE DAY, WHEN YOU THINK IT CAN'T GET ANY WORSE, THERE WILL BE A WAY.
IN ONE INCREDIBLE BLOW WE WILL DESTROY THE HEART OF EVIL.
WHAT ABOUT THE OTHER WORLD? MY DREAMS?
IT'S YOUR CHOICE, BUT THE FRUIT ON THIS TREE IS VERY SIMILAR TO THE RHAMBUTAN.
NOW, SWIM WITH ME!
AFTER THAT DAY THEY NEVER SAW THE BOY AGAIN. BUT THEY MADE THEIR HOME THERE BY THE LAKE. THOMAS DID EAT THE FRUIT, AND DIDN'T DREAM ONCE FOR FIFTEEN YEARS.
BUT THOMAS DID DREAM AGAIN...

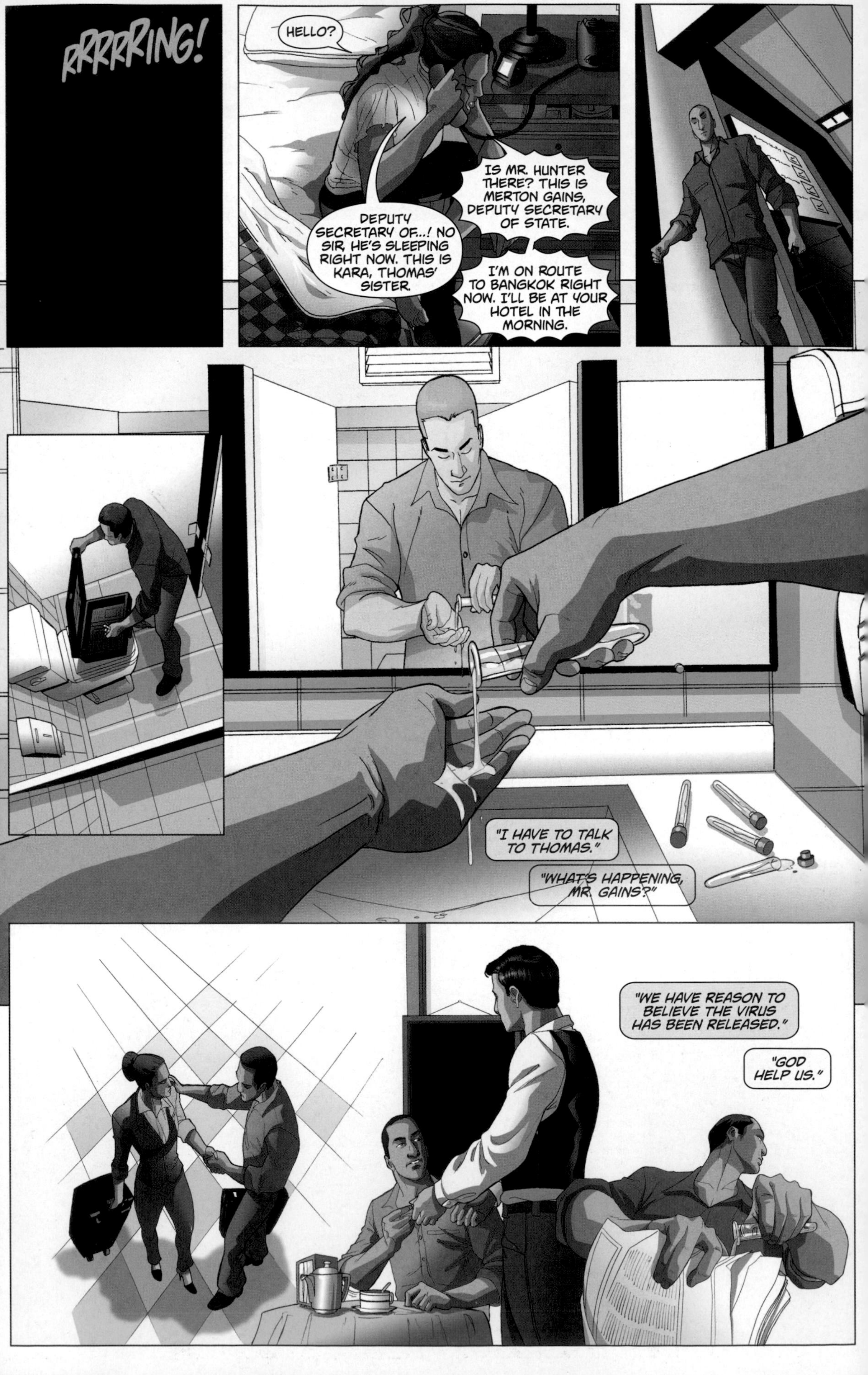
RRRRRING!
HELLO?
IS MR. HUNTER THERE? THIS IS MERTON GAINS, DEPUTY SECRETARY OF STATE.
DEPUTY SECRETARY OF...! NO SIR, HE'S SLEEPING RIGHT NOW. THIS IS KARA, THOMAS' SISTER.
I'M ON ROUTE TO BANGKOK RIGHT NOW. I'LL BE AT YOUR HOTEL IN THE MORNING.
"I HAVE TO TALK TO THOMAS."
"WHAT'S HAPPENING, MR. GAINS?"
"WE HAVE REASON TO BELIEVE THE VIRUS HAS BEEN RELEASED."
"GOD HELP US."

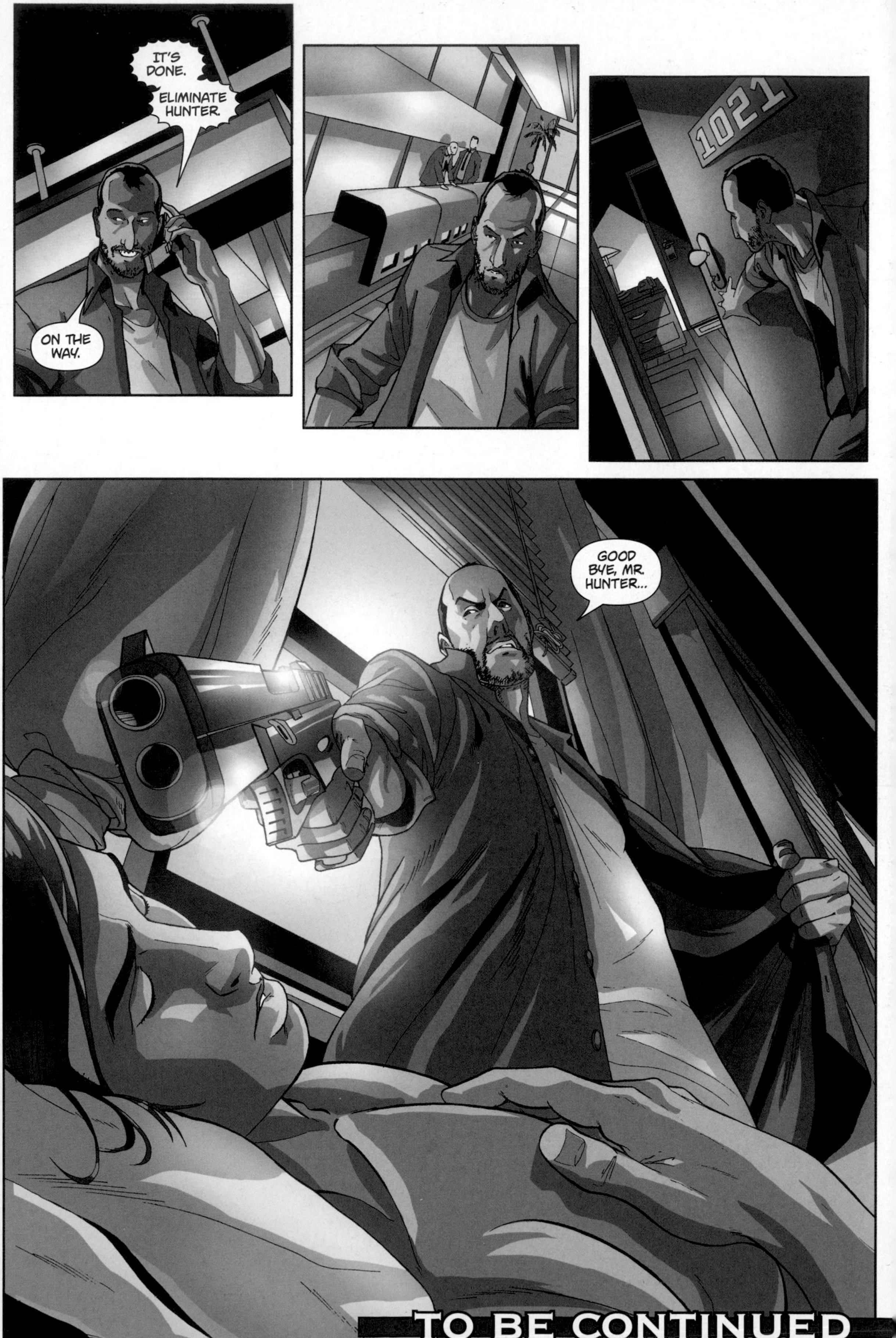
IT'S DONE.
ELIMINATE HUNTER.
ON THE WAY.
1021
GOOD BYE, MR. HUNTER...
TO BE CONTINUED

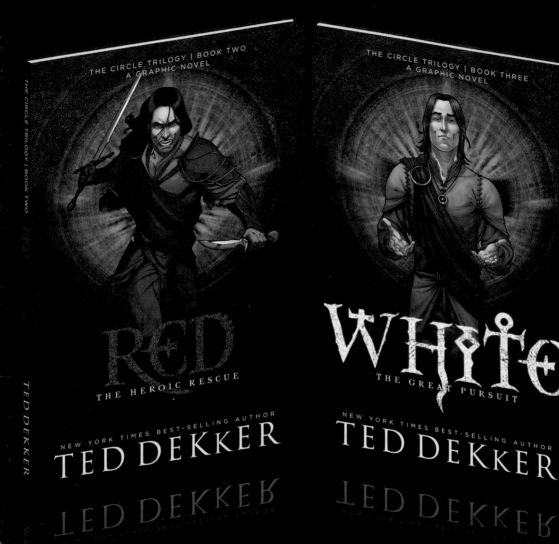

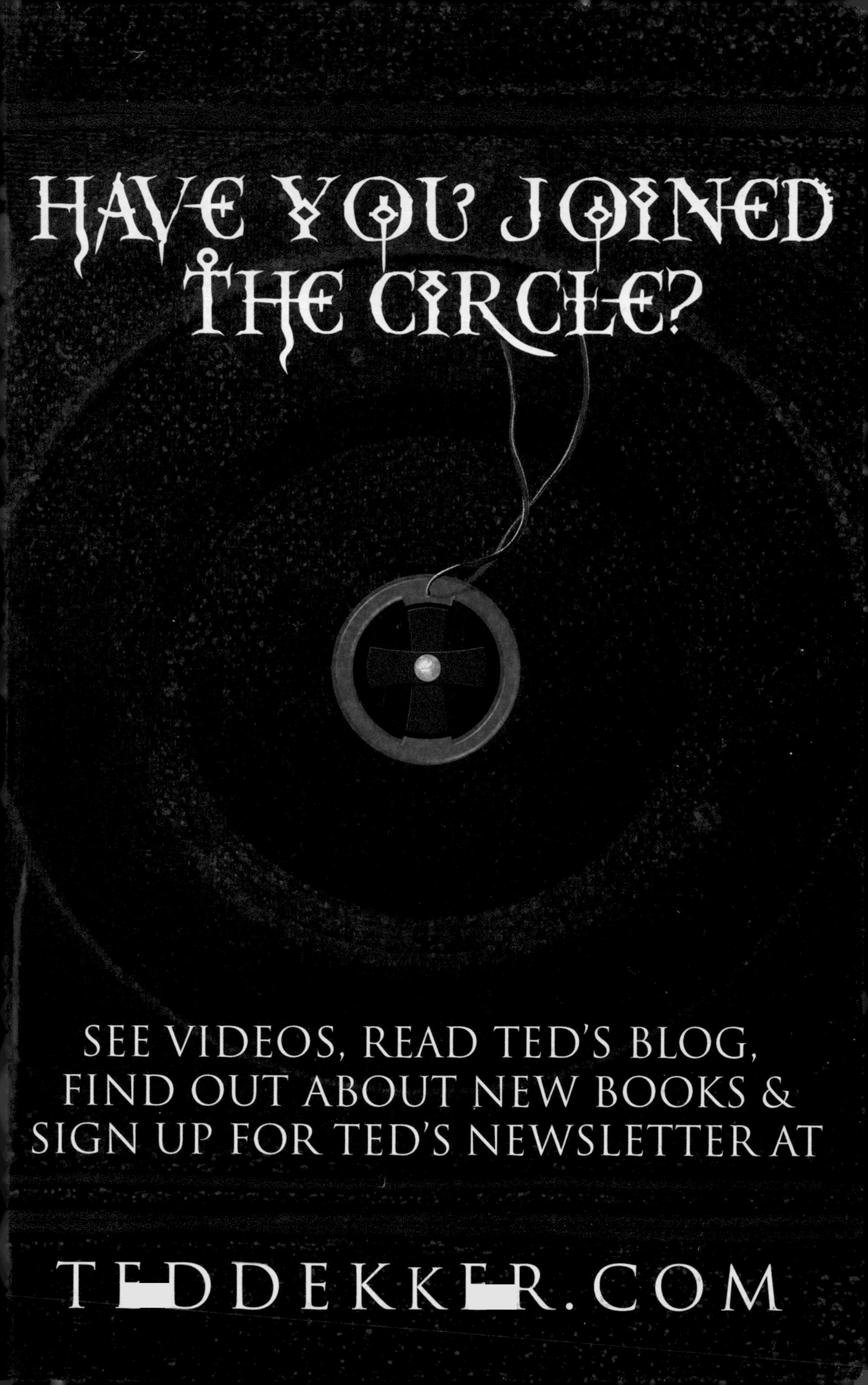
HAVE YOU JOINED THE CIRCLE?
SEE VIDEOS, READ TED'S BLOG, FIND OUT ABOUT NEW BOOKS & SIGN UP FOR TED'S NEWSLETTER AT
TEDDEKKER.COM

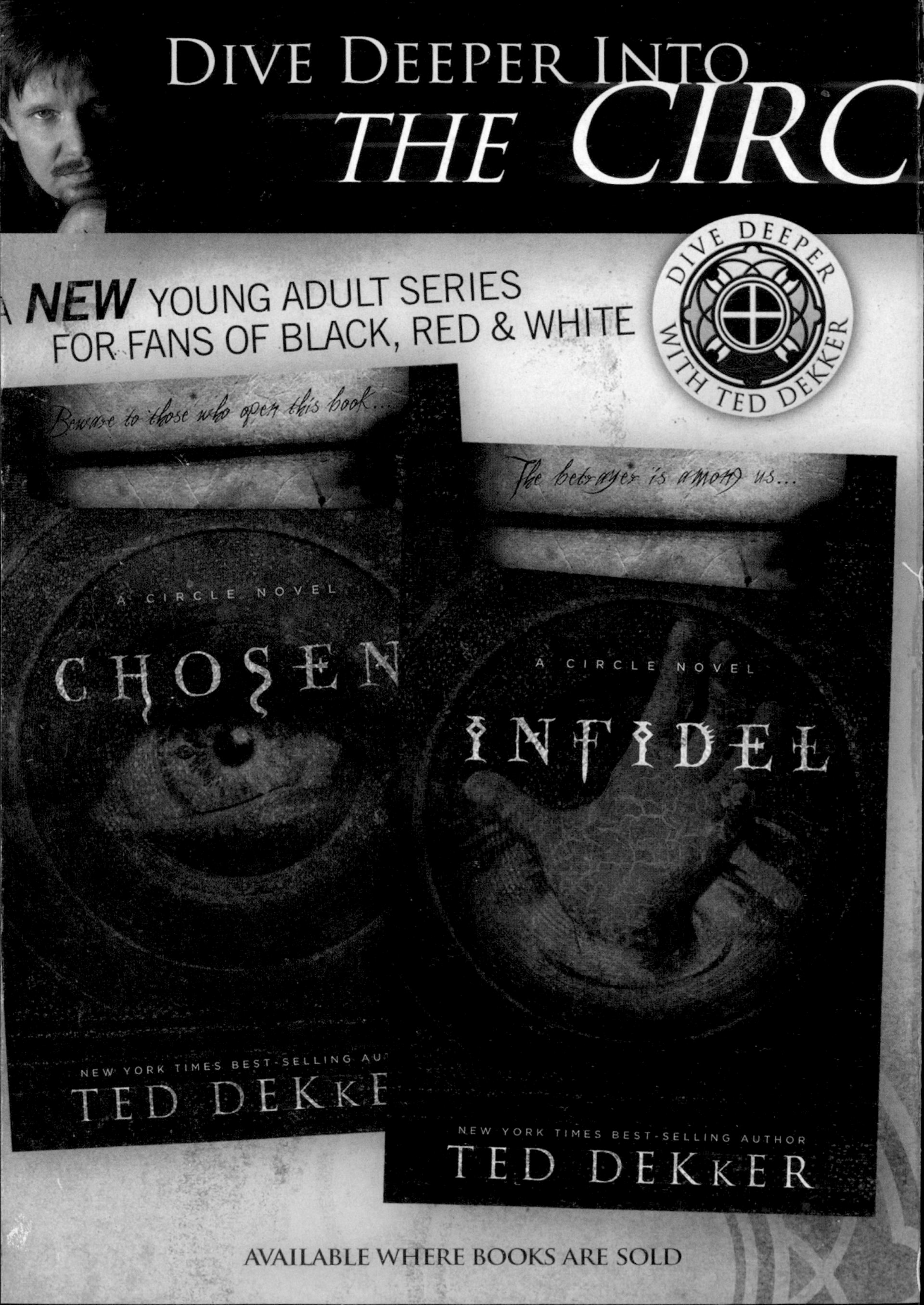
DIVE DEEPER INTO
THE CIRC
A NEW YOUNG ADULT SERIES
FOR FANS OF BLACK, RED & WHITE
DIVE DEEPER WITH TED DEKKER
Beware to those who open this book...
A CIRCLE NOVEL
CHOSEN
NEW YORK TIMES BEST-SELLING AU
TED DEKKE
The betrayer is among us...
A CIRCLE NOVEL
INFIDEL
NEW YORK TIMES BEST-SELLING AUTHOR
TED DEKKER
AVAILABLE WHERE BOOKS ARE SOLD